CW00766580

A Handbook On the Steam Engine with Especial Reference to Small and Medium-Sized Engines for the Use of the Engine Makers, Mechanical Draughtsmen, Engineering Students, and Users of Steam Power – Primary Source Edition

Hermann Haeder

NOT FOR LOAN

IF YOU REQUIRE ASSISTANCE PLEASE ASK

Book No.   1663191

Nabu Public Domain Reprints:

You are holding a reproduction of an original work published before 1923 that is in the public domain in the United States of America, and possibly other countries. You may freely copy and distribute this work as no entity (individual or corporate) has a copyright on the body of the work. This book may contain prior copyright references, and library stamps (as most of these works were scanned from library copies). These have been scanned and retained as part of the historical artifact.

This book may have occasional imperfections such as missing or blurred pages, poor pictures, errant marks, etc. that were either part of the original artifact, or were introduced by the scanning process. We believe this work is culturally important, and despite the imperfections, have elected to bring it back into print as part of our continuing commitment to the preservation of printed works worldwide. We appreciate your understanding of the imperfections in the preservation process, and hope you enjoy this valuable book.

A HANDBOOK

ON THE

STEAM ENGINE

WITH ESPECIAL REFERENCE TO

SMALL AND MEDIUM-SIZED ENGINES

*FOR THE USE OF ENGINE MAKERS, MECHANICAL
DRAUGHTSMEN, ENGINEERING STUDENTS,
AND USERS OF STEAM POWER*

By HERMAN HAEDER, CIVIL ENGINEER

English Edition

RE-EDITED BY THE AUTHOR FROM THE SECOND GERMAN EDITION, AND
TRANSLATED, WITH CONSIDERABLE ADDITIONS AND ALTERATIONS

By H. H. P. POWLES

ASSOC. MEMB. INST. C.E., M.I.M.E.
TRANSLATOR OF FRIEDRICH KICK'S "FLOUR MANUFACTURE"

Capio Lumen

LONDON

CROSBY LOCKWOOD AND SON

7, STATIONERS'-HALL COURT, LUDGATE HILL, E.C.

1893

JUL 19 1894

$150, 37

LONDON :
BRADBURY, AGNEW, & CO. LD., PRINTERS, WHITEFRIARS.

TORFAEN COUNTY BOROUGH BWRDEISTREF SIROL TORFAEN	
01663191	
Askews & Holts	15-Dec-2014
629	£21.99

TRANSLATOR'S PREFACE.

In preparing this work for an English edition, the plan of the Author has been adhered to as closely as possible, the theoretical part being treated very briefly, and formulæ given only when necessary; whilst numerous tables of dimensions of engine-details, taken from actual examples, and accompanied by illustrations, are appended. These will afford means of comparing the results of Continental with those of English practice.

To the present Edition there have been added examples, with tables and illustrations, of standard types of English Engines by several well-known makers, who have kindly supplied for the purpose dimensions and drawings.

As thus adapted to our own practice, it is hoped that the present edition of the work will be found by many English Engineers, and Mechanical Draughtsmen in particular, to answer a very useful purpose, not as yet fulfilled by any other publication.

To make the tables as clear as possible, the dimensions have been given, in almost every case, uniformly in inches.

London, *May*, 1893.

AUTHOR'S PREFACE TO FIRST EDITION.

IN the present condition of the markets, makers must not occupy too much time in calculations or mathematical research, but collecting results from actual practice, must note them in a convenient form, though not as formulæ, since formulæ are only useful within certain limits, there always being a risk of error in calculation. If anyone compares the results of the formulæ of one writer with those of another, he will often find great discrepancies between them.

The present work aims at showing the results of practical experience. Letterpress has been reduced as much as possible, to allow of the introduction of numerous tables and drawings, these being the language of technical people.

To those firms and others who have supplied me with information, I return my best thanks. May the book and its method gain many friends !

AUTHOR'S PREFACE TO SECOND EDITION.

THE first edition of this book had such a favourable reception in technical circles, that within a year a second edition has been found necessary.

Encouraged by this success, I have spared neither trouble nor expense to extend the usefulness of the work, and with that object have introduced a large number of additional figures.

To the numerous technical friends who have favoured me with communications on the subject, I return my grateful thanks, with a request for them to assist me with further exchange of ideas.

CONTENTS.

———•———

INTRODUCTION.

SECTION I.

TYPES OF STEAM ENGINES.

SECTION II.

DETAILS OF STEAM ENGINES.

SECTION III.

GOVERNORS.

SECTION IV.

VALVE GEARS.

HERM. HAEDER, C.E., DUISBURG o/RH.

SUPPLIES

GENERAL and DETAIL DRAWINGS of STEAM ENGINES of the best types, with ordinary Slide-valve, Corliss-, and Drop-valve Gear. Also of CONDENSING PLANTS, with or without Cooling Arrangements for the Condensing Water. Unsurpassed, simple and effective. The highest vacuum. Smallest quantity of Water required. Patents in the principal Countries of the World.

g. A valve opening outwards to allow steam to be blown through, but preventing air from entering the cylinder.

h. The main beam for transmitting the motion of the piston to the pump rod.

i. The pump rod.

Fig. 1.—Newcomen's Atmospheric Engine.

THE STEAM ENGINE.

INTRODUCTION.

THE knowledge that steam could be made use of as a motive power is very old, but it was not until about the year 1685 that the first model of a steam-engine was made by Dionysius Papin, a native of Blois in France, based on the fact that if cold water was applied or admitted to an enclosed vessel containing steam, the steam was condensed, and a vacuum resulted. In 1699, Captain Savery employed this principle for raising water, and in 1705 Newcomen, of Dartmouth, in Devonshire, constructed the first steam-engine properly so called. This first example was employed for raising water, and was known as "The Atmospheric Engine:" fig. 1 shows the general arrangement.

a. The steam cylinder.
b. The piston.
c. The steam generator or boiler.
d. The cock for admitting steam to the cylinder.
e. The cold water reservoir.
f. The cold water or "injection" cock.
g. A valve opening outwards to allow steam to be blown through, but preventing air from entering the cylinder.
h. The main beam for transmitting the motion of the piston to the pump rod.
i. The pump rod.

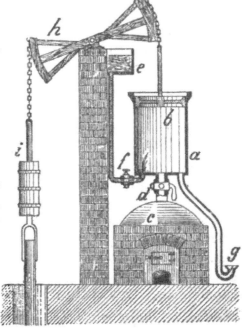

Fig. 1.—Newcomen's Atmospheric Engine.

The action of the engine is as follows :—In fig. 1 the weight of the pump rod, *i*, has brought the piston, *b*, to the top of the cylinder, the cylinder is then filled with steam from the boiler at atmospheric pressure through the cock, *d*, which is then closed. The cock, *f*, is now opened, and cold water from the tank, *e*, enters the cylinder in a jet ; the steam is condensed, and a vacuum produced below the piston. The atmospheric pressure above the piston forces the latter down to the bottom of the cylinder, at the same time raising the opposite end of the main beam, and with it the pump rod, *i*. By opening and closing the cocks, *d* and *f*, in succession, an alternate up and down movement is given to the piston.

James Watt introduced many improvements, especially the separate condensing chamber, in place of admitting the injection water into the cylinder, which tends to lower the temperature of the cylinder walls, and he remarked in one of his specifications "that the cylinder should be kept as hot as the steam that enters it." James Watt also invented mechanism for automatically opening and closing the valves, introduced the use of steam above atmospheric pressure, and discontinued the use of atmospheric pressure alone, by making use of the expansion of the steam for doing work on the piston. Watt's first engine was built in 1768. A year or two earlier, Smeaton had made many improvements ; but James Watt was amongst the first who really treated the steam-engine on a scientific basis.

Fig. 3 shows in diagram one of Boulton and Watt's condensing beam engines, working with a pressure of from 5 to 15 pounds on the square inch.

These early engines were invariably worked with low boiler pressures, and with condensation. High boiler pressures were regarded with distrust, and James Watt, although he gave attention to the idea, had strong prejudices against using high-pressure steam.

The first high-pressure engines using steam at 3 to 4 atmospheres were by Oliver Evans in America, 1786 to 1801, and Trevitick and Vivian in England, 1802.

The fact that the use of high pressures decreased the consumption of coal was soon recognised, and steam of 4 to 6 atmospheres was used, with and without condensation.

With high-pressure steam the advantage of expansion is very great. By using steam " expansively " is to be generally understood that the steam is admitted at high pressure for a short portion of the piston-stroke only, and then allowed to expand down to the end of the stroke, losing heat thereby in doing work. If the expansion is carried too far, the cooling becomes so great as to condense part of the steam. In order to prevent the waste from this cause, and to prevent the range of temperature between the entering and exhaust steam, the expansion is now carried on in two or more cylinders of different capacities; and engines on this principle are called "compound," if with two cylinders; triple expansion, if with three; quadruple expansion, if with four. Sometimes they are named "continuous" expansion engines, whether with two or more cylinders; also, when with three cylinders, they are occasionally termed "tri-compound."

The earliest attempt at a compound engine seems to have been that of Jonathan Hornblower in 1781, although he does not seem to have had any idea of what is understood now by a "compound" engine. He used two cylinders of unequal size, A and B (fig. 2); the steam was admitted first to the smaller cylinder, B, above the piston. On the piston arriving at the bottom of the stroke, the communication between the cylinder and boiler

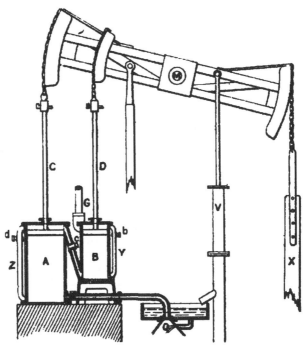

Fig. 2.—Hornblower's Engine.

was cut off, and a communication between top and bottom of the cylinder was opened by means of the pipe, Y, and cock, b. The piston then ascended by the weight of the pump-rod, X, and the steam displaced by the rising piston now filled the space below the piston. The cock, b, was then closed, and boiler steam admitted above the piston. The downstroke then commencing, the cock, c, opened the steam from the cylinder, B, then flowed into cylinder A, where it further expanded. On completion again of the downstroke, communication between upper and lower sides of the piston, A, was established, and the steam, after having done work on the upper side of the piston, passed to the lower side by means of the pipe, Z, and cock, d, during the downstroke; the steam eventually passed to the condenser, Q. It will be seen that the engine was really "compound," but it does not seem to have been more economical than the simple engines of James Watt of the same date, and was rather complicated. An outline of this machine is shown in fig. 2. Hornblower's engine was single acting.

In 1804 Arthur Woolf made a two-cylinder high-pressure engine with a condenser, together with a water-tube boiler, and took out an English patent for the same. Woolf's engine was an improvement on Hornblower's, being more simple in construction and double acting. It appears that one of Woolf's best engines was tried for coal consumption against one of Watt's in Cornwall, and resulted greatly in favour of Woolf's engine, probably from his using higher pressure steam, and from his carrying the expansion down in two separate cylinders.

In 1850 John Edler much improved the compound engine, and brought it into successful use for marine engines.

The annexed table shows the development in saving of fuel ; the figures give the coal consumption in pounds per horse-power per hour.

Atmospheric Engine. Savery. 1700	Low-pressure Engine. Watt. 1768	High-pressure Engine. Evans. 1804	Double Cylinder Engine. Woolf. 1804	Compound Engine. Edler. 1850—1891	Triple Expansion Engine. 1880—1891
31	8·8	6·7	4·5	2·25	1·76

It may appear that steam-engines have been brought to a high state of perfection, but it must be remembered that the efficiency of the best engines and boilers taken together is only about 15 per cent. of the theoretical value of the heat energy of the fuel.

SECTION I.

TYPES OF STEAM ENGINES.

Beam Engine, the original form as constructed by Boulton and Watt. This form owed its existence to the fact that all the earlier steam engines were used for pumping water, the beam forming a convenient means of attachment for the pump rods. Beam engines are still used for pumping, but are gradually giving way to more modern types.

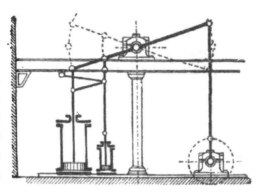

Fig. 3.—Beam Engine.

Horizontal Engine, with open frame cast iron bed-plate, a type much used for all sizes of engines for general purposes. The bed-plate frame is of U section, and is bolted down to a foundation of masonry or brickwork, the cylinder, main bearing and guides being bolted to the bed-plate.

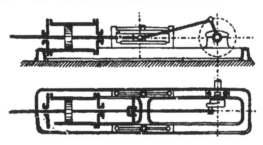

Figs. 4 and 5.—Horizontal Engine with Bed-Plate.

Vertical Engine.—A type now extensively used both for small and large engines; it has the advantage of occupying small floor space, and is not open to the objection so often put forward against horizontal engines,—that of the cylinder wearing oval. An endless number of varieties of this type are now in use, and it is the generally accepted type of marine screw-propeller engines.

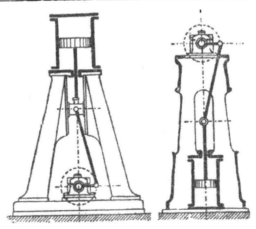

Figs. 6 and 7.—Vertical Engines.

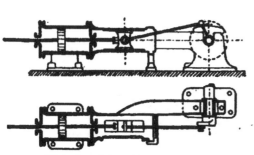

Figs. 8 and 9.—Girder Engine.

Corliss Frame or Girder Engines.—A type of horizontal engine now extensively used. Figs. 8 and 9 show an example with bored guides; they are also often made with flat-planed guides. In both cases the guides are formed in the main casting or girder which connects the cylinder to the main bearing. There are many varieties of this type.

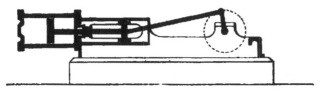

Fig. 10.—Self-contained Horizontal Engine.

Self - contained Horizontal Engines, with bent or slotted out cranks. This type, largely used for small power

short-stroke engines, has the cylinder bolted on to the end of an open bed-plate, which is widened out at the other end to take both bearings of the crank-shaft, so that the flywheel may be keyed on either side. The guides are usually formed in the bed-plate, the boring out of the guides and facing of the end flange being done at the same setting.

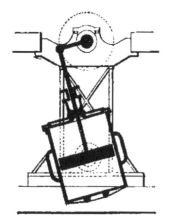

Fig. 11.—Oscillating Marine Engine.

Oscillating Engines, formerly much used as marine engines. Fig. 11 shows the usual type as made by Penn and others for driving paddle-wheels; this type has also been used for driving screw propellers, but is now almost superseded by the vertical type of marine engine.

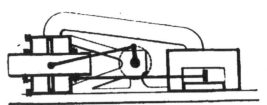

Fig. 12.—Penn's Trunk Engine.

Trunk Engines.—Fig. 12 shows an example of this type for driving a screw propeller as made by Penn. It has the advantage of being very compact and simple, but is open to the objection of the very large gland for the trunk, and that the trunk in its outward stroke is exposed to the cooling effect of the air. Very large engines of this type were formerly made. Two varieties are also shown in figs. 13 and 14.

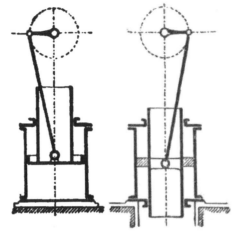

Figs. 13 and 14.—Trunk Engines.

Vertical Marine Engine, old type by Maudslay. Arrangement to reduce height, but at the expense of introducing heavy reciprocating masses.

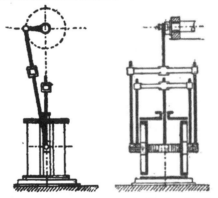

Figs. 15 and 16.—Maudslay's Marine Engine.

Steeple Engine, formerly, and still occasionally, used for driving paddle-wheels. A variety of this type has been used for small powers, and known as the Table Engine.

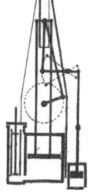

Fig. 17.—Steeple Engine.

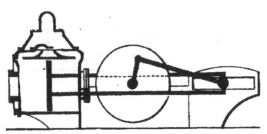

Fig. 18.—Bourne's Marine Engine.

Bourne's "return connecting-rod" engine, derived from the Steeple Engine, and used principally for driving screw propellers. There are two piston-rods in this engine, placed above and below the crank-shaft.

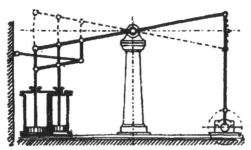

Fig. 19.—Woolf's Compound Beam Engine.

Beam Engine, Woolf's Compound. — Two unequal cylinders, side by side, at one end of the beam. Many pumping engines are of this type.

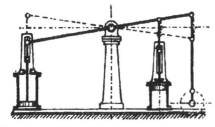

Fig. 20.—M'Naught's Compound Beam Engine.

M'Naught's Compound Beam Engine.—This system, consisting of a small cylinder (high pressure cylinder), placed at the opposite end of the beam to the larger cylinder used as a low-pressure cylinder, was introduced by M'Naught for increasing the power of existing engines. The high-pressure cylinder was the one added, the original cylinder being the low pressure cylinder. The power of the engine was thus increased by increase of boiler pressure and the addition of the new small cylinder, to which the boiler steam was admitted.

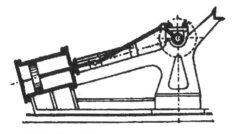

Fig. 21.—Inclined Frame Engine.

Inclined Frame Engines, now used extensively for paddle-steamers in several different varieties, usually compound engines.

A Double-Cylinder Engine variety derived from the above, with the cylinders inclined at an angle of about 45°, is occasionally used for driving rolling-mills in bar iron works.

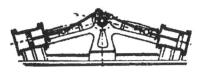

Fig. 22.—Inclined Frame Engine.

A variety of compound engine, with inclined cylinders, is shown in fig. 23.

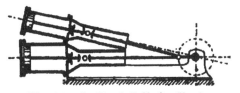

Fig. 23.—Inclined Cylinder Engine.

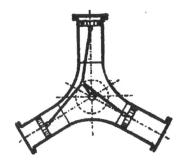

Fig. 24.—Radial Engine.

Fig. 25.—Four-Cylinder Radial Engine.

Radial Engines.—A modern type, of which there are many varieties. Fig. 24 shows Brotherhood's three-cylinder single-acting radial engine ; fig. 25, one with four cylinders. These are used for driving fans, steam-launches, and other purposes requiring speed and compactness.

Willan's Central Valve Engine.—One of the most modern types of engine, single-acting, compound or triple-expansion ; a special feature is the hollow piston-rod and central valve. Extensively used for driving dynamo-electric machines coupled direct on to the armature spindle.

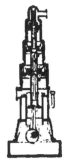

Fig. 26.—Willan's Central Valve Engine.

Various ways of arranging Cylinders and Cranks in Double and Three-cylinder, Compound, and Triple-expansion Engines.—Outline diagrams.

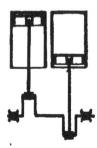

Fig. 27.—Double Cylinder, with cranks opposite or at 180 degrees.

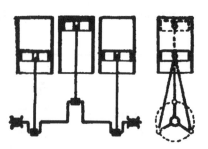

Fig. 28.—Three-cylinder Engine, with cranks at 120 degrees.

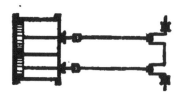

Fig. 29.—Compound Woolf Engine, with cranks together.

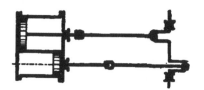

Fig. 30.—Compound Woolf Engine, with cranks opposite or at 180 degrees.

Fig. 31.—Compound Tandem Engine with receiver.

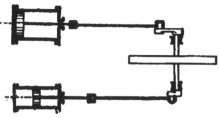

Fig. 32.—Compound Engine, with cylinders side by side with receiver; cranks at 90 degrees.

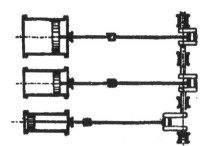

Fig. 33.—Triple Expansion Engine, with cylinders side by side; cranks at 120 degrees.

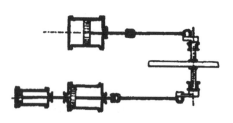

Fig. 34.—Triple Expansion Engine, semi-tandem; two cranks at 90 degrees.

Action of Pistons and Cranks in Woolf, Compound, and Triple-expansion Engines.*—Outline diagrams.

A crank is shown to each piston, to enable the action to be clearly followed ; in reality there is only one crank shaft to each engine.

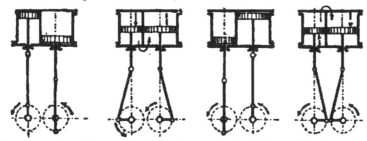

Fig. 35.—Woolf Engine, with cranks opposite (180°), without receiver.

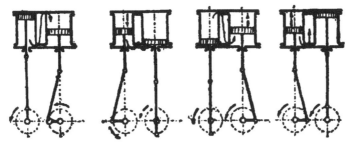

Fig. 36.—Compound Engine, with cranks at right angles, with receiver.

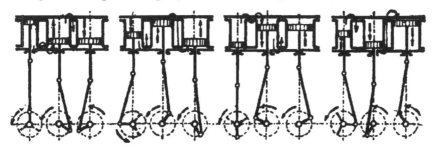

Fig. 37.—Triple Expansion Engine : cranks at 120 degrees, with two receivers.

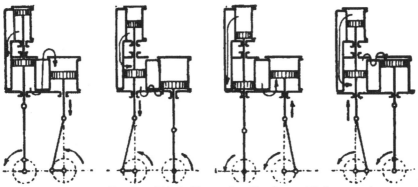

Fig. 38.—Semi-Tandem Triple-Expansion Engine, with two receivers.

* Further details of the action of these compound engines are given in the section on Compound Engines.

Names of the Parts of a simple Steam Engine.

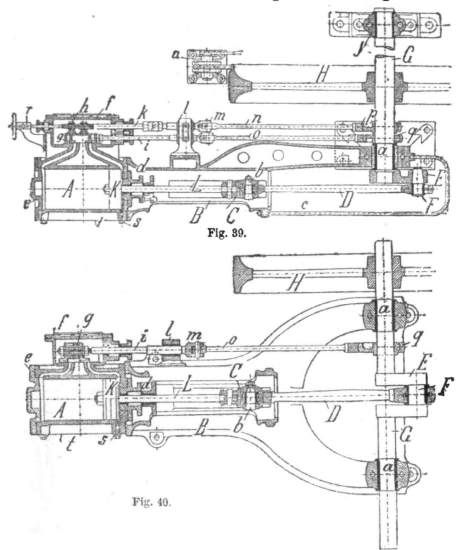

Fig. 39.

Fig. 40.

A. Cylinder.
B. Frame, bed, or bed plate.
C. Crosshead.
D. Connecting rod.
E. Crank.
F. Crank pin.
G. Crank shaft.
H. Fly wheel.
J. Outer bearing of crank shaft.
K. Piston.
L. Piston rod.
a. Crank shaft bearings, or main bearings
b. Crosshead pin or gudgeon.
c. Safety rail round engine.   [and gland.
d. Front cylinder cover with stuffing box
e. Back cylinder cover.

. Valve chest, or steam chest.
g. Main valve or main slide.
h. Cut off valve or expansion valve.
i. Main valve rod or spindle.
l. Valve rod guides.
m. Valve rod joints.
n. Cut off valve eccentric rod.
o. Main valve eccentric rod.
p. Cut off valve eccentric.
q. Main valve eccentric.   [expansion.
r. Hand adjustment for varying the
s. Bosses for indicator cocks.
t. Lagging, casing, or clothing.
u. Arrangement for turning the engine slowly round, "barring" arrangement.

Notes and General Remarks.

The size or perhaps better the power of an engine may be estimated by the diameter of the cylinder, the length of the stroke and the boiler pressure. The merits may be judged by the general design, workmanship, materials used, the construction of connecting rod ends, crosshead, crank shaft bearings, and by the nature of the valve gear.

The proportion of cylinder diameter to stroke, varies from 1.5 to 2.0 in ordinary engines for driving plants of machinery, and in special high speed engines from .75 to 1.25.

The steam engine maker must consider well before making a series of engines of one type, how best to make the minimum number of patterns serve for different sizes or powers required, and it is important to see that the parts are as far as possible symmetrical about the centre line, in order that engines may be readily built right or left-handed, in short before making either drawings or patterns, all possible dimensions should be tabulated out clearly, a few skeleton outlines being made for the different sizes showing centre lines only, the details such as pistons, crossheads, crank pins, main bearings, etc. can then be designed and a general drawing of each size prepared; from which the larger patterns can be made.

The most convenient starting points are obviously the diameter of the cylinder and the length of the stroke, then follow the speed, the maximum steam pressure and the subordinate details.

In making a set of drawings for a steam engine; for example of the horizontal girder type; the following method will be found both convenient and quick. Draw the centre line for the cylinder in plan and also the centre line for the crank shaft at right angles to the same, then from the table of dimensions draw in the crank pin where the two centre lines cross, on the centre line of crank shaft the width of the crank may then be set out which will give the position of the main bearing, the width of the same being taken from the tables; the same two centre lines are then drawn in elevation, and a circle for the path of the crank pin centre, the length of the connecting rod from the tables, will give the three positions of crosshead pin centre, an outline of crosshead at the two extreme positions will give the necessary length and positions of the guide surfaces for the crosshead slippers, the piston rod gland then drawn in will give the necessary clearance between it and the end of the crosshead boss. The stuffing box and cylinder cover then added will enable the position of the cylinder to be determined ; the remainder of the engine may then be filled in on the same principle, remembering that in all machine designing, whether they be steam engines or other machines of more or less special character, it is always well to have in view the fact that the complete machine to be designed is composed of a number of elementary parts or "units," which have to be brought together in a practical form, and in order to save time and labour all these "units" should be thoroughly worked out before the attempt is made to work out the complete machine.* It is, however, obvious that even elementary parts require modification, but the more thoroughly the smaller details are worked out, the less will be the labour and thought necessary to produce a complete machine for any special purpose. Speaking of the designing of steam engines of small powers, where a large number have to be made of few different sizes, the most successful makers have always been those who keep all the possible elementary parts in stock, this system enabling the cost of production to be greatly decreased, and leaving a margin for better design, material, and workmanship than is possible when each part is only made when actually wanted. Careful proportion of parts is not all that is wanted ; a detail that may work out well in one manufactory will not do so well in another. The designer must know the capabilities of the factory, nay, even the capabilities of the heads of the different workshops, before he can produce designs capable of being carried out so that the works may be run at their maximum efficiency.

---

* To many, these remarks may seem superfluous, but from neglect of these first principles of machine design much time is often lost in the drawing office.

SECTION II.

DETAILS OF STEAM ENGINES.

THE following leading points in steam engine design and construction are important.

Ample strength—it is not sufficient to trust to calculation alone but to compare calculated results, and to modify such results with judgment based on experience.

The selection of suitable materials for the different parts;—such as the best possible mixtures of cast iron for the cylinder, the use of phosphor bronze, good gun metal or even white metal in the bearings, and steel for all rods and spindles.

The form of those parts of which patterns have to be made is of importance; and especially in cast iron or cast steel very great care must be used in the distribution of the metal, any sudden transition from thick to thin metal being a source of unsoundness in the castings, and in most cases the designer should endeavour to study the different parts to be made in cast metal from the moulder's side of the question, the best castings being almost invariably produced from patterns so formed as to leave the sand with ease, without rendering it necessary to "mend up" the mould;—it being obvious that all mending up of a mould means a source of inaccuracy in the resulting casting, *i.e.* that it will differ from the pattern and no two castings will be obtained alike.

Good workmanship;—the dearest is not always the best. Special attention should be given to the wearing surfaces, and in order to prevent hot bearings the brasses should always be bored out a fraction larger than the measured diameter of the shaft which runs in them; it is often difficult to make a workman do this as he is apt to think that such a practice is against the idea of a "good fit;" hot bearings often cost a factory considerable sums of money and may damage the reputation of an engine maker. Good lubrication is a necessity, and all oil holes in brasses or joints should be supplemented by distributing oil grooves or channels, deep enough to keep clear for a long time, a simple oil hole in a long bearing especially, is totally inadequate.

"An excessive or exaggerated seeking after improvements or originality is very objectionable, one holds to good and well tried schemes. Every innovation should be discussed with a partner or a practical man, four eyes seeing more than two." The seeking after improvements or new appliances should always be encouraged, many useful schemes are lost by diffidence on the part of the schemer, which a little encouragement would allay.

Besides one's own experience we may often make use of that of others, and notes of what we see, systematically arranged, so as to be easy to find, will afford much assistance.

Frames for small Self-contained Horizontal Engines up to 15 inches stroke.

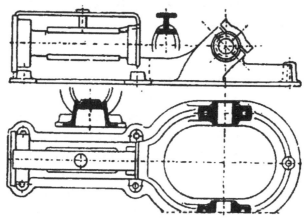

Figs. 41 and 42.—Frame, with double (top and bottom) slipper guides with flat surfaces.

The crank shaft is bent or slotted out and admits of the flywheel being carried at either side of the engine outside the bearings, and if required a driving pulley at the opposite side. The crank shaft bearing brasses are generally in two pieces with a cap and two or four bolts.

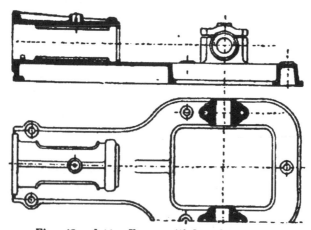

Figs. 43 and 44.—Frame with bored Guides.

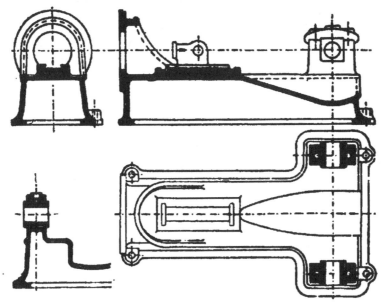

Figs. 45 and 46.—Frame with single slipper guide.

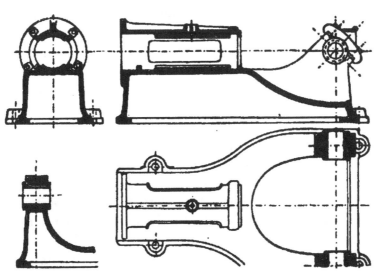

Figs. 47 and 48.—Frames with bored guides.

All the above frames are symmetrical about the centre line in plan.

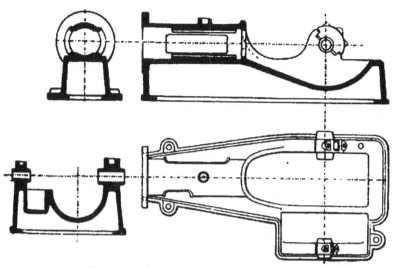

Figs. 49 and 50.—Frame with bored guides.

These frames are not symmetrical about the centre line and but little used, as right and left hand patterns would be required.

These engines can be used as wall engines by being bolted vertically with either the cylinder or crank shaft above; to a substantial wall; they are convenient also for transit as they can be packed complete with everything in its place except the fly-wheel.

The development of steam engine frames from earliest times to the present day is quite an interesting study, and has been progressing so quietly that it often escapes notice; formerly architectural features were always introduced, now smoothness of outline is almost universal, and the even disposition of metal is studied.

In horizontal engines of old types the bed was treated more or less as a plate whereon to bolt cylinders, guides and bearings; the metal was placed below, and far away from the centre line of the piston rod, so that the bed plate was subjected to a bending stress at each stroke of the piston, and these beds in some measure depended on the mass of masonry to which they were bolted for stiffness. In modern designing the tendency is to dispose the metal as nearly in the right place to resist stresses as possible. In girder engines the metal is disposed around the same horizontal plane as the piston rod, and as near to it as possible sideways; in vertical marine engines the frame is a stiff triangle, placed over the crank shaft; in marine paddle engines, &c., of diagonal type the metal is disposed in a most advantageous manner.

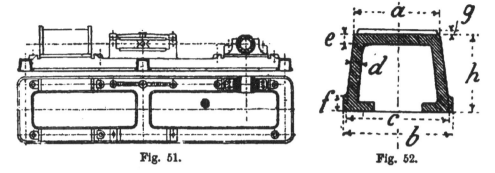

Fig. 51.   Fig. 52.

Bed-plate Frames of U-form section ; an old type, but still used for large engines.

TABLE 1.—Dimensions of the above Frames.

Engine.		All Dimensions are in Inches.							
H*	D	h	b	a	c	d	e	f	g
12	6	$5\frac{1}{2}$	5	$3\frac{1}{2}$	4	$\frac{11}{16}$	$\frac{5}{8}$	$\frac{3}{4}$	$\frac{1}{4}$
16	8	7	6	$4\frac{1}{2}$	5	$\frac{3}{4}$	$\frac{3}{4}$	$\frac{7}{8}$	$\frac{1}{4}$
24	12	$8\frac{1}{2}$	$7\frac{1}{2}$	$5\frac{1}{2}$	$6\frac{1}{2}$	$\frac{3}{4}$	$\frac{3}{4}$	$\frac{7}{8}$	$\frac{3}{8}$
32	16	$10\frac{1}{2}$	9	7	8	$\frac{7}{8}$	$\frac{7}{8}$	1	$\frac{3}{8}$
40	20	12	10	9	$9\frac{1}{2}$	1	1	$1\frac{1}{8}$	$\frac{1}{2}$
48	24	14	12	$9\frac{1}{2}$	11	$1\frac{1}{8}$	$1\frac{1}{8}$	$1\frac{1}{4}$	$\frac{1}{2}$
56	28	16	$13\frac{1}{2}$	$10\frac{1}{2}$	12	$1\frac{1}{4}$	$1\frac{1}{4}$	$1\frac{3}{8}$	$\frac{5}{8}$
64	32	18	15	$11\frac{1}{2}$	13	$1\frac{3}{8}$	$1\frac{3}{8}$	$1\frac{1}{2}$	$\frac{5}{8}$
72	36	20	$16\frac{1}{2}$	13	15	$1\frac{3}{8}$	$1\frac{3}{8}$	$1\frac{1}{2}$	$\frac{3}{4}$
80	40	22	18	14	16	$1\frac{1}{2}$	$1\frac{1}{2}$	$1\frac{5}{8}$	$\frac{3}{4}$

*Note.—Throughout the Tables the letter H signifies the stroke of the engine, and D the diameter of the cylinder.

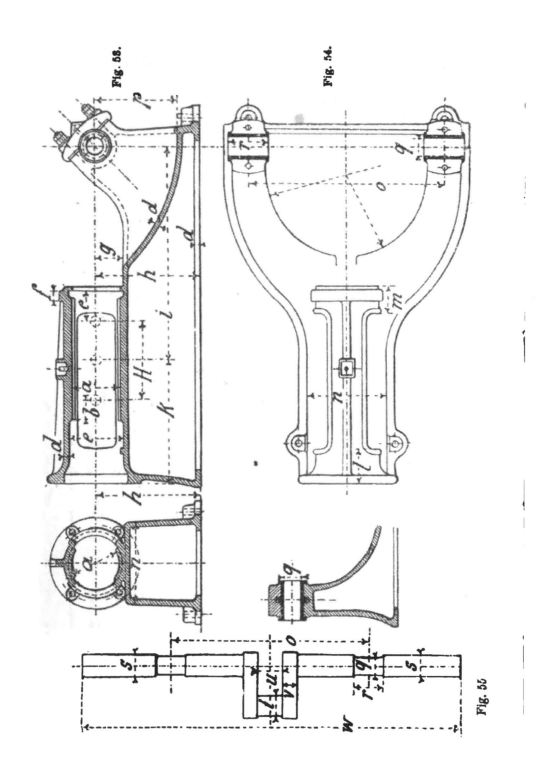

Fig. 53.

Fig. 54.

Fig. 55.

TABLE 2.—**Dimensions of Frames and Crank Shafts for small Engines** (Figs. 53—55).

Engine.		Frame.															Main bearing.		Crank Shaft.				
H	D	*a*	*b*	*c*	*d*	*e*	*f*	*g*	*h*	*i*	*k*	*l*	*m*	*n*	*o*	*p*	*q*	*r*	*s*	*t*	*u*	*v*	*w*
8	4	6	2	$3\frac{1}{4}$	$\frac{1}{2}$	$6\frac{1}{2}$	$1\frac{3}{8}$	$3\frac{1}{2}$	12	22	14	4	$3\frac{1}{2}$	10	22	$9\frac{1}{2}$	$2\frac{1}{2}$	5	3	$2\frac{3}{4}$	$3\frac{1}{4}$	2	48
12	6	$7\frac{1}{2}$	3	$4\frac{1}{4}$	$\frac{5}{8}$	$8\frac{1}{4}$	$1\frac{5}{8}$	$4\frac{1}{2}$	16	32	18	$4\frac{3}{4}$	4	12	32	$10\frac{1}{2}$	3	6	$3\frac{1}{2}$	$3\frac{1}{4}$	$3\frac{1}{2}$	$2\frac{3}{8}$	58

All Dimensions in this Table are given in Inches.

Frames for Medium and Large Engines.

The bed plate frame as in page 19, fig. 51, was formerly largely used but now has given place to the more modern types given below; it has the advantage of taking firm hold of the foundation and is still much used for winding engines of large size.

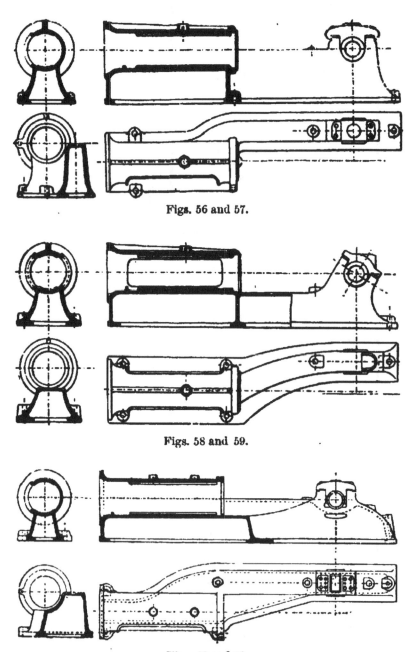

Figs. 56 and 57.

Figs. 58 and 59.

Figs. 60 and 61.

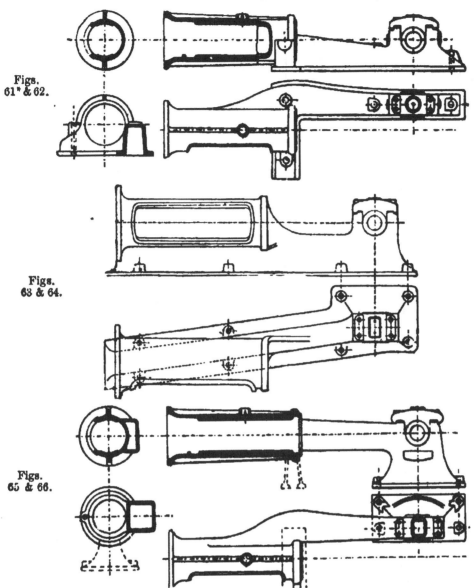

Figs.
61* & 62.

Figs.
63 & 64.

Figs.
65 & 66.

All the above frames Figs. 56—66 are of the semi-girder type having the frame supported throughout its length on the foundation except fig. 65, which is of the true girder type, the girder being free from the foundation, supports being at the ends, one under the cylinder the other at the main bearing. In the semi-girder type the cylinder usually overhangs the end of the frame.

Note.—The frame of a girder-winding engine at Herne, of 5'3″ stroke, cracked at (*a*), fig. 67, and the bending of the girder in the middle

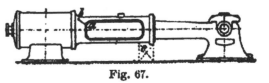

Fig. 67.

could be seen distinctly. A hole was drilled at the end of crack (*b*), and a supporting foot fixed under the girder at C.

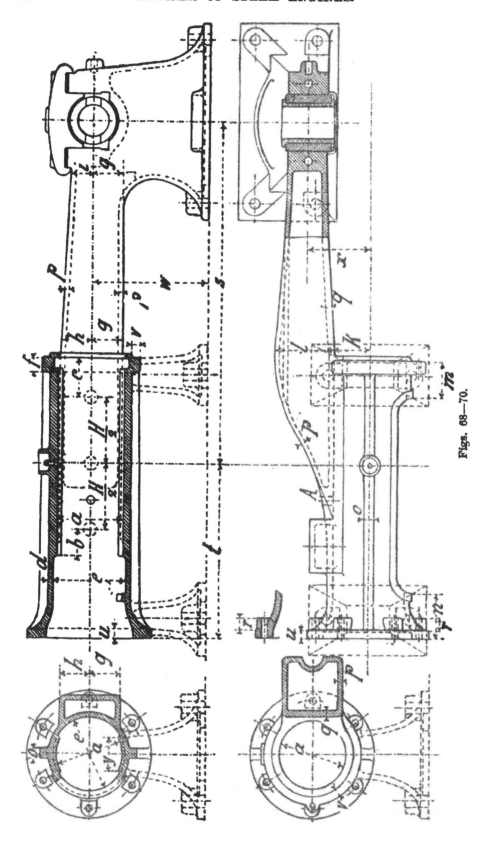

Figs. 68—70.

TABLE 3.—**Dimensions of Girder Frames with Bored Guides** (Figs. 68—70).

All Dimensions are given in Inches.

Engine. H	Engine. D	a	b	c	d	e	f	g	h	i	k	l	m	n	o	p	q	r	s	t	u	v	w	x	y
20	10	11	4¼	5¾	11/16	11⅞	2¼	4¾	4½	2¾	5½	9	5½	6½	1⅜	¾	⅞	1¾	50	27	1⅜	1⅛	18	9¼	5
24	12	12	4¾	6½	¾	13	2⅜	5½	5	3¼	6½	10	6½	7½	1½	¾	1	2	60	30¾	1½	1⅜	20	10¾	6¼
28	14	13½	5½	7¼	13/16	14⅝	2½	6¼	6	3¾	7½	11½	7	8	1¾	⅞	1	2¼	70	34	1½	1½	22	12¼	7¼
32	16	15	6	8	⅞	16½	2¾	7¼	6¾	4½	8¼	13	8	9	2	⅞	1⅛	2½	80	37½	1⅝	1¾	24	14	8
36	18	17	6¼	8¾	⅞	18½	3	8	7½	5	9½	14½	8½	9½	2¼	⅞	1⅛	2⅞	90	41	1¾	2	26	15⅝	8¾
40	20	19	6¾	9½	15/16	20½	3¼	8¾	8	5½	10½	15½	9½	10½	2½	1	1¼	3¼	100	44¼	2	2¼	28	17¼	9½
44	22	21	7	10	1	22½	3½	9½	8¾	6	11½	16½	10	11	2¾	1	1¼	3½	110	48¾	2¼	2½	30	18½	10

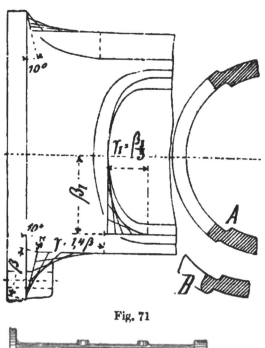

The opening or window for the crosshead has ends in the form of a parabola with axes as 1 to 3 and a fillet is carried round the window either as at A or B. Fig. 71 also shows the blending of the round part of the frame with the flange to which the cylinder is bolted; the guides are sometimes finished as shown in Figs. 72, 73.

Fig. 71

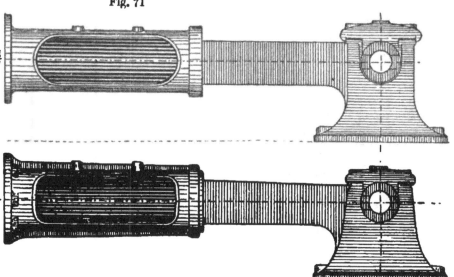

Figs. 72 and 73.

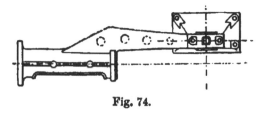

Fig. 74.

Fig. 74 shows the connection between the part of the frame with the bored out guides and the main crankshaft-bearing, the straight line forms shown in the figure, makes the pattern simple; the dotted circles show the holes for venting the core and for getting it out of the casting.

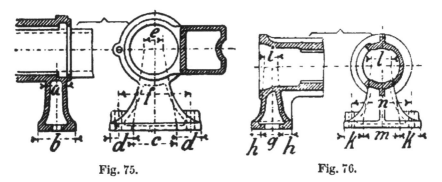

Fig. 75.   Fig. 76.

TABLE 4.—**Feet for supporting Girder Frames** (Figs. 75—77).

Engines.		Feet supporting middle of Girder.						Feet at Cylinder end of Girder.						
H	D	a	b	c	d	e	f	g	h	i	k	l	m	n
20	10	—	—	—	—	—	—	6	2½	4½	5½	4¾	8	15
24	12	—	—	—	—	—	—	6¾	2½	5	6¼	5¾	9½	17
28	14	—	—	—	—	—	—	7½	2¾	6½	6¾	6¾	11½	19½
32	16	5½	10	12	7¼	6½	21	—	—	—	—	—	—	—
36	18	6¾	10½	12¾	7½	6¾	22	—	—	—	—	—	—	—
40	20	7¼	11	13½	8	7¼	23	—	—	—	—	—	—	—
44	22	7½	11½	14½	8¾	7½	25½	—	—	—	—	—	—	—

All Dimensions are in Inches.

Small engines up to 12″ diameter of cylinder are frequently made with overhanging cylinders and with the foot cast in one with the girder as shown in fig. 76.

For larger engines an intermediate supporting foot is sometimes cast or bolted on to the girder. The curve of the sides of these feet is parabolic, fig. 77

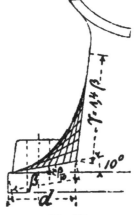

Fig. 77.

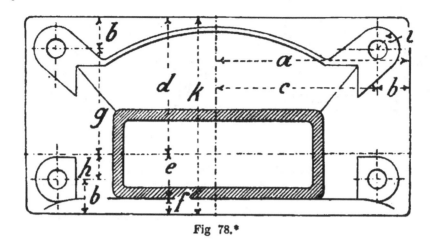

Fig 78.*

TABLE 5.—**Main Bearing Foot** (Fig. 78).

Engines.		All Dimensions are in Inches.									
H	D	a	b	c	d	e	f	g	h	i	k
20	10	$13\frac{1}{4}$	2	$11\frac{1}{4}$	9	$2\frac{7}{8}$	$1\frac{1}{8}$	7	2	$1\frac{3}{4}$	13
24	12	$14\frac{3}{4}$	$2\frac{1}{2}$	$12\frac{1}{4}$	11	$3\frac{3}{8}$	$1\frac{5}{8}$	$8\frac{1}{2}$	$2\frac{1}{2}$	2	16
28	14	18	$2\frac{1}{2}$	$15\frac{1}{2}$	12	$3\frac{7}{8}$	$2\frac{1}{8}$	$9\frac{1}{2}$	$3\frac{1}{2}$	$2\frac{1}{4}$	18
32	16	20	$2\frac{3}{4}$	$17\frac{1}{4}$	13	$4\frac{3}{8}$	$2\frac{1}{8}$	$10\frac{1}{4}$	$3\frac{3}{4}$	$2\frac{1}{4}$	$19\frac{1}{2}$
36	18	$21\frac{1}{2}$	$2\frac{3}{4}$	$18\frac{3}{4}$	15	$4\frac{7}{8}$	$1\frac{5}{8}$	$12\frac{1}{4}$	$3\frac{3}{4}$	$2\frac{1}{2}$	$21\frac{1}{2}$
40	20	24	$3\frac{1}{4}$	$21\frac{3}{4}$	16	$5\frac{3}{8}$	$2\frac{1}{8}$	$12\frac{3}{4}$	$4\frac{1}{4}$	$2\frac{1}{2}$	$23\frac{1}{2}$
44	22	26	$3\frac{1}{2}$	$22\frac{3}{4}$	18	6	$2\frac{1}{2}$	$14\frac{3}{4}$	$5\frac{1}{4}$	$2\frac{3}{4}$	$26\frac{1}{2}$

* This foot is not symmetrical about the longitudinal centre line, and therefore cannot be used for both right and left-hand engines without alteration to patterns unless bolted to girders by a flange.

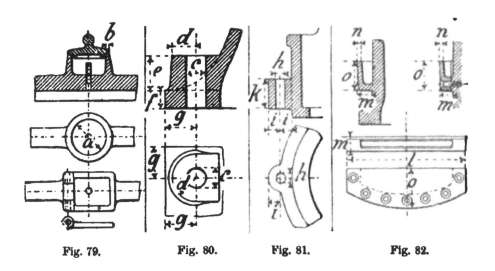

Fig. 79.　　Fig. 80.　　Fig. 81.　　Fig. 82.

TABLE 6.—Sundry Details for Girder Frames (Figs. 79—82).

H	No.	a	b	c	d	e	f	g	h	i	k	l	m	n	o
	Oil Cup for Guides.			Bosses for Foundation Bolts.					Boss for Guard Rail.			Oil Catcher for Main Bearing.			
8	1	$1\frac{1}{2}$	$\frac{1}{4}$	$1\frac{1}{8}$	$1\frac{1}{4}$	$1\frac{3}{8}$	1	$1\frac{1}{2}$	—	—	—	—	—	—	—
12	1	2	$\frac{1}{4}$	$1\frac{1}{4}$	$1\frac{3}{8}$	$1\frac{1}{2}$	$1\frac{1}{4}$	$1\frac{3}{4}$	—	—	—	—	—	—	—
16	1	$2\frac{1}{2}$	$\frac{1}{4}$	$1\frac{3}{8}$	$1\frac{1}{2}$	$1\frac{3}{4}$	$1\frac{3}{8}$	2	$\frac{5}{8}$	$\frac{3}{4}$	2	9	1	$\frac{1}{4}$	2
20	1	$2\frac{3}{4}$	$\frac{3}{8}$	$1\frac{1}{2}$	$1\frac{3}{4}$	2	$1\frac{1}{2}$	$2\frac{1}{4}$	$\frac{3}{4}$	$\frac{7}{8}$	$2\frac{1}{4}$	10	1	$\frac{1}{4}$	$2\frac{1}{4}$
24	1	$3\frac{1}{4}$	$\frac{3}{8}$	$1\frac{3}{4}$	2	2	$1\frac{3}{4}$	$2\frac{1}{2}$	$\frac{3}{4}$	1	$2\frac{3}{8}$	11	$1\frac{1}{8}$	$\frac{1}{4}$	$2\frac{3}{8}$
28	1	$3\frac{3}{4}$	$\frac{3}{8}$	2	$2\frac{1}{4}$	$2\frac{3}{8}$	2	$2\frac{3}{4}$	$\frac{7}{8}$	1	$2\frac{1}{2}$	12	$1\frac{1}{8}$	$\frac{1}{4}$	$2\frac{1}{2}$
32	2	$3\frac{1}{4}$	$\frac{3}{8}$	$2\frac{1}{8}$	$2\frac{1}{4}$	$2\frac{1}{2}$	$2\frac{1}{4}$	3	1	1	$2\frac{3}{4}$	13	$1\frac{1}{4}$	$\frac{3}{8}$	$2\frac{3}{4}$
36	2	$3\frac{1}{2}$	$\frac{1}{2}$	$2\frac{1}{4}$	$2\frac{1}{2}$	$2\frac{3}{4}$	$2\frac{3}{8}$	$3\frac{1}{4}$	1	$1\frac{1}{8}$	3	14	$1\frac{1}{4}$	$\frac{3}{8}$	3
40	2	$3\frac{3}{4}$	$\frac{1}{2}$	$2\frac{1}{4}$	$2\frac{1}{2}$	3	$2\frac{1}{2}$	$3\frac{1}{4}$	1	$1\frac{1}{4}$	$3\frac{1}{4}$	15	$1\frac{3}{8}$	$\frac{3}{8}$	$3\frac{1}{4}$
44	2	4	$\frac{1}{2}$	$2\frac{3}{8}$	$2\frac{3}{4}$	$3\frac{1}{4}$	$2\frac{5}{8}$	$3\frac{1}{2}$	$1\frac{1}{8}$	$1\frac{3}{8}$	$3\frac{1}{2}$	16	$1\frac{1}{2}$	$\frac{1}{2}$	$3\frac{1}{2}$
	All Dimensions are in Inches.														

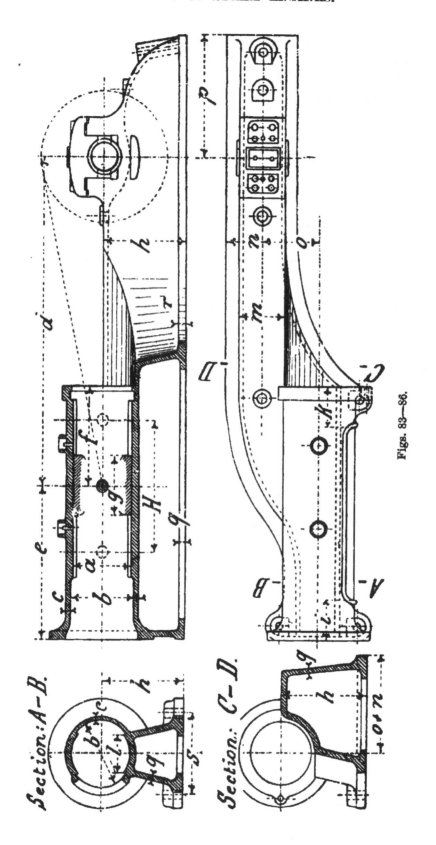

Figs. 83—86.

TABLE 7.—**Dimensions of Frames with bored Guides supported on Foundation from end to end, "semi-girder" type** (Figs. 83—86).

All Dimensions are in Inches.

Engine. H	Engine. D	a	b	c	d	f	g	h	i	k	l	m	n	o	p	q	r	s	No. of Bolts
16	8	9	10	5/8	42	12¾	8¾	14	5½	5	4½	5¾	7¼	9¼	28	¾	¾	17¼	7
20	12	12	13	¾	62	19¼	12	19	7½	6½	6¼	8	8¾	12⅜	38	¾	1	19½	7
32	16	15	16½	¾	80	24¾	15¼	24	8¾	7½	8	9½	10½	15¼	48	⅞	1¼	22	8
40	20	19	20½	⅞	100	30½	17½	28	10½	8½	9½	12	12	19¼	56	1	1⅜	25	8
48	24	23	24½	1	120	36	20½	32	11½	9¼	11¼	15¼	13½	23⅝	67	1⅛	1½	28	9
56	28	27	28½	1⅛	140	42	27¼	36	12½	10	12¾	17¾	15¼	27¼	72	1¼	2	31	10
64	32	31	32½	1¼	160	48	30	40	13½	11	14½	20	16¾	30¾	80	1¼	2½	34	11
72	36	34½	36	1⅜	176	54	32¾	42	14½	11¾	17¼	22	18½	33⅝	84	1⅜	2¾	37	12
80	40	38½	40	1⅜	192	60	36	44	15¼	12¾	20	24¾	20	37⅝	88	1⅜	3¼	40	12

Frames for Horizontal Engines with more than One Cylinder.

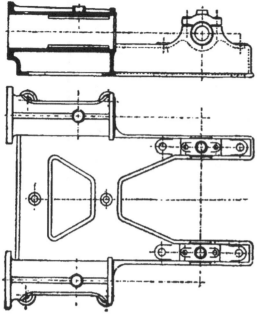

Figs. 87, 88 show a frame for a double cylinder engine with fly-wheel between the two cylinders. A very convenient and cheap type for small self-contained engines. The size of the fly-wheel is limited in this arrangement to about three and a half times the crank radius.

Figs. 87 and 88.

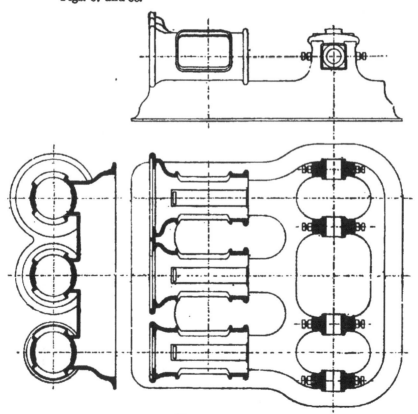

Figs. 89—91.

Figs. 89—91 show a frame for a triple expansion horizontal engine of 20 inches stroke, the arrangement for adjusting the crank shaft brasses by set screws is not recommended, although formerly it was a very common practice.*

Frames for Vertical Engines.

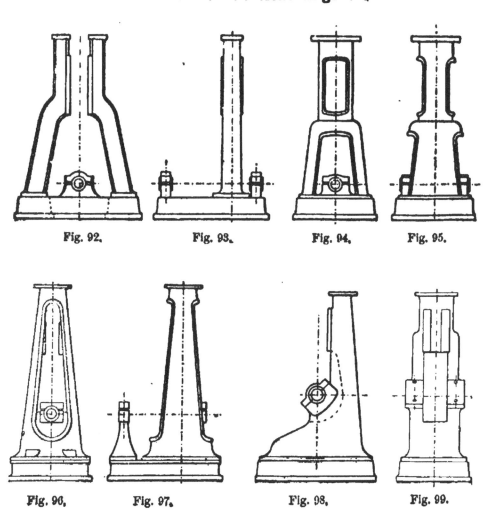

Fig. 92.   Fig. 93.   Fig. 94.   Fig. 95.

Fig. 96,   Fig. 97.   Fig. 98,   Fig. 99.

The above figs. 92—99 show some early types of vertical engine frames for small engines, a modification of fig. 98 is now used for small quick running engines, and has a wrought-iron stay bar brought from a lug on the cylinder down to the front of the base of the frame.

---

* See "Zeitschrift der Verein deutsch. Ingenieur, 1888," page 226.

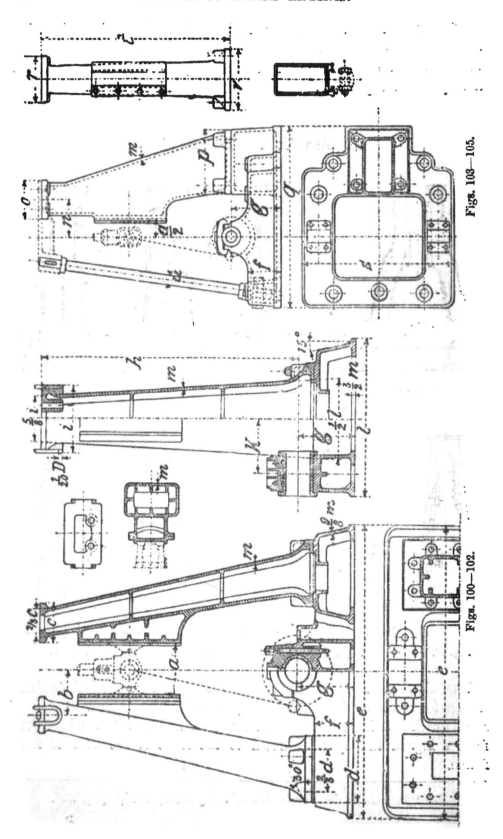

Figs. 103—105.

Figs. 100—102.

TABLE 8.—Dimensions of Frames for Vertical Engines (Figs. 100—165).

S	D	a	b	c	d	e	f	g	h	i	k	l	m	n	o	p	q	r	s	t	u	v	w
8	6	11	—	—	—	—	11	18	—	—	—	—	$\frac{5}{8}$	11	11	18	48	12	48	42	—	16	—
12	10	13	—	—	—	—	12	19	—	—	—	—	$\frac{11}{16}$	13	13	21	60	15	57	60	—	2	—
16	14	15	—	—	—	—	13	20	—	—	—	—	$\frac{3}{4}$	15	15	25	72	18	66	78	—	24	—
20	18	17	—	—	—	—	14	21	—	—	—	—	$\frac{5}{8}$	17	17	29	84	21	75	96	—	26	—
24	22	19	—	—	—	—	15	22	—	—	—	—	$\frac{7}{8}$	19	19	32	96	24	84	114	—	32	—
28	26	21	17	15	26½	120	16	23	108	26½	22	64	$\frac{15}{16}$	—	—	—	—	—	—	—	—	—	—
32	30	23	18½	16	29	132	17½	25	120	29	24	70	1	—	—	—	—	—	—	—	—	—	—
36	34	25	20	17½	31½	144	19	27	132	31½	26	76	$1\frac{1}{16}$	—	—	—	—	—	—	—	—	—	—
40	38	27	21½	19	34	156	20½	29	144	34	28	82	$1\frac{1}{8}$	—	—	—	—	—	—	—	—	—	—
44	44	29	23	20½	36	168	22	31	156	36½	30	88	$1\frac{3}{16}$	—	—	—	—	—	—	—	—	—	—

All Dimensions are given in Inches.

Figs. 100—102 show a vertical engine frame of cast iron for large engines of the marine type, the outer bearing is here on a separate bed outside the fly-wheel when used as a land engine.

Figs. 103—105 show a vertical engine frame of cast iron with wrought-iron stay bar in front, and both crank shaft bearings on one bed thus making the engine self-contained.

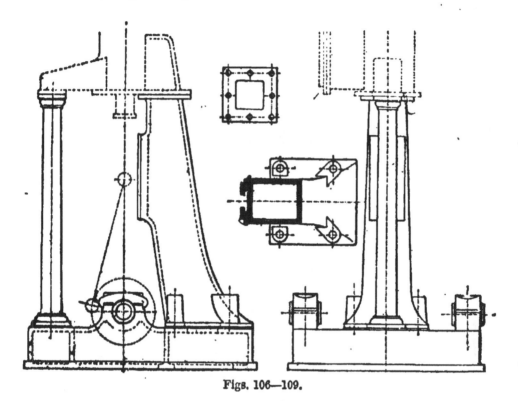

Figs. 106—109.

Figs. 106—109 show a frame of the marine type modified for self-contained vertical land engines.

Crank Shaft Bearings.

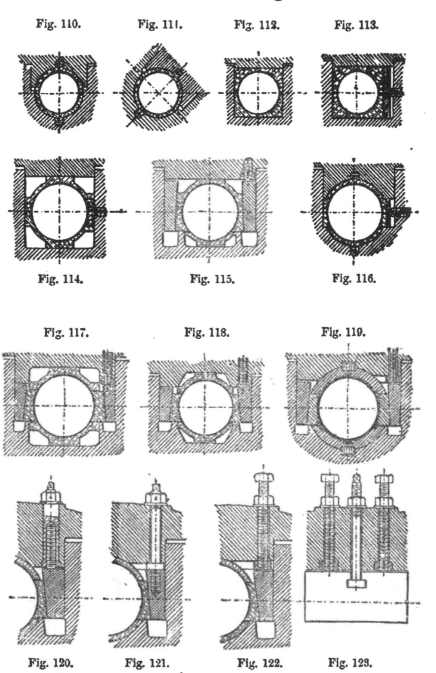

Fig. 110. Fig. 111. Fig. 112. Fig. 113.

Fig. 114. Fig. 115. Fig. 116.

Fig. 117. Fig. 118. Fig. 119.

Fig. 120. Fig. 121. Fig. 122. Fig. 123.

Figs. 110—113.—Bearings with brasses in two parts for small engines.
Figs. 114—116.—Bearings with brasses in three parts for medium-sized engines.
Figs. 117—123.—Bearings with brasses in four parts for large engines.

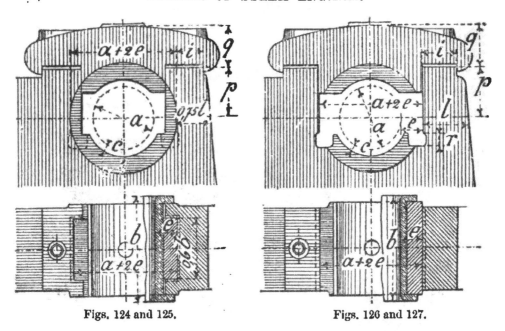

Figs. 124 and 125.   Figs. 126 and 127.

Figs. 124—127 show two different designs of bearings; in one, Fig. 124, the adjusting wedge is difficult to fit in, and in fig. 126, if desirable to cover up the wedge at the sides, the flanges of the brasses require to be very deep.

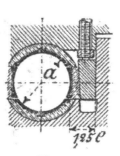

Fig. 128.

Fig. 128 shows the bearings of cast iron or cast steel lined with white metal. In large bearings the caps are often cored out to lighten them, as shown in section in figs. 129—131; these figures also show two methods of adjusting the brasses endways or horizontally. The outline of the bearing foot is made approximately parabolic, a curve which gives perhaps the neatest appearance.

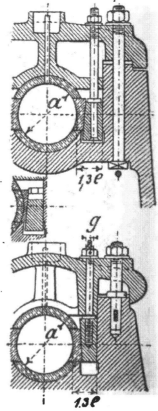

Figs. 129—131.

It will be noted in fig. 128 that the adjusting wedge is shown with the *small end* downwards ; it is generally better to have all adjusting wedges with the *large end* downwards, as then, if the bolt jars loose, the wedge will work down, and not jamb as it might do when put in the other way.

The crank shaft or main bearing, being a very important part of the engine, requires special care both in design and construction. The adjustment of bearings with the brasses in three or more parts by means of wedges placed so as to take up the wear in definite directions, has many advantages if skilfully handled, but may lead to bad results and prove to be far worse than the ordinary bearing with two-part brasses if badly handled. On this ground, many firms make even large engines with two-part brasses and no wedge adjustment. It is noticeable that both in marine and locomotive practice the bearings are made as simple as possible without any elaborations.

The part of the brass step which rests on the body casting of the bearing should always be well fitted and have ample surface. Figs. 132, 133, show the section of a crank shaft brass when new and after many years wear, the lower fig. shows how the material of the brass spreads

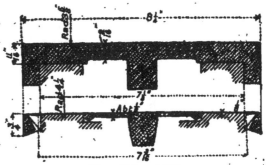

Figs. 132 and 133.

out in the direction of its length by the continual pressure and jarring of ordinary work.*

Crank shaft and other similar brasses have a tendency to close in and pinch the shaft as they become warm, to avoid this trouble two-part brasses should be bored out 0·5 per cent. and four-part brasses 0·8 per cent. larger than the diameter of the shaft, attention to this point would often save trouble in ordinary shafting, the brasses of which are often sent out a tight fit on the shaft and have generally to be filed or scraped out until they are a comparatively loose fit.

To bore out and fit up brasses, especially when in many pieces, they are planed up on the flat joint surfaces and soldered together, and can then be bored out, turned or machined where required, and fitted to their places, and afterwards readily separated by heat ; sometimes, where possible, they are held together by clamps and steady pins.

---

* Zeitschrift der Verein deutsches Ingenieur, 1890, page 931.

A suitable mixture for white metal is, according to Kirchweger, composed of 9½ parts copper, 13 parts antimony, 59 parts of pure zinc : the copper should be first melted, then the antimony and zinc

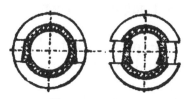

Figs. 134 and 135.

added and the mixture well stirred and granulated ; 27 parts of this granulated metal should then be melted, and 29½ parts of pure zinc added, the mixture well stirred and run into bars. There are numbers of different metals now used for lining engine and other bearings, one of the first used was Babbit's metal, said to be composed of 1 part copper, 10 parts tin, and 1 part antimony. All these alloys of metals, differing much in their melting points, should be mixed with care, otherwise the easily fusible metals will volatilize, and unsatisfactory results will be obtained. Other standard metals used for engine brasses vary in their composition according to the judgment and experience of the manufacturer, they usually are composed of copper, tin and zinc, copper and tin being the chief ingredients.

The heating of bearings may proceed from the construction, maintenance or attention, or rather want of attention, whilst at work, and even when at rest.

The causes of heating may be tabulated as follows:—

1. Too high pressure per unit of surface P.

2. Too great speed of the shaft for the given pressure, *i.e.*, $p\,v$ too great.

3. Too much pressure from the shaft being not sufficiently stiff for the work, *i.e.*, shaft too elastic.

4. Unsuitable material for the brasses or steps.

5. Insufficient means of lubrication.

6. Blows or jars.

Then let d = diameter of journal in inches.

$\qquad l$ = length of journal in inches.

$\qquad n$ = speed in revolutions per minute.

$\qquad$ P = total pressure in lbs.

$\qquad p$ = pressure per square inch in lbs.

$\qquad v$ = periphery speed of the journal in feet per second,

then, for ordinary engines :

$$p \lesseqgtr 270 \; ; \; p\,v \lesseqgtr 840.$$

These figures do not give the limit to which the pressure and speed may be carried, the table gives some examples taken from engines which have been running for some years.

TABLE 9.—**Examples of Main Bearings from Actual Practice.**

Diam. of Steam Cyl. in.	Stroke. in.	Revolution per min.	d. in.	l. in.	P. lbs.	p. lbs. per sq. in.	p. v. foot-lbs. p. sec. & sq. in.	Material of Bearings.	Machinery driven by engine.
17·7	27·5	66	6·7	10·8	28200	381	750	Babbited Gun metal	Electric light
23·6	43·3	75	12·6	24·4	37500	122	503	Gun metal	Roller mills
{ 23·6 35·4	41·3	60	8·6	14·2	46100	378	851	Babbit	Flour mill
{ 23·6 39·3	39·4	120	9·8	14·5	30800	277	1113	Gun metal	Roller mills
25·6	25·6	150 180	9·6	15·7	34800	235	1477 1772	Babbit	Roller mills
27·5	39·4	100	10·2	16·5	49500	290	1549	Babbit	Roller mills
31·5	47·2	80	12·2	19·7	52300	217	924	Gun metal	Roller mills
35·4	53·1	80	14·2	22·8	78200	242	1095	Gun metal	Roller mills
49·2	49·2	80 90	17·1	23·6	156200	387	2310 2599	Babbit	Roller mills

The Lubrication of Bearings is of great importance, and efficient means should always be provided for supply and distribution of the oil or other lubricant. Figs. 136, 137, give a section through the crank-shaft bearing of an engine used for driving a rolling mill. The lubricant is a stiff grease, and is delivered into the bearing by six pistons of gas tube, shown in the fig. 136 in their respective holes in the cap; from these the grease is forced by the weight of the pistons into channels formed at the joints of the different parts of the brass. The engine from which this example is taken has a cylinder of 39 ins. diameter, and the stroke is 55 ins.

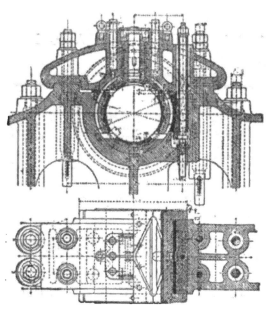

Figs. 136 and 137.

The large opening in the centre of the cap can be filled up with lard (*speck*), a material largely used in rolling mills. The adjusting wedge is of the same form as that shown in fig. 127.

Water is occasionally used to cool down hot bearings, applied as shown in fig. 138; with marine engines water is laid on to most of the bearings through small copper pipes from a cistern, each pipe being provided with a tap. Figs. 139—142 give

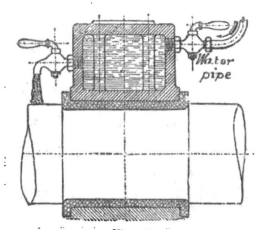

Fig. 138.

examples of a large crank shaft bearing, with the dimensions given in inches in Table 10 below.

Solidified oil or grease has been successfully introduced for the lubrication of engine and other bearings; it is forced into the oil grooves by a special screw cap to the lubricator, such as those of Stauffer and others.

Fig. 139. Fig. 141.

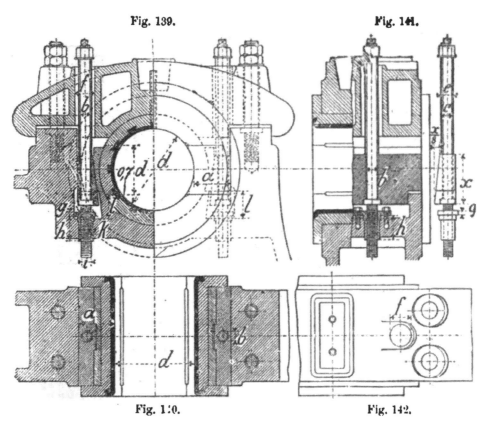

Fig. 140. Fig. 142.

Figs. 139—142.—Bearing with Brasses in Four Parts.

TABLE 10.—**Dimensions of Bearings** (Figs. 139—142).

d	a	b	c	e	f	g	h	i	k	l
7	$3\frac{5}{8}$	$\frac{7}{8}$	1	$1\frac{1}{4}$	$2\frac{1}{2}$	$\frac{3}{8}$	$2\frac{1}{8}$	$\frac{7}{8}$	$\frac{1}{4}$	$2\frac{1}{2}$
$7\frac{1}{2}$	$3\frac{7}{8}$	1	$1\frac{1}{4}$	$1\frac{1}{2}$	$2\frac{1}{2}$	$\frac{3}{8}$	$2\frac{1}{4}$	1	$\frac{1}{4}$	$2\frac{1}{2}$
8	4	1	$1\frac{1}{4}$	$1\frac{1}{2}$	$2\frac{1}{2}$	$\frac{3}{8}$	$2\frac{3}{8}$	1	$\frac{1}{4}$	$2\frac{3}{4}$
$8\frac{1}{2}$	$4\frac{1}{4}$	$1\frac{1}{8}$	$1\frac{1}{4}$	$1\frac{3}{4}$	$2\frac{3}{4}$	$\frac{1}{2}$	$2\frac{1}{2}$	$1\frac{1}{8}$	$\frac{5}{16}$	3
9	$4\frac{1}{2}$	$1\frac{1}{8}$	$1\frac{1}{2}$	$1\frac{3}{4}$	$2\frac{3}{4}$	$\frac{1}{2}$	$2\frac{3}{4}$	$1\frac{1}{8}$	$\frac{5}{16}$	$3\frac{1}{8}$
10	$4\frac{7}{8}$	$1\frac{1}{4}$	$1\frac{1}{2}$	$1\frac{3}{4}$	$3\frac{1}{8}$	$\frac{1}{2}$	3	$1\frac{1}{4}$	$\frac{3}{8}$	$3\frac{1}{4}$
11	$5\frac{3}{8}$	$1\frac{1}{4}$	$1\frac{1}{2}$	$2\frac{3}{8}$	$3\frac{1}{8}$	$\frac{1}{2}$	$3\frac{1}{4}$	$1\frac{1}{4}$	$\frac{3}{8}$	$3\frac{1}{2}$
12	$5\frac{3}{4}$	$1\frac{3}{8}$	2	$2\frac{3}{8}$	$3\frac{1}{2}$	$\frac{1}{2}$	$3\frac{3}{8}$	$1\frac{3}{8}$	$\frac{7}{16}$	$3\frac{3}{4}$
13	$6\frac{1}{4}$	$1\frac{1}{2}$	2	$2\frac{3}{8}$	$3\frac{3}{4}$	$\frac{5}{8}$	$3\frac{3}{4}$	$1\frac{1}{2}$	$\frac{1}{2}$	4
14	$6\frac{1}{2}$	$1\frac{1}{2}$	2	3	$3\frac{3}{4}$	$\frac{5}{8}$	4	$1\frac{1}{2}$	$\frac{1}{2}$	$4\frac{1}{4}$
15	7	$1\frac{3}{4}$	$2\frac{1}{2}$	3	$4\frac{1}{8}$	$\frac{5}{8}$	$4\frac{1}{4}$	$1\frac{3}{4}$	$\frac{5}{8}$	$4\frac{1}{2}$
16	$7\frac{1}{2}$	$1\frac{3}{4}$	$2\frac{1}{2}$	3	$4\frac{3}{8}$	$\frac{5}{8}$	$4\frac{1}{2}$	$1\frac{3}{4}$	$\frac{5}{8}$	$4\frac{3}{4}$

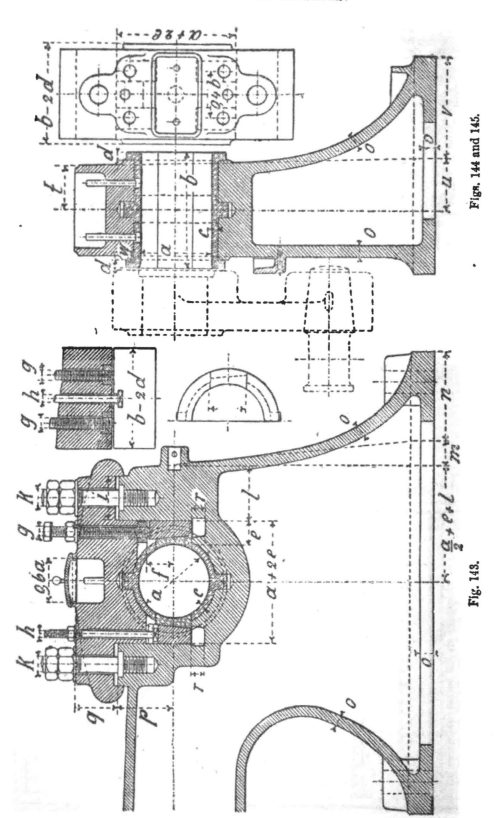

Figs. 144 and 145.

Fig. 143.

TABLE 11.—**Dimensions of Crank Shaft Bearings** (Figs. 143—145).

Engine.		Brasses.									Bolts.												
H	D	*a*	*b*	*c*	*d*	*e*	*f*	*g*	*h*	*i*	No.	*k*	*l*	*m*	*n*	*o*	*p*	*q*	*r*	*t*	*u*	*v*	*w*
16	8	3⅝	5⅞	7/16	½	1¼	1⅜	⅝	½	2¼	2	⅞	2⅝	—	4¼	¾	2½	2¼	⅞	2	2½	—	¼
20	10	4½	7¼	7/16	½	1⅜	1⅝	⅝	½	2½	2	1	3	1⅝	5	¾	3¼	2⅝	1	2¾	3¼	5¾	¼
24	12	5¼	8½	½	⅝	1½	2	⅝	½	2¾	2	1⅛	3⅝	1⅞	6⅛	⅞	4	3	1¼	3⅛	3¾	7¼	¼
28	14	6⅜	9½	9/16	⅝	1¾	2⅜	¾	½	3¼	2	1¼	4¼	2 3/16	6⅝	1	4¾	3⅜	1⅜	3⅝	4¼	7¾	¼
32	16	7	10¾	⅝	¾	1¾	2¾	¾	½	3⅝	2	1¼	4¾	2⅜	7⅝	1	5⅝	3¾	1½	4¼	4¾	8¼	¼
36	18	7⅝	12	⅝	¾	2⅛	3¼	⅞	⅝	4	4	1¼	5⅜	2 7/16	7¾	1⅛	6½	4¼	1¾	4¾	5½	9½	⅜
40	20	8¾	13¼	¾	⅞	2⅜	3⅝	⅞	⅝	4⅝	4	1⅜	6	2⅞	8⅜	1¼	7¼	4⅝	2	5¼	6	10	⅜
44	22	10	14¾	13/16	1	2½	4	⅞	⅝	5¼	4	1⅜	6¾	3	8¾	1¼	7¾	5	2¼	5¾	6½	11½	⅜

All the Dimensions are given in Inches.

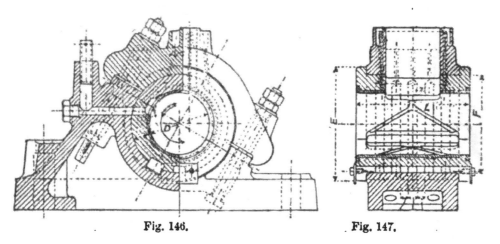

Fig. 146.   Fig. 147.

Figs. 146, 147 show an example of inclined main bearing for high speed rope pulley, and is arranged for water circulation.

Crank Shafts, Cranks, and Crank Discs.

Crank shafts were usually made of wrought iron, but now almost always of mild steel. For very large marine engines they are built

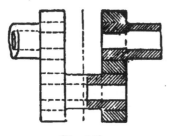

Fig. 148.

up of steel, often Whitworth's compressed steel, and are made hollow to save weight; the diameter of the hollow being about ·6 of the external diameter of the shaft. Fig. 148 shows a built-up hollow crank.

In high speed engines the weight of the connecting rod and crank should be balanced.

Let W_1 = the necessary balance weight.

R   = radius of the centre of gravity of the balance weight.

W_2 = weight of the crank pin plus half the weight of the connecting rod.

r = the radius of the crank.

W_3 = weight of the piston, piston rod and crosshead.

Then for horizontal engines

$$W_1 = W_2 \frac{r}{R} \; ;$$

for vertical engines

$$W_1 = \tfrac{2}{3} (W_2 + W_3) \frac{r}{R} \; ;$$

for locomotives it may be taken that

$$W_1 = W_2 \frac{r}{R}.$$

The balance weight should act in the same plane in which the parts to be balanced move ; hence it is wrong to balance the crank, connecting rod, piston, and crosshead by applying the balance weight to the fly-wheel. The employment of crank discs, figs. 160, 163, although somewhat easy to balance, is often objectionable on account of their acting as resonant bodies, and tend to magnify the noise caused by any knock in the engine.* A balanced crank disc is shown in figs. 156, 157.

Cranks, Crank Discs slotted out, and bent Crank Shafts.

Figs. 149 and 150. Figs. 151—155.

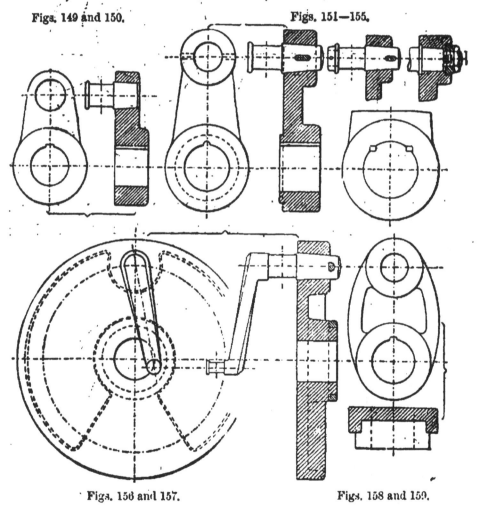

Figs. 156 and 157. Figs. 158 and 159.

Figs. 149, 150, show a form of ordinary crank, formerly made of cast iron ; figs. 151—155, a crank of wrought iron or cast steel ; figs.

---

* This may be true in some cases, but if the disc is sufficiently massive the effect is not very noticeable, especially if the balance weight is applied as is shown in figs. 182, 184.—ED.

156, 157, a crank disc of cast iron ; figs. 158, 159, a crank of either cast iron or cast steel, the former material is not now much used, except in small cheap engines.

Crank Shafts with Balance Weights.

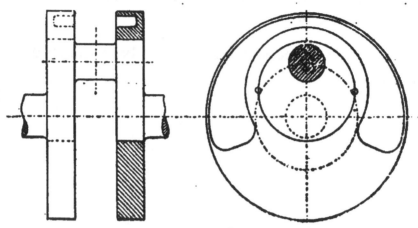

Figs. 160 and 161.

Figs. 160, 161, show a slotted or machined-out crank, with disc balance weights applied in a special manner to the round cheeks of the crank dip.

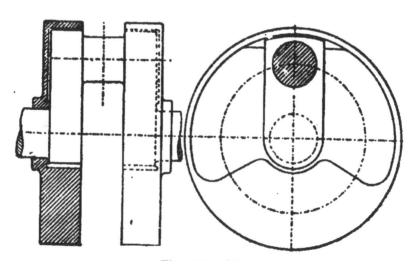

Figs. 162 and 163.

Figs. 162, 163, show an arrangement for applying the balance weights to the cheeks of an ordinary slotted-out crank.

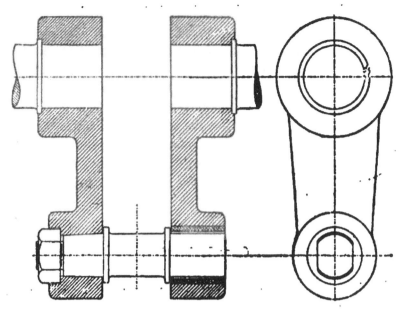

Figs. 164 and 165.

Figs. 164, 165, show a wrought-iron or steel crank, with the crank pin free in one side of the crank; this type is much used for paddle engines, the engine crank shaft being separate from the paddle-wheel shafts, the latter being driven by the crank pin as shown, the left crank being on the engine shaft, the right-hand one on the paddle-wheel shaft.

Cranks, Crank Discs, Slotted-out and Bent Crank Shafts.

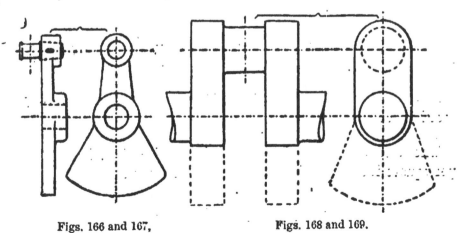

Figs. 166 and 167,   Figs. 168 and 169.

Figs. 166, 167 show a form of crank with balance weight in one piece; figs. 168, 169, a slotted-out crank a form much used in

E

" undertype" and other engines where it is desirable to save room in the width of the engine, this form being narrower than the common form of bent crank, which is almost exclusively used on portable

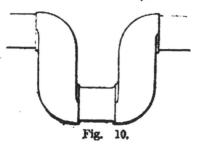

Fig. 10.

engines, fig. 170. In the fig. 169 the slotted crank is shown with the sides shaped off concentric with the shaft and pin respectively at the two ends, but it is usual to turn these ends in the lathe on a centre, midway between the crank pin and shaft centres.

Crank Shafts.

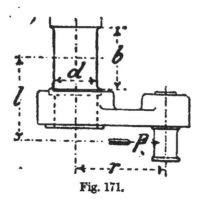

Fig. 171.

Particulars of the neck or journal.

In fig. 171 :—

P = Pressure on piston in lbs. ;

$M_b = Pl$ = the bending moment in inch or foot lbs. ;

$M_d = Pr$ = the turning moment in inch or foot lbs. ;

k = the stress on the material in pounds per square inch ;

so the ideal bending moment (if, as usually the case, $M_b < M_d$)
$(M_b)_i = {\cdot}625 \ M_b + {\cdot}6 \ M_d = Wk$.

Example.—An engine with piston $15\frac{3}{4}$" diameter, stroke $27\frac{1}{2}$", $l = 13\frac{3}{4}$", $p = 103$ lbs. per square inch, P = 20064 lbs.

$(M_b)_i = ({\cdot}625 \times 20064 \times 13{\cdot}75 + 20064 \times {\cdot}6 \times 13{\cdot}75) \div 12 = 28400$ foot lbs., or 340600 inch lbs.

The stress on the metal may be taken as $k = 9960$ lbs., or $4{\cdot}4$ tons per square inch, this gives the resistance moment

$$W = {\cdot}1 \ d^3 = \frac{340600}{9960} = 34{\cdot}0$$

$$d = 6{\cdot}9 \text{ inches.}$$

Material: Wrought Iron or Mild Steel.

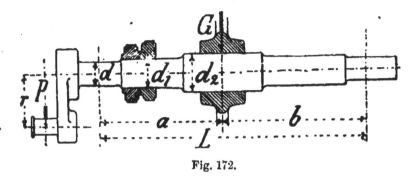

Fig. 172.

The diameter of the neck or journal being d, the diameters at the other parts of the shaft in fig. 172, $d_1 = 1\cdot15\,d$, $d_2 = 1\cdot4\,d$.

With usual proportions the stress on the metal at d_2 may be taken as from 2,800 to 5,600 lbs., or $1\frac{1}{4}$ to $2\frac{1}{2}$ tons per square inch.

If G = the weight of the fly-wheel in pounds, the ideal bending moment for d_2, taking as before, page 50, $M_b < M_d$,

$$(M_b)_i = Wk = 0\cdot625\ G\frac{ab}{L} + 0\cdot6\ Pr.$$

Cranks and Crank Pins.

Wrought-iron or cast steel cranks (fig. 173).

Length of boss $b = \cdot9$ to $1\cdot3\,d$;
Thickness of metal $W = \cdot4$ to $\cdot5\,d$;

The crank web will be exposed to a bending and twisting stress,

$$M_b = Pr\ ;\ M_d = Pa.$$

The diameter of the boss for the crank pin will be about $\frac{2}{3}$ of the larger boss for the shaft. The bore of the boss is made from $\frac{1}{1000}$ to $\frac{1}{2000}$ smaller than the end of the crank shaft, put on hot, in workshop language "shrunk on," and fitted with one or two keys.

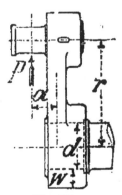

Fig. 173.

Crank Shafts for Engines with Two Cylinders.

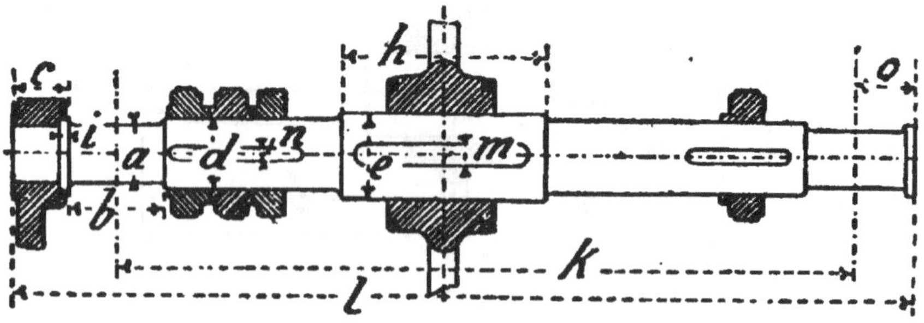

Fig. 174.

TABLE 12.—**Dimensions of Crank Shafts** (Fig. 174).

Diam. of Piston and Stroke.		Journal or Neck.											
H	D	*a*	*b*	*c*	*d*	*e*	*h*	*i*	*k*	*l*	*m*	*n*	*o*
20	10	$4\frac{1}{2}$	$7\frac{1}{4}$	$3\frac{15}{16}$	$5\frac{1}{4}$	$5\frac{1}{4}$	—	$\frac{1}{4}$	4′ 4″	5′ $3\frac{3}{4}$″	$1\frac{3}{8}$	$\frac{5}{8}$	$4\frac{1}{4}$
24	12	$5\frac{1}{4}$	$8\frac{1}{2}$	5	6	6	—	$\frac{1}{4}$	4′ 10″	6′ $0\frac{1}{4}$″	$1\frac{5}{8}$	$\frac{5}{8}$	5
28	14	$6\frac{3}{8}$	$9\frac{1}{2}$	$5\frac{3}{4}$	$7\frac{3}{8}$	$8\frac{3}{8}$	1′ 8″	$\frac{3}{8}$	5′ 4″	6′ $8\frac{1}{8}$″	2	$\frac{3}{4}$	$5\frac{5}{8}$
32	16	7	$10\frac{3}{4}$	$6\frac{5}{8}$	8	$9\frac{3}{8}$	2′ 0″	$\frac{3}{8}$	5′ 10″	7′ $4\frac{3}{4}$″	$2\frac{1}{4}$	$\frac{3}{4}$	$6\frac{3}{4}$
36	18	$7\frac{5}{8}$	12	$7\frac{3}{8}$	$8\frac{5}{8}$	$10\frac{5}{8}$	2′ 4″	$\frac{1}{2}$	6′ 4″	8′ $0\frac{3}{8}$″	$2\frac{5}{8}$	$\frac{3}{4}$	7
40	20	$8\frac{3}{4}$	$13\frac{1}{4}$	$8\frac{1}{8}$	10	12	2′ 8″	$\frac{1}{2}$	7′ 0″	8′ $10\frac{1}{2}$″	$2\frac{3}{4}$	$\frac{3}{4}$	$7\frac{3}{4}$
44	22	10	$14\frac{3}{4}$	$8\frac{3}{8}$	$11\frac{1}{4}$	$13\frac{1}{4}$	3′ 0″	$\frac{1}{2}$	7′ 8″	9′ $8\frac{3}{4}$″	3	$\frac{7}{8}$	$8\frac{5}{8}$

All Dimensions are given in Feet and Inches.

Crank Pins.

These are invariably of mild steel.

d = diameter of pin in inches.

b = length of pin in inches.

P = maximum pressure on piston in lbs.,

then $M_i = P \dfrac{b}{2} = Wk = \cdot 1 \, d^3 k.$

Fig. 175.

The stress k may be taken as from 6,720 to 11,200 lbs. or 3 to 5 tons per square inch. In order to avoid heating, the crank pin is usually made larger than given by the above formula, let $p = \dfrac{P}{db}$ = the pressure per square inch in lbs. on the surface of the crank pin and $v = \dfrac{d\pi n}{12}$ = speed of crank pin surface in feet per minute, then for ordinary workmanship $p \leq 1,130$ lbs. per square inch $vp \leq 845$ with very high class workmanship we may go higher, see table on page 63.

Methods of fixing crank pins into the crank arm.—A very usual method is with cone and key (fig. 177), the pin being shrunk in, the taper of the cone being about 1 in 32. There is always difficulty in boring a tapered hole and making a pin to be an exact fit, an easier and better method of fixing crank pins is by making the pin with a collar and turning the shank parallel to fit a parallel hole in the crank arm, the pin can, when small, be secured by riveting the end over or by a key transversely through crank arm and pin, but in all cases the pin should be shrunk in, or squeezed in with a hydraulic press. A special method of fixing the pin is shown in fig. 174, which also shows an elaborate system of lubrication.

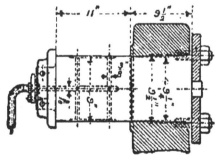

Fig. 176.

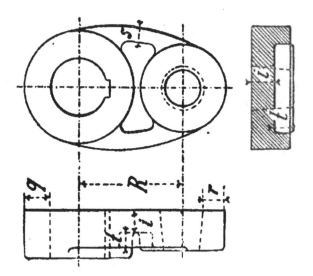

Figs. 179—181.

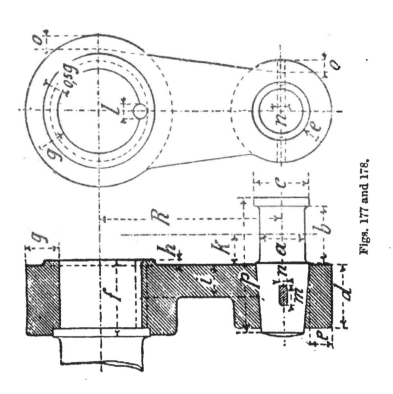

Figs. 177 and 178.

TABLE 13.—**Dimensions of Cranks and Crank Pins** (Figs. 177—181).

Diameter of Piston, Stroke and Radius of Crank.			Wrought iron or cast steel.															Cast iron.			
H	D	R	*a*	*b*	*c*	*d*	*e*	*f*	*g*	*h*	*i*	*k*	*l*	*m*	*n*	*o*	*p*	*q*	*r*	*s*	*t*
20	10	10	$2\frac{5}{8}$	$3\frac{1}{4}$	$3\frac{1}{4}$	$3\frac{1}{4}$	$1\frac{1}{4}$	$3\frac{15}{16}$	2	$\frac{5}{16}$	$1\frac{3}{4}$	$1\frac{11}{16}$	$\frac{3}{4}$	1	$\frac{3}{8}$	$\frac{3}{4}$	7	2	$1\frac{1}{2}$	$1\frac{1}{8}$	$1\frac{1}{4}$
24	12	12	$2\frac{3}{4}$	$3\frac{5}{8}$	$3\frac{5}{8}$	4	$1\frac{3}{8}$	5	$2\frac{3}{8}$	$\frac{3}{8}$	2	$1\frac{7}{8}$	$\frac{7}{8}$	$1\frac{1}{8}$	$\frac{7}{16}$	$\frac{7}{8}$	$8\frac{1}{4}$	$2\frac{3}{8}$	$1\frac{3}{4}$	$1\frac{1}{4}$	$1\frac{3}{8}$
28	14	14	$3\frac{1}{4}$	$4\frac{1}{4}$	4	$4\frac{3}{8}$	$1\frac{1}{2}$	$5\frac{3}{4}$	$2\frac{5}{8}$	$\frac{7}{16}$	$2\frac{1}{4}$	$2\frac{3}{16}$	1	$1\frac{3}{8}$	$\frac{1}{2}$	1	$9\frac{1}{2}$	$2\frac{5}{8}$	2	$1\frac{3}{8}$	$1\frac{1}{2}$
32	16	16	$3\frac{3}{4}$	$4\frac{5}{8}$	$4\frac{5}{8}$	$4\frac{3}{4}$	$1\frac{3}{4}$	$6\frac{5}{8}$	$2\frac{7}{8}$	$\frac{7}{16}$	$2\frac{5}{8}$	$2\frac{3}{8}$	$1\frac{1}{8}$	$1\frac{1}{2}$	$\frac{9}{16}$	1	$10\frac{1}{4}$	3	$2\frac{1}{4}$	$1\frac{1}{2}$	$1\frac{3}{4}$
36	18	18	$4\frac{1}{4}$	$5\frac{1}{4}$	5	$5\frac{1}{4}$	2	$7\frac{3}{8}$	$3\frac{1}{4}$	$\frac{1}{2}$	3	$2\frac{3}{4}$	$1\frac{1}{4}$	$1\frac{5}{8}$	$\frac{5}{8}$	$1\frac{1}{8}$	$11\frac{1}{4}$	—	—	—	—
40	20	20	$4\frac{3}{4}$	$5\frac{3}{4}$	$5\frac{3}{4}$	$5\frac{3}{4}$	$2\frac{1}{4}$	$8\frac{1}{8}$	$3\frac{1}{2}$	$\frac{1}{2}$	$3\frac{3}{8}$	3	$1\frac{1}{4}$	$1\frac{3}{4}$	$\frac{11}{16}$	$1\frac{1}{4}$	$12\frac{1}{2}$	—	—	—	—
44	22	22	$5\frac{1}{4}$	$6\frac{3}{8}$	$6\frac{1}{4}$	$6\frac{3}{8}$	$2\frac{3}{8}$	$8\frac{3}{8}$	$3\frac{3}{4}$	$\frac{9}{16}$	4	$3\frac{5}{16}$	$1\frac{3}{8}$	2	$\frac{3}{4}$	$1\frac{1}{4}$	$13\frac{1}{2}$	—	—	—	—

All Dimensions are given in Inches.

Crank Discs of Cast Iron.

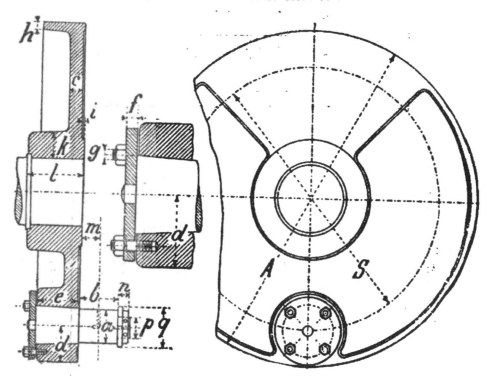

Figs. 182—184.

TABLE 14.—Dimensions of Crank Discs (Figs. 182—184).

Diameter of piston and stroke.		Crank Pin.							Bolts.									
H	D	A	a	b	c	d	e	f	No.	g	h	i	k	l	m	n	p	q
16	8	22	$2\frac{1}{2}$	$3\frac{1}{2}$	$1\frac{1}{8}$	3	3	$\frac{3}{8}$	3	$\frac{5}{8}$	$\frac{5}{8}$	$\frac{1}{8}$	2	4	$1\frac{3}{4}$	1	$1\frac{3}{4}$	3
20	10	26	$2\frac{3}{4}$	4	$1\frac{1}{4}$	3	$3\frac{1}{2}$	$\frac{7}{16}$	3	$\frac{5}{8}$	$\frac{5}{8}$	$\frac{1}{4}$	$2\frac{1}{4}$	5	$1\frac{3}{4}$	$1\frac{1}{8}$	$1\frac{7}{8}$	$3\frac{1}{2}$
24	12	31	$3\frac{1}{4}$	$4\frac{1}{2}$	$1\frac{3}{8}$	$3\frac{1}{2}$	4	$\frac{1}{2}$	3	$\frac{3}{4}$	$\frac{3}{4}$	$\frac{1}{4}$	$2\frac{1}{2}$	6	2	$1\frac{1}{4}$	$2\frac{1}{4}$	4
28	14	36	$3\frac{1}{2}$	5	$1\frac{5}{8}$	4	$4\frac{1}{2}$	$\frac{9}{16}$	4	$\frac{5}{8}$	$\frac{3}{4}$	$\frac{3}{8}$	$2\frac{3}{4}$	7	$2\frac{1}{8}$	$1\frac{3}{8}$	$2\frac{5}{8}$	$4\frac{1}{2}$
32	16	41	$4\frac{1}{4}$	$5\frac{1}{2}$	$1\frac{3}{4}$	$4\frac{1}{2}$	5	$\frac{5}{8}$	4	$\frac{5}{8}$	$\frac{7}{8}$	$\frac{3}{8}$	3	$7\frac{1}{2}$	$2\frac{3}{8}$	$1\frac{1}{2}$	$2\frac{7}{8}$	5
36	18	46	$4\frac{3}{4}$	6	2	5	$5\frac{1}{2}$	$\frac{11}{16}$	4	$\frac{3}{4}$	$\frac{7}{8}$	$\frac{1}{2}$	$3\frac{1}{2}$	8	$2\frac{1}{2}$	$1\frac{3}{4}$	$3\frac{1}{4}$	$5\frac{1}{2}$
40	20	51	5	$6\frac{1}{2}$	$2\frac{1}{8}$	$5\frac{1}{2}$	6	$\frac{3}{4}$	4	$\frac{3}{4}$	1	$\frac{1}{2}$	4	$8\frac{1}{2}$	$2\frac{3}{4}$	2	$3\frac{1}{2}$	6

Preparation of Crank Pins in Special Cases.

Crank pins are sometimes case-hardened and ground up true in a grinding machine. This has been done in America, and also in Germany and other countries. The journals in the Allen engine by Whitworth were ground up perfectly true; no doubt this is conducive to cool running, but with crank pins the heating is not always caused by want of truth in the form of the pin, but probably from the pin not being perfectly in line with the crank shaft.

Lubrication of Crank Pins.

In small engines the necessary lubrication is obtained from an oil cup in the connecting rod end (fig. 185).

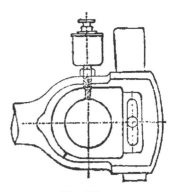

Fig. 185.

An arrangement for oiling the crank pin whilst the engine is running is shown in fig. 186. The oil cup is supported on the guard rail of the engine. The oil from the cup runs down a tube into a hollow ring at the end of a tube fixed into the crank pin. This hollow ring receives the oil which by centrifugal force makes its way through the holes in the crank pin, and thus supplies the pin

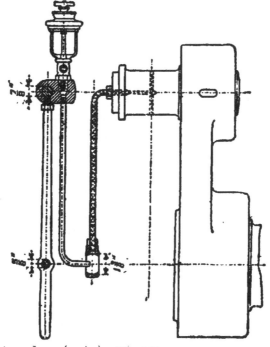

Fig. 186.

and connecting rod end with oil. Two other methods of lubricating with special grease are shown in figs. 187, 188, one with the "Stauffer"

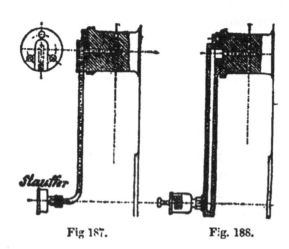

Fig 187.   Fig. 188.

grease cup. The cap of this cup is screwed down by hand, and forces the grease along the tube to the pin.

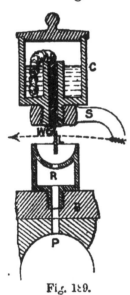

Fig. 189.

Another method much used in large engines is shown in fig. 189. The oil cup, C, is supported on a wrought-iron standard carried up from the main bearing pedestal, so as to stand just over the crank pin when at the highest position. A cotton wick is provided in the cup, and is allowed to project through the bottom of the cup far enough to be wiped by the lip, L, in the cup R, fixed to the connecting rod end, B; at every revolution of the crank a small quantity of oil is wiped off by the lip, and falls down the oil hole to the crank pin, P. This method answers very well with engines running at ordinary speed, is very simple and inexpensive, and easily kept clean, there being no long pipes through which the oil must pass, and which frequently get stopped up with gummy matter and dirt.

Slotted or Machined-out Cranks.

Formerly these were forged solid out of wrought iron, and then the dip drilled and slotted out; now they are usually made of mild steel, and machined out to the required form and dimensions. Small cranks are occasionally cast to form from a pattern in steel.*

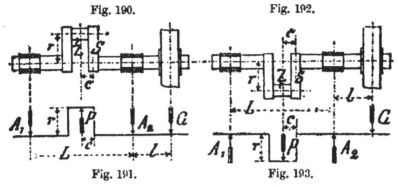

Fig. 190.   Fig. 192.

Fig. 191.   Fig. 193.

Let P = the pressure on the crank pin in lbs.

     G = the weight of the fly-wheel in lbs.

(a.) Single Crank Shaft as in the above figs. 190, 193.

The maximum supported pressure is first to be calculated.

In figs. 190, 191—

$$A_1 = \frac{P \cdot \frac{L}{2} + G \cdot l}{L} = \frac{P}{2} + G \frac{l}{L} \quad . \quad . \quad (3)$$

In figs. 192, 193—

$$A_2 = \frac{P \cdot \frac{L}{2} + G(L + l)}{L} = \frac{P}{2} + G + G \frac{l}{L} \quad . \quad (4)$$

For calculating the crank checks or dips, S, imagine the right-hand cheek as rigidly fixed; then in figs. 190, 191—

$$\text{I.} \begin{cases} M_b = A_1 \left(\frac{L}{2} + c \right) - Pc \quad . \quad . \quad . \quad (5) \\ M_d = 0 \quad . \quad . \quad . \quad . \quad . \quad (6) \end{cases}$$

---

* There is some risk of confusion in speaking of "mild steel," "cast steel," and "steel castings," or "cast in steel." Generally speaking "mild steel" means such steels as are worked up from open hearth or Bessemer ingots into bars, plates, angles, &c. Such steel is not supposed to harden perceptibly when heated and quenched in cold water. "Cast steel" is a somewhat vague term, but may be generally taken to mean steel worked up from ingots made from melted shear steel, and is usually highly carbonized, and capable of being hardened in the ordinary way. One kind of this steel is known as tool steel. "Cast in steel" or "steel castings" means that the object is actually cast in form from melted steel poured into a mould. Steel castings of the very best quality are often advertised as "crucible steel," meaning obviously that the steel is melted in crucibles, and poured from them into the mould. Other more direct processes than this are used for large steel castings.

When turned 90°—

$$\text{II.} \begin{cases} M_b = Pr & \text{. . . . . . . (7)} \\ M_d = A_1 \left(\dfrac{L}{2} + c\right) - Pc & \text{. . (8)} \end{cases}$$

To calculate the cross section, that value is to be introduced which, according to equations I. or II., gives the $(M_i)_i$.

$$\text{For the pin Z take} \begin{cases} M_b = A_1 \dfrac{L}{2} & \text{. . . . . (9)} \\ M_d = 0. \end{cases}$$

$$\text{At the bearing } A_2 \begin{cases} M_b = Gb & \text{. . . . . (10)} \\ M_d = Pr & \text{. . . . . . (11)} \end{cases}$$

M_b and M_d may be combined into the ideal bending moment $(M_b)_i$ according to the formula given on page 50.

Example.—Calculation from above formulæ for the shaft of an engine with piston 8″ diameter, and stroke 11¾″, working pressure 75 lbs. per square inch. The engine frame is shown on page 20, fig. 54.

$$P = 3306 \text{ lbs., } G = 880 \text{ lbs., } r = \frac{11 \cdot 75}{2} = 5 \cdot 875 \text{ inches.}$$

$$L = 29 \cdot 5 \text{ inches, } l = 8 \cdot 67 \text{ inches, } c = 2 \cdot 95 \text{ inches.}$$

$$A_1 = \frac{3306}{2} + 880 \frac{8 \cdot 67}{29 \cdot 5} = 1912 \text{ lbs.}$$

$$A_2 = \frac{3306}{2} + 880 + 880 \frac{8 \cdot 67}{29 \cdot 5} = 2792 \text{ lbs.}$$

Fig. 194.

For the crank cheeks or dips—

$$\text{II.} \begin{cases} M_b = 3306 \times 5 \cdot 875 = 19423 \text{ inch-lbs.,} \\ M_d = 1913 \, (14 \cdot 76 + 2 \cdot 95) - 3306 \times 2 \cdot 95 = 24110 \text{ inch-lbs. ;} \end{cases}$$

then $(M_b)_i = \cdot 625 \times 19423 + \cdot 6 \times 24126 = 12139 + 14466 = $
26605 inch-lbs.

The cross-section of the crank cheek $= 3 \cdot 5'' \times 2 \cdot 4'' = 8 \cdot 4$ sq. ins. the value of the smallest cross-section of metal.

$$\frac{26605}{8 \cdot 4} = 3170 \text{ inch-lbs. per square inch nearly.}$$

For the bearing A_2, figs. 190—193,

$$(M_b)_i = \cdot625 \times 880 \times 8\cdot625 + \cdot6 \times 3306 \times 5\cdot9 =$$
$$4744 + 11706 = 16450 \text{ inch-lbs.}$$

Cross-section $=$ area of $2\cdot95$ inches $= 6\cdot83$ sq. ins.

$$\frac{16450}{6\cdot83} = 2406 \text{ inch-lbs. per square inch.}$$

For the crank pin, Z, $M_t = 1913 \times \dfrac{29\cdot5}{2} = 28216$ inch-lbs.

Cross-section $=$ area of $3\cdot14 = 7\cdot74$

$$\frac{28216}{7\cdot74} = 3644 \text{ inch-lbs. per square inch.}$$

(b.) Double Crank Shafts.

Also here the first point to be determined is the pressure on the bearings; for simple calculation the pressure on the two pistons may be taken as equal.

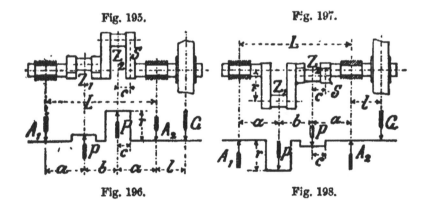

Fig. 195. Fig. 197.

Fig. 196. Fig. 198.

In figs. 195, 196,

$$A_1 = \frac{Pa + P(a + b) + Gl}{L} = P + G\frac{l}{L} \qquad . \qquad . \qquad . \quad (12)$$

In figs. 197, 198,

$$A_2 = \frac{Pa + P(a + b) + G(L + l)}{L} = P + G + G\frac{l}{L} \quad . \quad (13)$$

The twisting and bending moments for the cheeks, S, crank pin, Z_2, and bearing, A_2, can be determined by the same method as above.

A useful formula for calculating the diameter of a crank shaft is as follows : $d = \sqrt[3]{\dfrac{HP}{N}} \times c$. Where N = number of revolutions per minute, c = a constant based on practice. When using the somewhat vague term of "nominal" horse-power, the constant may be taken as 560; $d = \sqrt[3]{\dfrac{HP}{N}} \times 560$. When using indicated horse-power, the constant may be taken as 190; $d = \sqrt[3]{\dfrac{IHP}{N}} \times 190$, this will give ample strength for mild steel shafts.

Methods of oiling Crank Pins of Bent and Slotted-out Cranks.—The usual method is based on that shown on page 57, fig. 185, where the crank pin is oiled through the connecting rod end. Another method, but certainly not so good, is shown in fig. 199,

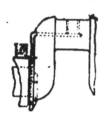

where a hole is drilled in the pin shown in dotted lines, and fed with oil by a cup fixed to a ring held concentric with the shaft. No doubt this would freely oil the pin, but the long holes through which the oil has to travel are liable to get choked up, and may do so without being noticed until the pin runs hot.

Fig. 199.

Connecting Rods.

Of almost equal importance to the crank shaft main bearing is the connecting rod end which works on the crank pin. The desire to make a perfect connecting rod end has led to a large number of

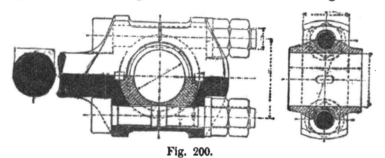

Fig. 200.

varieties being designed, but the general tendency has been to settle down into two or three types, such as the marine type with bolts, the strap and cotter type, the solid end type, and a few others for special cases.

Fig. 200 shows an example of connecting rod end fitted with bolts, and the seating faces of the brasses of spherical form to allow of slight self-adjustment should any part be out of truth. The example is taken from a pumping engine, with a crank pin 9·84 inches diameter.

TABLE 15.—Engine Crank Pins from Actual Practice.
(Kiesselbach.)

Diam. of Cyl. in.	Stroke in.	Revs. per min.	d ins.	l ins.	P lbs.	p lbs. p. per. sq. in.	$p v$ ft. lbs. p. sec. &sq.in.	Material of bearings.	Machinery driven by Engine.
17·7	27·5	66	4·5	4·7	22500	1113	1381	Babbit	Electric light
23·6	43·3	75	8·5	13·0	30900	280	779	Gun metal	Roller mills
23·6 35·4	41·1	60	6·1	6·1	38200	1027	1640	Babbit	Flour mills
23·6 39·3	39·4	120	5·1	5·1	24700	950	1537	Gun metal	Roller mills
25·6	25·6	150 180	5·9	6·3	28200	750	2896 3475	Babbit	Roller mills
27·5	39·4	100	6·3	6·7	40400	957	2631	Babbit	Roller mills
31·5	47·2	80	7·1	8·6	41900	686	1700	Gun metal	Roller mills
35·4	53·1	80	7·9	9·8	65300	861	2374	Gun motal	Roller mills
49·2	49·2	80 90	9·8	11·0	127800	1186	4057 4567	Babbit	Roller mills

Connecting Rod Ends.

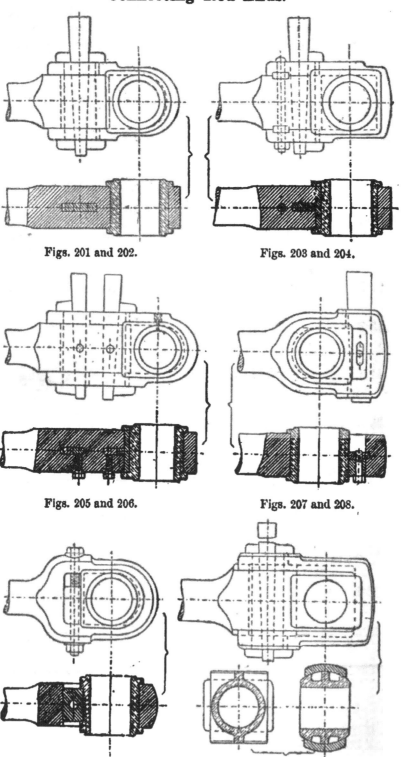

Figs. 201 and 202.

Figs. 203 and 204.

Figs. 205 and 206.

Figs. 207 and 208.

Figs. 209 and 210.

Figs. 211 and 212.

TABLE 22.—Dimensions of Crossheads (Figs. 260—263) for Engine Frame, page 24.

Engines		Cast Iron.																	Wrought Iron with Cast-iron Slippers.						
H	D	a	b	c	d	e	f	g	h	i	k	l	m	n	o	p	q	r	s	t	u	v	w	x
12	6	6	$3\frac{3}{8}$	7	$1\frac{1}{8}$	$1\frac{3}{4}$	1	2	$\frac{1}{2}$	$\frac{3}{4}$	1	$2\frac{3}{4}$	$\frac{3}{8}$	$1\frac{3}{4}$	$\frac{3}{8}$	$1\frac{1}{8}$	$\frac{3}{8}$	—	—	—	—	—	—	$5\frac{1}{4}$
16	8	$7\frac{7}{8}$	$4\frac{1}{2}$	9	$1\frac{1}{2}$	$2\frac{1}{8}$	$1\frac{1}{4}$	$2\frac{1}{4}$	$\frac{5}{8}$	$1\frac{1}{8}$	$1\frac{1}{4}$	$3\frac{3}{8}$	$\frac{3}{8}$	$2\frac{1}{8}$	$\frac{1}{2}$	$1\frac{3}{8}$	$\frac{3}{8}$	—	—	—	—	—	—	$6\frac{1}{4}$
20	10	$8\frac{3}{4}$	5	11	2	$2\frac{3}{4}$	$1\frac{1}{2}$	$2\frac{3}{4}$	$\frac{5}{8}$	$1\frac{1}{4}$	$1\frac{3}{8}$	$4\frac{1}{8}$	$\frac{7}{16}$	$2\frac{3}{4}$	$1\frac{1}{4}$	$\frac{3}{4}$	$\frac{3}{8}$	—	—	—	—	—	—	$7\frac{1}{2}$
24	12	$10\frac{3}{4}$	$6\frac{1}{4}$	12	$2\frac{1}{4}$	$3\frac{1}{4}$	$1\frac{7}{8}$	$3\frac{1}{8}$	$\frac{3}{4}$	$1\frac{3}{8}$	$1\frac{3}{8}$	$4\frac{1}{4}$	$\frac{1}{2}$	$3\frac{1}{8}$	$\frac{5}{8}$	1	$\frac{1}{2}$	$1\frac{1}{8}$	$1\frac{1}{8}$	$6\frac{3}{8}$	1	$1\frac{3}{8}$	$\frac{5}{8}$	$8\frac{1}{2}$
28	14	12	$7\frac{1}{4}$	$13\frac{1}{2}$	$2\frac{5}{8}$	$3\frac{5}{8}$	$2\frac{1}{8}$	$3\frac{3}{8}$	$\frac{7}{8}$	$1\frac{1}{2}$	$1\frac{3}{4}$	5	$\frac{9}{16}$	$3\frac{3}{4}$	$\frac{5}{8}$	$1\frac{1}{8}$	$\frac{1}{2}$	$1\frac{1}{4}$	$1\frac{1}{4}$	$7\frac{1}{4}$	$1\frac{1}{4}$	$1\frac{5}{8}$	$\frac{5}{8}$	$9\frac{1}{4}$
32	16	$13\frac{5}{8}$	8	15	3	4	$2\frac{1}{4}$	$3\frac{7}{8}$	$\frac{7}{8}$	$1\frac{5}{8}$	2	$5\frac{3}{4}$	$\frac{5}{8}$	$3\frac{3}{4}$	$\frac{3}{4}$	$1\frac{1}{8}$	$\frac{5}{8}$	$1\frac{3}{8}$	$1\frac{3}{8}$	8	$1\frac{3}{8}$	$1\frac{7}{8}$	$\frac{3}{4}$	$10\frac{1}{2}$
36	18	$14\frac{3}{4}$	$8\frac{3}{4}$	17	$3\frac{3}{8}$	$4\frac{3}{8}$	$2\frac{1}{2}$	$4\frac{1}{4}$	$1\frac{1}{8}$	$1\frac{3}{4}$	$2\frac{1}{8}$	$6\frac{1}{8}$	$\frac{11}{16}$	$4\frac{1}{8}$	$\frac{5}{8}$	$1\frac{1}{4}$	$\frac{5}{8}$	$1\frac{3}{8}$	$1\frac{1}{2}$	$8\frac{1}{2}$	$1\frac{1}{2}$	$2\frac{1}{8}$	$\frac{3}{4}$	$11\frac{1}{2}$
40	20	$16\frac{1}{8}$	$9\frac{1}{2}$	19	$3\frac{3}{4}$	$4\frac{3}{4}$	$2\frac{5}{8}$	$4\frac{5}{8}$	$1\frac{1}{4}$	$1\frac{7}{8}$	$2\frac{1}{4}$	$6\frac{5}{8}$	$\frac{3}{4}$	$4\frac{3}{8}$	$\frac{3}{4}$	$1\frac{3}{8}$	$\frac{3}{4}$	$1\frac{1}{2}$	$1\frac{5}{8}$	$9\frac{1}{4}$	$1\frac{3}{4}$	$2\frac{3}{8}$	$\frac{7}{8}$	$12\frac{1}{2}$
44	22	$21\frac{1}{2}$	10	21	4	$5\frac{1}{4}$	$3\frac{1}{8}$	5	$1\frac{5}{8}$	$2\frac{1}{4}$	$2\frac{5}{8}$	$7\frac{7}{8}$	$\frac{13}{16}$	$4\frac{3}{8}$	$\frac{3}{4}$	$1\frac{3}{8}$	$\frac{3}{4}$	$1\frac{3}{4}$	$1\frac{7}{8}$	10	2	$2\frac{5}{8}$	$\frac{7}{8}$	14

All Dimensions are given in Inches.

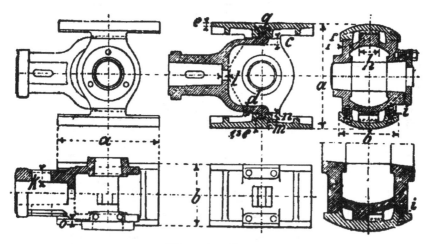

Figs. 264 and 265.

TABLE 23.—Dimensions of Cast Steel Crossheads with Cast-iron Slippers (Figs. 264, 265).

Engines.															
H	D	a	b	c	d	e	f	g	h	i	k	l	m	n	o
24	12	12	$6\frac{1}{4}$	$\frac{5}{8}$	$\frac{1}{2}$	$\frac{3}{8}$	1	$\frac{3}{4}$	2	$\frac{1}{2}$	$\frac{7}{8}$	$\frac{5}{8}$	$\frac{1}{2}$	$\frac{7}{8}$	$\frac{1}{16}$
32	16	15	8	$\frac{3}{4}$	$\frac{5}{8}$	$\frac{1}{2}$	$1\frac{1}{4}$	$1\frac{1}{4}$	$2\frac{3}{4}$	$\frac{1}{2}$	$1\frac{1}{8}$	$\frac{7}{8}$	$\frac{5}{8}$	$1\frac{1}{8}$	$\frac{1}{16}$
40	20	19	$9\frac{1}{2}$	$\frac{7}{8}$	$\frac{3}{4}$	$\frac{5}{8}$	$1\frac{3}{8}$	$1\frac{1}{4}$	3	$\frac{5}{8}$	$1\frac{1}{4}$	$1\frac{1}{8}$	$\frac{5}{8}$	$1\frac{1}{4}$	$\frac{1}{8}$
48	24	23	$11\frac{1}{4}$	1	$\frac{7}{8}$	$\frac{3}{4}$	$1\frac{5}{8}$	$1\frac{1}{2}$	$3\frac{5}{8}$	$\frac{5}{8}$	$1\frac{1}{2}$	$1\frac{3}{8}$	$\frac{3}{4}$	$1\frac{3}{8}$	$\frac{1}{8}$
56	28	27	$12\frac{3}{4}$	$1\frac{1}{8}$	1	$\frac{7}{8}$	2	$1\frac{5}{8}$	4	$\frac{3}{4}$	$1\frac{3}{4}$	$1\frac{5}{8}$	$\frac{7}{8}$	$1\frac{5}{8}$	$\frac{1}{8}$
64	32	31	$14\frac{1}{2}$	$1\frac{1}{4}$	$1\frac{1}{8}$	1	$2\frac{1}{4}$	2	$4\frac{3}{4}$	$\frac{3}{4}$	2	$1\frac{7}{8}$	1	$1\frac{7}{8}$	$\frac{1}{8}$
72	36	$34\frac{1}{2}$	$17\frac{1}{4}$	$1\frac{3}{8}$	$1\frac{1}{4}$	$1\frac{1}{8}$	$2\frac{5}{8}$	$2\frac{1}{4}$	$5\frac{3}{8}$	$\frac{7}{8}$	$2\frac{1}{4}$	$2\frac{1}{4}$	$1\frac{1}{8}$	$2\frac{1}{8}$	$\frac{3}{16}$
80	40	$38\frac{1}{2}$	20	$1\frac{1}{2}$	$1\frac{3}{8}$	$1\frac{1}{4}$	$2\frac{3}{4}$	$2\frac{3}{8}$	6	$\frac{7}{8}$	$2\frac{3}{8}$	$2\frac{3}{8}$	$1\frac{1}{4}$	$2\frac{3}{8}$	$\frac{3}{16}$

All Dimensions are given in Inches.

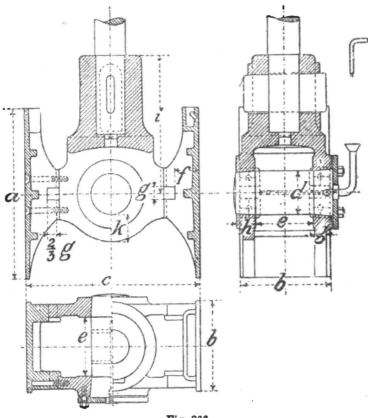

Fig. 266.

TABLE 24.—Dimensions of Cast-steel Crossheads with Cast-iron Slippers (Fig. 266).

Engine.		a	b	c	d	e	f	g	h	i	k
H	D										
28	26	18	11	21	$4\frac{1}{2}$	$6\frac{1}{2}$	$2\frac{1}{2}$	$1\frac{3}{8}$	2	15	$2\frac{1}{2}$
30	28	20	$11\frac{1}{2}$	22	5	7	$2\frac{3}{4}$	$1\frac{1}{2}$	$2\frac{1}{4}$	16	$2\frac{3}{4}$
32	30	22	12	23	$5\frac{1}{2}$	$7\frac{1}{2}$	3	$1\frac{5}{8}$	$2\frac{1}{2}$	17	3
34	32	23	$12\frac{1}{2}$	24	$5\frac{3}{4}$	8	$3\frac{1}{4}$	$1\frac{3}{4}$	$2\frac{3}{4}$	18	$3\frac{1}{4}$
36	34	24	13	25	6	$8\frac{1}{2}$	$3\frac{1}{2}$	$1\frac{7}{8}$	3	19	$3\frac{1}{2}$
38	36	25	$13\frac{1}{2}$	26	$6\frac{1}{4}$	9	$3\frac{3}{4}$	2	$3\frac{1}{4}$	20	$3\frac{3}{4}$
40	38	26	14	27	$6\frac{1}{2}$	$9\frac{1}{2}$	4	$2\frac{1}{4}$	$3\frac{1}{2}$	21	4
42	40	27	15	28	$6\frac{3}{4}$	10	$4\frac{1}{4}$	$2\frac{1}{2}$	$3\frac{3}{4}$	22	$4\frac{1}{4}$
44	44	28	16	29	7	$10\frac{1}{2}$	$4\frac{1}{2}$	$2\frac{3}{4}$	4	23	$4\frac{1}{2}$

All Dimensions are given in Inches.

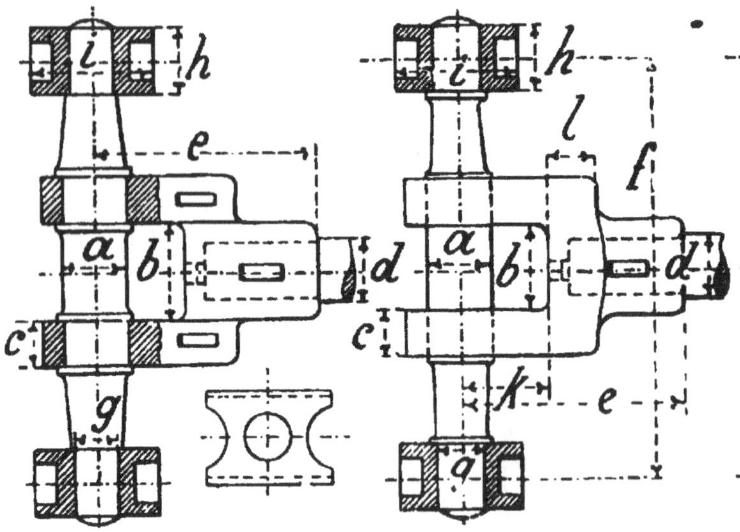

Fig. 267.

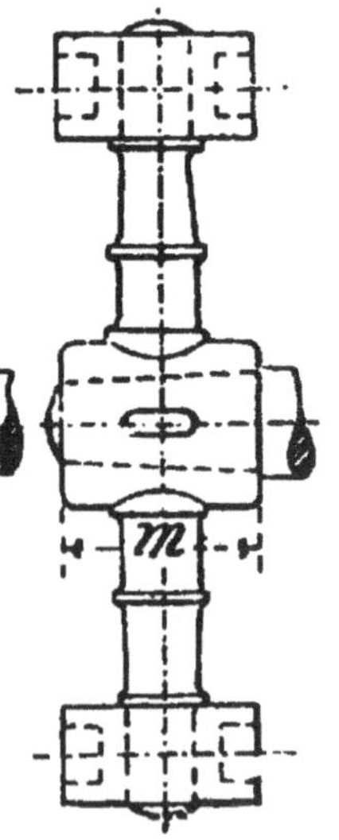

Fig. 268.

TABLE 25.—**Dimensions of Crossheads** (Figs. 267, 268) **for Bed-plate Engines**, page 19.

Engines.													
H	D	*d*	*a*	*b*	*c*	*e*	*f*	*g*	*h*	*i*	*k*	*l*	*m*
12	6	1¾	2⅛	3	1½	8	14	1¼	2	3½	3	1¼	4¼
16	8	2	2⅜	3¼	1¾	9	16	1½	2⅜	4¾	3⅜	1½	4¾
20	10	2¼	2¾	3⅝	2	10	19½	1¾	3	6	3¾	1¾	5¼
24	12	2⅝	3	4	2¼	11	21½	2	3⅝	7¼	4	2⅛	5⅝
28	14	2¾	3¼	4¼	2⅜	12	24	2¼	4⅝	8⅜	4¼	2¼	6⅝
32	16	3	3⅝	4⅝	2⅝	13	26	2⅜	5¼	9⅝	4⅝	2⅜	7
36	18	3¼	4	5	2¾	14	28	2⅝	6	10¾	5	2⅝	7⅝
40	20	3⅝	4⅜	5¼	3	15	30	2¾	6¾	12	5⅜	2⅞	8⅜
48	24	4⅜	5⅜	6⅜	3⅜	19	32	3⅜	7⅝	13⅝	6⅜	3½	10
56	28	5¼	6⅜	7⅝	3¾	23	36	4	8⅜	15¼	7⅜	4⅛	12⅜
64	32	6	7⅜	8¾	4⅜	26	42	4⅝	9⅝	16¾	8⅜	4¾	14¾
72	36	7	8⅜	10	5	30	52	5¼	10¾	18⅜	9⅜	5⅝	17¼
80	40	8	9⅝	11¼	5⅜	34	60	6	12	20	10⅝	6⅜	20

All Dimensions are given in Inches.

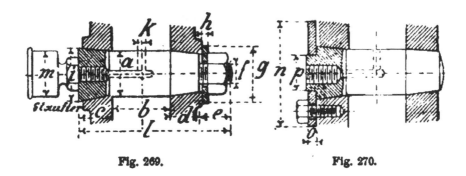

Fig. 269. Fig. 270.

The above figs. show two methods of fixing crosshead pins, another method is shown on page 66, fig. 226, under connecting rods with remarks on different ways of fixing pins.

TABLE 26.—**Dimensions of Crosshead Pins** (Figs. 269, 270).

Engines.		a	b	c	d	e	f	g	h	i	k	l	m	n	o	p
H	D															
12	6	$1\frac{3}{8}$	$1\frac{3}{4}$	$1\frac{1}{4}$	1	$1\frac{1}{4}$	$\frac{5}{8}$	2	$\frac{3}{16}$	$1\frac{5}{8}$	$\frac{1}{4}$	$5\frac{1}{4}$	$\frac{3}{4}$	—	—	—
16	8	$1\frac{1}{2}$	$2\frac{1}{8}$	$1\frac{3}{8}$	$1\frac{1}{4}$	$1\frac{1}{8}$	$\frac{3}{4}$	$2\frac{3}{8}$	$\frac{3}{16}$	$1\frac{7}{8}$	$\frac{1}{4}$	$6\frac{1}{8}$	$1\frac{1}{4}$	—	—	—
20	10	2	$2\frac{3}{4}$	$1\frac{3}{4}$	$1\frac{1}{2}$	$1\frac{1}{8}$	$\frac{3}{4}$	$2\frac{5}{8}$	$\frac{3}{16}$	$2\frac{3}{8}$	$\frac{1}{4}$	$7\frac{3}{8}$	$1\frac{1}{4}$	—	—	—
24	12	$2\frac{1}{4}$	$3\frac{1}{4}$	2	$1\frac{3}{4}$	$1\frac{1}{2}$	$\frac{7}{8}$	3	$\frac{1}{4}$	$2\frac{3}{4}$	$\frac{5}{16}$	$8\frac{1}{2}$	$1\frac{1}{2}$	4	$\frac{3}{8}$	$1\frac{1}{2}$
28	14	$2\frac{5}{8}$	$3\frac{5}{8}$	$2\frac{1}{4}$	2	$1\frac{1}{2}$	$\frac{7}{8}$	$3\frac{3}{8}$	$\frac{1}{4}$	3	$\frac{5}{16}$	$9\frac{3}{8}$	$1\frac{1}{2}$	$4\frac{5}{8}$	$\frac{1}{2}$	$1\frac{3}{4}$
32	16	3	4	$2\frac{3}{8}$	$2\frac{1}{4}$	$1\frac{3}{4}$	1	$3\frac{3}{4}$	$\frac{5}{16}$	$3\frac{1}{2}$	$\frac{5}{16}$	$10\frac{3}{8}$	2	$5\frac{3}{8}$	$\frac{5}{8}$	2
36	18	$3\frac{3}{8}$	$4\frac{1}{8}$	$2\frac{3}{4}$	$2\frac{5}{8}$	$1\frac{3}{4}$	1	$4\frac{1}{4}$	$\frac{3}{8}$	4	$\frac{3}{8}$	$11\frac{1}{2}$	2	6	$\frac{5}{8}$	$2\frac{1}{4}$
40	20	$3\frac{3}{4}$	$4\frac{3}{4}$	$3\frac{1}{4}$	$2\frac{3}{4}$	2	$1\frac{1}{8}$	$4\frac{5}{8}$	$\frac{3}{8}$	$4\frac{1}{4}$	$\frac{3}{8}$	$12\frac{3}{4}$	$2\frac{3}{8}$	$6\frac{3}{8}$	$\frac{5}{8}$	$2\frac{3}{8}$
44	22	4	$5\frac{1}{4}$	$3\frac{5}{8}$	$3\frac{1}{4}$	$2\frac{3}{8}$	$1\frac{1}{4}$	$4\frac{3}{4}$	$\frac{3}{8}$	$4\frac{5}{8}$	$\frac{3}{8}$	$14\frac{1}{2}$	$2\frac{3}{8}$	$6\frac{3}{4}$	$\frac{3}{4}$	$2\frac{3}{4}$

All Dimensions are given in Inches.

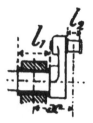

Fig. 271.

The length of the main-bearing journal and the dimension x, depend in some measure on the design of the engine. In the Table d = diameter, l = length of journals and the upper figures are for 110, and the lower for 90 lbs. working pressure.

TABLE 27.—Dimensions of Main Bearings, Crank Pins, and Crosshead Pins.

Diam. of Cylinder.	Main Bearing.		Crank Pin.		Crosshead Pin.		Dimension of x.
D	d_1	l_1	d_2	l_2	d_3	l_3	$x = 0.9\,(l_1 + l_3)$
10	$4\frac{1}{2}$	$7\frac{1}{4}$	$2\frac{5}{8}$	$3\frac{1}{4}$	2	$2\frac{3}{4}$	$9\frac{1}{4}$
	4	$7\frac{1}{4}$	$2\frac{1}{4}$	$3\frac{1}{4}$	2	$2\frac{3}{4}$	
12	$5\frac{1}{4}$	$8\frac{1}{2}$	$2\frac{3}{4}$	$3\frac{5}{8}$	$2\frac{1}{4}$	$3\frac{1}{4}$	$10\frac{3}{4}$
	$4\frac{5}{8}$	$8\frac{1}{2}$	$2\frac{5}{8}$	$3\frac{5}{8}$	$2\frac{1}{4}$	$3\frac{1}{4}$	
14	$6\frac{3}{8}$	$9\frac{1}{2}$	$3\frac{1}{4}$	$4\frac{1}{4}$	$2\frac{5}{8}$	$3\frac{5}{8}$	$12\frac{1}{4}$
	$5\frac{1}{4}$	$9\frac{1}{2}$	3	$4\frac{1}{4}$	$2\frac{5}{8}$	$3\frac{5}{8}$	
16	7	$10\frac{3}{4}$	$3\frac{3}{4}$	$4\frac{5}{8}$	3	4	14
	6	$10\frac{3}{4}$	$3\frac{3}{8}$	$4\frac{5}{8}$	3	4	
18	$7\frac{5}{8}$	12	$4\frac{1}{4}$	$5\frac{1}{4}$	$3\frac{3}{8}$	$4\frac{3}{8}$	$15\frac{5}{8}$
	$6\frac{3}{4}$	12	$3\frac{3}{4}$	$5\frac{1}{4}$	$3\frac{3}{8}$	$4\frac{3}{8}$	
20	$8\frac{3}{4}$	$13\frac{1}{4}$	$4\frac{3}{4}$	$5\frac{3}{4}$	$3\frac{3}{4}$	$4\frac{3}{4}$	$17\frac{1}{4}$
	$7\frac{5}{8}$	$13\frac{1}{4}$	$4\frac{1}{4}$	$5\frac{3}{4}$	$3\frac{3}{4}$	$4\frac{3}{4}$	
22	10	$14\frac{3}{4}$	$5\frac{1}{4}$	$6\frac{3}{8}$	4	$5\frac{1}{4}$	$18\frac{1}{2}$
	$8\frac{3}{8}$	$14\frac{3}{4}$	$4\frac{5}{8}$	$6\frac{3}{8}$	4	$5\frac{1}{4}$	

All Dimensions are given in Inches.

TABLE 28.—Dimensions of Piston Rods, Main Bearings, Crank Pins and Crosshead Pins for Engines with 90 to 110 lbs. Working Pressure. (For Engine Frame, see page 30.)

Engines.		Revs. per Min.	Piston speed ft. per min.	Piston Rods.	Main Bearings.		Crank Pins.		Crosshead Pins.	
H	D	n	c	d	d	l	d	l	d	l
12	6	125	250	$1\frac{1}{8}$	—	—	—	—	$1\frac{3}{8}$	$1\frac{3}{4}$
16	8	110	283	$1\frac{3}{8}$	—	—	—	—	$1\frac{1}{2}$	$2\frac{1}{8}$
20	10	100	334	$1\frac{5}{8}$	$4\frac{1}{2}$	$7\frac{1}{4}$	$2\frac{5}{8}$	$3\frac{1}{4}$	2	$2\frac{3}{4}$
24	12	90	360	2	$5\frac{1}{4}$	$8\frac{1}{2}$	$2\frac{3}{4}$	$3\frac{5}{8}$	$2\frac{1}{4}$	$3\frac{1}{4}$
28	14	85	396	$2\frac{1}{4}$	$6\frac{3}{8}$	$9\frac{1}{2}$	$3\frac{1}{4}$	$4\frac{1}{4}$	$2\frac{5}{8}$	$3\frac{5}{8}$
32	16	80	426	$2\frac{3}{8}$	7	$10\frac{3}{4}$	$3\frac{3}{4}$	$4\frac{5}{8}$	3	4
36	18	78	468	$2\frac{5}{8}$	$7\frac{5}{8}$	12	$4\frac{1}{4}$	$5\frac{1}{4}$	$3\frac{3}{8}$	$4\frac{3}{8}$
40	20	75	500	$2\frac{3}{4}$	$8\frac{3}{4}$	$13\frac{1}{4}$	$4\frac{3}{4}$	$5\frac{3}{4}$	$3\frac{3}{4}$	$4\frac{3}{4}$
44	22	72	528	$3\frac{1}{4}$	10	$14\frac{3}{4}$	$5\frac{1}{4}$	$6\frac{3}{8}$	4	$5\frac{1}{4}$
48	24	70	560	$3\frac{3}{4}$	$11\frac{1}{4}$	$16\frac{3}{4}$	$5\frac{3}{4}$	$7\frac{1}{4}$	5	$5\frac{3}{4}$
56	28	61	570	$4\frac{3}{8}$	$12\frac{1}{2}$	$18\frac{3}{4}$	$6\frac{1}{2}$	8	$5\frac{3}{4}$	$6\frac{3}{8}$
64	32	$54\frac{1}{2}$	580	$5\frac{1}{4}$	14	$21\frac{1}{4}$	$7\frac{3}{4}$	$9\frac{1}{4}$	$6\frac{1}{2}$	$7\frac{1}{4}$
72	36	49	590	6	$15\frac{3}{4}$	24	$8\frac{3}{4}$	$10\frac{3}{8}$	$7\frac{1}{4}$	8
80	40	45	600	$6\frac{3}{4}$	$17\frac{1}{4}$	26	$9\frac{1}{2}$	$11\frac{5}{8}$	8	$9\frac{1}{4}$
88	44	41	600	$7\frac{5}{8}$	$18\frac{3}{4}$	$28\frac{3}{4}$	$10\frac{1}{2}$	$13\frac{1}{4}$	$8\frac{3}{4}$	$10\frac{3}{8}$

All Dimensions are given in Inches, except those in Column c.

Piston Rods.

Piston rods are now almost always made of either Bessemer or open-hearth steel.

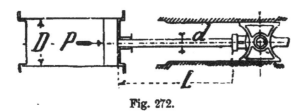

Fig. 272.

Both ends of the piston rod can be taken as fixed, then the diameter to resist crushing may be taken from the formula
$d = \cdot 0324 \sqrt[4]{P\,L^3}$ where d = diameter of rod in inches, P the maximum pressure on the piston in lbs., and L the length of the rod. A more direct method of determining the diameter of the piston rod is in proportion to the area of the piston and the maximum pressure thereon.

Thus if A = area of piston and a = area of piston rod, then for a maximum boiler pressure of 80 lbs. $\dfrac{A}{41} = a$ or A $\times \cdot 0244 = a$ gives a very safe strength for the smallest part of the rod, usually that part of the rod around the cottar hole at crosshead end, and as the rod has to be of a somewhat larger diameter in that part which passes through the cylinder cover, there is ample strength to resist crushing or bending.

Another way is to give sufficient metal in the smallest area of the rod to give a maximum stress of $1\frac{3}{4}$ tons per square inch, in some cases the stress may be as high as 2 tons per square inch. The staff or main part of the rod is often made about $\frac{1}{16}''$ to $\frac{1}{8}''$ larger than the largest diameter where it enters the crosshead, thus giving a small shoulder, this is for allowing the rod to be trued up after wear, without disturbing the part which fits into the crosshead.

Pistons.

Of pistons for steam engines there are endless varieties, high speeds and high pressures rendering it difficult to construct a perfect piston, and in fact this difficulty is well shown by the number of new pistons that are constantly being advertised in the technical journals. A perfect piston should work silently, and keep steam tight for a reasonable length of time, and should be as near frictionless as possible; the number of parts should be few, and all bolts and nuts secured from working loose. The attachment of the piston to the rod is a matter of great importance, the cone and nut shown in figs. 273, 276 has been successfully used on small pistons, but it is questionable whether a parallel rod with collar and nut is not better for very large pistons, accidents having happened from the piston body being burst by gradually mounting up the cone, especially when the taper of the latter has been too slight; a good proportion for the cone is a taper of $1\frac{1}{2}$ inches of diameter to one foot of length.

Figs. 273, 274 show a form of plain piston fitted with Ramsbottom rings, figs. 275, 276, 277, a good and cheap form for small pistons with one inside and two outside rings, all of cast iron, fig. 284, a spiral coil-spring piston of cast iron, with cast-iron outside rings.

Fig. 273. Fig. 274. Fig. 275.

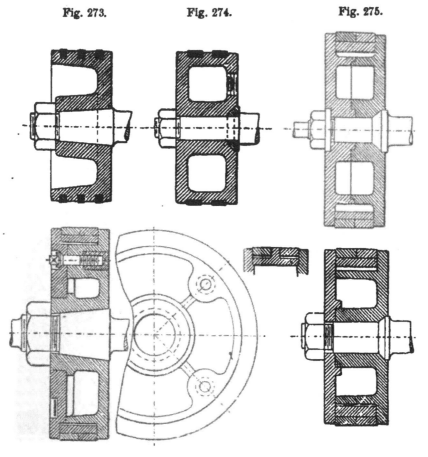

Fig. 276. Fig. 277.

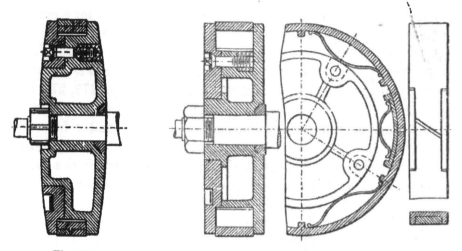

Fig. 278.   Fig. 279.

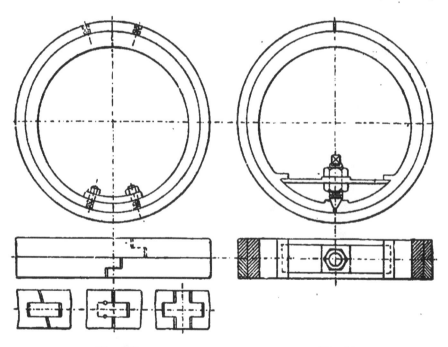

Fig. 280.   Fig. 281

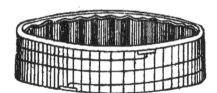

Fig. 282.—Cremer's Piston with spiral ring.

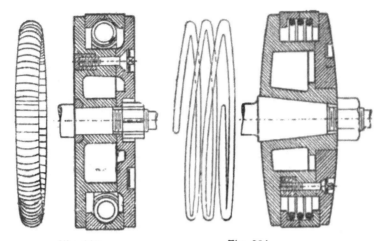

Fig. 283.   Fig. 284.

Fig. 284.—A Piston with helical spring bearing on outside cast-iron rings.

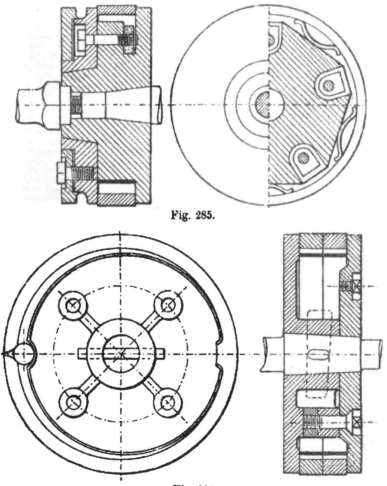

Fig. 285.

Fig. 286

Fig. 286.—Piston with two outside cast-iron rings and steel spring ring, with block at joint. This is a cheap form derived from an older form of locomotive piston, and has been much used for portable engines.

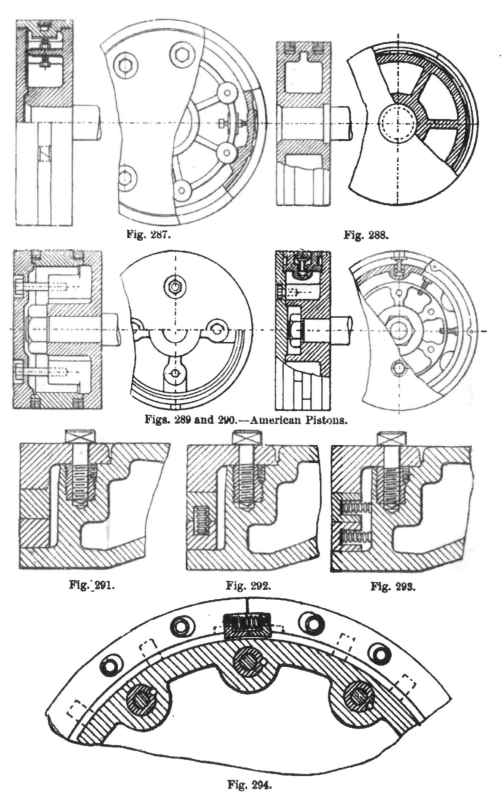

Fig. 287.

Fig. 288.

Figs. 289 and 290.—American Pistons.

Fig. 291.

Fig. 292.

Fig. 293.

Fig. 294.

Figs. 291 to 298.—Marine Pistons.

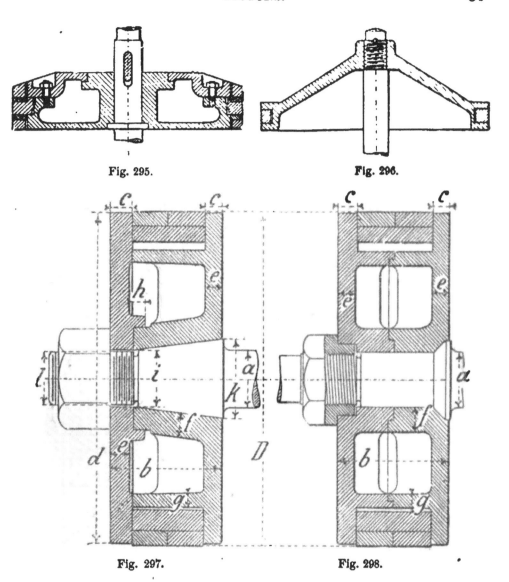

Fig. 295. Fig. 296.

Fig. 297. Fig. 298.

TABLE 29.—**Dimensions of Pistons from 6″ to 16″ Diameter, with Cover held on by Piston-rod Nut** (Figs. 297, 298.)

D	a	b	b_1	c	e	f	g	h	i	k	l
6	$1\frac{1}{8}$	3	2	$\frac{1}{2}$	$\frac{1}{2}$	$\frac{9}{16}$	$\frac{5}{16}$	$\frac{5}{16}$	$1\frac{1}{4}$	$1\frac{3}{4}$	1
8	$1\frac{3}{8}$	$3\frac{1}{4}$	$2\frac{1}{8}$	$\frac{9}{16}$	$\frac{1}{2}$	$\frac{5}{8}$	$\frac{3}{8}$	$\frac{5}{16}$	$1\frac{3}{8}$	2	$1\frac{1}{4}$
10	$1\frac{5}{8}$	$3\frac{5}{8}$	$2\frac{3}{8}$	$\frac{5}{8}$	$\frac{9}{16}$	$\frac{11}{16}$	$\frac{3}{8}$	$\frac{3}{8}$	$1\frac{5}{8}$	$2\frac{3}{8}$	$1\frac{1}{2}$
12	2	4	$2\frac{5}{8}$	$\frac{11}{16}$	$\frac{5}{8}$	$\frac{3}{4}$	$\frac{1}{2}$	$\frac{3}{8}$	$1\frac{7}{8}$	$2\frac{3}{4}$	$1\frac{7}{8}$
14	$2\frac{1}{4}$	$4\frac{1}{2}$	3	$\frac{3}{4}$	$\frac{5}{8}$	$\frac{13}{16}$	$\frac{1}{2}$	$\frac{3}{8}$	$2\frac{1}{8}$	$3\frac{1}{4}$	2
16	$2\frac{3}{8}$	$4\frac{3}{4}$	$3\frac{1}{4}$	$\frac{3}{4}$	$\frac{11}{16}$	$\frac{7}{8}$	$\frac{1}{2}$	$\frac{3}{8}$	$2\frac{5}{16}$	$3\frac{5}{8}$	$2\frac{1}{4}$

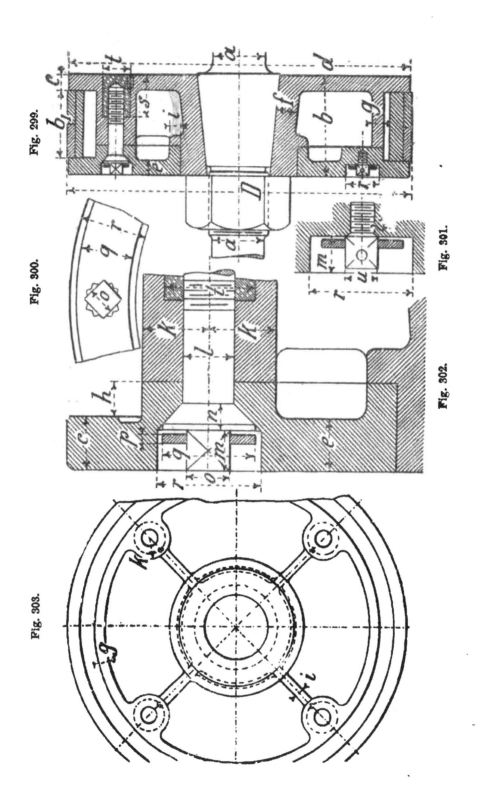

Fig. 299.

Fig. 300.

Fig. 301.

Fig. 302.

Fig. 303.

TABLE 30.—Dimensions of Pistons with Cover held on by Bolts. From 14″ up to 40″ Diameter (Fig. 299).

	NOTE.—All Dimensions are in Inches.										Cover bolts.										
D	a	b	b_1	c	e	f	g	h	i	k	No.	l	m	n	o	p	q	r	s	t	u
14	2 1/4	4 1/2	3	3/4	5/8	7/8	1/2	1/2	3/8	1	4	3/4	1/2	7/16	5/8	1/8	1 3/8	1 1/2	2	1 3/8	1/2
16	2 3/8	4 3/4	3 1/4	3/4	11/16	7/8	1/2	1/2	1/2	1	5	3/4	1/2	7/16	5/8	1/8	1 3/8	1 1/2	2	1 3/8	1/2
18	2 5/8	5	3 3/8	13/16	11/16	1	9/16	9/16	1/2	1 1/4	5	7/8	5/8	1/2	3/4	1/8	1 1/2	1 3/4	2 1/4	1 1/2	1/2
20	2 3/4	5 1/4	3 1/2	7/8	3/4	1	5/8	9/16	9/16	1 1/4	5	7/8	5/8	1/2	3/4	1/8	1 1/2	1 3/4	2 1/4	1 1/2	1/2
22	3 1/4	5 1/2	3 5/8	15/16	3/4	1	5/8	9/16	5/8	1 1/4	6	7/8	5/8	1/2	3/4	1/8	1 1/2	1 3/4	2 1/4	1 1/2	1/2
24	3 3/4	6	4	1	13/16	1 1/4	3/4	5/8	5/8	1 3/8	6	1	5/8	1/2	7/8	3/16	1 3/4	2 1/8	2 5/8	1 3/4	5/8
28	4 3/8	6 3/4	4 3/4	1	7/8	1 3/8	3/4	3/4	3/4	1 3/8	7	1	5/8	1/2	7/8	3/16	1 3/4	2 1/8	2 5/8	1 3/4	5/8
32	5 1/4	7 3/4	5 1/4	1 1/4	1	1 1/2	3/4	3/4	3/4	1 1/2	7	1 1/8	3/4	5/8	1	3/16	2 1/8	2 3/8	2 3/4	2	3/4
36	6	8 3/8	5 7/8	1 1/4	1	1 3/4	7/8	7/8	7/8	1 1/2	8	1 1/8	3/4	5/8	1	3/16	2 1/8	2 3/8	2 3/4	2	3/4
40	6 3/4	8 3/4	6	1 3/8	1 1/16	2	1	1	1	1 5/8	8	1 1/4	3/4	5/8	1	1/4	2 1/4	2 1/2	3	2 1/8	3/4

Fig. 306.

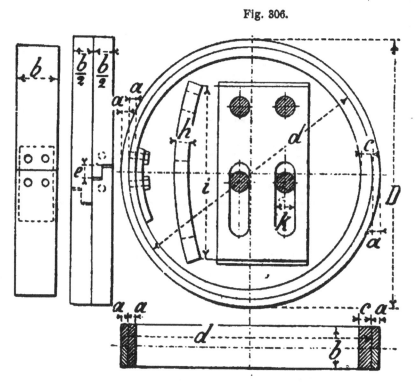

Figs. 308 and 307. Fig. 305.

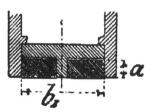

Fig. 304.

Figures 304 to 308 show an ordinary set of piston rings with tongue piece on inside ring, and the outside ring cut so as to prevent marking the cylinder and also to prevent the leakage of steam. This way of cutting the rings is not usually considered necessary, a diagonal cut being generally sufficient with or without the tongue pieces. Table 31 gives the dimensions of these rings.

TABLE 31.—**Dimensions of Piston Rings** (Figs. 304 to 308).

D	b	a	c	D_1	f	e	D	d	d_1	g	d	h	i	k
4	$1\frac{3}{4}$	$\frac{5}{16}$	$\frac{1}{2}$	$4\frac{1}{4}$	—	$\frac{3}{8}$	4	$3\frac{3}{8}$	$3\frac{7}{16}$	—	$3\frac{3}{8}$	$\frac{1}{4}$	2	$\frac{5}{16}$
6	2	$\frac{5}{16}$	$\frac{9}{16}$	$6\frac{1}{4}$	—	$\frac{1}{2}$	6	$5\frac{3}{8}$	$5\frac{7}{16}$	$\frac{1}{16}$	$5\frac{3}{8}$	$\frac{1}{4}$	$2\frac{3}{8}$	$\frac{5}{16}$
8	$2\frac{1}{8}$	$\frac{3}{8}$	$\frac{5}{8}$	$8\frac{5}{16}$	—	$\frac{5}{8}$	8	$7\frac{1}{4}$	$7\frac{5}{16}$	$\frac{1}{8}$	$7\frac{1}{4}$	$\frac{1}{4}$	$2\frac{3}{4}$	$\frac{5}{16}$
10	$2\frac{3}{8}$	$\frac{3}{8}$	$\frac{5}{8}$	$10\frac{3}{8}$	$\frac{3}{16}$	$\frac{5}{8}$	10	$9\frac{1}{4}$	$9\frac{3}{8}$	$\frac{3}{16}$	$9\frac{1}{4}$	$\frac{5}{16}$	$3\frac{1}{4}$	$\frac{3}{8}$
12	$2\frac{5}{8}$	$\frac{7}{16}$	$\frac{3}{4}$	$12\frac{7}{16}$	$\frac{5}{16}$	$\frac{5}{8}$	12	$11\frac{1}{8}$	$11\frac{1}{4}$	$\frac{3}{16}$	$11\frac{1}{8}$	$\frac{5}{16}$	$3\frac{5}{8}$	$\frac{3}{8}$
14	3	$\frac{1}{2}$	$\frac{3}{4}$	$14\frac{1}{2}$	$\frac{3}{8}$	$\frac{3}{4}$	14	13	$13\frac{5}{16}$	$\frac{1}{4}$	13	$\frac{3}{8}$	4	$\frac{3}{8}$
16	$3\frac{1}{4}$	$\frac{1}{2}$	$\frac{13}{16}$	$16\frac{9}{16}$	$\frac{1}{2}$	$\frac{3}{4}$	16	15	$15\frac{1}{4}$	$\frac{3}{8}$	15	$\frac{3}{8}$	$4\frac{3}{8}$	$\frac{1}{2}$
18	$3\frac{3}{8}$	$\frac{5}{8}$	$\frac{7}{8}$	$18\frac{5}{8}$	$\frac{5}{8}$	$\frac{3}{4}$	18	$16\frac{3}{4}$	16	$\frac{1}{2}$	$16\frac{3}{4}$	$\frac{1}{2}$	$4\frac{3}{4}$	$\frac{1}{2}$
20	$3\frac{1}{2}$	$\frac{5}{8}$	$\frac{7}{8}$	$20\frac{5}{8}$	$\frac{11}{16}$	$\frac{7}{8}$	20	$18\frac{3}{4}$	$19\frac{1}{4}$	$\frac{5}{8}$	$18\frac{3}{4}$	$\frac{1}{2}$	$5\frac{1}{4}$	$\frac{1}{2}$
22	$3\frac{5}{8}$	$\frac{11}{16}$	1	$22\frac{11}{16}$	$\frac{3}{4}$	$\frac{7}{8}$	22	$20\frac{5}{8}$	21	$\frac{3}{4}$	$20\frac{5}{8}$	$\frac{1}{2}$	$5\frac{5}{8}$	$\frac{1}{2}$
24	4	$\frac{11}{16}$	1	$24\frac{3}{4}$	$\frac{7}{8}$	1	24	$22\frac{5}{8}$	23	1	$22\frac{5}{8}$	$\frac{1}{2}$	6	$\frac{5}{8}$
28	$4\frac{3}{4}$	$\frac{3}{4}$	$1\frac{1}{8}$	$28\frac{7}{8}$	$1\frac{1}{8}$	$1\frac{1}{16}$	28	$26\frac{1}{2}$	27	$1\frac{1}{4}$	$26\frac{1}{2}$	$\frac{1}{2}$	$6\frac{3}{8}$	$\frac{5}{8}$
32	$5\frac{1}{4}$	$\frac{3}{4}$	$1\frac{1}{4}$	33	$1\frac{1}{4}$	$1\frac{1}{4}$	32	$30\frac{1}{2}$	31	$1\frac{3}{8}$	$30\frac{1}{2}$	$\frac{9}{16}$	$6\frac{3}{4}$	$\frac{5}{8}$
36	$5\frac{7}{8}$	$\frac{7}{8}$	$1\frac{1}{4}$	37	$1\frac{3}{8}$	$1\frac{1}{2}$	36	$34\frac{1}{4}$	$34\frac{7}{8}$	$1\frac{1}{2}$	$34\frac{1}{4}$	$\frac{5}{8}$	$7\frac{1}{4}$	$\frac{5}{8}$
40	6	$\frac{7}{8}$	$1\frac{3}{8}$	$41\frac{1}{4}$	$1\frac{1}{2}$	$1\frac{1}{2}$	40	$38\frac{1}{4}$	39	$1\frac{7}{8}$	$38\frac{1}{4}$	$\frac{5}{8}$	$7\frac{5}{8}$	$\frac{5}{8}$

All Dimensions are given in Inches.

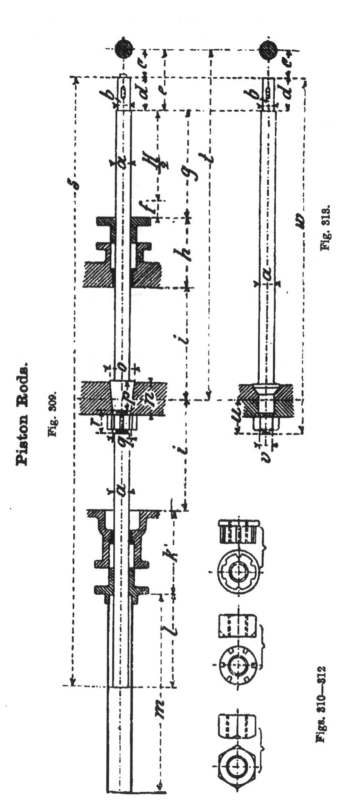

Piston Rods.

Fig. 309.

Fig. 313.

Figs. 310—312.

TABLE 32.—Dimensions of Piston Rods (Figs. 309, 313).

NOTE.—All Dimensions are given in Inches.

Engine.																							
H	D	a	b	c	d	e	f	g	h	i	k	l	m	n	o	p	q	r	s	t	u	v	w
12	6	1 1/8	1	2 1/2	2 3/4	5 1/4	1 1/16	7 1/16	7	7 11/16	—	—	—	3	—	2 3/4	—	—	—	27	2 3/4	1 1/8	27 1/4
16	8	1 3/8	1 1/4	2 7/8	3 5/8	6 1/2	1 1/16	9 1/16	8 1/4	9 13/16	—	—	—	3 1/4	—	3	—	—	—	33 5/8	3 1/4	1 3/8	34
20	10	1 5/8	1 1/2	3 3/8	4 1/8	7 1/2	1 1/16	11 1/8	9 3/8	12	—	—	—	3 5/8	—	3 1/2	—	—	—	40	3 3/4	1 3/4	40 3/8
24	12	2	1 7/8	3 7/8	4 5/8	8 1/2	1 1/16	13 1/16	10 1/2	14 3/16	—	12	28	4	3 1/4	3 3/4	2 3/8	2 3/8	—	46 1/4	—	—	—
28	14	2 1/4	2 1/8	4 1/4	5	9 1/4	1 1/8	15 1/8	11 1/8	16 1/2	—	14	32	4 1/2	3 1/2	4	2 1/2	2 1/2	—	52	—	—	—
32	16	2 3/8	2 1/4	4 3/4	5 3/4	10 1/2	1 3/8	17 3/8	11 1/2	18 5/8	—	16	36	4 3/4	3 3/4	4 1/2	2 3/4	2 3/4	—	58	—	—	—
36	18	2 5/8	2 1/2	5 3/8	6 1/8	11 1/2	1 9/16	19 9/16	12 1/8	20 13/16	—	18	40	5	4	4 5/8	3	3	—	64	—	—	—
40	20	2 3/4	2 5/8	5 7/8	6 5/8	12 1/2	1 9/16	21 9/16	12 3/4	22 15/16	—	20	44	5 1/4	4 1/2	4 3/4	3 1/4	3 1/4	—	69 3/4	—	—	—
44	22	3 1/4	3 1/8	6 5/8	7 3/8	14	1 9/16	23 9/16	14 1/8	25 1/16	—	22	48	5 1/2	4 3/4	5	3 5/8	3 5/8	—	76 3/4	—	—	—

Steam Engine Cylinders.

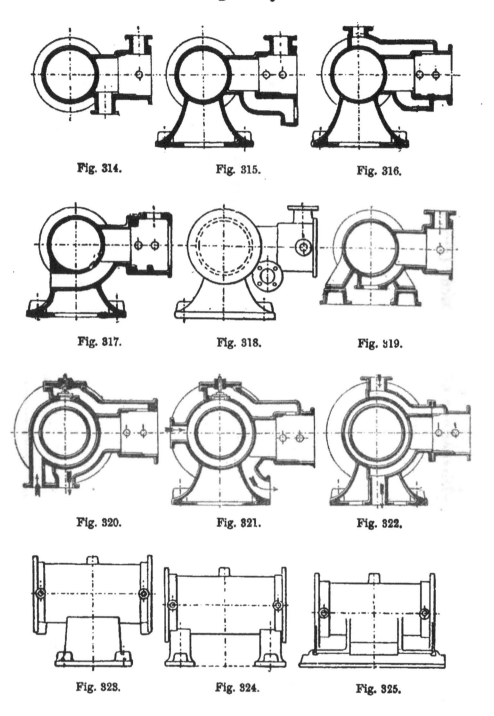

Fig. 314. Fig. 315. Fig. 316.

Fig. 317. Fig. 318. Fig. 319.

Fig. 320. Fig. 321. Fig. 322.

Fig. 323. Fig. 324. Fig. 325.

The above figures show different designs for cylinders of horizontal engines with and without steam jackets.

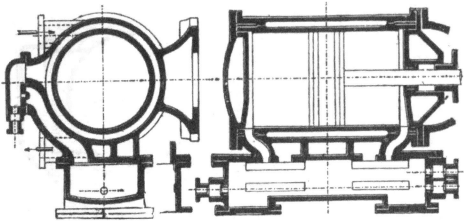

Figs. 327 and 328.—Cylinder for double slide valve gear, with the valves in two parts; an arrangement which reduces the length of the steam ports to the shortest length possible with slide valves.

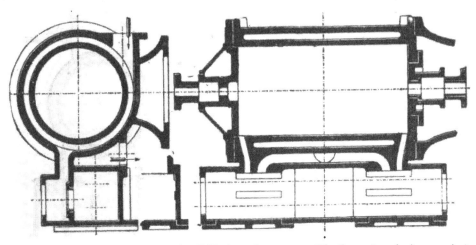

Figs. 329 and 330.—Cylinder for Rider's valve gear, with the valves in two parts to reduce length of steam ports.

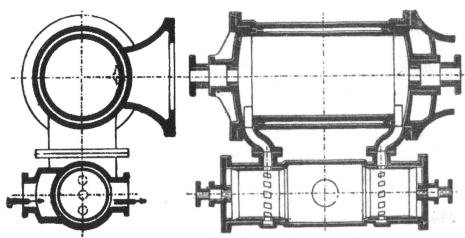

Figs 331 and 332.—Cylinder for piston slide valve.

H

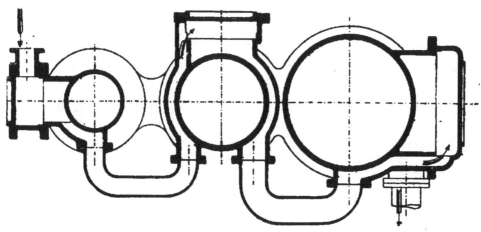

Fig. 333.—Cylinders for triple-expansion engine, designed for use with frame shown in fig. 89, page 32. In this arrangement all the three slide valves are easy of access.

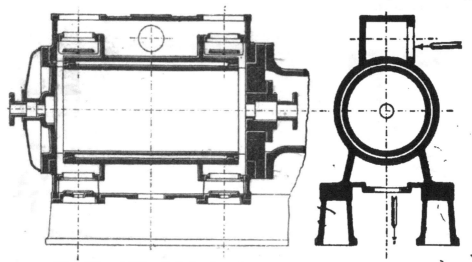

Figs. 334 and 335.—Cylinder for valve gear, with mushroom valves.

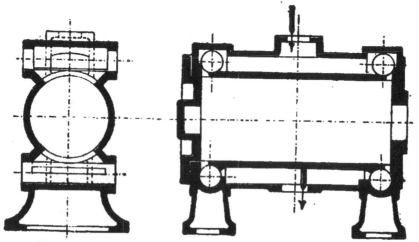

Figs. 336 and 337.—Cylinder for valve gear, with Corliss valves.

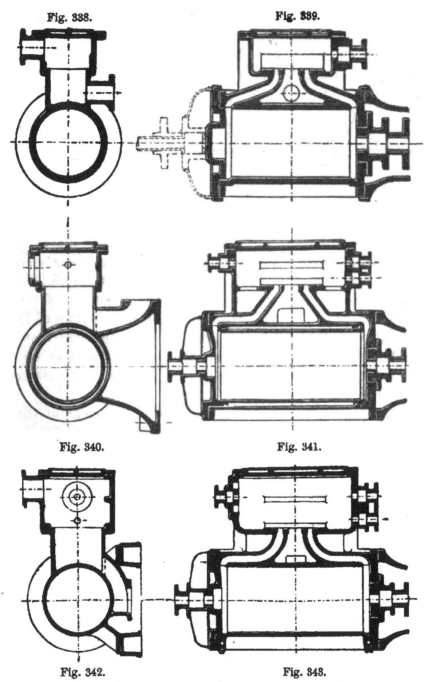

Fig. 338. Fig. 339.

Fig. 340. Fig. 341.

Fig. 342. Fig. 343.

Figs. 338 and 339.—Cylinder for ordinary simple slide valve gear.
Figs. 340 and 341.—Cylinder for Meyer's slide valve gear.
Figs. 342 and 343.—Cylinder for Rider's valve gear.

In the above examples the slide valve chest is shown shorter than the cylinder; this arrangement saves weight, but it is often more convenient to make it the same length as the cylinder and to bolt the stuffing boxes on.

H 2

The thickness of the cylinder walls in small or medium sized engines has been determined from practice more than from calculation, and ranges from ⅜" in small cylinders up to 9" bore; beyond that size an approximate formula is t = thickness of walls in inches = ·75 + $\dfrac{D}{100}$, where D = bore of cylinder in inches; this formula gives the thickness rather high for small cylinders. The thickness of the cylinder covers has also been determined by practice and depends on the steam pressure and also on the construction of the cover, whether strengthened by ribs for the larger cylinders or plain for the smaller ones. The thickness of the cover at the bolt circle is often made a little less than that of the cylinder flange; the thickness of the flange being about 1·25 times the thickness of the cylinder walls. The bolts for holding the cover on must be spaced according to the load on the cover, the strain on the bolts being about 2 tons per square inch of section at bottom of thread; (see table 151, page 411, which gives the areas at bottom of thread of the usual sizes of bolts), but it should be remembered that bolts smaller than ⅝" diameter may be overstrained by tightening up with an ordinary spanner and seriously injured before any pressure or working stress comes upon them.

The bosses on the ends of the cylinder for attachment of the Indicator cocks are tapped with ¾" Whitworth thread, and fitted with screw plugs often made of iron, but if not occasionally removed are apt to rust in and must be drilled out; they should therefore be of brass. The steam ports should be sufficiently large to admit the steam at a maximum velocity of 100 feet per second; as in some valve gears the port is not opened to its full width to steam, care should be taken in calculating the speed of the entering steam to reckon only for the opening of the port to steam up to the edge of the valve. If the steam is cut off early when the engine is running on full load it is obvious that the ports need not be so large as for the later cut off, as the piston speed is naturally less near the beginning than towards the middle of the stroke.

The length of the port, i.e. the dimension measured at right angles to the length of the cylinder, depends on the design of the cylinder, and this being determined, the other dimension is readily calculated from the area.

In cylinder construction it is important to arrange bosses for connection of all pipes required, and specially to arrange for efficient means of draining and lubricating the cylinder barrel, for admitting steam to the jacket and draining the same in an efficient manner. Other important points are the means for neatly clothing the cylinder with some non-conducting medium.

It may be again mentioned here that in order to save multiplications of patterns, the cylinder as well as other parts of engines should be designed symmetrically about their centre lines, so that a cylinder by being turned end for end may be used for either a right or a left hand engine.

Clearance space in Steam Engine Cylinders.—A small distance between the piston at each end of the stroke and the cylinder covers is necessary in order to prevent the piston from coming into contact with the covers. This space, called "clearance," should be as small as possible, but cannot be reduced beyond a certain limit, as the length of the connecting rod alters by wear and adjustment; therefore the clearance is seldom less

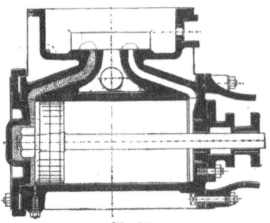

Fig. 344.

than $\frac{5}{16}''$ in small engines and somewhat more in larger engines. In calculating the amount of steam used in an engine this space has to be added to the volume swept by the piston in its stroke; in addition to the clearance space at the end of the stroke, there are the steam passages, and if a double slide valve gear, the hollow part of the main valve to be taken in. Fig. 344 shows the clearance space and steam passage shaded at the left hand end of the cylinder. In this case it amounts to 450 cubic inches, the volume swept by the piston equals 7320 cubic inches $\frac{450 \times 100}{7320} = 6 \cdot 1$ per cent., so the clearance space amounts to 6·1 per cent. of the volume of the stroke. Table 33 shows the clearance spaces for different varieties of ports.

TABLE 33.—Percentage of Clearance Space with Steam Ports of different Design.

Engine.	For the Normal Velocity of the Steam.	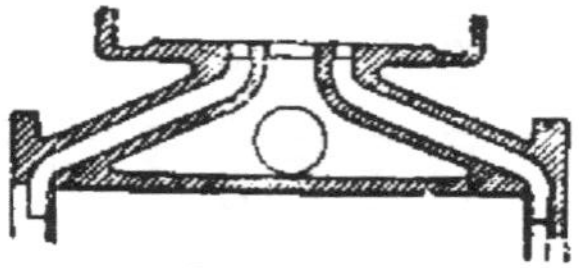 Fig. 345.	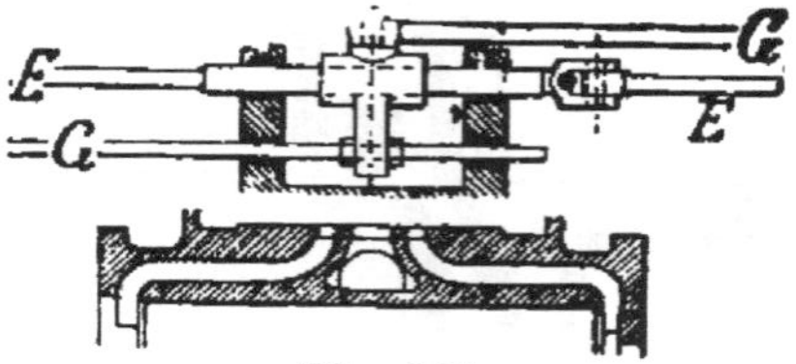 Fig. 346.	 Fig. 347.
D = 10	Steam port .	52·5	45·5	23·5
	Clearance .	16·2	16·2	16·2
H = 16	Recess in cover .	8·6	8·6	8·6
	Recess in cover .	1·5	1·5	1·5
n = 120	Ring in cylinder	3·4	3·4	3·4
	Total .	82·2 cube in.	75·2 cube in.	53·2 cube in.
	Per cent. of cylinder capacity	7	6·5	4·5
D = 22	Steam port .	687·3	633·3	244·3
	Clearance .	114·7	114·7	114·7
H = 40	Recess in cover .	24·6	24·6	24·6
	Recess in cover .	21·5	21·5	21·5
n = 65	Ring in cylinder	20·0	20·0	20·0
	Total .	868·1 cube in.	814·1 cube in.	425·1 cube in.
	Per cent. of cylinder capacity	6	5·7	3

Feet for Cylinders.

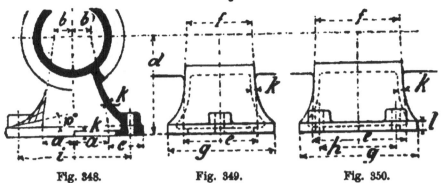

Fig. 348.   Fig. 349.   Fig. 350.

TABLE 34.—Dimensions of Cylinder Feet (Figs. 348—350).

Engines.		NOTE.—All Dimensions are in Inches.										
H	D	a	b	c	d	e	f	g	h	i	k	l
20	10	5	3	5	18	12	$10\frac{1}{2}$	17	—	16	$\frac{3}{4}$	$1\frac{1}{2}$
24	12	$5\frac{1}{2}$	$3\frac{1}{2}$	6	20	14	12	20	14	18	$\frac{3}{4}$	$1\frac{3}{4}$
28	14	$6\frac{1}{2}$	4	$6\frac{1}{2}$	22	16	14	22	16	21	$\frac{7}{8}$	2
32	16	$7\frac{1}{2}$	$4\frac{1}{2}$	$7\frac{1}{4}$	24	18	16	25	18	23	1	$2\frac{1}{4}$
36	18	8	$5\frac{1}{2}$	8	26	20	$18\frac{1}{2}$	$27\frac{1}{2}$	19	26	$1\frac{1}{8}$	$2\frac{3}{8}$
40	20	9	6	$8\frac{1}{2}$	28	22	19	30	20	28	$1\frac{1}{4}$	$2\frac{1}{2}$
44	22	$9\frac{1}{2}$	7	9	30	24	21	32	22	30	$1\frac{1}{4}$	$2\frac{3}{4}$

The expansion of the metal of the cylinder due to the difference in temperature between the cylinder at atmospheric and working heat has occasionally been allowed for by arranging the cylinder foot on a sliding bed, as in fig. 351. The difference in length is given in Table 35. It will be seen that the amount is small, and usually no allowance need be made for it.

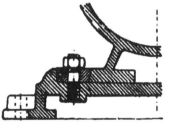

Fig. 351.

TABLE 35.

Stroke of Engine in Inches.	16	24	32	89	78
Amount of expansion, or increase of length —inches . . .	·0196	·0315	·0432	·0629	·1377

Cylinder with Steam Jacket (see TABLE 36).

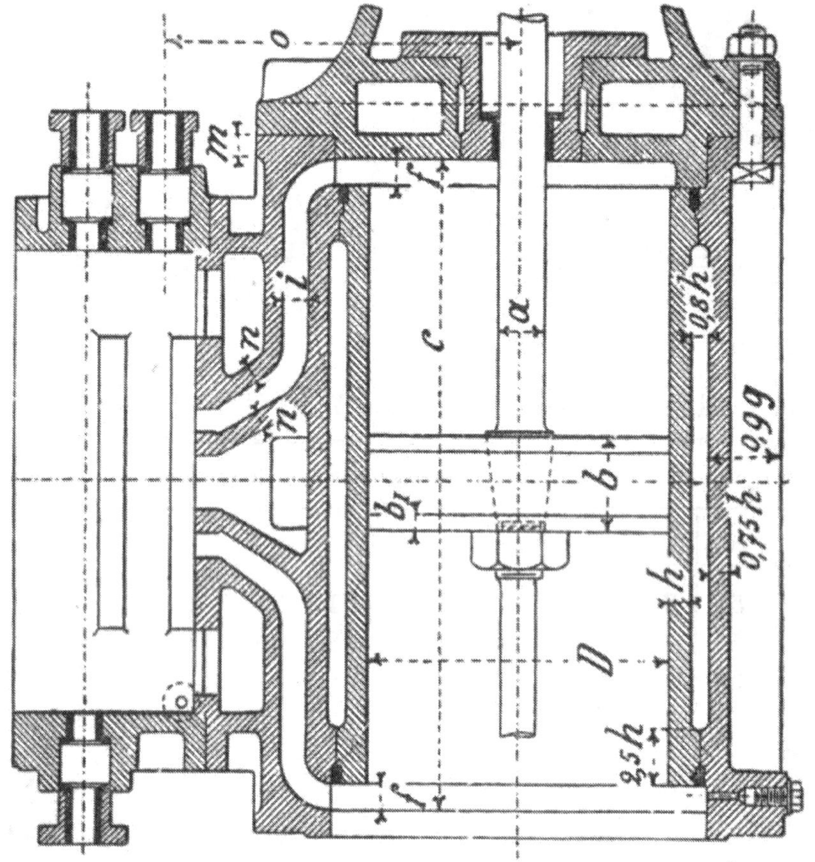

Fig. 353.

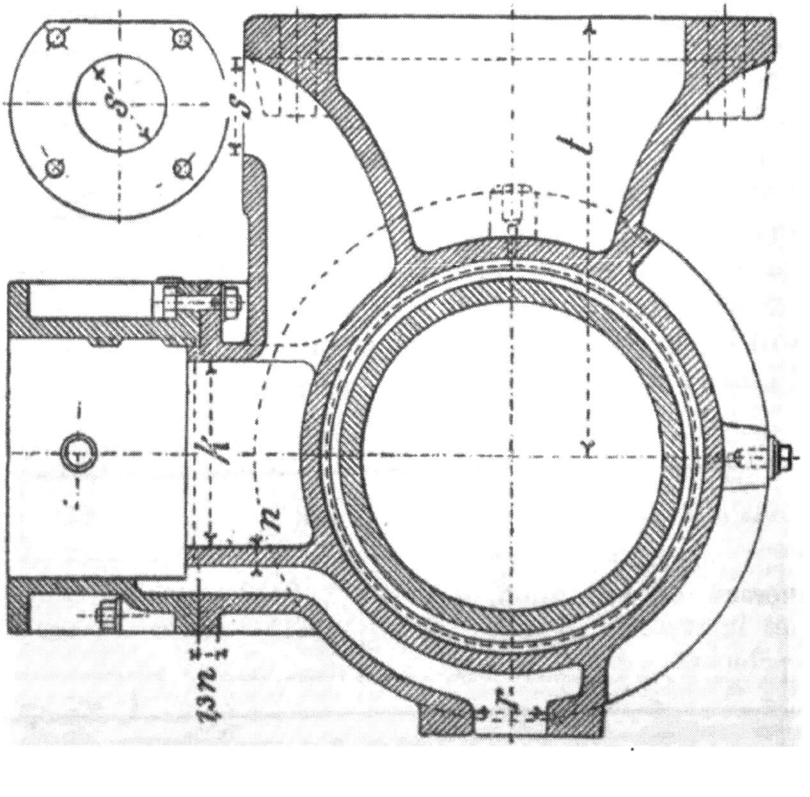

Fig. 352.

TABLE 36.—Dimensions of Cylinders from 10″ up to 22″ diameter for Double Slide Valves (Figs. 352, 353).

Engine.		Piston.									Steam Ports.						Bolts.		Bolts.					
H	D	a	b	b_1	c	d	e	f	g	h	i	k	l	m	n	o	No.	p	No.	q	r	s	t	u
16	8	—	—	—	—	—	—	—	—	—	—	—	—	—	—	—	—	—	—	—	—	—	—	—
20	10	$1\frac{5}{8}$	$3\frac{5}{8}$	$\frac{5}{8}$	24	1	13	$\frac{13}{16}$	$4\frac{1}{8}$	$\frac{7}{8}$	$\frac{3}{4}$	$5\frac{3}{8}$	$18\frac{1}{4}$	1	$\frac{5}{8}$	$14\frac{1}{4}$	4	$\frac{7}{8}$	8	$\frac{3}{4}$	$2\frac{3}{8}$	$2\frac{3}{4}$	18	$5\frac{1}{4}$
24	12	2	4	$\frac{11}{16}$	$28\frac{3}{8}$	$1\frac{5}{16}$	$15\frac{1}{2}$	$\frac{7}{8}$	$4\frac{1}{4}$	$\frac{7}{8}$	1	$6\frac{3}{4}$	$20\frac{1}{2}$	$1\frac{1}{8}$	$\frac{3}{4}$	$16\frac{1}{2}$	5	1	8	$\frac{7}{8}$	3	$3\frac{5}{8}$	20	$6\frac{3}{8}$
28	14	$2\frac{1}{4}$	$4\frac{1}{2}$	$\frac{3}{4}$	33	$1\frac{1}{2}$	18	1	$4\frac{5}{8}$	$\frac{15}{16}$	$1\frac{1}{8}$	$8\frac{3}{8}$	$23\frac{1}{4}$	$1\frac{1}{4}$	$\frac{3}{4}$	$18\frac{3}{4}$	5	$1\frac{1}{8}$	10	$\frac{7}{8}$	$3\frac{5}{8}$	$4\frac{3}{8}$	22	$7\frac{5}{8}$
32	16	$2\frac{3}{8}$	$4\frac{3}{4}$	$\frac{3}{4}$	$37\frac{1}{4}$	$1\frac{7}{8}$	$20\frac{1}{2}$	$1\frac{1}{16}$	$4\frac{7}{8}$	$\frac{15}{16}$	$1\frac{1}{4}$	10	$25\frac{3}{4}$	$1\frac{3}{8}$	$\frac{7}{8}$	$21\frac{1}{4}$	6	$1\frac{1}{8}$	10	$\frac{7}{8}$	$4\frac{1}{4}$	5	24	$8\frac{3}{4}$
36	18	$2\frac{5}{8}$	5	$\frac{13}{16}$	$41\frac{5}{8}$	$2\frac{3}{16}$	23	$1\frac{3}{16}$	$5\frac{1}{4}$	1	$1\frac{3}{8}$	$11\frac{5}{8}$	$28\frac{1}{2}$	$1\frac{3}{8}$	$\frac{7}{8}$	$22\frac{1}{2}$	6	$1\frac{1}{4}$	10	1	$4\frac{5}{8}$	$5\frac{5}{8}$	26	$9\frac{5}{8}$
40	20	$2\frac{3}{4}$	$5\frac{1}{4}$	$\frac{7}{8}$	$45\frac{7}{8}$	$2\frac{9}{16}$	$25\frac{1}{2}$	$1\frac{1}{4}$	$5\frac{1}{2}$	1	$1\frac{5}{8}$	$13\frac{1}{4}$	31	$1\frac{1}{2}$	1	$25\frac{5}{8}$	8	$1\frac{1}{4}$	12	1	$5\frac{1}{4}$	$6\frac{3}{8}$	28	10
44	22	$3\frac{1}{4}$	$5\frac{1}{2}$	$\frac{15}{16}$	$50\frac{1}{8}$	$2\frac{3}{4}$	28	$1\frac{5}{16}$	$5\frac{1}{2}$	$1\frac{1}{16}$	$1\frac{3}{4}$	15	33	$1\frac{1}{2}$	1	$28\frac{1}{4}$	8	$1\frac{3}{8}$	14	1	$5\frac{3}{4}$	$7\frac{1}{4}$	30	$10\frac{3}{8}$

All Dimensions are given in Inches.

Steam Jackets.

The use of steam jackets is now almost universally adopted in all but very small cheap engines. A well arranged steam jacket tends to keep the steam dry in the cylinder, and slightly reduces the

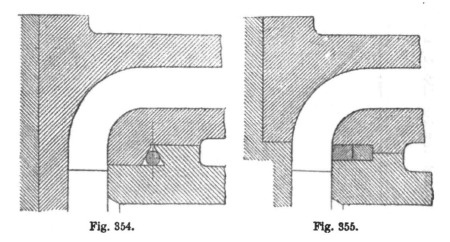

Fig. 354.   Fig. 355.

amount of steam used per horse power. In some cases the cylinder and jacket are in one casting, but usually the working barrel or liner is separate from the cylinder body, and forced steam tight into it by a hydraulic press. The liner can be made of harder iron than would

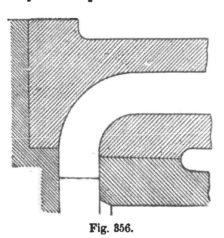

Fig. 356.

be safe, if the whole were in one casting. Figs. 352, 353 show methods of rendering the joint between liner and body tight by means of packing. In fig. 353, the packing consists of a copper ring caulked in, but for small work this is quite unnecessary. A good fit is not difficult to obtain, and when the liner is either shrunk in by warming the body, or forced in cold by the hydraulic press, a leak is of very rare occurrence.

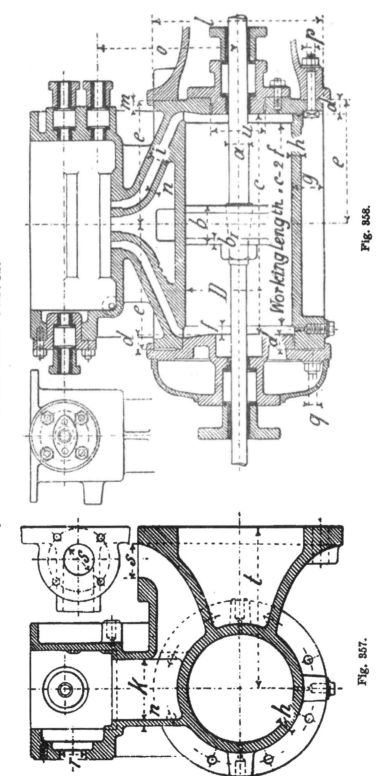

Cylinder for Double Slide Valves.

Fig. 358.

Fig. 357.

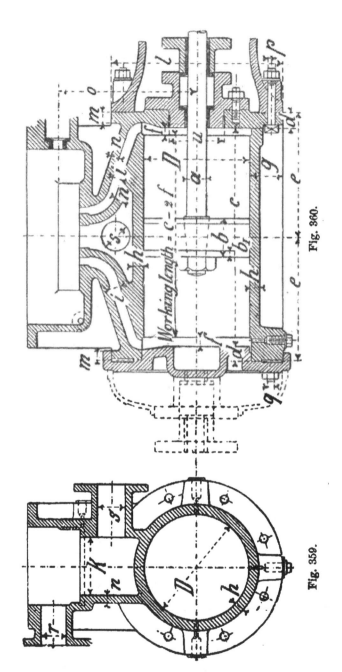

Cylinder for Single Slide Valve (see Table 37).

Working length = C - 2f.

Fig. 360.

Fig. 359.

TABLE 37.—Dimensions of Cylinders from 6″ up to 14″ diameter for Single Slide Valve (Figs. 359, 360).

Engine.		Piston.			c	d	e	f	g	h	Steam Ports.		l	m	n	o	Bolts.		Bolts.				
H	D	a	b	b_1							i	k		m	n	o	No. p	p	No. q	q	r	s	u
12	6	$1\frac{1}{8}$	3	$\frac{1}{2}$	$15\frac{3}{8}$	$\frac{9}{16}$	$8\frac{1}{4}$	$\frac{3}{4}$	$3\frac{7}{8}$	$\frac{3}{4}$	$\frac{1}{2}$	$3\frac{1}{4}$	$13\frac{3}{4}$	$\frac{7}{8}$	$\frac{1}{2}$	—	4	$\frac{3}{4}$	6	$\frac{3}{4}$	$1\frac{1}{8}$	$1\frac{3}{4}$	$3\frac{1}{4}$
16	8	$1\frac{1}{4}$	$3\frac{1}{4}$	$\frac{9}{16}$	$19\frac{1}{4}$	$\frac{11}{16}$	$10\frac{1}{2}$	$\frac{3}{4}$	4	$\frac{3}{4}$	$\frac{5}{8}$	$4\frac{3}{8}$	16	$\frac{7}{8}$	$\frac{5}{8}$	—	4	$\frac{3}{4}$	6	$\frac{3}{4}$	$1\frac{1}{4}$	$2\frac{1}{4}$	$4\frac{1}{4}$
20	10	$1\frac{5}{8}$	$3\frac{3}{8}$	$\frac{5}{8}$	24	1	13	$\frac{13}{16}$	$4\frac{1}{8}$	$\frac{7}{8}$	$\frac{3}{4}$	$5\frac{5}{8}$	$18\frac{1}{4}$	1	$\frac{5}{8}$	$14\frac{1}{4}$	4	$\frac{7}{8}$	8	$\frac{3}{4}$	$2\frac{3}{8}$	$2\frac{3}{4}$	$5\frac{1}{4}$
24	12	2	4	$\frac{11}{16}$	$28\frac{3}{8}$	$1\frac{5}{16}$	$15\frac{1}{2}$	$\frac{7}{8}$	$4\frac{1}{4}$	$\frac{7}{8}$	1	$6\frac{3}{4}$	$20\frac{1}{2}$	$1\frac{1}{8}$	$\frac{3}{4}$	$16\frac{1}{2}$	5	1	8	$\frac{7}{8}$	3	$3\frac{3}{8}$	$6\frac{3}{8}$
28	14	$2\frac{1}{4}$	$4\frac{1}{2}$	$\frac{3}{4}$	33	$1\frac{1}{2}$	18	1	$4\frac{5}{8}$	$\frac{15}{16}$	$1\frac{1}{8}$	$8\frac{3}{8}$	$23\frac{1}{4}$	$1\frac{1}{4}$	$\frac{3}{4}$	$18\frac{3}{4}$	5	$1\frac{1}{4}$	10	$1\frac{1}{8}$	$3\frac{3}{8}$	$4\frac{3}{8}$	$7\frac{7}{8}$

All Dimensions are given in Inches.

Attachment of Cylinders to Girder Frames.

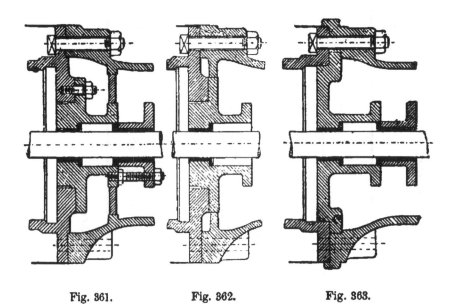

Fig. 361.   Fig. 362.   Fig. 363.

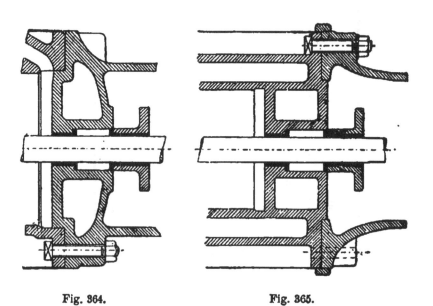

Fig. 364.   Fig. 365.

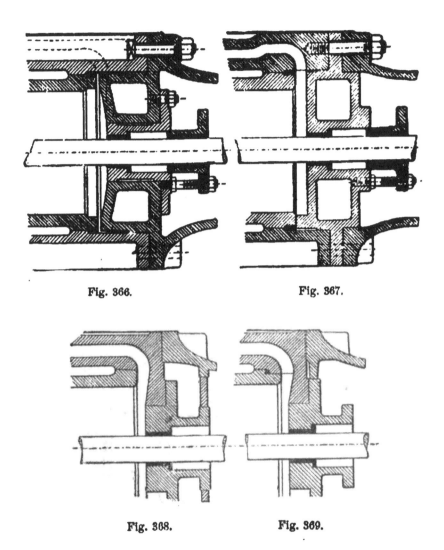

Fig. 366.   Fig. 367.

Fig. 368.   Fig. 369.

Figs. 361 to 369 show different ways of bolting cylinders on to girder frames. Figs. 362, 363, 369 show the simplest and perhaps best way; in fig. 362 the small cover can be removed without disturbing any other part, but in fig. 363 the girder and cylinder must be parted in order to take the cover off, and is therefore not so convenient as figs. 362 and 369. In figs. 364, 366, the girder makes a steam joint with the cylinder; not a good arrangement.

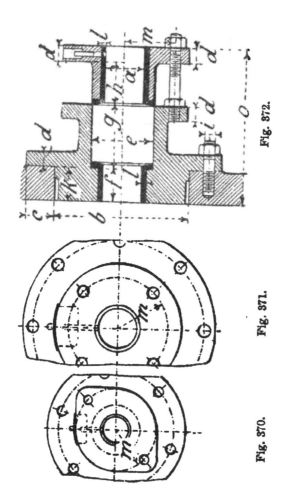

Fig. 372.

Fig. 371.

Fig. 370.

TABLE 38.—**Dimensions of Front Cylinder Covers and Glands** (Figs. 370—372).

Engine.										Bolts.					Bolts.		
H	D	*a*	*b*	*c*	*d*	*e*	*f*	*g*	*h*	No.	*i*	*k*	*l*	*m*	No.	*n*	*o*
12	6	$1\frac{1}{8}$	$3\frac{1}{4}$	$1\frac{1}{2}$	$\frac{3}{4}$	$2\frac{3}{8}$	$\frac{3}{4}$	$2\frac{5}{8}$	$1\frac{3}{4}$	4	$\frac{5}{8}$	$1\frac{3}{8}$	$\frac{3}{16}$	$2\frac{3}{8}$	2	$\frac{5}{8}$	7
16	8	$1\frac{3}{8}$	$4\frac{1}{4}$	2	$\frac{7}{8}$	$2\frac{3}{4}$	$1\frac{1}{4}$	3	$1\frac{7}{8}$	4	$\frac{5}{8}$	$1\frac{1}{2}$	$\frac{3}{16}$	$2\frac{1}{2}$	2	$\frac{5}{8}$	$8\frac{1}{4}$
20	10	$1\frac{5}{8}$	$5\frac{1}{4}$	$2\frac{1}{4}$	1	3	$1\frac{3}{8}$	$3\frac{3}{8}$	$2\frac{1}{8}$	6	$\frac{5}{8}$	$1\frac{1}{2}$	$\frac{3}{16}$	$2\frac{7}{8}$	2	$\frac{3}{4}$	$9\frac{3}{8}$
24	12	2	$6\frac{3}{8}$	$2\frac{1}{4}$	1	$3\frac{5}{8}$	$1\frac{5}{8}$	4	$2\frac{3}{8}$	6	$\frac{3}{4}$	$1\frac{3}{4}$	$\frac{1}{4}$	$3\frac{3}{16}$	3	$\frac{3}{4}$	$10\frac{1}{2}$
28	14	$2\frac{1}{4}$	$7\frac{5}{8}$	$2\frac{1}{4}$	1	$3\frac{3}{4}$	$1\frac{3}{4}$	$4\frac{1}{4}$	$2\frac{1}{2}$	6	$\frac{3}{4}$	2	$\frac{1}{4}$	$3\frac{1}{4}$	3	$\frac{3}{4}$	$11\frac{1}{8}$
32	16	$2\frac{3}{8}$	$8\frac{3}{4}$	$2\frac{3}{8}$	$1\frac{1}{8}$	4	2	$4\frac{1}{4}$	$2\frac{5}{8}$	6	$\frac{3}{4}$	$2\frac{1}{2}$	$\frac{5}{16}$	$3\frac{3}{8}$	3	$\frac{3}{4}$	$11\frac{1}{2}$
36	18	$2\frac{5}{8}$	$9\frac{5}{8}$	$2\frac{3}{8}$	$1\frac{1}{8}$	$4\frac{1}{4}$	$2\frac{1}{4}$	$4\frac{3}{8}$	$2\frac{3}{4}$	6	$\frac{3}{4}$	$2\frac{3}{4}$	$\frac{5}{16}$	$3\frac{1}{2}$	3	$\frac{3}{4}$	$12\frac{1}{8}$
40	20	$2\frac{3}{4}$	10	$2\frac{3}{8}$	$1\frac{1}{4}$	$4\frac{3}{8}$	$2\frac{3}{8}$	$4\frac{5}{8}$	3	8	$\frac{3}{4}$	3	$\frac{5}{16}$	$3\frac{9}{16}$	3	$\frac{3}{4}$	$12\frac{3}{4}$
44	22	$3\frac{1}{4}$	$10\frac{3}{8}$	$2\frac{3}{8}$	$1\frac{1}{4}$	5	$2\frac{3}{4}$	5	$3\frac{3}{8}$	8	$\frac{3}{4}$	$3\frac{1}{4}$	$\frac{5}{16}$	4	4	$\frac{7}{8}$	$14\frac{1}{8}$

All Dimensions are given in Inches.

Back Cylinder Covers, with and without Tail Rod Guides.

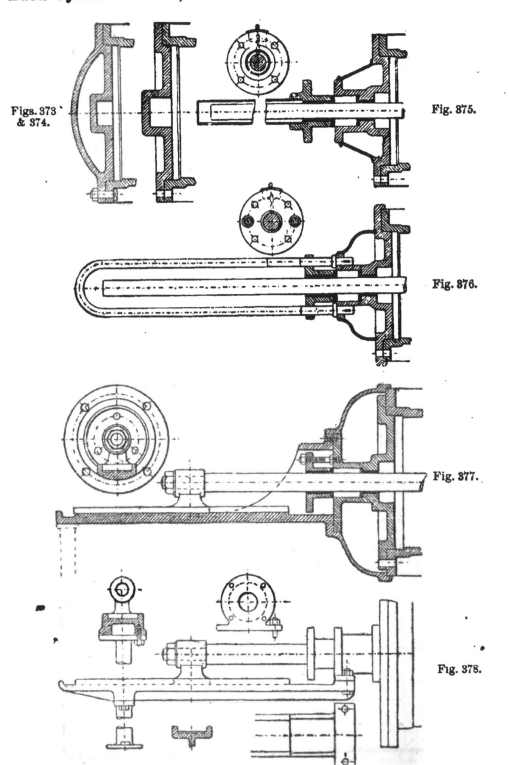

Figs. 373 & 374.

Fig. 375.

Fig. 376.

Fig. 377.

Fig. 378.

Fig. 373 shows a chambered cover cast in one piece ; fig. 374 a plain back cover. Fig. 375 a simple tail rod guide formed by a stuffing box and gland in back cover and protected by a covering of iron pipe, a very neat arrangement and one that is much used ; fig. 376, the guide for the tail rod, is the same as in the last figure ; the rod is protected by a pair of guard rails, an arrangement which is neither so neat nor good as the tube in fig. 375. In figs. 377, 378 the tail rod guide is more elaborate, being guided by a planed bar and slipper, a more expensive arrangement than those of figs. 375, 376, but more suitable for large engines. Figs. 379, 380 show further methods of guiding the tail rod.

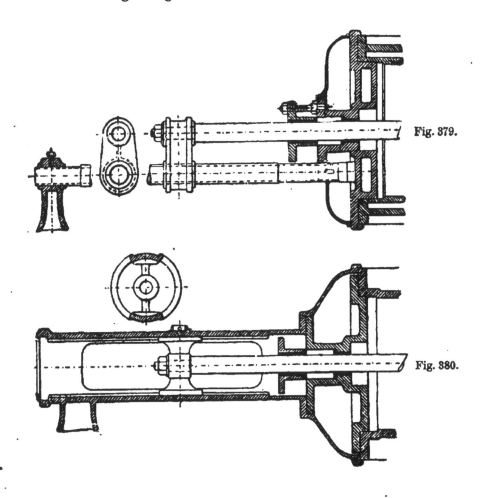

Fig. 379.

Fig. 380.

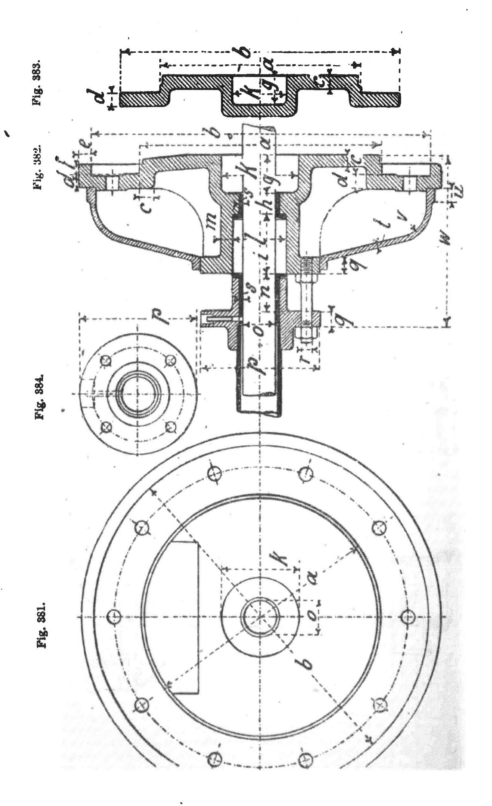

Fig. 383.

Fig. 382.

Fig. 384.

Fig. 381.

TABLE 39.—**Dimensions of Back Cylinder Covers** (Figs. 381—384).

Engines.																		Bolts.			Cover casing.		
H.	D.	a	b	c	d	e	f	g	h	i	k	l	m	n	o	p	q	No.	r	s	t	u	v
12	6	6½	13⅞	¾	1	—	—	1⅜	—	—	2¾	—	—	—	—	—	—	—	—	—	—	—	—
16	8	8½	16	¾	1	—	—	1¾	—	—	3½	—	—	—	—	—	—	—	—	—	—	—	—
20	10	10½	18¼	⅞	1	—	—	2¼	—	—	4½	—	—	—	—	—	—	—	—	—	—	—	—
24	12	12½	20½	⅞	1	⅝	⅝	2⅜	1⅝	4	4⅝	3⅝	¾	2⅜	2	8¼	1	3	¾	¼	5/16	⅝	
28	14	14¾	23¼	1	1¼	⅝	⅝	2⅝	1¾	4¼	4¾	3¾	¾	2½	2¼	8½	1	3	¾	¼	5/16	⅝	2½
32	16	16¾	25¾	1	1¼	¾	⅝	2¾	2	4¼	5¼	4	⅞	2⅝	2⅜	8⅝	1⅛	3	¾	5/16	⅜	¾	2½
36	18	18¾	28½	1⅛	1⅜	⅞	¾	3	2¼	4⅜	6	4¼	⅞	2¾	2⅝	9¼	1⅛	3	¾	5/16	⅜	¾	2¾
40	20	20¾	31	1¼	1½	1	¾	3¼	2⅜	4⅝	6¼	4⅜	⅞	3	2¾	9⅜	1¼	3	¾	5/16	7/16	⅞	3
44	22	22¾	33	1¼	1½	1	1	3½	2¾	5	6½	5	1	3⅝	3¼	10⅛	1¼	4	⅞	5/16	½	1	3¼

All Dimensions are given in Inches.

Stuffing Boxes and Glands for Piston Rods.

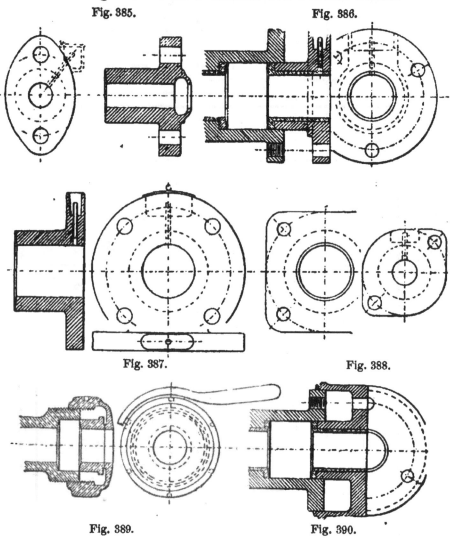

Fig. 385.   Fig. 386.

Fig. 387.   Fig. 388.

Fig. 389.   Fig. 390.

Figs. 385, 386 show ordinary simple stuffing boxes and glands; figs. 389, 390 glands of old fashioned type having the disadvantage of often corroding up round the outside of the stuffing box where the cap goes over. Fig. 391 shows the very ingenious device of Mr.

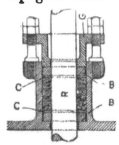

Fig. 391.

Yarrow especially adapted for high speed engines. The piston rod has often given trouble in high speed engines by getting very hot, the reason being that the crosshead guides and cylinder bore are seldom in perfect truth with one another, so that a severe side strain is exerted by the rod against the gland. In Mr. Yarrow's gland this is obviated by introducing loose collars B, B, between the packing and the gland G ; these collars are a good fit on the rod but free from touching the sides of the stuffing box ; the gland is bored larger than the rod R, but is turned a good fit in the stuffing box. It will be seen in this arrangement if the rod R is guided by the crosshead slightly out of truth with the cylinder bore, the loose collars will allow it to move in its own path freely, the elasticity of the packing allowing of this, and that no severe strain can come upon the gland causing the rod to heat.

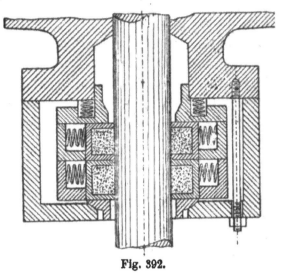

Fig. 392.

Fig. 392 shows a gland and packing made by the United States Metallic Packing Co., Ltd., of Bradford.

Slide Valve Chests and Covers.

Slide valve chests and their covers are made of cast iron ; for calculating the strength of the cover and chest walls, they are considered as plates held fast round the edges (figs. 393, 394).

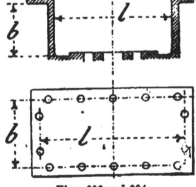

Figs. 393 and 394.

Thickness of walls, $\delta = \cdot 5l \sqrt{\dfrac{Ph}{k\bar{l}}}$

Stress $k = 0\cdot 25 \dfrac{Pbl}{\delta^2} =$ for cast iron 6400 lbs. per square inch.

P = press in lbs. per square inch.
h = breadth of walls.
l = length.

Example.—An engine with $15\frac{3}{4}''$ diameter of piston $27\frac{1}{2}''$ stroke, 88·2 lbs. pressure of steam.

(1.) For the valve chest walls,

$l = 22''$; $b = 11''$; $k = 6400$ lbs. per square inch.

$$\delta = \cdot 5 \times 22 \sqrt{\frac{88\cdot 2 \times 11}{6400 \times 22}} = \cdot 91'' \text{ about } \tfrac{7}{8}''.$$

(2.) For the valve chest cover,

$$l = 25'' \; ; \; b = 15'' \; ; \; k = 6400 \text{ lbs. per square inch.}$$

$$\delta = \cdot 5 \times 25 \sqrt{\frac{88 \cdot 2 \times 15}{6400 \times 25}} = 1\tfrac{1}{16}'' \text{ inches.}$$

This $1\tfrac{1}{16}''$ would be the necessary thickness if the cover were a plain flat plate without stiffening ribs, but as ribs are generally used, except in the case of very small covers, the thickness may be reduced in proportion to the depth and number of ribs. In small engines the valve chest is cast in one with the cylinder, but with very large engines it is often cast separate and bolted on.

Valve Chest Covers.

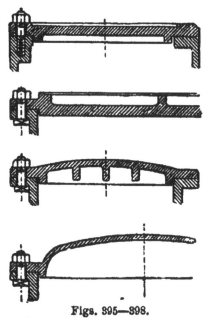

Valve chests have either internal flanges as figs. 395 and 402, or external flanges as figs. 396 to 401; the stiffening ribs are usually on the outside as figs. 396, 402.

The design shown in fig. 402, where the valve chest is finished off with a bold curve, is one that has been largely used on portable engines, and gives an exceedingly neat appearance; but it is not easy to clothe a valve chest with lagging when the corners are round, as when the corners are square and a small external flange cast on the chest to receive the lagging screws. The cover when ribbed as in fig.

Figs. 395—398.

402, is often filled up with non-conducting material and neatly covered over with sheet iron or steel.

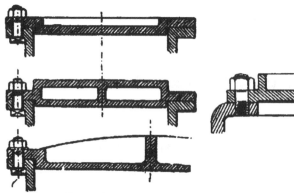

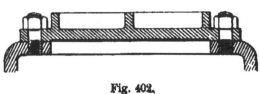

Fig. 402.

Figs. 399—401.

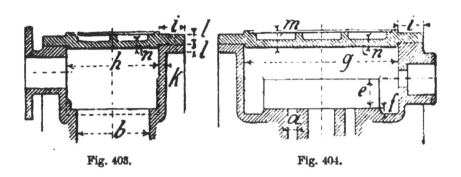

Fig. 403.   Fig. 404.

TABLE 40.—Dimensions of Valve Chests of Single Slide Valves (Figs. 403, 404).

Engines.		a	b	e	f	g	h	i	k	l	m	n
H	D											
12	6	$\frac{3}{8}$	$3\frac{1}{4}$	$1\frac{1}{2}$	$\frac{1}{2}$	6	$4\frac{3}{4}$	$1\frac{7}{8}$	$\frac{1}{2}$	$\frac{5}{8}$	1	$\frac{3}{8}$
16	8	$\frac{1}{2}$	$4\frac{3}{4}$	2	$\frac{1}{2}$	$7\frac{5}{8}$	6	2	$\frac{1}{2}$	$\frac{5}{8}$	$1\frac{1}{8}$	$\frac{1}{2}$
20	10	$\frac{5}{8}$	$5\frac{5}{8}$	$2\frac{1}{4}$	$\frac{1}{2}$	$9\frac{1}{4}$	$7\frac{1}{2}$	$2\frac{1}{8}$	$\frac{5}{8}$	$\frac{3}{4}$	$1\frac{3}{4}$	$\frac{1}{2}$
24	12	$\frac{3}{4}$	$6\frac{3}{4}$	$2\frac{3}{8}$	$\frac{1}{2}$	12	9	$2\frac{3}{8}$	$\frac{5}{8}$	$\frac{3}{4}$	$1\frac{1}{2}$	$\frac{5}{8}$
28	14	1	$8\frac{3}{4}$	$2\frac{5}{8}$	$\frac{1}{2}$	$14\frac{1}{2}$	$10\frac{3}{4}$	$2\frac{1}{2}$	$\frac{3}{4}$	$\frac{7}{8}$	$1\frac{5}{8}$	$\frac{5}{8}$

All Dimensions are given in Inches.

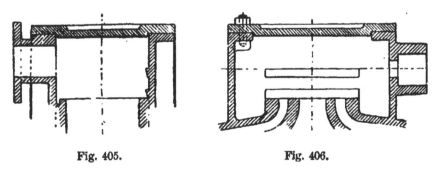

Fig. 405.   Fig. 406.

Figs. 405, 406 show two sections of a slide valve chest of ordinary construction with raised port face.

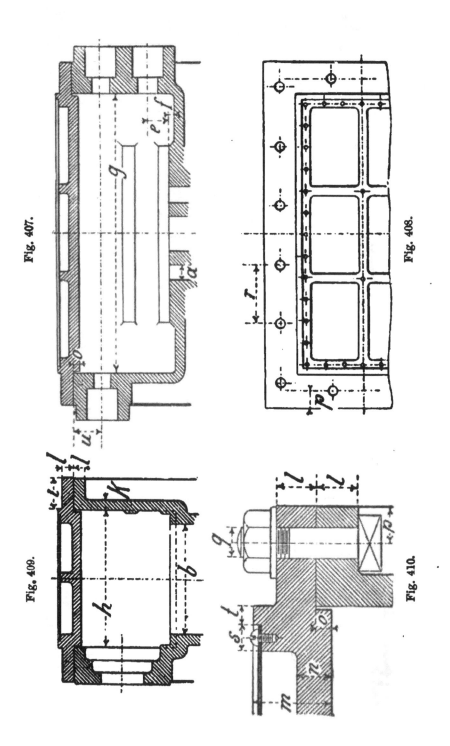

Fig. 407.

Fig. 408.

Fig. 409.

Fig. 410.

TABLE 41.—**Dimensions of Valve Chests with Cover for Meyer's Slide Valves** (Figs. 407—410).

Engines.														Bolts.					
H	D	*a*	*b*	*e*	*f*	*g*	*h*	*i*	*k*	*l*	*m*	*n*	*o*	*p*	No.	*q*	*r*	*s*	*t*	*u*
16	8	½	4⅜	1	½	11¼	6	2	½	⅝	1⅜	⅝	¼	⅝	10	½	4	⅝	⅜	1¾
20	10	⅝	5⅝	1¼	½	13¼	7½	2⅛	⅝	¾	1½	¾	¼	¾	12	⅝	4⅜	⅝	⅜	2
24	12	¾	6¾	1⅜	½	16	9	2⅜	¾	⅞	1¾	⅞	¼	¾	14	⅝	4⅝	⅝	⅜	2¼
28	14	1	8⅜	1½	½	18½	10¾	2½	¾	1	2	1	⅜	1	16	¾	4¾	⅝	⅜	2⅜
32	16	1⅛	10	1¾	⅝	21¼	12½	2¾	⅞	1⅛	2¼	1⅛	⅜	1	18	¾	4¾	⅝	½	2⅝
36	18	1¼	11⅝	2	⅝	24	14¾	3	1	1¼	2⅜	1¼	⅜	1⅛	20	⅞	4¾	⅝	½	2¾
40	20	1½	13¼	2	¾	27¼	16½	3¼	1⅛	1¼	2⅝	1¼	½	1⅛	20	⅞	5	⅝	½	3
44	22	1⅝	15	2¼	¾	30	18	3½	1⅜	1½	2¾	1⅜	½	1⅜	22	1	5¼	⅝	½	3¼

All Dimensions are given in Inches.

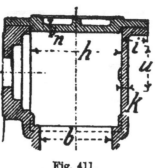

Fig. 411.

TABLE 42.—**Dimensions of Valve Chests for Rider's Slide Valves** (Figs. 411, 412).

H	20	24	28	32	36	40	44
D	10	12	14	16	18	20	22
u	$3\frac{1}{2}$	$4\frac{1}{2}$	5	6	7	8	9
y	15	$17\frac{1}{2}$	$20\frac{1}{2}$	$23\frac{1}{2}$	$26\frac{1}{2}$	30	33

All Dimensions are given in Inches.

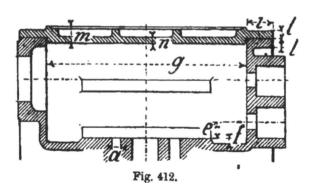

Fig. 412.

Fly-wheels.

The fly-wheel of an engine may be looked upon as a speed regulator, especially for reducing those irregularities which occur in the engine itself when passing the centres ; the fly also serves to soften down the irregularities proceeding from external causes, such as sudden variations in the load, and thus assists the governor, whose special duty is to control the speed of the engine when under a varying load.

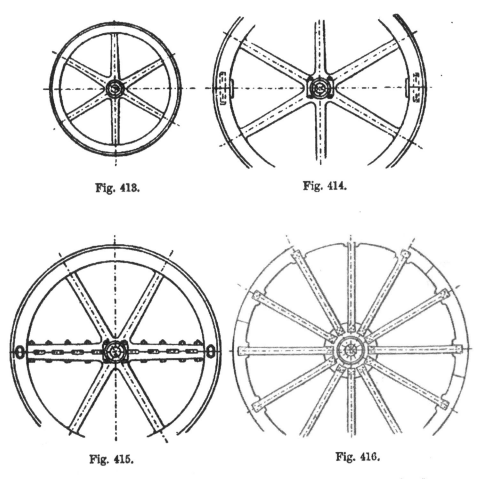

Fig. 413.   Fig. 414.

Fig. 415.   Fig. 416.

The above figs. show examples of fly-wheels : fig. 414 is the most usual method of making a fly-wheel in halves; fig. 416 shows a built-up wheel with wrought-iron arms, figs. 420 and 431, on page 126 show respectively the section of rim and boss of such a wheel.

Various rules can be given for the weight of fly-wheels, but it should always be remembered that where very steady running is required the fly-wheel should be heavier than most formulæ give, especially if the engine is used, as is often the case, with electric lighting to drive one machine direct; this is perhaps the severest test of steady running that can be given. Where a number of machines are driven from an engine by means of shafting, steady running is not nearly so difficult of attainment, on account of the steadying power of the shafting pulleys, belting, &c.

Engines working with a high rate of expansion require heavy fly-wheels on account of the internal irregularities being greater than when steam is admitted for more than half the stroke.

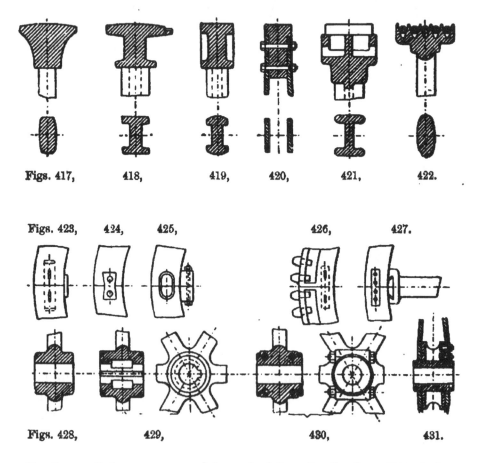

Figs. 417,　　418,　　419,　　420,　　421,　　422.

Figs. 423,　424,　425,　　　　426,　　427.

Figs. 428,　　429,　　　　430,　　431.

Sections of rims, arms, and bosses of fly-wheels, figs. 417, 418, 419, are ordinary sections of rims and arms; fig. 430, an ordinary fly-wheel boss in halves; other figs. show special examples.

Let N = the effective horse power of the engine.

n = the number of revs. per minute.

r = the crank radius in inches.

l = the length of the connecting rod in inches.

$\dfrac{r}{l}$ = the ratio of crank radius to length of connecting rod.

G = the weight of the fly-wheel rim in lbs.

R = the mean radius of the fly-wheel rim in feet.

v = the mean speed of the rim in feet per second.

$\dfrac{1}{\delta} = \dfrac{v \text{ max.} - v \text{ min.}}{v}$ = the extent of irregularity.

δ = regularity.

Values of δ—

For ordinary steam engines δ = 40 to 60.

For engines driving spinning machinery $\Big\}$ δ = 60 to 100
or for electric lighting,

For a single cylinder engine,

$$G = 100\,i\ \frac{\delta\,N}{v^2\,n} \text{ and } \delta = \frac{G\,v^2 n}{100\,i\,N}$$

The coefficient i is dependent on the rate of expansion and may be taken from the table where the values of i are given for $\dfrac{r}{l} = \frac{1}{4}$ to $\frac{1}{6}$ and the clearance space s = from 2 to 7 per cent. of the stroke, and p = absolute initial pressure, w = absolute pressure of release, then $\dfrac{P}{w}$ — total expansion, and h = the cut off.

TABLE 43.—**Values of** i.

$\dfrac{P}{w}$	1	2	3	4	5	6	7	8	9
h	1	·5	·33	·25	·20	·15	·10	·08	·06
i	1265	1610	1840	2070	2185	2300	2415	2530	2645

Example.—For an engine with piston $15\frac{3}{4}''$ diameter, $27\frac{1}{2}''$ stroke, 85 revolutions per minute, 55 effective HP, $\dfrac{r}{l} = \frac{1}{5}$, R = 5' 3''

$$v = \frac{85 \times 2\pi \times 5\cdot25}{60} = 46\cdot5 \text{ feet per second}; h = \cdot17, \delta = 50.$$

$$G = 100 \times 2185\ \frac{50 \times 55}{(46.5)^2 \times 85} = 3270 \text{ lbs.}$$

The total weight of the fly-wheel, including the arms and boss, is about 1·35 times that of the rim.

For double-cylinder or compound engines, the weight of the wheel may be somewhat less if the cranks are at right angles. $G = 30\,i\,\dfrac{\delta\,N}{v^2\,n}$ where $N =$ the total effective HP of the engine and the value of δ for such engines being rather greater than 70.

Let $Gs =$ the weight in lbs. of a segment whose length is l, then $C = \dfrac{Gsv^2}{gR} =$ the centrifugal force.

The piece l, fig. 432, may be taken as a beam with an equally distributed load and fixed at the two ends; the centrifugal force acting outwards will then be the sum of these equal loads. In order to

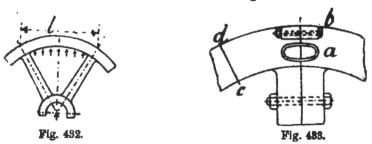

Fig. 432.   Fig. 433.

increase the strength of the joint in the rim when the fly-wheels are made in halves a wrought iron ring, a, fig. 433, is shrunk on over lugs cast on the rim; (the joint in fig. 433 is of unusual construction, see those shown in figs. 438, 440). The stress S_1 on the rim in lbs. per square inch of section may be calculated by the formula, $S_1 = ·144\,v^2$, where v is in feet per second; this includes the bending strain on the arms. The total stress on the cross section, $c-d$, fig. 433, is $f \times S_1$, where f is the cross section in square inches. If q is the cross section of the two rings taken together and q_1 the cross section of the bolts or dowells according to which plan of construction is adopted, then the stress in rings and bolts is $S = \dfrac{fS_1}{q + q_1}$.

The arms are exposed to a tearing stress from the centrifugal force, and to a bending stress from the variations of the force communicated to the wheel; the stress may be for cast iron, 1300 lbs. per square inch, for wrought iron, 5000 lbs. per square inch.

The maximum safe velocity for the periphery of a cast iron fly-wheel is usually taken as 80 feet per second, and care must be taken that when the fly-wheel is in halves, that the joints are sufficiently strong to resist bursting, and if not made in halves the boss should be split to allow of contraction in cooling, a hoop being shrunk on after the wheel is cool.*

Fly-wheels are often used as pulleys for driving machinery by means of belts ; the rim is then turned slightly arched, or if ropes are used, the rim is grooved, as shown in fig. 434.

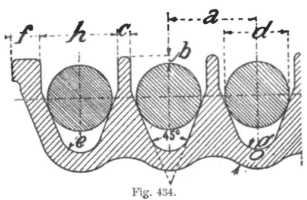

Fig. 434.

TABLE 44.—**Dimensions of Grooves for Rope Pulleys** (Fig. 434).

d	a	b	c	e	f	g	h
$1\frac{9}{16}$	$2\frac{1}{8}$	$\frac{3}{16}$	$\frac{5}{16}$	about $\frac{7}{16}$	$\frac{5}{8}$	$\frac{7}{16}$	$1\frac{13}{16}$
$1\frac{3}{4}$	$2\frac{3}{8}$	$\frac{5}{16}$	$\frac{3}{8}$	$\frac{1}{2}$	$\frac{3}{4}$	$\frac{1}{2}$	2
2	$2\frac{5}{8}$	$\frac{3}{4}$	$\frac{7}{16}$	$\frac{5}{8}$	$\frac{7}{8}$	$\frac{5}{8}$	$2\frac{1}{4}$

All Dimensions are given in Inches.

TABLE 45.—**Dimensions and Particulars of Rope Drives.**

Circumference of ropes . .	$2\frac{3}{4}$	3	$3\frac{1}{2}$	$4\frac{1}{4}$	$5\frac{1}{4}$	6	$6\frac{1}{2}$
Diameter of ropes . . .	$\frac{3}{4}$	$\frac{7}{8}$	1	$1\frac{1}{4}$	$1\frac{1}{2}$	$1\frac{3}{4}$	2
Weight in lbs. per foot, Hemp	·37	·46	·56	·66	1·00	1·37	1·62
,, ,, ,, Cotton	·27	·30	·39	·59	·87	1·17	1·50
†Diameter of smallest pulley .	18	24	30	36	46	60	66
Pitch of grooves . . .	$1\frac{3}{8}$	$1\frac{1}{2}$	$1\frac{3}{4}$	2	$2\frac{1}{2}$	$2\frac{3}{4}$	3
Indicated HP transmitted by one rope for the above pulleys at 100 revolutions per minute	For ropes running horizonal or nearly so.						
	2	3	5	12	20	28	36
	For ropes running vertical or nearly so.						
	1	2	4	8	14	20	26

All Dimensions are given in Inches.

* A fly-wheel, 20 feet diameter, running at 70 revolutions per minute, burst, and the pieces were carried to great distances—the speed in this case being about 70 feet per second.—*Engineer*, Oct. 7th, 1892.

† By "diameter of smallest pulley," it is to be understood that it is best not to use smaller pulleys, except in cases of emergency.

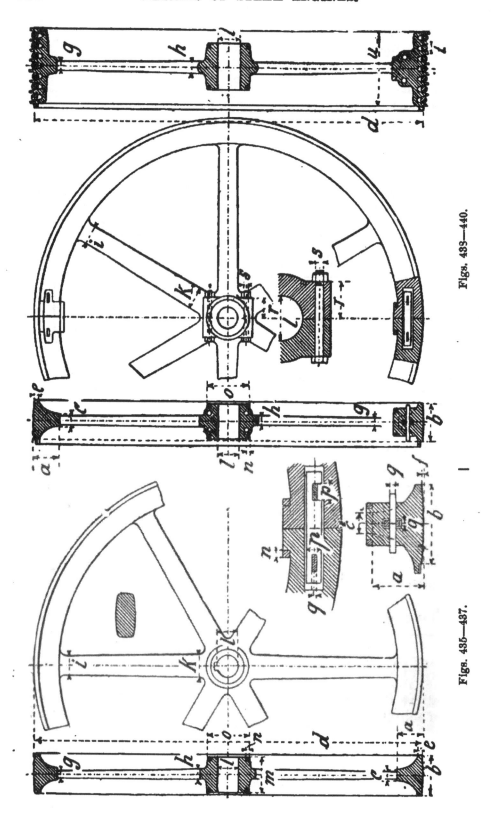

Figs. 438—440.

Figs. 435—437.

TABLE 46.—**Dimensions of Fly-Wheels** (Figs. 435—440).

Engines.																				Centre of gravity of Rim.	Weight of Rim.	Rope Pulleys.		
H.	D.	*d*	*b*	*a*	*c*	*e*	*f*	*g*	*h*	*i*	*k*	*l*	*m*	*n*	*o*	*p*	*q*	*r*	*s*	d_1	lbs.	Ropes No.	*t*	*u*
12	6	42	6	3	2	⅜	⅛	⅞	1¼	2	2½	3	5	—	6	—	—	—	—	40	300	—	—	—
16	8	60	7	3½	2¼	⅜	⅛	1¼	1½	2½	3¼	3½	6	—	7	—	—	—	—	58	800	—	—	—
20	10	78	8	4	2½	⅜	3/16	1½	2	3½	4½	5¼	7½	1	10	—	—	—	—	75	1,250	3	1½	7
24	12	96	10	5	2¾	⅜	3/16	2	2½	4½	5½	6	9	1¼	12	—	—	—	—	93	1,900	4	1½	8½
28	14	114	12	5½	3¼	⅜	¼	2½	2⅞	5½	6½	8⅜	9½	1⅜	14	2½	1	5	1⅜	110½	2,700	4	1¾	10
32	16	132	15	6	3½	⅜	¼	2¾	3¼	6½	7⅝	9⅜	11	1⅜	16	3	1⅛	5¾	1½	128	3,800	5	2	13½
36	18	156	18	6½	4	⅜	5/16	3¼	3¾	7	8⅜	10⅝	12½	1½	17	3¼	1¼	6½	1⅝	152	5,100	6	2	16½
40	20	168	20	7½	4½	½	⅜	3½	4½	7½	9	12	14	1⅝	20	3½	1⅜	7½	1¾	163	6,850	7	2	19
44	22	192	22	8	5	½	⅜	4	5	8	9½	13¼	16	1¾	22	4	1½	8	2	187	10,000	8	2	22

All Dimensions are given in Inches.

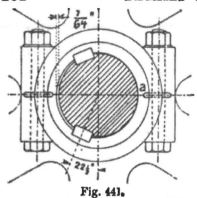

Fig. 441.

An American practice for fly-wheels is to bore out the boss exactly to the size of the shaft, and then machine or slot out a clearance, as shown to the left of the figure 441, two keys being fitted and driven home. The wheel is thus pulled hard over on to the true part of the original bore.

Throttle Valves.

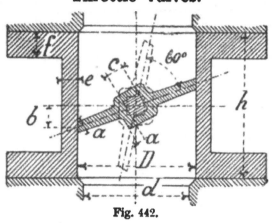

Fig. 442.

TABLE 47.—Dimensions of Throttle Valves.

d	D.	a	b	c	e	f	h
$\frac{3}{4}$	$1\frac{1}{4}$	$\frac{1}{8}$	$\frac{1}{4}$	$\frac{5}{16}$	$\frac{3}{8}$	$\frac{5}{8}$	2
$1\frac{1}{4}$	$1\frac{1}{2}$	$\frac{1}{8}$	$\frac{1}{4}$	$\frac{3}{8}$	$\frac{3}{8}$	$\frac{5}{8}$	$2\frac{1}{2}$
$1\frac{1}{2}$	2	$\frac{1}{8}$	$\frac{3}{8}$	$\frac{3}{8}$	$\frac{3}{8}$	$\frac{5}{8}$	3
2	$2\frac{1}{2}$	$\frac{1}{8}$	$\frac{3}{8}$	$\frac{3}{8}$	$\frac{1}{2}$	$\frac{3}{4}$	$3\frac{1}{2}$
$2\frac{1}{2}$	$2\frac{3}{4}$	$\frac{3}{16}$	$\frac{1}{2}$	$\frac{1}{2}$	$\frac{1}{2}$	$\frac{3}{4}$	4
$2\frac{3}{4}$	$3\frac{1}{4}$	$\frac{3}{16}$	$\frac{1}{2}$	$\frac{1}{2}$	$\frac{1}{2}$	$\frac{3}{4}$	$4\frac{1}{2}$
$3\frac{1}{4}$	$3\frac{1}{2}$	$\frac{3}{16}$	$\frac{5}{8}$	$\frac{1}{2}$	$\frac{1}{2}$	$\frac{3}{4}$	5
$3\frac{1}{2}$	4	$\frac{3}{16}$	$\frac{3}{4}$	$\frac{5}{8}$	$\frac{1}{2}$	$\frac{3}{4}$	$5\frac{1}{2}$
4	$4\frac{1}{4}$	$\frac{1}{4}$	$\frac{3}{4}$	$\frac{5}{8}$	$\frac{1}{2}$	$\frac{3}{4}$	6
$4\frac{1}{2}$	5	$\frac{1}{4}$	$\frac{7}{8}$	$\frac{5}{8}$	$\frac{1}{2}$	$\frac{7}{8}$	$6\frac{1}{2}$
$4\frac{3}{4}$	$5\frac{1}{2}$	$\frac{1}{4}$	1	$\frac{3}{4}$	$\frac{5}{8}$	$\frac{7}{8}$	7
$5\frac{1}{4}$	6	$\frac{1}{4}$	1	$\frac{3}{4}$	$\frac{5}{8}$	$\frac{7}{8}$	$7\frac{1}{2}$
$5\frac{1}{2}$	$6\frac{1}{2}$	$\frac{5}{16}$	$1\frac{1}{8}$	$\frac{7}{8}$	$\frac{5}{8}$	1	8
6	7	$\frac{5}{16}$	$1\frac{1}{8}$	1	$\frac{5}{8}$	1	$8\frac{1}{2}$

SECTION III.

GOVERNORS.

STEAM-ENGINE GOVERNORS have been greatly elaborated since the time of James Watt's simple conical pendulum governor, and new varieties have been introduced. Governors may be roughly divided into two main types, those in which some form of revolving pendulum is the basis, and those in which the centrifugal force of weights carried on levers is balanced against a spring; the former with a few exceptions revolve on vertical spindles, the latter are usually keyed direct on the engine crank shaft, and are sometimes called "crank shaft" governors. These latter also act directly, in some cases, on the valve eccentric and govern the engine by altering the degree of expansion; the former at the present time are seldom used to control the engine by means of a throttle valve, as in the earliest engines, but are connected indirectly to the valve gear and control the engine by altering the degree of expansion. There are further sub-divisions into which governors may be divided, such as static, pseudo-astatic, and astatic.

The simple ball governor of Watt is an example of the static governor, and each different speed of revolution corresponds to a definite position of the balls. Astatic governors are too sensitive to be of any use unless indirectly connected with the controlling mechanism, the slightest increase of speed of revolution causing the balls to fly out to their fullest limit; they have, however, been used, when connected to the controlling mechanism, through the medium of three bevel wheels and a clutch (fig. 465).

Pseudo-astatic governors approach nearer to the static governors and are much used; the cross-armed governor of Mr. J. Head (fig. 445) is an example in this kind, and any degree of sensitiveness can be attained by suitable proportions of the arms. When these pendulum governors are combined with a sliding weight as in Porter's governor (fig. 452), they are then called loaded governors, and are better adapted to control an engine than the simple governor of Watt.

Outlines of Different Types of Governors.

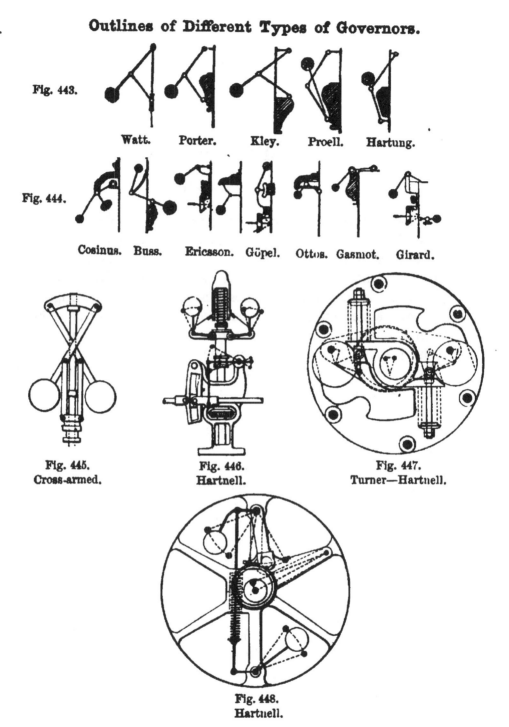

Fig. 443.

Watt.   Porter.   Kley.   Proell.   Hartung.

Fig. 444.

Cosinus.   Buss.   Ericsson.   Göpel.   Ottos.   Gasmot.   Girard.

Fig. 445.
Cross-armed.

Fig. 446.
Hartnell.

Fig. 447.
Turner—Hartnell.

Fig. 448.
Hartnell.

Figs. 443—445 show varieties of loaded and unloaded ball governors without springs ; fig. 446, one of Hartnell's loaded centrifugal governors (with spring) on a vertical spindle ; figs. 447, 448 two examples of crank-shaft governors.

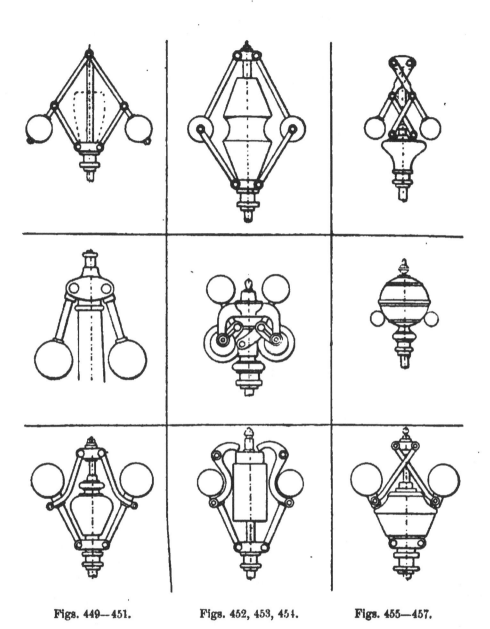

Figs. 449—451.   Figs. 452, 453, 454.   Figs. 455—457.

Varieties of Governors of the Pendulum and Loaded Pendulum Types.

Fig. 449.—Watt.   Fig. 452.—Porter.   Fig. 455.—Crossarm.
Fig. 450.—Tangye.   Fig. 453.—Buss.   loaded.
F g. 451.—Proell.   Fig. 454.—Proell.   Fig. 456.—Cosine.

The formulæ given below serve to show the action of pendulum governors and to calculate the proportions for any given normal speed.

Let P = the weight in lbs. of one ball plus one half the weight of the rod to which it is attached.

Q = the weight in lbs. of the sliding weight plus half the weight of the rod.

R = the resistance offered by the throttle valve or expansion gear actuated by the governor together with the resistance of the governor itself.

$n_1, n, n_{11},$ = the greatest, normal and least number of revolutions per minute of the governor.

$\beta_1, \beta, \beta_{11},$ = the greatest, normal and least angle between the rods and the spindle.

$\dfrac{1}{\delta_0}$ = the irregularity of the fly-wheel speed.

$\dfrac{1}{\delta} = \dfrac{n_1 - n_{11}}{n}$ the irregularity of the speed of the engine and consequently also of the governor ; $\dfrac{1}{\delta}$ = about $\cdot 9 \dfrac{1}{\delta_0}$.

S = the distance in inches which the sliding weight moves up and down.

An ordinary approximate formula for calculating the height of cone of revolving pendulum governor for any number of revolutions per minute N, is ; $N = \dfrac{187 \cdot 5}{\sqrt{L}}$ and $L = \left(\dfrac{187 \cdot 5}{N}\right)^2$ where L = height of cone in inches measured from plane of rotation of the centre of the balls to the point where the centre lines of the arms carrying the balls cross on the centre line of spindle. For a loaded governor the height of the cone is increased for a given speed in the ratio $2P + 2Q : 2P$; where P = weight of one ball and half the arm in lbs., and Q the load or sliding weight and half arm in lbs.

d = diameter in inches of the balls. For the normal speed n, R is taken to equal 0 in the equations.

Watt's governor, fig. 458.

$$n^2 = \dfrac{2936}{a \cos. \beta}\left(1 + \dfrac{Qb}{Pa}\right) ; \quad \dfrac{1}{\delta} = \dfrac{Rb}{Pa + Qb}.$$

Dimensions in feet ; the constant 2936, in from $\dfrac{3600g}{4\pi^2}$ where $g = 32 \cdot 2$.

The following proportions will be found to give good results—

$$\frac{Q}{P} = 0 \text{ to } 4, \quad \frac{b}{a} = \cdot6, \quad S = \cdot12b, \quad \beta = 25^\circ, \quad \frac{1}{\delta} = \cdot03.$$

For Porter's governor, fig. 459.

$$n^2 = 2936 \; \frac{1 + \dfrac{Q \pm R}{P}}{a \cos \beta + e \cot \beta}$$

$$\frac{1}{\delta} = \frac{R}{P + Q}, \text{ dimensions in feet.}$$

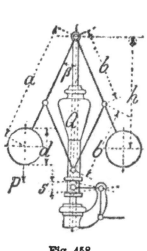

Fig. 458.

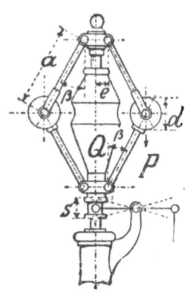

Fig. 459.

Table 48 gives the leading dimensions for a few examples of Porter's governor.

TABLE 48.

$n =$	150	140	130	120	110	100	90
$a =$	$8\frac{3}{4}$	$10\frac{3}{8}$	12	$14\frac{3}{8}$	$18\frac{1}{4}$	20	24
$e =$	$\frac{7}{8}$	1	$1\frac{1}{4}$	$1\frac{3}{8}$	$1\frac{5}{8}$	2	$2\frac{3}{8}$
$s =$	$1\frac{1}{8}$	$1\frac{1}{2}$	2	$2\frac{3}{8}$	$2\frac{3}{4}$	$3\frac{1}{4}$	$3\frac{5}{8}$
$d =$	$3\frac{1}{4}$	$4\frac{1}{4}$	$5\frac{1}{4}$	6	$6\frac{3}{4}$	$7\frac{5}{8}$	8

All Dimensions are given in Inches

Kley's governor (astatic), fig. 460.

$$n^2 = \frac{2936}{a \cos \beta - e \cot \beta} \left(1 + \frac{Qb}{Pa}\right)$$

$$\frac{1}{\delta} = \frac{Rb}{Pa + Qb}$$

Proell's governor (pseudo-astatic), fig. 461.

$$n^2 = 2936 \; \frac{-1 + \dfrac{Q + 2P + R}{P} \times \dfrac{b}{a} \times \dfrac{\sin \gamma}{\sin \beta}}{a \cos \beta + e \cot \beta}$$

$$\frac{1}{\delta} = \frac{R}{- P\dfrac{a}{b} \times \dfrac{\sin \gamma}{\sin \beta} + Q + 2P}$$

dimensions in feet.

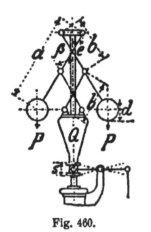

Fig. 460.

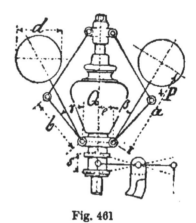

Fig. 461.

TABLE 49.—**Leading Dimensions of Kley's Governor**
(Fig. 460).

$\dfrac{a}{b} = \cdot 7$ to $\cdot 5$.

$\dfrac{Q}{P} = $ about 4.

$\beta = 30°$.

$n =$	110	100	90	85	80	75	70
$a =$	$13\frac{3}{8}$	$15\frac{5}{8}$	18	$21\frac{3}{4}$	$25\frac{3}{8}$	30	36
$e =$	$\frac{7}{8}$	1	$1\frac{1}{4}$	$1\frac{3}{8}$	$1\frac{5}{8}$	2	$2\frac{3}{8}$
$s =$	$2\frac{1}{4}$	$2\frac{3}{8}$	$2\frac{3}{4}$	$3\frac{3}{8}$	4	$4\frac{3}{4}$	$5\frac{5}{8}$
$d =$	$4\frac{5}{8}$	$5\frac{3}{8}$	6	$7\frac{1}{4}$	$8\frac{3}{8}$	10	$11\frac{1}{4}$

All Dimensions are given in Inches

TABLE 50.—Leading Dimensions of Proell's Governor (Fig. 461).

$$\frac{Q}{P} = \text{about } 4.$$

$\beta = 20°.$

$\gamma = 30°.$

$n =$	135	125	115	110	105	100	95
$a =$	8	$9\frac{5}{8}$	$11\frac{1}{4}$	$12\frac{3}{4}$	$14\frac{3}{8}$	$16\frac{3}{8}$	$18\frac{3}{8}$
$b =$	$5\frac{3}{8}$	$6\frac{3}{4}$	$7\frac{3}{4}$	9	10	$11\frac{3}{8}$	$12\frac{3}{4}$
$e =$	$\frac{7}{8}$	1	$1\frac{1}{4}$	$1\frac{3}{8}$	$1\frac{5}{8}$	2	$2\frac{3}{8}$
$s =$	2	$2\frac{1}{4}$	$2\frac{3}{8}$	$2\frac{5}{8}$	$2\frac{3}{4}$	3	$3\frac{1}{4}$
$d =$	4	$4\frac{3}{4}$	$5\frac{5}{8}$	$6\frac{3}{8}$	$7\frac{1}{4}$	$8\frac{1}{4}$	$9\frac{1}{4}$

All Dimensions are given in Inches.

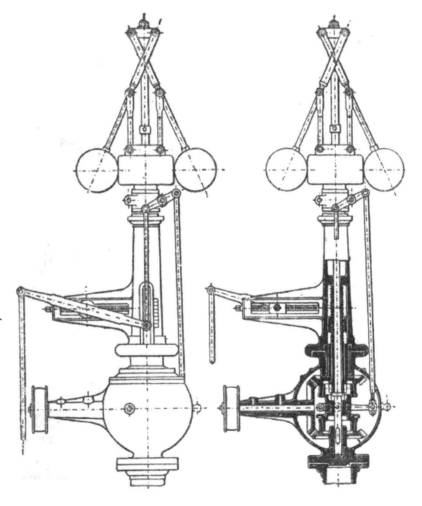

Fig. 462.   Fig. 463.

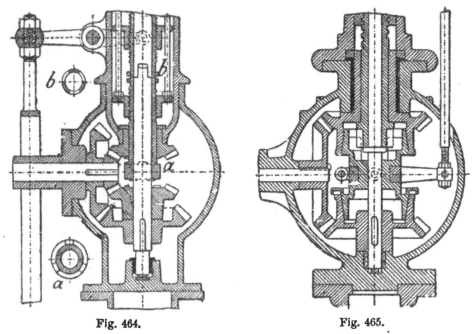

Fig. 464. Fig. 465.

Figs. 462—465 give examples of cross-armed governors on stands with clutch and bevel-wheel gear.

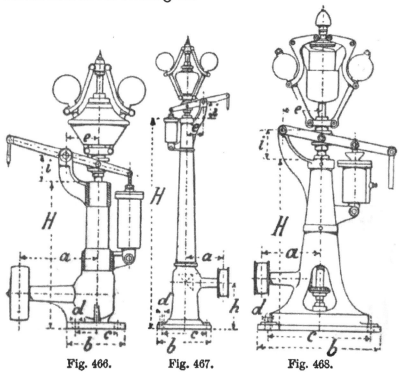

Fig. 466. Fig. 467. Fig. 468.

Figs. 466—468 give examples of governors made by the Lauchammer Iron Works fitted with an oil-brake or dash-pot, with a table of dimensions.

TABLE 51.—**Leading Dimensions of the Lauchammer Governors** (Figs. 466—468).

Distinguishing No.	I.	II.	III.	IV.
Height of stand, H	$21\frac{5}{8}$	61	$37\frac{3}{8}$	$42\frac{1}{2}$
Dimension *a*	$9\frac{7}{8}$	$11\frac{1}{2}$	13	$14\frac{3}{4}$
„ *b*	$8\frac{5}{8}$	$15\frac{3}{4}$	$27\frac{5}{8}$	$31\frac{1}{2}$
„ *c*	$6\frac{1}{4}$	13	$23\frac{5}{8}$	$27\frac{1}{8}$
„ *d*	$\frac{3}{4}$	1	$1\frac{1}{8}$	$1\frac{1}{4}$
„ *e*	$4\frac{3}{8}$	$4\frac{7}{8}$	$8\frac{5}{8}$	$9\frac{7}{8}$
„ *i*	$4\frac{7}{8}$	$4\frac{1}{2}$	$6\frac{3}{8}$	$7\frac{1}{8}$
Weight in lbs. complete as shown in figures	660	704	750	840

All Dimensions are given in Inches.

Fig. 466 is especially adapted for horizontal engines; fig. 467 for vertical engines; fig. 468 a heavy type with a spring enclosed in a case in place of the sliding weight.

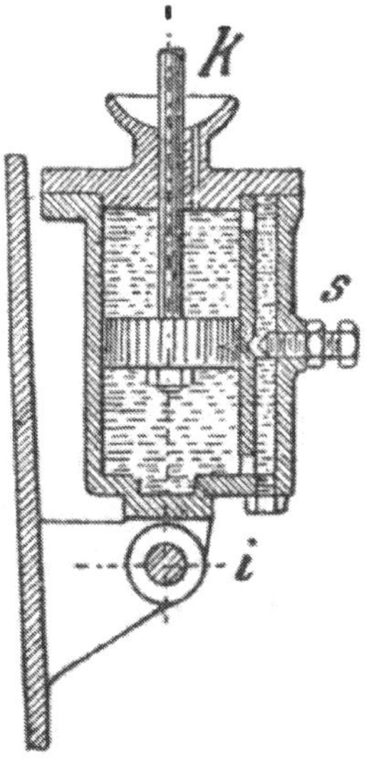

Fig. 469.

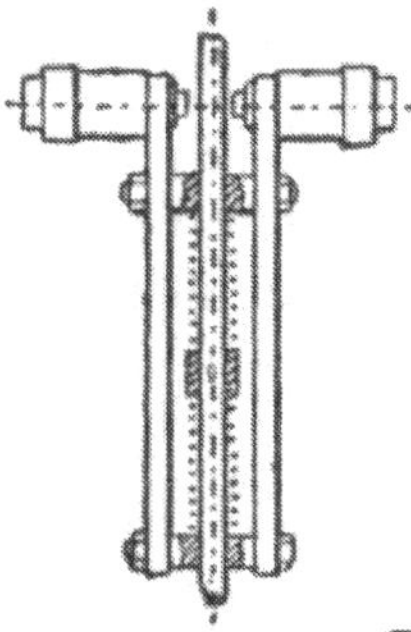

Fig. 472.

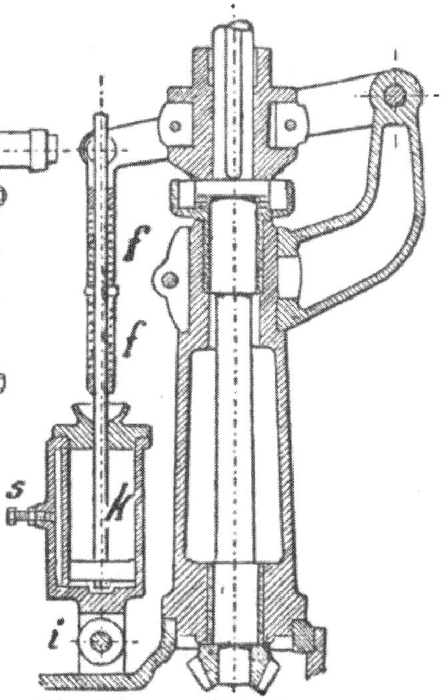

Fig. 470. Fig. 471.

To prevent sudden and violent fluctuations of the governor an oil-brake or "dash-pot" is often added; examples of dash-pots applied to governors are shown in Figs. 469—471. The cylinder of the dash-pot, fig. 469, is jointed to the frame or stand of the governor, by the pin *i*.

The cylinder is filled with oil or glycerine, and as the piston is moved up or down, the oil passes from the upper to the lower side of the piston by a passage shown at the side of the cylinder; this passage can be more or less throttled by the screw S, so as to give more or less resistance to the movement of the piston, and thus "damp" the tendency to violent fluctuations in the governor. The screw S can be adjusted whilst the engine is running. Fig. 471 shows a combination of dash-pot with an elastic connection between the governor lever and piston rod of dash-pot, a spiral spring being inserted as shown at ff, fig. 471. This elastic connection assists the damping action of the dash-pot and should be conducive to very steady running. In some cases the dash-pot is incorporated with the governor, and enclosed in a neat case.

Automatic Expansion Governor by Wilson Hartnell (Fig. 473).

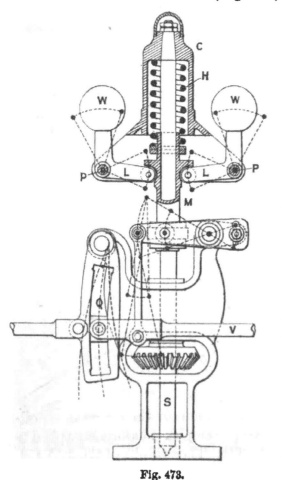

Fig. 473.

This governor is driven by bevel wheels and pulleys from the crank shaft of the engine, and consists essentially of a vertical spindle, S, carrying a casting, C; two weights, W W, on bell-crank levers, L L, are jointed on to C, by means of pins, P P; the inner ends of the levers are in contact with the sleeve M, against which the spring H presses; the lower part of the sleeve M is connected by means of a ring and rods, to the valve rod V; when the sleeve M rises, the block in the link Q is raised, and thus a varying stroke is given to the valve, the link Q being moved by an eccentric. The centrifugal force of the weights W W, through the medium of the levers L L, tends to compress the spring H. The motion of the different parts is clearly shown in the fig. by the dotted lines.

This governor is much used for controlling the speed of engines, by varying the cut-off, and is usually applied to valve gears with two valves, the main valve driven by an eccentric in the usual way, the cut-off by a separate eccentric through the medium of the link on the governor by which the cut-off is varied.

Crank Shaft Governors.

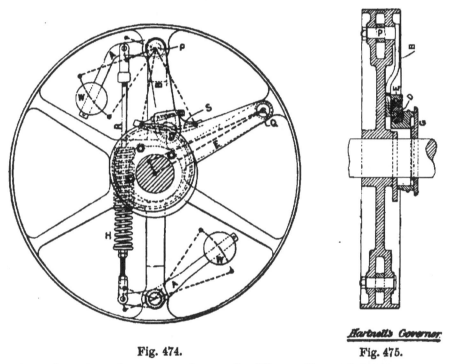

Fig. 474.   Fig. 475.

Figs. 474, 475, show two views of a Hartnell crank-shaft governor for controlling the speed of an engine by varying the cut-off. In the above figures the governor is shown in a six-armed wheel or pulley ; in some cases the governor is carried in the fly-wheel itself. Two weights, W W, are carried on two levers, A A, turning on pins in the arms of the wheel ; the two levers are connected together by the rod R by means of joints and pins, and when the weights move outwards by centrifugal force they tend to compress the spring H. The upper lever, fig. 474, is rigidly fixed to its centre pin, and this pin carries the arm B, terminating at the lower end in the sector S, so that when the weight W moves outwards or inwards the sector S moves to the right or left. The sector is formed as shown in the cross section, fig. 475, and engages in the swivel block D. The block D is free to turn in a recess formed to receive it, in the arm of the eccentric E, this arm being centred on the pin Q. On referring to fig. 474 it will be seen that the sector S is not concentric with the centre P, upon which it swings, but its centre lies to the right hand of the centre P, so that the sector is inclined, the right hand end being the lower. Now as the sector swings on centre P towards the left, and in sliding through the block D pushes the eccentric arm E downwards, and as the eccentric itself is attached to the arm E, its centre will approach towards the centre of the crank-shaft, and thus the stroke of the eccentric will be reduced and the steam cut off earlier. In the figure the line in which the centre of the eccentric approaches the centre of the shaft is radial, and the governor is for application to a separate cut-off valve of the gridiron type working on the balk of the main valve. For engines with only a single valve, the line in which the centre of the eccentric approaches the centre of the crank-shaft is not radial but parallel to radial line such as that in the figure, but at a distance equal to the lap and lead from the crank-shaft centre. It will be seen that one important feature in these crank-shaft governors, is that they are keyed fast on the shaft, and not being driven by means of belts or gear, can lead to no accident from belt slipping or gears breaking ; and if the spring should break, the weights would fly out to their extreme limits and diminish the supply of steam to nothing, so the engine would slow down until nearly stopped. These governors are extremely sensitive and well adapted for high speeds : with very slow running-engines they become rather heavy. For calculating the springs the following simple formula is used :—

W = weight in lbs. of one of the weights.

N = normal speed in revolutions per minute.

N_1 = minimum speed in revolutions per minute.

N_2 = maximum speed in revolutions per minute.

$N_2 - N_1$ = allowed variation, upon the limit of this variation the sensitiveness of the governor largely depends ; about 3 per cent. under and 4 per cent. over the normal speed gives good results, and the usual variations in load of an engine in ordinary working conditions will not give nearly as much variation in speed.

R_1 = the radius in inches from centre of shaft to centre of weight when the latter is nearest to the centre of the shaft and corresponds to the speed of N_1.

R_2 = the corresponding radius to the speed of N_2.

L = the length in inches of the lever carrying the weight.

l = the length in inches of the lever to which the spring rod **R** is attached.

r = the distance through which the spring is compressed by the action of the governor.

P_1 = the load on the spring in lbs. due to the centrifugal force at the minimum speed.

P_2 = the corresponding load in lbs. due to the maximum speed.

The $P_2 - P_1$ will equal the difference of maximum and minimum loads and $\left(\dfrac{P_2 - P_1}{r} \right)$ 2 will equal the load in lbs. per inch of compression of the spring as the two weights act together on the spring.

$$P_1 = \frac{W \times R_1 \times N_1{}^2 \times L \times \cdot 000028}{l},$$

$$P_2 = \frac{W \times R_2 \times N_2{}^2 \times L \times \cdot 000028}{l}.$$

Spring-makers seem to be very successful in making springs accurate enough for such purposes as centrifugal governors from such data as stiffness per inch required, maximum load to which the spring will be subjected, external diameter and length when uncompressed.

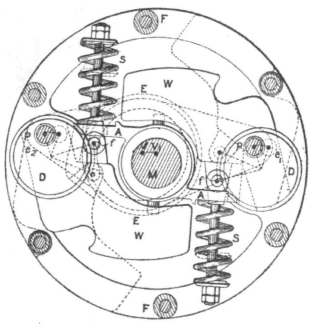

Fig. 476.

A modification of Hartnell's crank shaft governor, has been introduced by Messrs. Turner, of Ipswich, shown in diagram in fig. 476, and in perspective in figs. 477, 478.

Referring to fig. 476, two weights, W W, are formed with turned bosses, D D, fitted to and free to turn in holes in the plates or discs which form the governor body, and which are keyed on the crank shaft, M, the weights thus turning with the shaft and discs, and having their centrifugal force balanced by the springs, S S; the weights are connected by the eccentric, E (shown in dotted lines), by means of the pins, P P; the weights are shown in fig. 476, closed in full lines, and open in dotted lines. It will be seen that by the weights open-

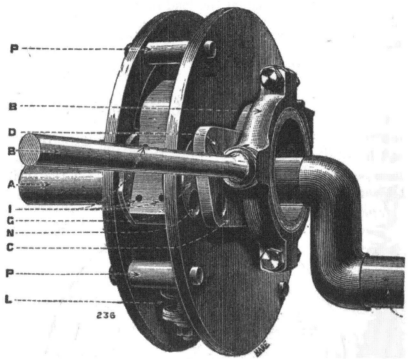

Fig. 477.

ing outwards, the pins, P P, move towards the left, and carry the eccentric with them, the centre of the eccentric moving from V to V₁ the stroke being thereby reduced, the result being nearly the same as in the Hartnell governor, and the action on the valve almost as if the variation in the cut-off were effected by an ordinary Stephenson link motion.

In fig. 477, the outside view of the Turner-Hartnell governor is shown with the eccentric rod attached; in fig. 478, one side disc is removed, and the weights shown open.

The reference letters are, A, the engine crank shaft; B, the valve eccentric rod; C, the eccentric; D D, pins carrying the eccentric, and passing through the bosses of the weights; H H, the weights;

P, bolts with collars and nuts, forming stanchions or pillars for holding the discs together.

Fig. 478.

Another variety of crank shaft governor, is that of Mr. Moore, made by Messrs. Marshall, of Gainsborough. Figs. 479—482, show the different parts, and the governor consists of a heavy loose rim, A, attached to the shaft through an elastic arrangement of links carrying the weights; C C, are the weights turning on centres attached to the rim; D D, the springs; B B, links connected at one end to the weights and at the other to the points, H H, on the tripod G, fig. 482; the arm of the eccentric, E, fig. 481, is centred on the single end of G, fig. 482, at I; the link F connects the eccentric E to the rim A.

The rim A revolves with the shaft, but is capable of running round the shaft to a small extent, defined by the limit of extension and contraction of the link centres, that is, by the extent to which the weights will open out, which can be regulated by stops on the back of the weights.

In connection with the loose rim is a variable expansion eccentric shifting with the rim and increasing or decreasing the stroke of the eccentric and valve, and thus varying the cut-off. The action of this governor is peculiar, and may be explained as follows:—The inertia of the rim assists the weights to rise; the momentum of the rim, by

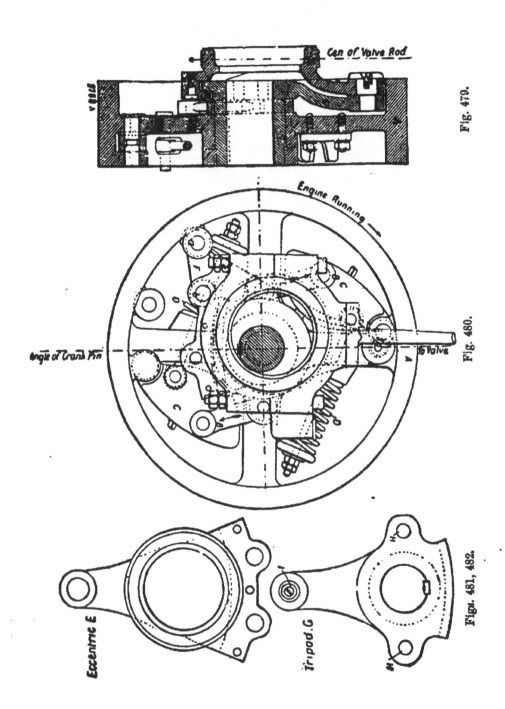

Cen of Valve Rod

Fig. 479.

Engine Running

Angle of Crank Pin

To Valve

Fig. 480.

Eccentric E

Tripod G

Fig. 481, 482.

straightening out the link and weight when the speed of the shaft diminishes, assists the weights to fall.

When the governor is expanding (rising), with an increasing speed, the shaft acts against the rim, through the link and weight, as shown by the arrow. When the governor is closing (falling) with a diminishing speed, the rim acts against it, tending to pull it forward, straightening out the link and weight. The weights are maintained in a larger plane of revolution, so to speak, than that due to centrifugal force, by the governor acting against the inertia of the rim when rising, *i.e.*, speed increasing. The weights are maintained in a smaller plane of revolution than that due to centrifugal force by the momentum of the rim acting against the governor, tending to pull it forward when closing, *i.e.*, speed decreasing.

The governor has a tendency to go too far both ways, either up or down, whenever there is the slightest variation above or below the normal speed, this tendency is checked by the work done by the governor in shifting the eccentric and valve. From the assistance given to the action of the governor weights by the rim, this governor is extremely sensitive.

SECTION IV.

VALVE GEARS.

Indicator Diagrams.

In order to follow the effect of the different distribution of steam effected by different valve gears, it is necessary to understand the indicator diagram. By the term "indicator diagram" is to be understood the graphic representation of the varying pressure of the steam on the engine piston at all positions of the crank. The steam engine "Indicator" invented by James Watt is the instrument by which the diagrams are automatically drawn. A brief description of indicators will be found on page 368. Figs. 483—488 show a few ideal forms of diagrams, with the following letters of reference :—

H = the stroke of the piston.

h = length of the period during which steam is admitted. If H be taken to equal 1, then $\dfrac{H}{h}$ = the ratio of expansion.

p = the initial absolute pressure measured from the line of perfect vacuum. p is usually taken in lbs. per square inch, but may sometimes be conveniently taken in atmospheres.

p_m = the average or mean effective pressure on the piston.

w = the terminal pressure.

p_o = the back pressure.

s = the clearance and steam passage for one end of the cylinder, usually taken in cubic inches or feet, and in diagrams figs. 483—488 it is expressed in terms of the piston area, so that the line s represents the volume of the clearance space.

va = the line of perfect vacuum.

at = the atmospheric line.

ve = the portion of the stroke from the point where the exhaust opens to the end of the stroke ; in the diagrams the line ve represents the volume of that portion of the stroke alluded to.

oC, diagrams for non-condensing engines.

mC, diagrams for condensing engines.

Figs. 483, 484, show the diagram for an engine with steam admitted for the whole stroke and in which the average pressure throughout the whole stroke is equal to the initial pressure—the back pressure

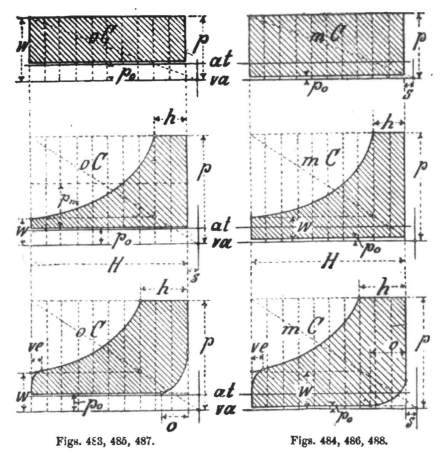

Figs. 483, 485, 487. Figs. 484, 486, 488.

and the diagram is a rectangle; such a case seldom if ever occurs in practice. The figures 485, 486 show imaginary diagrams with steam cut off at ·2 of the stroke; figures 487, 488, show diagrams of a more or less perfect form, with steam cut off at ·3 of the stroke and the corners rounded off as they always come in practice from compression as at o and early opening of the exhaust as at ve.

The curve formed in these diagrams by the expansion of steam is approximately a rectangular hyperbola, and knowing the initial absolute pressure and the point of cut off, the mean pressure can be calculated by the formula :—

$$p_m = p \left(\frac{1 + \text{hyp. log. R}}{R} \right)$$

from the value of p_m from this formula the deductions for back pressure, &c., must be made. In the formula R = the ratio of expansion and in the diagrams is the ratio $\frac{H}{h}$. The approximate expansion curve may be graphically laid down in the following manner, see figs. 489, 490, which is very convenient for comparing the actual curve formed by the indicator and that which would be formed were the action of the steam unaltered by the condensation which always takes place in the cylinder of a steam engine.

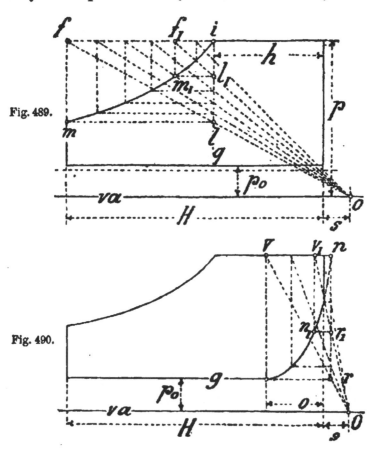

Fig. 489.

Fig. 490.

H = the length of the diagram and represents the stroke of the piston, and as the cylinder is parallel throughout its length, the line H also represents the volume swept by the piston in making one complete stroke.

h = the period of admission.

s = the clearance expressed in terms of the piston area, so that s in line H represents the volume of the clearance.

p = the initial absolute pressure in lbs. per square inch laid off to any convenient scale.

va = the line of perfect vacuum.

p_o = the back pressure of the exhaust steam.

o = the length of the compression period or the remainder of the stroke left to be completed after the exhaust has closed.

Complete the rectangle on the lines pH, then from point O draw the line $o f$, and the line $i q$ parallel to the line p; from the point where $o f$ cuts $i q$ draw $l m$ parallel to H, then m is the terminal point of the curve; the remaining points are found by drawing lines from O to points on the upper side of the rectangle, and the horizontal lines from where they cut the line $i q$, fig. 489.

Fig. 490 shows the same process for drawing the compression curve.

For obtaining the mean pressure on the piston from a diagram thus drawn, it may be either measured by means of a planimeter, or by dividing the figure into equal parts by vertical lines and measuring the sum of the vertical heights of these parts and dividing by their number for the average. Further explanation of these diagrams and their uses will be found at page 373. The above curve does not actually represent the expansion curve, only an approximation; a truer curve may be obtained by Rankine's formula:

$$\text{Pressure} \times \text{(volume)}^{\frac{17}{16}} = \text{constant.}$$

If the pressure be expressed in lbs. per square inch, and the volumes in cubic feet, the constant has a value of 475, when adopting Zeuner's modification of Rankine's formula $\text{Pressure} \times \text{(volume)}^{1.0646} = 475$ The formula is referring to one pound of steam. The volume occupied by one pound of steam at different pressures is called the specific volume for that pressure.

The back pressure (p_o) of exhaust in lbs. per square inch absolute for a speed of about 80 feet per second is given in the table.

TABLE 52.

Terminal pressure, w =	8·8	11·7	14·7	17·6	22·0	29·4	44·0	58·8
For non-condensing engine, p_o =	—	—	14·7	15·4	16·2	17·1	18·0	18·5
For condensing engine, p_o =	3·23	3·7	4·1	4·4	4·7	4·9	5·3	5·6

All pressures are given in lbs. per square inch absolute.

For ordinary work p_o may be taken as 17 lbs. absolute for non-condensing engines, and 3·7 for condensing engines.

Classification of Valves and Valve Gears.

Valves and valve gears may be divided under the following heads :

A. Gears of simple kind, with eccentrics working either ordinary slide valves or piston valves.

B. Trip valve gears with Corliss valves.

C. Trip or positive motion gears with mushroom valves.

A. Simple Slide or Piston Valve Gears.

(a) With one slide or piston valve, rate of expansion usually fixed ; or when combined with a Hartnell governor or link motion, the rate of expansion is variable.

(b) Double slide valve gears, with two separate slide valves ; the expansion or cut-off valve working on the back of the main or exhaust valve, including Meyer's valve gear, Rider's, and others also, in which the expansion valve is controlled by the governor. In these gears both valves are worked by separate eccentrics, with the exception of one or two special examples

B. Trip Valve Gears with Corliss Valves.

(a) Gears in which the valves, such as Corliss valves, are opened positively, and let go at a period determined by the governor, by a so-called " trip " gear, the closing of the valves being effected by springs or dash-pots. The valves are parts of cylinders, and work to and fro in bored-out seatings.

(b) Gears in which the Corliss valves revolve continuously, such as those of Siegel and Ehrhardt.

In Corliss valve gears there are usually two steam valves and two exhaust valves. The advantages of this system will be referred to when treating of Corliss engines, pages 252 *et seq.*

C. Gears with Mushroom Valves.

(a) Gears with positively driven valves of mushroom form.

(b) Gears with valves driven through the medium of trip gear, the valves being of mushroom form. Examples of these are given on pages 234 *et seq.*

Slide Valves.

The figures 491—500 show longtitudinal and cross sections of simple slide valves, such as are used in small steam engines.

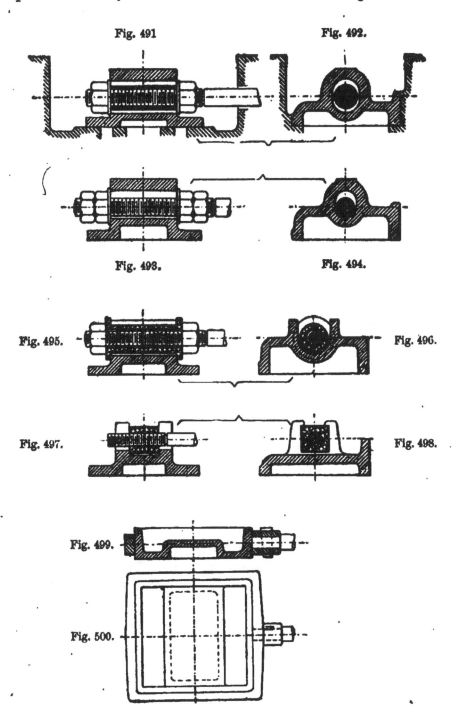

Fig. 491. Fig. 492.

Fig. 493. Fig. 494.

Fig. 495. Fig. 496.

Fig. 497. Fig. 498.

Fig. 499.

Fig. 500.

Figs. 501—503 show sections of the "Trick" valve, with the double opening for steam shown by the arrows; this is a good form of slide valve for quick running engines. The width of the port, $a = 2c + d$, and the eccentric radius or half stroke, $r = e + 2c$.

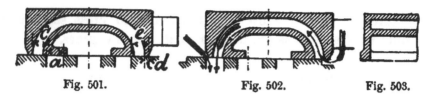

Fig. 501. Fig. 502. Fig. 503.

Figs. 504 and 505, show a main and cut-off slide valve, each worked by a separate eccentric, and for a fixed rate of expansion. Only one port is shown in the example given at each end of the main valve, but it is generally better to have a number of ports, 4 to 6, or even more. They are then termed multiple ported, or " gridiron slide valves.

Fig. 504.   Fig. 505.

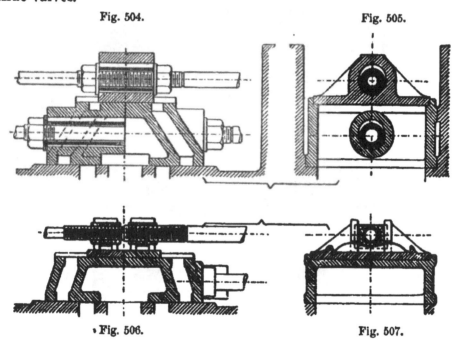

Fig. 506.   Fig. 507.

Figs. 506 and 507 show an example of Meyer's valves for variable expansion, in which the cut-off is varied by increasing the distance between the outer edges of the cut-off valve. The valve is in two parts, one part having a right hand nut, the other a left hand, and a corresponding thread cut on the valve spindle, which is capable of being turned round by a hand wheel, or, in some cases, by being actuated by the governor.

In Rider's valve gear, of which the valves are shown in figs. 508—511, the cut-off valve itself corresponds to the right and left hand screw of Meyer's. The rate of expansion is varied by turning the cut-off valve on its seat, which is formed by boring out a recess on

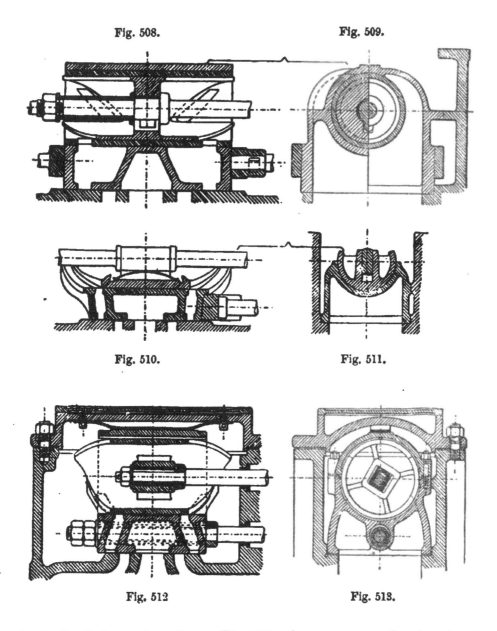

Fig. 508.

Fig. 509.

Fig. 510.

Fig. 511.

Fig. 512

Fig. 513.

the back of the main valve. Fig. 508 gives an example of a closed Rider valve, and fig. 510, an open one; the cut-off valve is usually connected with the governor.

Figs. 512 and 513 give another example of closed Rider valves.

A modification of Rider's valves is shown in figs. 514—516, where in place of the cut-off valve being cylindrical it is flat with inclined edges, and is moved across the back of the main valve by means of a rack and pinion. The figs. are taken from valves by Heinrich Lanz of Mannheim.

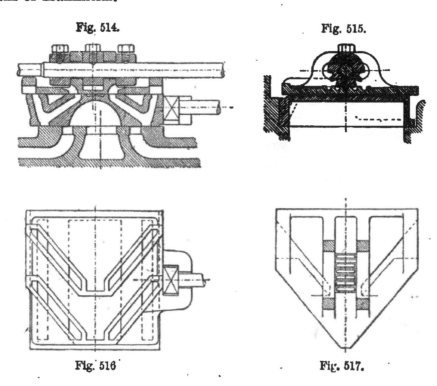

Fig. 514. Fig. 515.

Fig. 516. Fig. 517.

An arrangement of valve for a tandem compound portable engine by Messrs. Garrett, Smith & Co., of Buckau-Magdeburg, is shown in fig. 518, the arrows indicating the passage of steam and exhaust.

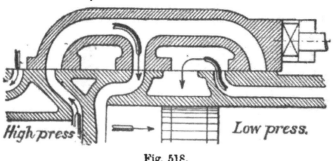

High press. Low press.

Fig. 518.

The double ported valve, fig. 519, is a form where the two end ports of the main valve are separate. This is necessary where a variation in the cut-off is effected by turning the cut-off valve

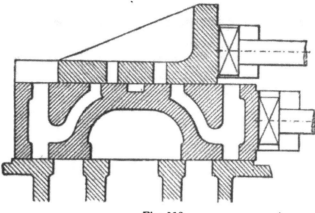

Fig. 519.

e centric round on the shaft; in other words, by increasing the angle of advance of the cut-off valve eccentric. When the variation is effected by altering the stroke of the cut-off valve eccentric, the main valve may be a hollow case, with a number of ports at the back, all o which ports will be in use, admitting steam to whichever end of the cylinder the main valve allows it to enter. The advantages of having a number of ports are, that the cut-off is much more rapid than with only one or two ports.

A double slide valve arrangement, fig. 520, has a separate chamber for the expansion valve. There are some advantages in this, and it

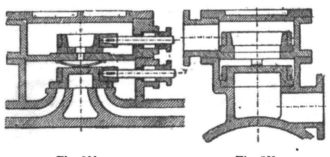

Fig. 520.   Fig. 521

has been very successfully used by Messrs. Davey, Paxman & Co., of Colchester.

In order to reduce the stroke of a slide valve, the double ported single valve, figs. 522, 523, was introduced by Messrs. Penn for marine engines: a equalling the total width of the steam passage, then the radius of the eccentric, or half stroke, $r = \cdot 5a + e$. The lead and lap are half the amount which would be required for a simple valve for the same width of port. The steam enters by the passages E E, as well as over the back of the valve.

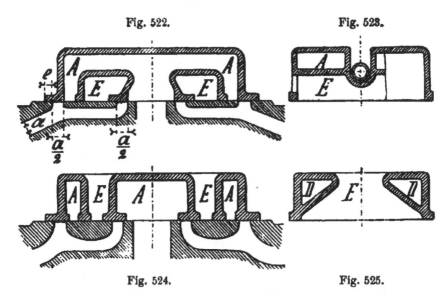

Fig. 522.　　　　　　Fig. 523.

Fig. 524.　　　　　　Fig. 525.

A variety of Penn's valve, by Borsig, is shown in figs. 524, 525. The passages, A A, are in connection with the side passages, D D, fig. 525.

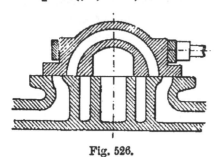

Fig. 526.

This arrangement allows of an expansion valve to be used on the back of the main valve in the usual way.

Fig. 526 shows the valve of Hick for a compound engine, with both pistons moving in the same direction.

Fig. 527.

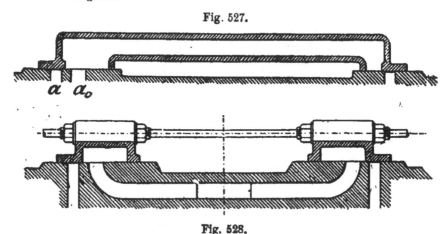

Fig. 528.

In order to reduce the length of the ports to a minimum, valves are often made in two parts, fig. 528. The same effect is produced by the long valve, fig. 527, but is not so good as separating the two ends as in fig. 528. In Meyer's and Rider's valve gears they can be arranged as in figs. 529, 530, where the two ends are separate, and the ports thus made very short.

Fig. 529.

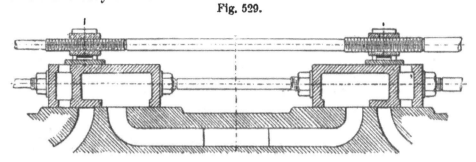

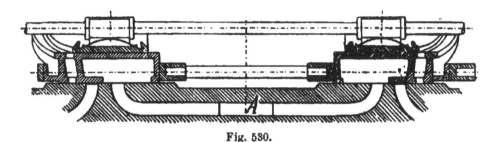

Fig. 530.

The attachment of the valve to the valve rod or spindle, is effected in various ways, and it should always be remembered that the centre line of the rod should be as near the port face as possible, so that the push and pull may be near to the line of greatest resistance, and thus to move the valve as quietly and steadily as possible.

In order to place the rod close to the port face, the rod is often made with a T head, fitting into a recess in the end of valve,

Fig. 531.

Fig. 533.

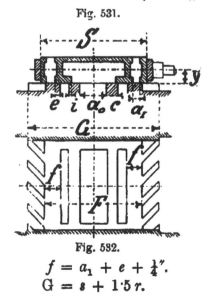

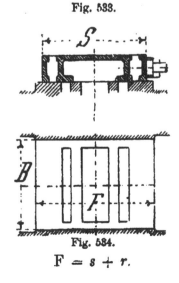

Fig. 532.

Fig. 534.

$$f = a_1 + e + \tfrac{1}{4}''.$$
$$G = s + 1.5\,r.$$

$$F = s + r.$$

fig. 533, or a bridle, figs. 536, 531, is used. Considering the small surface given by these T headed rods, it is somewhat surprising how long they will last without undue slackness from wear.

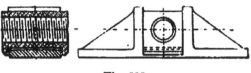

Fig. 535.

Expansion valves are often attached, as shown in fig. 535, by means of a block through which the rod passes, and in the case of Meyer's valves, is screwed into the block, or, with other valves for ordinary work, secured by a cottar.

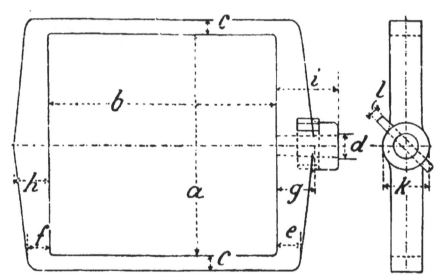

Figs. 536 and 537.—Valve bridle for valves of the kind shown in fig. 531.

The great pressure exerted by the steam on slide valves has induced many schemes to be brought out to relieve this pressure. To construct a perfect "balanced" slide valve, is a point of great

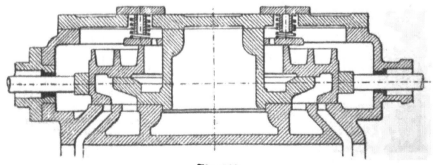

Fig. 538.

difficulty; many so-called balanced valves remaining so for a **very** short time after the engine has been working. A few examples are shown in figs. 538—541. In fig. 539, the valve is balanced by a ring

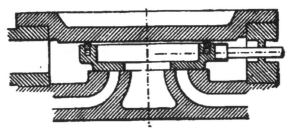

Fig. 539.

on the back, held up by light springs against the cover, so as to prevent the pressure of steam from acting on the back of the valve.

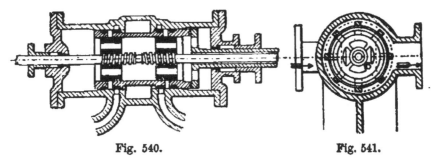

Fig. 540. Fig. 541.

Perhaps the best form of balanced valve is the piston valve, which has been successfully used in marine engines with very high pressures. Examples of these will be found on pages 222, 223.

Simple Valve Gears.

The following reference letters are used throughout the investigations of valve gear diagrams and valves in the next pages 164—204.

a. The admission or steam port.

a_0. The exhaust port.

c. The breadth of the bars between the ports.

e. The outside lap.

i. The inside lap.

r. The radius of the eccentric, or half the stroke of valve.

v. The lead or length of steam port open to steam at beginning of stroke.

v_0. The inner lead on exhaust side.

The simple valve, worked by an eccentric, is chiefly used in small engines with cut off at from ·5 to ·8 of stroke, much better results being obtained from valve gears with two valves, worked by separate eccentrics. A single valve, however, attached to a link motion, has been used as a variable expansion apparatus, as well as for reversing.

Single valves in combination with a Hartnell governor, figs. 474, 476, page 145, have given good results,* the action on the valve being nearly the same in this case as with the link motion. Simple slide valves with the reference letters are shown in figs. 542 and 543.

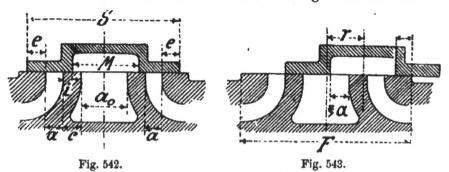

Fig. 542.   Fig. 543.

The proportions for given rates of expansion are :—

For cut off at ·5	at ·6	at ·7
$e = 2\,a$	$e = 1·3\,a$	$e = ·8\,a$
$i = ·7\,a$	$i = ·5\,a$	$i = ·3\,a$
$r = ·8\,a + e$	$r = a + e$	$r = a + e$
$v = ·25\,a$ to $0·5\,a$	$v = ·2\,a$ to $·4\,a$	$v = ·2\,a$ to $·3\,a$.

The greater values of v are for quick running.

Figs. 544—547 show in diagram the relative positions of the crank and valve in a simple valve gear, at four different points in the stroke.

In fig. 544 the piston is at the left hand end, and crank is at the beginning of the stroke, or, at the dead point ; the steam port is open to the extent of the lead v, the exhaust port is open v_0 ; $x = e + v$.

In fig. 545 the steam port is full open, and the valve, at its extreme position, to the right ; $x = r$.

In fig. 546 the steam port is closed and the expansion has begun ; $x = e$.

In fig. 547 the exhaust is closed, and the compression has begun ; $x = i$.

In these figures, K is the crank, δ, the angular advance of the eccentric radius E, and the arrows show the direction of running, and the direction of the flow of steam in the ports and passages.

---

* See report of judges at the Cardiff Meeting of the Royal Agricultural Society.

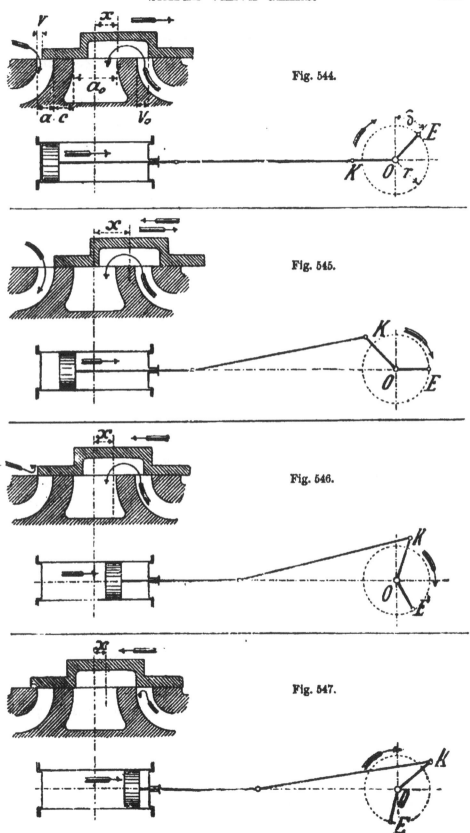

Fig. 544.

Fig. 545.

Fig. 546.

Fig. 547.

Zeuner's Valve Diagram.

By means of Zeuner's valve diagram, the relative positions of crank and valve can be shown graphically; the construction is briefly as follows: Draw the two axes at right angles to each other, O X, O Y, figs. 548, 549, then make $O E = e =$ the outside lap; $E V = v =$ the lead; with radius $= \frac{r}{2}$ describe the circle O V G cutting O and V, then M will be the centre of this circle, called the valve circle, O G will $= r$, and will give the position of the eccentric radius,

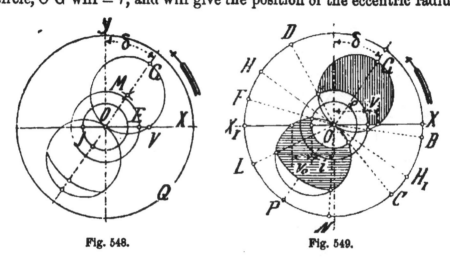

Fig. 548.　　　　　　　Fig. 549.

and δ will be the angle of advance on O G produced. A circle of the same radius is then drawn below O X. Make $O J = i$ the inside lap, and draw the crank circle from centre O of any convenient size. Note that in this diagram the crank moves in the direction of the arrow, the contrary way to that in which the engine crank moves.

Looking at fig. 549, when the crank is at—

O B, the steam port is beginning to open at right hand.

O X, the right hand steam port is open to the extent of the lead v (crank at dead point to the right hand).

O G, valve at its furthest position to the left.

O D, the right hand steam port closes and expansion begins.

O H, valve in its middle position.

O F, beginning of exhaust at the right hand.

$O X_1$, exhaust port open v_0 at the right hand (crank at dead point to the left hand).

O P, valve at its furthest position to the right.

O L to O N, exhaust open fully to right hand.

O C, exhaust closes, beginning of compression.

$O H_1$, valve in its middle position.

From P to G (in direction of arrow), through H_1, the valve moves to the left.   From G to P, through H, the valve moves to the right. The half stroke or radius of eccentricity equals the port + the lap.

$$r = a + e \; ; \text{ but } r \text{ can be } \substack{< \\ >} a + e.$$

Fig. 550.	Fig. 551.
$r < a + e = a_1 + e$	$r > a + e = a + e + m$
$a = 12$	$a = 12$
$a_1 = 10$	$m = 2$
$e = 18$	$e = 18$
$i = 7$	$i = 7$
$v = 4$	$v = 4$
$r = 10 + 18 = 28$	$r = 12 + 18 + 2 = 32$

Fig. 550.   Fig. 551.

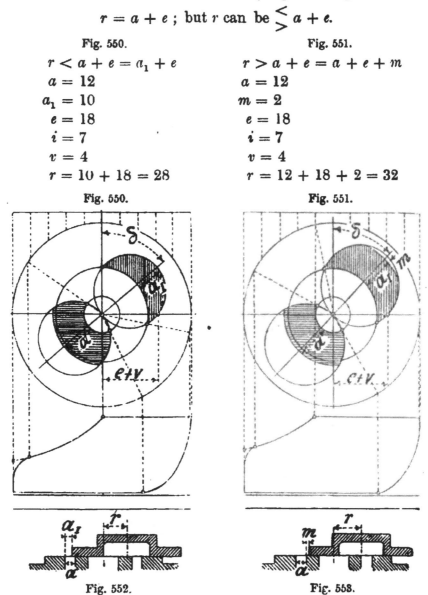

Fig. 552.   Fig. 553.

The point of cut off will be earlier with the shorter stroke, and it is often sufficient that the greatest opening of port to steam $a_1 = \cdot 8\, a$.   This smaller opening of port to steam, takes place in the single valve gears connected with a governor of the Hartnell type, in order to keep the range of the governor as short as possible, and can be arranged to give very good admission and exhaust, as the exhaust side of the valve allows of full opening of the port.

Figs. 554 and 555.

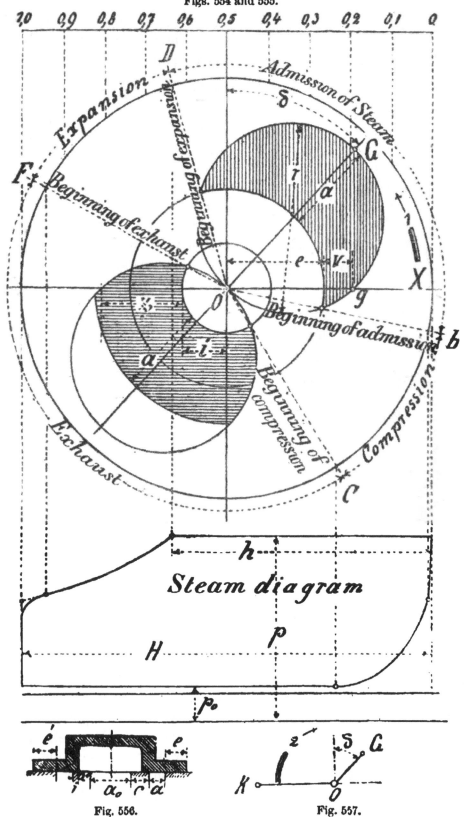

Fig. 556.   Fig. 557.

Valve Diagram for a Simple Valve Gear.

O X, direction of valve motion.

O, centre of the diagram.

e, outside lap (circle 2 e diameter about centre O, called lap circle).

i, inside lap (circle 2 i diameter about centre O).

v, lead of the valve, O $g = e + v$.

$r = a + e$ the radius or half stroke of the eccentric (valve circle through g and O).

H, diameter of the crank circle (any convenient size)

Then in figures 554 to 557—

$v_0 =$ inner or exhaust lead.

O G, position of the eccentric radius.

$\delta =$ the angle of advance.

O B, the position of the crank for beginning of admission.

O D,	,,	,,	,,	of expansion.
O F,	,,	,,	,,	of exhaust.
O C,	,,	,,	,, ·	of compression.

$h =$ the position of cut off.

If there is no inside lap, then the beginning of compression and exhaust take place on a line at right angles to the original position of the eccentric radius.

The diagram crank moves in the direction of the arrow 1, in fig. 554; the engine crank moves in the direction of the arrow 2, in fig. 557; the radius of the eccentric is in advance of the crank to the extent of $90° + \delta$; O K is the position of the crank, O G that of the eccentric, fig. 557. In order to understand this valve diagram, it is better to draw the steam diagram under, as shown in fig. 555.

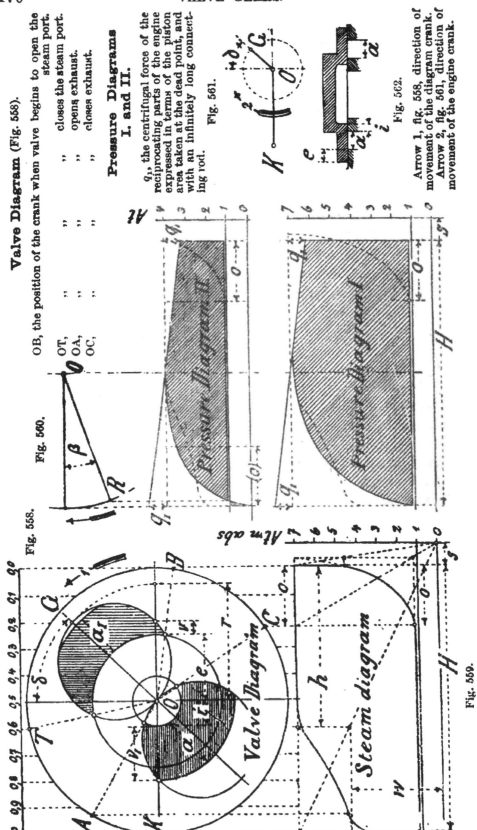

Valve Diagram (Fig. 558).

OB, the position of the crank when valve begins to open the steam port.

OT,   ,,   ,,   closes the steam port.

OA,   ,,   ,,   opens exhaust.

OC,   ,,   ,,   closes exhaust.

Pressure Diagrams I. and II.

q_1, the centrifugal force of the reciprocating parts of the engine expressed in terms of the piston area taken at the dead point, and with an infinitely long connecting rod.

Fig. 561.

Fig. 562.

Arrow 1, fig. 558, direction of movement of the diagram crank.
Arrow 2, fig. 561, direction of movement of the engine crank.

Fig. 560.

Fig. 558.

Pressure Diagram II.

Pressure Diagram I.

Valve Diagram

Steam diagram

Fig. 559.

TABLE 53.—Valve Diagram for Simple Valve Gear (Fig. 558).

		12	16	20	24	28
Stroke	H	12	16	20	24	28
Diameter of piston	D	6	8	10	12	14
Revolutions per minute	n	125	110	100	90	85
Width of steam ports in port face	a	$\frac{7}{8}$	$\frac{1}{2}$	$\frac{5}{8}$	$\frac{3}{4}$	1
Necessary width of opening to steam	a_1	$\frac{5}{16}$	$\frac{3}{8}$	$\frac{1}{2}$	$\frac{5}{8}$	$\frac{13}{16}$
Outside lap	e	$\frac{7}{16}$	$\frac{5}{8}$	$\frac{3}{4}$	1	$1\frac{1}{4}$
Inside lap	i	$\frac{3}{16}$	$\frac{1}{4}$	$\frac{5}{16}$	$\frac{3}{8}$	$\frac{7}{16}$
Radius of eccentric	r	$\frac{3}{4}$	$1\frac{1}{8}$	$1\frac{3}{8}$	$1\frac{3}{4}$	$2\frac{1}{4}$
Lead, outer	v	$\frac{1}{16}$	$\frac{1}{8}$	$\frac{3}{16}$	$\frac{1}{4}$	$\frac{1}{4}$
Lead, inner	v_1	$\frac{5}{16}$	$\frac{1}{2}$	$\frac{3}{4}$	$\frac{7}{8}$	$\frac{15}{16}$
Cut off	h	·6	·6	·6	·6	·6
Exhaust	f	·07	·07	·07	·07	·06
Compression	o	·2	·2	·2	·2	·2
Angle of advance in degrees	δ	42	41	41	41	41

All Dimensions are given in Inches.

From the pressure diagram I it will be seen that with 7 atmospheres absolute pressure and full load the direction of pressure in the connecting rod changes at the dead point, but with 4 atmospheres absolute pressure, diagram II, it changes before the dead point at O R, angle β.

Slide Valves.

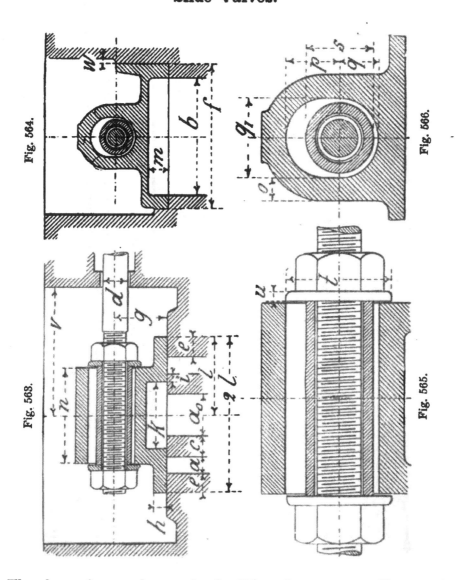

The above figures show a simple slide valve corresponding to the valve diagram, fig. 558, and a table of dimensions is given on next page.

TABLE 54.—**Dimensions of Simple Slide Valve** (Figs. 563—566, and for Valve Diagram, see Fig. 558).

Engine.																								
H	D	a_o	a	b	c	d	e	f	g	h	i	k	l	m	n	o	p	q	q_1	s	t	u	v	w	r
12	6	$\frac{3}{4}$	$\frac{3}{8}$	$3\frac{1}{4}$	$\frac{9}{16}$	$\frac{7}{8}$	$\frac{7}{16}$	$4\frac{1}{4}$	$1\frac{1}{2}$	$\frac{3}{8}$	$\frac{3}{16}$	$1\frac{5}{8}$	$1\frac{13}{16}$	$\frac{5}{8}$	$2\frac{1}{2}$	$\frac{3}{8}$	1	$\frac{3}{4}$	$1\frac{3}{8}$	$\frac{1}{4}$	$1\frac{1}{2}$	$\frac{3}{16}$	3	$\frac{3}{16}$	$\frac{3}{4}$
16	8	$1\frac{1}{8}$	$\frac{1}{2}$	$4\frac{3}{8}$	$\frac{5}{8}$	1	$\frac{5}{8}$	$5\frac{3}{8}$	2	$\frac{1}{2}$	$\frac{1}{4}$	2	$2\frac{3}{8}$	$\frac{5}{8}$	$2\frac{3}{4}$	$\frac{1}{2}$	1	$\frac{3}{4}$	$1\frac{1}{2}$	$1\frac{3}{8}$	2	$\frac{3}{16}$	$3\frac{3}{4}$	$\frac{3}{16}$	$1\frac{1}{8}$
20	10	$1\frac{1}{2}$	$\frac{5}{8}$	$5\frac{5}{8}$	$\frac{11}{16}$	$1\frac{1}{8}$	$\frac{3}{4}$	$6\frac{3}{4}$	$2\frac{1}{4}$	$\frac{5}{8}$	$\frac{5}{16}$	$2\frac{3}{8}$	$2\frac{7}{8}$	$\frac{3}{4}$	$3\frac{1}{2}$	$\frac{5}{8}$	$1\frac{1}{8}$	$\frac{7}{8}$	$1\frac{7}{8}$	$1\frac{5}{8}$	$2\frac{3}{8}$	$\frac{3}{16}$	$4\frac{5}{8}$	$\frac{3}{16}$	$1\frac{3}{8}$
24	12	$2\frac{1}{8}$	$\frac{3}{4}$	$6\frac{3}{4}$	$\frac{3}{4}$	$1\frac{3}{16}$	1	$8\frac{3}{8}$	$2\frac{3}{8}$	$\frac{11}{16}$	$\frac{3}{8}$	$2\frac{7}{8}$	$3\frac{9}{16}$	1	$4\frac{1}{4}$	$\frac{5}{8}$	$1\frac{1}{4}$	1	$1\frac{7}{8}$	$1\frac{5}{8}$	$2\frac{5}{8}$	$\frac{1}{4}$	6	$\frac{5}{16}$	$1\frac{3}{4}$
28	14	$2\frac{3}{8}$	1	$8\frac{3}{8}$	$\frac{7}{8}$	$1\frac{1}{4}$	$1\frac{1}{4}$	10	$2\frac{5}{8}$	$\frac{3}{4}$	$\frac{7}{16}$	$3\frac{3}{4}$	$4\frac{9}{16}$	$1\frac{1}{4}$	5	$\frac{3}{4}$	$1\frac{1}{4}$	1	$1\frac{7}{8}$	$1\frac{5}{8}$	$2\frac{3}{4}$	$\frac{1}{4}$	$7\frac{1}{4}$	$\frac{5}{16}$	$2\frac{1}{4}$

All Dimensions are given in Inches.

Valve Gears with Two Valves.

Meyer's Valve Gear.

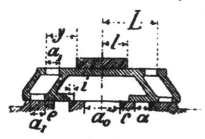

Fig. 567.

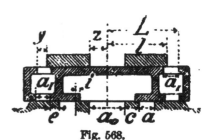

Fig. 568.

Fig. 567 shows the two valves arranged for a fixed rate of expansion; fig. 568 for variable expansion, with the following reference letters.

a, width of steam ports in port face.

a_1, width of steam ports in main valve.

a_0, width of exhaust port.

c, width of bars between ports.

e, outside lap.

i, inside lap.

v, outside lead.

v_0, inside lead or exhaust lead.

r, half stroke of main valve.

r_1, half stroke of cut-off valve.

δ, angle of advance of main valve eccentric.

δ_1, angle of advance of cut-off valve eccentric.

$y = L - l$, distance between working edges of valves; in fig. 568 an ideal middle position is taken for any selected point of cut off.

z, the horizontal distance from centre line of the back edge of cut-off valve for any selected point of cut off.

I, the valve circle of main valve, fig. 569.

II, the valve circle of cut-off valve.

III, the relative valve circle.

Valve diagram, fig. 569.

The outside lap circle, $2e$ diameter.

The inside lap circle, $2i$ diameter.

The valve circle I, with a diameter of $O G = r =$ half stroke of main valve, is drawn the same as for the simple valve gear. The advance angle of the cut-off valve eccentric δ_1 may be taken from 60° to 90°, and the cut-off valve circle II described with

diameter $O E = r_1 =$ half stroke of cut-off valve eccentric. Draw
G P parallel to O E, and O P parallel to E G, then O P will be the
diameter of the relative valve circle III. The chord of valve circle
III gives the distance between the centres of the two valves which
is greatest when the crank is in the position O P, and then is equal
to the line O P; for a fixed period of admission or point of cut off,
for example ·7, $O S = L - l$, and the shaded part of the diagram
shows the opening of the port to steam. When the crank is at O N,
the port in the main valve is fully open; when at O m, the port is

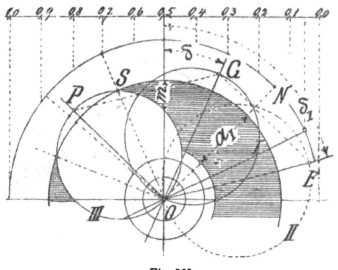

Fig. 569.

open to the extent of m; when at O S, the port is closed: the
greater the distance between the working edges of the cut-off plates
or valves, the greater is l, and so $L - l$ is less. For very early cut
off, $L - l$ is negative; example, for a cut off at ·05, the crank centre
line cuts the circle III in the lower quadrant.

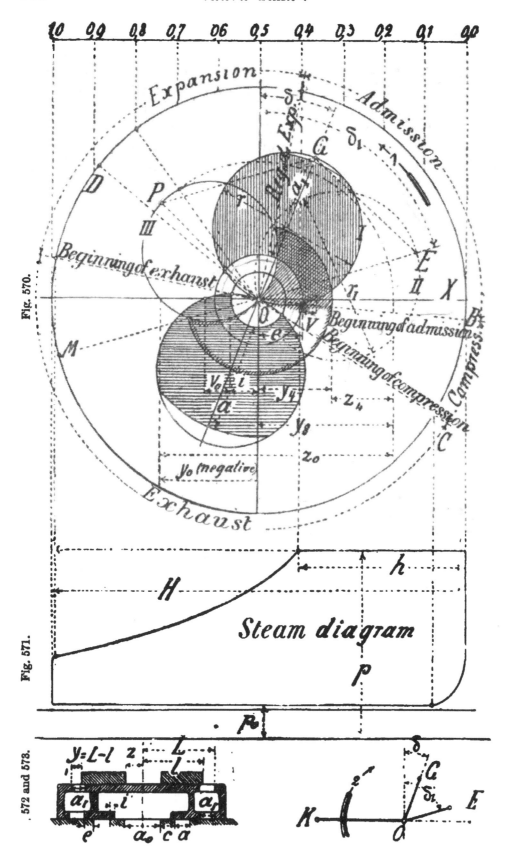

Fig. 570.

Fig. 571.

572 and 573.

Steam diagram

Valve Diagram for Meyer's Valve Gear (Figs. 570—573).

O X, direction of the valve motion, that is, plane of port face.

e, outside lap.

i, inside lap.

r, lead.

r, half stroke of main valve eccentric.

O E, position of cut-off valve eccentric radius.

r_1 half stroke of cut-off valve eccentric.

G P_1, parallel to O E.

O P_1, diameter of relative or resultant valve circle

V_0, inside lead.

δ, angle of advance of main valve eccentric.

δ_1, angle of advance of cut-off valve eccentric.

$y_8 = L - l$, for cut-off at ·8 ; chord of circle III.

$y_4 = L - l$, for cut-off at ·4 ; chord of circle III.

$y_0 = L - l$, for cut-off at ·0 ; chord of circle III., negative.

·8 is taken as the latest cut-off.

O B, position of crank for beginning of admission.

O, ·4   ,,   ,,   for beginning of expansion for cut-off at ·4.

O D,   ,,   ,,   when main valve closes the steam port.

O F,   ,,   ,,   when exhaust opens.

O M,   ,,   ,,   when port in main valve reopens to steam
                       for cut-off at ·4.

O C,   ,,   ,,   when exhaust closes and compression begins.

The chord of valve circle I. gives the distance of the middle of the main valve from the centre of the port face.

The chord of valve circle II. gives the distance of the middle of the cut-off valve from the centre of the port face.

The chord of the valve circle III. gives the distance between the centres of the two valves.

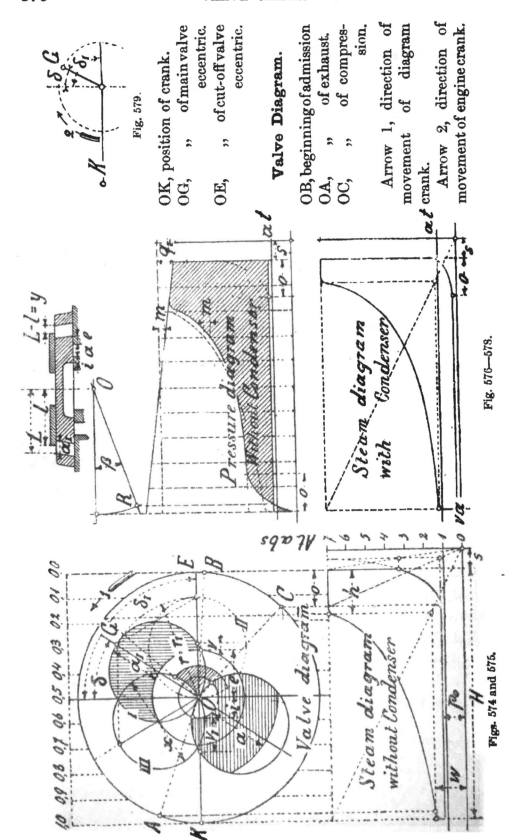

Fig. 579.

OK, position of crank.
OG, „ of main valve eccentric.
OE, „ of cut-off valve eccentric.

Valve Diagram.

OB, beginning of admission
OA, „ of exhaust.
OC, „ of compression.

Arrow 1, direction of movement of diagram crank.

Arrow 2, direction of movement of engine crank.

$L - l = y$

Pressure diagram without Condenser

Steam diagram with Condenser

Fig. 576—578.

Valve diagram

Steam diagram without Condenser

Fig. 574 and 575.

TABLE 55.—Valve Diagram for Meyer's Valve Gear (Figs. 574—578).

Stroke	H	16	20	24	28	32	36	40	44
Diameter of piston	D	8	10	12	14	16	18	20	22
Revolutions per minute	n	110	100	90	85	80	78	75	72
Width of steam ports	$a.$	$\frac{1}{2}$	$\frac{5}{8}$	$\frac{3}{4}$	1	$1\frac{1}{8}$	$1\frac{1}{4}$	$1\frac{1}{2}$	$1\frac{5}{8}$
Width of ports in main valve	a_1	$\frac{3}{8}$	$\frac{1}{2}$	$\frac{11}{16}$	$\frac{7}{8}$	1	$1\frac{1}{8}$	$1\frac{3}{8}$	$1\frac{1}{2}$
Outside lap	e	$\frac{3}{8}$	$\frac{1}{2}$	$\frac{5}{8}$	$\frac{3}{4}$	$\frac{7}{8}$	1	$1\frac{1}{8}$	$1\frac{1}{4}$
Inside lap	i	$\frac{1}{4}$	$\frac{1}{4}$	$\frac{5}{16}$	$\frac{5}{16}$	$\frac{3}{8}$	$\frac{1}{2}$	$\frac{1}{2}$	$\frac{5}{8}$
Half stroke of both valves	$r = r_1$	$\frac{3}{4}$	1	$1\frac{5}{16}$	$1\frac{5}{8}$	$1\frac{7}{8}$	$2\frac{1}{8}$	$2\frac{1}{2}$	$2\frac{3}{4}$
Lead, outside	v	$\frac{1}{16}$	$\frac{1}{16}$	$\frac{1}{8}$	$\frac{1}{8}$	$\frac{1}{8}$	$\frac{3}{16}$	$\frac{1}{4}$	$\frac{1}{4}$
Lead, inside	v_1	$\frac{3}{16}$	$\frac{5}{16}$	$\frac{7}{16}$	$\frac{9}{16}$	$\frac{5}{8}$	$\frac{11}{16}$	$\frac{7}{8}$	$\frac{7}{8}$
Angle of advance, main valve eccentric in degrees	δ	33	33	33	33	33	33	33	33
Angle of advance, cut-off eccentric in degrees	δ_1	90	90	90	90	90	90	90	90
Greatest distance between both valves	x	$\frac{3}{4}$	$\frac{15}{16}$	$1\frac{1}{4}$	$1\frac{3}{8}$	$1\frac{7}{8}$	$2\frac{1}{4}$	$2\frac{3}{8}$	$2\frac{3}{4}$
cut-off at ·73	y	$\frac{3}{4}$	$\frac{15}{16}$	$1\frac{1}{4}$	$1\frac{3}{8}$	$1\frac{7}{8}$	$2\frac{1}{4}$	$2\frac{3}{8}$	$2\frac{3}{4}$
,, ·60	y	$\frac{11}{16}$	$\frac{7}{8}$	$1\frac{3}{16}$	$1\frac{5}{16}$	$1\frac{13}{16}$	$2\frac{1}{8}$	$2\frac{5}{16}$	$2\frac{5}{8}$
,, ·50	y	$\frac{5}{8}$	$\frac{3}{4}$	$1\frac{1}{16}$	$1\frac{1}{4}$	$1\frac{1}{2}$	2	$2\frac{1}{8}$	$2\frac{3}{8}$
,, ·40	y	$\frac{9}{16}$	$\frac{11}{16}$	$\frac{15}{16}$	$1\frac{3}{16}$	$1\frac{7}{16}$	$1\frac{1}{4}$	$1\frac{7}{8}$	$2\frac{1}{8}$
,, ·30	y	$\frac{1}{2}$	$\frac{5}{8}$	$\frac{3}{4}$	$\frac{7}{8}$	$1\frac{1}{16}$	$1\frac{3}{8}$	$1\frac{1}{2}$	$1\frac{5}{8}$
,, ·20	y	$\frac{7}{16}$	$\frac{3}{8}$	$\frac{1}{2}$	$\frac{5}{8}$	$\frac{11}{16}$	$\frac{7}{8}$	1	$1\frac{1}{8}$
,, ·10	y	$\frac{1}{8}$	$\frac{1}{8}$	$\frac{3}{16}$	$\frac{1}{4}$	$\frac{5}{16}$	$\frac{5}{16}$	$\frac{3}{8}$	$\frac{3}{8}$
,, ·00	y	$\frac{3}{8}$	$\frac{7}{16}$	$\frac{1}{2}$	$\frac{11}{16}$	$\frac{3}{4}$	1	$1\frac{1}{8}$	$1\frac{1}{4}$

The variable distance $L-l$ between the working edges, y, is for different points of cut-off

All Dimensions are given in Inches.

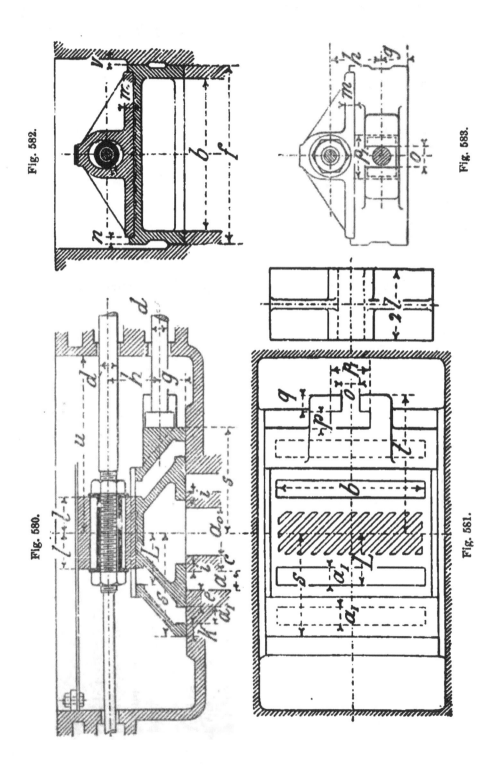

Fig. 582.

Fig. 583.

Fig. 580.

Fig. 581.

TABLE 56.—Double Valves, for Fixed Expansion (Figs. 580—583).

H	D	a_0	a	a_1	b	c	d	e	f	g	h	i	k	m	n	o	p	p_1	q	s	t	u	r	$r=r_1$
16	8	1	$\frac{1}{2}$	$\frac{3}{8}$	$4\frac{3}{8}$	$\frac{5}{8}$	1	$\frac{3}{8}$	$5\frac{3}{8}$	1	3	$\frac{1}{4}$	$\frac{5}{8}$	$\frac{1}{2}$	$\frac{5}{16}$	$1\frac{1}{8}$	$\frac{5}{8}$	$2\frac{1}{4}$	$\frac{3}{4}$	3	$4\frac{3}{8}$	$5\frac{5}{8}$	$\frac{1}{4}$	$\frac{3}{4}$
20	10	$1\frac{3}{8}$	$\frac{5}{8}$	$\frac{1}{2}$	$5\frac{5}{8}$	$\frac{11}{16}$	$1\frac{1}{8}$	$\frac{1}{2}$	$6\frac{1}{4}$	$1\frac{1}{4}$	$3\frac{1}{4}$	$\frac{1}{4}$	$\frac{5}{8}$	$\frac{1}{2}$	$\frac{5}{16}$	$1\frac{1}{8}$	$\frac{11}{16}$	$2\frac{3}{8}$	$\frac{7}{8}$	$3\frac{3}{8}$	$5\frac{3}{16}$	$6\frac{5}{8}$	$\frac{1}{4}$	1
24	12	$1\frac{7}{8}$	$\frac{3}{4}$	$\frac{11}{16}$	$6\frac{1}{4}$	$\frac{3}{4}$	$1\frac{1}{4}$	$\frac{5}{8}$	$8\frac{1}{8}$	$1\frac{3}{8}$	$3\frac{3}{8}$	$\frac{5}{16}$	$\frac{5}{8}$	$\frac{5}{8}$	$\frac{3}{8}$	$1\frac{1}{4}$	$\frac{3}{4}$	$2\frac{5}{8}$	1	$4\frac{3}{8}$	$6\frac{1}{4}$	8	$\frac{3}{8}$	$1\frac{5}{16}$
28	14	$2\frac{3}{8}$	1	$\frac{7}{8}$	$8\frac{3}{8}$	$\frac{7}{8}$	$1\frac{1}{4}$	$\frac{3}{4}$	10	$1\frac{5}{8}$	$3\frac{5}{8}$	$\frac{5}{16}$	$\frac{5}{8}$	$\frac{5}{8}$	$\frac{3}{8}$	$1\frac{3}{8}$	$\frac{7}{8}$	$2\frac{3}{4}$	1	$5\frac{5}{16}$	$7\frac{3}{16}$	$9\frac{1}{4}$	$\frac{3}{8}$	$1\frac{5}{8}$
32	16	$2\frac{3}{4}$	$1\frac{1}{8}$	1	10	1	$1\frac{3}{8}$	$\frac{7}{8}$	$11\frac{1}{2}$	$1\frac{3}{4}$	$3\frac{3}{4}$	$\frac{3}{8}$	$\frac{3}{4}$	$\frac{5}{8}$	$\frac{3}{8}$	$1\frac{1}{2}$	1	3	$1\frac{1}{8}$	$6\frac{1}{4}$	$8\frac{1}{4}$	$10\frac{5}{8}$	$\frac{3}{8}$	$1\frac{7}{8}$
36	18	$3\frac{1}{8}$	$1\frac{1}{4}$	$1\frac{1}{8}$	$11\frac{5}{8}$	$1\frac{1}{8}$	$1\frac{3}{8}$	1	$13\frac{3}{8}$	$1\frac{3}{4}$	4	$\frac{1}{2}$	$\frac{3}{4}$	$\frac{3}{4}$	$\frac{7}{16}$	$1\frac{5}{8}$	1	$3\frac{1}{4}$	$1\frac{1}{4}$	$6\frac{13}{16}$	$9\frac{3}{16}$	12	$\frac{3}{8}$	$2\frac{1}{8}$
40	20	$3\frac{5}{8}$	$1\frac{1}{2}$	$1\frac{3}{8}$	$13\frac{1}{4}$	$1\frac{1}{4}$	$1\frac{1}{2}$	$1\frac{1}{8}$	$15\frac{1}{4}$	2	$4\frac{1}{4}$	$\frac{1}{2}$	$\frac{7}{8}$	$\frac{3}{4}$	$\frac{1}{2}$	$1\frac{7}{8}$	$1\frac{1}{8}$	$3\frac{3}{8}$	$1\frac{3}{8}$	$7\frac{15}{16}$	$10\frac{7}{16}$	$13\frac{3}{4}$	$\frac{3}{8}$	$2\frac{3}{8}$
44	22	4	$1\frac{5}{8}$	$1\frac{1}{2}$	$14\frac{3}{4}$	$1\frac{1}{4}$	$1\frac{5}{8}$	$1\frac{1}{4}$	$16\frac{1}{4}$	$2\frac{1}{4}$	$4\frac{7}{8}$	$\frac{5}{8}$	1	$\frac{3}{4}$	$\frac{1}{2}$	2	$1\frac{1}{4}$	$3\frac{5}{8}$	$1\frac{1}{2}$	$8\frac{1}{2}$	$11\frac{1}{8}$	15	$\frac{3}{8}$	$2\frac{3}{4}$

All Dimensions are given in Inches

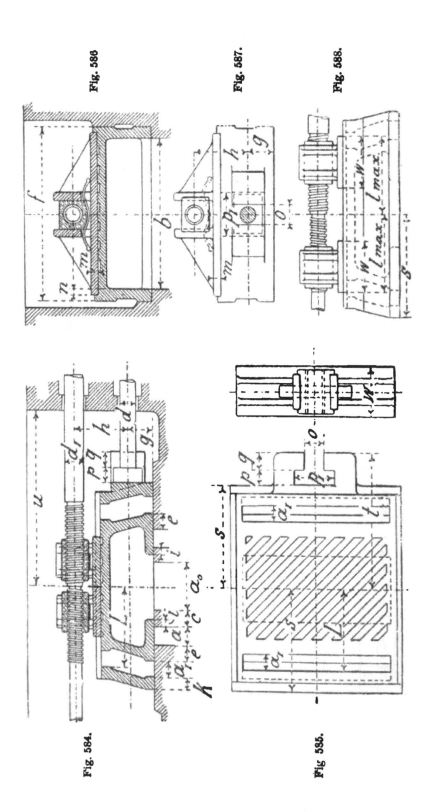

Fig. 586.

Fig. 587.

Fig. 588.

Fig. 584.

Fig 585.

TABLE 57.—Valves for Meyer's Variable Expansion Gear (Figs. 584—588).

H	D	a_0	a	a_1	b	c	d	d_1	e	f	g	h	i	k	m	n	o	p	p_1	q	s	t	u	v	$r=r_1$
16	8	1	$\frac{1}{2}$	$\frac{3}{8}$	$4\frac{3}{8}$	$\frac{5}{8}$	1	$1\frac{3}{16}$	$\frac{3}{8}$	$5\frac{3}{8}$	1	3	$\frac{1}{4}$	$\frac{5}{8}$	$\frac{1}{2}$	$\frac{5}{16}$	$1\frac{1}{8}$	$\frac{5}{8}$	$2\frac{1}{4}$	$\frac{3}{4}$	3	$4\frac{3}{8}$	$5\frac{5}{8}$	$\frac{1}{4}$	$\frac{3}{4}$
20	10	$1\frac{1}{8}$	$\frac{5}{8}$	$\frac{1}{2}$	$5\frac{5}{8}$	$\frac{11}{16}$	$1\frac{1}{8}$	$1\frac{5}{16}$	$\frac{1}{2}$	$6\frac{3}{4}$	$1\frac{1}{4}$	$3\frac{1}{4}$	$\frac{1}{4}$	$\frac{5}{8}$	$\frac{1}{2}$	$\frac{5}{16}$	$1\frac{1}{4}$	$\frac{11}{16}$	$2\frac{3}{8}$	$\frac{7}{8}$	$3\frac{3}{8}$	$5\frac{3}{16}$	$6\frac{5}{8}$	$\frac{1}{4}$	1
24	12	$1\frac{7}{8}$	$\frac{3}{4}$	$\frac{11}{16}$	$6\frac{3}{4}$	$\frac{3}{4}$	$1\frac{1}{4}$	$1\frac{3}{8}$	$\frac{5}{8}$	$8\frac{3}{8}$	$1\frac{3}{8}$	$3\frac{3}{8}$	$\frac{5}{16}$	$\frac{5}{8}$	$\frac{5}{8}$	$\frac{3}{8}$	$1\frac{1}{4}$	$\frac{3}{4}$	$2\frac{5}{8}$	1	$4\frac{3}{8}$	$6\frac{1}{4}$	8	$\frac{3}{8}$	$1\frac{5}{16}$
28	14	$2\frac{3}{8}$	1	$\frac{7}{8}$	$8\frac{3}{8}$	$\frac{7}{8}$	$1\frac{1}{4}$	$1\frac{1}{2}$	$\frac{3}{4}$	10	$1\frac{5}{8}$	$3\frac{5}{8}$	$\frac{5}{16}$	$\frac{5}{8}$	$\frac{5}{8}$	$\frac{3}{8}$	$1\frac{3}{8}$	$\frac{7}{8}$	$2\frac{3}{4}$	1	$5\frac{5}{16}$	$7\frac{3}{16}$	$9\frac{1}{4}$	$\frac{3}{8}$	$1\frac{7}{8}$
32	16	$2\frac{1}{4}$	$1\frac{1}{8}$	1	10	1	$1\frac{3}{8}$	$1\frac{5}{8}$	$\frac{7}{8}$	$11\frac{5}{8}$	$1\frac{3}{4}$	$3\frac{7}{8}$	$\frac{3}{8}$	$\frac{3}{4}$	$\frac{5}{8}$	$\frac{3}{8}$	$1\frac{1}{2}$	1	3	$1\frac{1}{8}$	$6\frac{1}{8}$	$8\frac{1}{4}$	$10\frac{5}{8}$	$\frac{3}{8}$	$1\frac{7}{8}$
36	18	$3\frac{1}{8}$	$1\frac{1}{4}$	$1\frac{1}{8}$	$11\frac{5}{8}$	$1\frac{1}{8}$	$1\frac{3}{8}$	$1\frac{7}{8}$	1	$13\frac{3}{8}$	$1\frac{3}{4}$	$4\frac{1}{4}$	$\frac{3}{8}$	$\frac{3}{4}$	$\frac{3}{4}$	$\frac{7}{16}$	$1\frac{5}{8}$	1	$3\frac{1}{4}$	$1\frac{1}{4}$	$6\frac{13}{16}$	$9\frac{1}{16}$	12	$\frac{3}{8}$	$2\frac{1}{8}$
40	20	$3\frac{3}{8}$	$1\frac{1}{2}$	$1\frac{3}{8}$	$13\frac{1}{4}$	$1\frac{1}{4}$	$1\frac{1}{2}$	2	$1\frac{1}{8}$	$15\frac{1}{4}$	2	$4\frac{3}{8}$	$\frac{1}{2}$	$\frac{7}{8}$	$\frac{3}{4}$	$\frac{1}{2}$	$1\frac{7}{8}$	$1\frac{1}{8}$	$3\frac{3}{8}$	$1\frac{3}{8}$	$7\frac{15}{16}$	$10\frac{7}{16}$	$13\frac{3}{8}$	$\frac{3}{8}$	$2\frac{1}{2}$
44	22	4	$1\frac{5}{8}$	$1\frac{1}{2}$	$14\frac{1}{4}$	$1\frac{1}{4}$	$1\frac{1}{2}$	$2\frac{1}{8}$	$1\frac{1}{4}$	$16\frac{3}{4}$	$2\frac{1}{4}$	$4\frac{5}{8}$	$\frac{5}{8}$	1	$\frac{7}{8}$	$\frac{1}{2}$	2	$1\frac{1}{4}$	$3\frac{5}{8}$	$1\frac{1}{2}$	$8\frac{5}{8}$	$11\frac{1}{8}$	15	$\frac{3}{8}$	$2\frac{3}{4}$

All Dimensions are given in Inches.

OK, position of crank (figs. 589, 591).
OG, ,, of main valve eccentric.
OE, ,, of cut-off valve eccentric.
OB, position of crank at beginning of admission.

OT, ,, ,, at cut-off, h.
OA, ,, ,, at beginning of exhaust.
OC, ,, ,, at beginning of compression.

Pressure Diagram (fig. 593).

q_1 is the centrifugal force of the reciprocating parts expressed in terms of the piston area at the dead point with indefinitely long connecting-rod.

Arrow 1, fig. 589, the direction of the movement of the diagram crank.

Arrow 2, fig. 591, the direction of the movement of the engine crank.

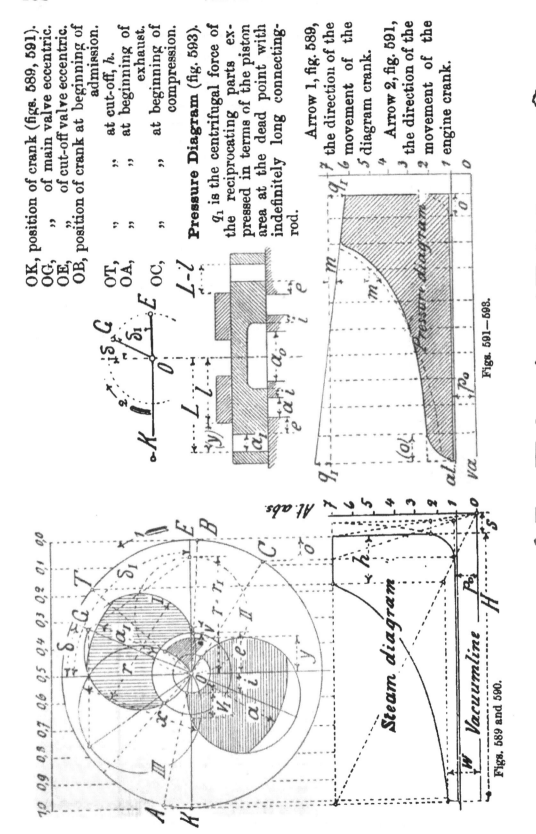

Figs. 591—593.

Figs. 589 and 590.

TABLE 58.—Diagram of Expansion Valves for Small Clearance Space (Figs. 589—593).

		16	20	24	28	32	36	40	44
Stroke	H	16	20	24	28	32	36	40	44
Diameter of piston	D	8	10	12	14	16	18	20	22
Revolutions per minute	n	110	100	90	85	80	78	75	72
Width of port in port face	a	$\frac{1}{2}$	$\frac{5}{8}$	$\frac{3}{4}$	1	$1\frac{1}{8}$	$1\frac{1}{4}$	$1\frac{1}{2}$	$1\frac{5}{8}$
,, ,, in main valve	a_1	$\frac{3}{8}$	$\frac{1}{2}$	$\frac{11}{16}$	$\frac{7}{8}$	1	$1\frac{1}{8}$	$1\frac{1}{8}$	$1\frac{1}{2}$
Outside lap	e	$\frac{1}{4}$	$\frac{3}{8}$	$\frac{7}{16}$	$\frac{5}{8}$	$\frac{5}{8}$	$\frac{3}{4}$	$\frac{3}{4}$	$\frac{13}{16}$
Inside lap	i	$\frac{1}{8}$	$\frac{3}{16}$	$\frac{1}{4}$	$\frac{1}{2}$	$\frac{1}{4}$	$\frac{5}{16}$	$\frac{5}{16}$	$\frac{3}{8}$
Half stroke of both valves	$r=r_1$	$\frac{3}{4}$	1	$1\frac{3}{16}$	$1\frac{1}{2}$	$1\frac{3}{4}$	2	$2\frac{1}{4}$	$2\frac{7}{16}$
Lead outside	v	$\frac{1}{16}$	$\frac{1}{16}$	$\frac{1}{16}$	$\frac{1}{16}$	$\frac{5}{16}$	$\frac{1}{8}$	$\frac{3}{16}$	$\frac{1}{4}$
,, inside	v_1	$\frac{9}{16}$	$\frac{1}{4}$	$\frac{1}{4}$	$\frac{5}{16}$	$\frac{1}{2}$	$\frac{9}{16}$	$\frac{5}{8}$	$\frac{11}{16}$
Angle of advance, main valve eccentric in degrees	δ	26	26	25	24	24	25	25	25
,, ,, cut-off in degrees	δ_1	90	90	90	90	90	90	90	90
Greatest distance between valves	x	$\frac{3}{4}$	$1\frac{1}{16}$	$1\frac{5}{16}$	$1\frac{9}{16}$	$1\frac{7}{8}$	$2\frac{1}{8}$	$2\frac{7}{16}$	$2\frac{11}{16}$
Variable distance $L-l$ between the working edges of the valves, y, in the diagram for different points of cut-off — ·76	y	$\frac{3}{4}$	$1\frac{1}{16}$	$1\frac{5}{16}$	$1\frac{9}{16}$	$1\frac{7}{8}$	$2\frac{1}{8}$	$2\frac{7}{16}$	$2\frac{11}{16}$
·60	y	$\frac{11}{16}$	1	$1\frac{1}{4}$	$1\frac{9}{16}$	$1\frac{7}{8}$	$2\frac{1}{8}$	$2\frac{7}{16}$	$2\frac{11}{16}$
·50	y	$\frac{5}{8}$	$\frac{7}{8}$	$1\frac{1}{4}$	$1\frac{1}{2}$	$1\frac{3}{4}$	2	$2\frac{1}{4}$	$2\frac{1}{4}$
·40	y	$\frac{1}{2}$	$\frac{3}{4}$	$1\frac{1}{4}$	$1\frac{3}{8}$	$1\frac{1}{2}$	$1\frac{3}{4}$	2	$2\frac{5}{16}$
·30	y	$\frac{3}{8}$	$\frac{3}{4}$	1	$1\frac{1}{4}$	$1\frac{3}{8}$	$1\frac{1}{2}$	$1\frac{3}{4}$	2
·20	y	$\frac{1}{4}$	$\frac{1}{2}$	$\frac{11}{16}$	$\frac{7}{8}$	1	$1\frac{1}{4}$	$1\frac{3}{8}$	$1\frac{1}{2}$
·10	y	$\frac{1}{16}$	$\frac{3}{8}$	$\frac{1}{2}$	$\frac{9}{14}$	$\frac{5}{8}$	$\frac{3}{4}$	$\frac{3}{4}$	1
·00	y	$-\frac{3}{8}$	$-\frac{1}{2}$	$-\frac{5}{8}$	$-\frac{7}{8}$	-1	$-1\frac{1}{8}$	$-1\frac{1}{4}$	$-1\frac{1}{8}$

All Dimensions are given in Inches.

The Valve Ellipse.

(a.) For Simple Valve Gear.

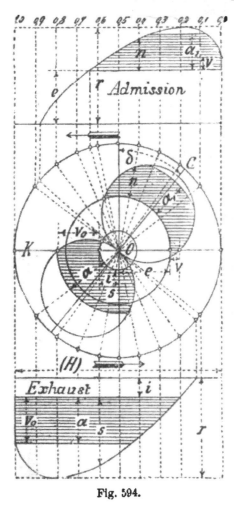

Fig. 594.

The valve ellipse, fig. 594, is a great assistance in understanding Zeuner's valve diagram, and it also shows the speed with which the valve moves at different parts of its stroke, when opening or closing the ports. The length of the connecting-rod is disregarded and is taken to be infinite. The diameter of the crank circle is divided in 10 equal parts, and perpendicular lines are drawn through these points terminating in horizontal lines as in the fig. 594 placed for convenience above and below the valve diagram, and the distances from the centre of the valve to the centre of the port face (chords of the valve circle) are laid off on the perpendicular lines, through the points thus found the curve called the valve ellipse is drawn, the lap e is laid off and the port width a_1, then the shaded part of the diagram gives the actual opening of the port by the valve; at the dead point, for example, the port is open to the extent of v, when the crank is at the position ·4 the port is open the amount n. The scale of fig. 594 is $\frac{2}{5}$ natural size:

$$\text{Width of port, } a_1 = \text{ ·67 inch.}$$
$$\text{,, } \quad a = \text{ ·78 ,,}$$
$$\text{Half stroke of valve } r = 1\text{·77 inch.}$$
$$\text{Lap (outside) } e = \text{ ·98 ,,}$$
$$\text{,, (inside) } \quad i = \text{ ·35 ,,}$$
$$\text{Lead (outside) } v = \text{ ·196 inch.}$$
$$\text{,, (inside) } v_0 = \text{ ·78 ,,}$$
$$\text{Angle of advance } \delta = 41°.$$

(b.) For Rider's and Meyer's Valve Gears.

The diagram and ellipse for the main slide is constructed in the same manner as for the simple valve gear. In the figs. 595, 596, the influence of the magnitude of the angle of advance δ_1 (of the cut-off

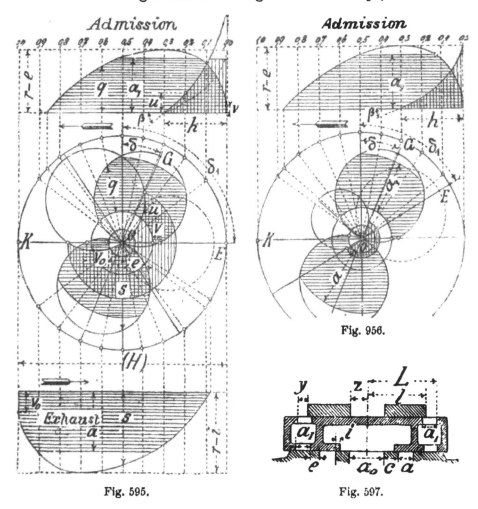

Fig. 595.

Fig. 956.

Fig. 597.

valve eccentric) on the speed with which the ports are closed is shown, and the following data are taken as starting points :—

Admission period or cut-off, $h = \cdot 3$ port in back of main valve $a_1 = \cdot 98$ inch ; steam port, $a = 1 \cdot 14$ inch ; outside lap, $e = \cdot 59$ inch ; inside lap, $i = 2 \cdot 55$ inch ; half stroke of main and cut-off valves r and $r_1 = 1 \cdot 73$ inch ; outside lead $= \cdot 12$ inch angle of advance of main valve eccentric $= 24°$ scale $\frac{2}{5}$ natural size. In fig. 595 the advance angle of cut-off valve eccentric $= 90°$, in fig. 596 $= 60°$. To show the opening of the ports in back of main valve, lay off the distances between the acting edges of the main and cut-off valves as

ordinates, then the area shaded with vertical lines gives the opening
of the ports, a comparison of fig. 595 with fig. 596 shows there is a
better admission of steam with an advance angle of 90° than with
60°; the magnitude of the angle β shows this clearly.

Defect in Arrangement of Valve Gears.

By defective arrangement of valve gears with two valves worked by
separate eccentrics, a second admission of steam may take place
towards the end of the stroke before the main valve has closed the
steam port.   The diagram fig. 598 shows an example of this, the ex-

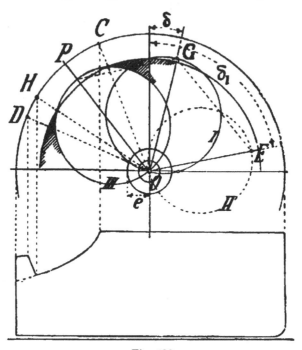

Fig. 598.

pansion will begin when the crank is at O C when the cut-off valve
has closed the port; but they will reopen again when the crank is at
O H, and second admission will take place as the main valve only
closes the port when the crank is at O D.   This fault can be avoided
by a proper advance angle δ_1 and stroke of valve $2\,r_1$, the position of
the diameter O P of the valve circle III. fig. 598 must be near the
position O D the point at which the main valve closes the port.   To
avoid this fault requires great care in valve gears where the expansion is varied by varying the stroke of the cut-off valve eccentric
as in Hartnell's expansion governor.   Under indicator diagrams
will be found an example which occurred in practice, but from a
different cause to that above mentioned.

Arrangement for Variation of Expansion by Band.

The expansion may be varied by increasing the advance angle of the cut-off eccentric by turning the eccentric round on the shaft and fixing it by means of a bolt to the main valve eccentric as shown in fig. 599, this has usually to be adjusted when the engine is stopped, but it has also been arranged to be varied automatically. The diagram fig. 600 shows the effect of altering the advance angle δ_1 from 90° to 60° and the cut will be thus altered from ·6 to ·25 of the stroke. It should be noted that for this kind of variable expansion the two ends of the main valve must be separated from each other as in fig. 584, so that each end is independent, but for valve gears where the

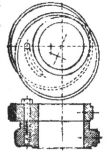

Fig. 599.

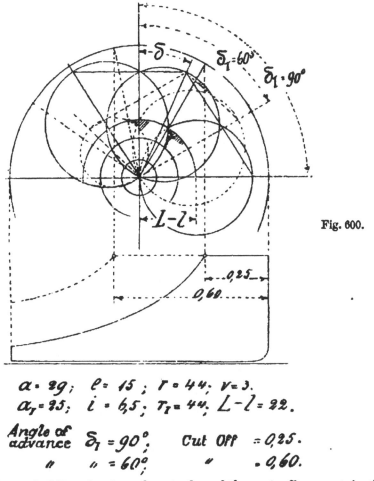

Fig. 600.

$$a \cdot 29; \quad \ell = 15; \quad r = 44; \quad v = 3.$$
$$a_1 = 25; \quad i = 65; \quad r_1 = 44; \quad L - l = 22.$$

Angle of advance $\delta_1 = 90°;$ Cut Off $= 0.25.$

   "   " $= 60°;$ " $.0.60.$

expansion is varied by altering the stroke of the cut-off eccentric the two ends need not be independent of each other, so that all the ports in the back of the main valve are used for each end of the cylinder.

Valve Diagram for Valve Gears with Two Slide Valves, each Worked by a Separate Eccentric.

The construction of the diagram is as follows:—

First describe a circle (fig. 601) whose diameter equals the stroke of the main valve eccentric and draw the horizontal and vertical diameters, $R Q = N T$. On the horizontal, $R Q$ set off the lap of the valve, plus the lead, $O L$; from $O L$ erect a perpendicular, cutting the circle VI. in K, draw the radial line, $O K$, then $O K$ will be the position of the main valve eccentric radius when the crank is at one of the dead points R, and the angle $K O N$, will be the "angle of advance" of main eccentric. The steam port in cylinder may be represented by the perpendiculars drawn below $R Q$ from the points P and J, the distance $O P$ being equal to the lap of the valve. If now the radial line $O K$ be imagined to move round on the centre O, in the direction of the arrow VI. from K to the point K_1, it will show the angular movement of the crank-pin and eccentric radius from the dead point of the former until the valve has returned and closed the port. If the distance $K K_1$ is taken with the compasses and set off from R to x_a in circle VI. and a perpendicular dropped cutting $R Q$ in x_a, the proportion of $R x_a$ to the diameter of the circle VI. will give the portion of the piston-stroke during which steam is admitted. It is easy to follow this motion and obtain the position of the crank, and from thence the position of the piston for the admission, cut-off, release and compression, by setting out the steam ports and exhaust in their proper position at the right of the port $P J$; and by setting out the valve on a separate piece of paper and moving it backwards and forwards along the line $R Q$, and holding a set-square against the left-hand edge of the valve so as to mark the different phases on the circle or on the diameter $R Q$, all the positions of the piston may be marked on $R Q$ for admission, cut-off, release and compression, and if $R Q$ be divided into tenths, the percentage of stroke may be read off; always bearing in mind that no account in this kind of valve diagram is taken of the difference in the distribution of steam caused by the angle of the connecting and eccentric rods.

For valve gears with two valves, having the cut-off valve worked on the back of the main valve by a separate eccentric, a further construction is necessary. The example given is one with a "gridiron" or many-ported cut-off valve, and with a varying stroke, the maximum stroke being taken as equal to the stroke of the main valve.

On K in the circle VI., describe a circle XII. of a diameter equal to the width of one port in back of main valve, and touching this circle, draw the perpendiculars C D, F G. On a point in circle VI. describe a circle equal in diameter, to width of one port in cut-off valve, so that this circle overlaps the line of port in main valve F G, by a small amount, say, $\frac{1}{16}$th of an inch, more or less; this may be called the lead of cut-off valve. The line O A, gives the position of the cut-off

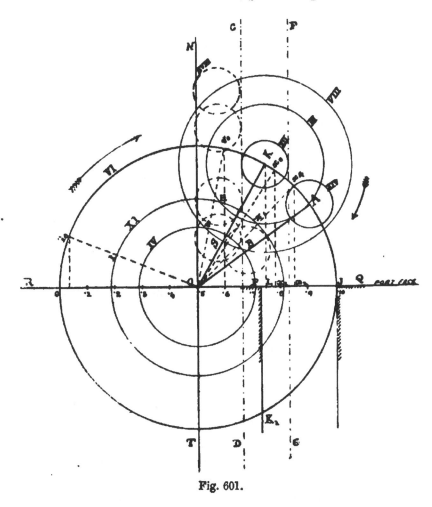

Fig. 601.

eccentric radius, when the crank is at one of the dead points R, and angle N O A "angle of advance" of cut-off valve eccentric.

From point K at radius K A, draw circle III. If closely observed, it will be seen that when the system of circles XII. and XIV. are revolved round on centre O, at radius O K, and at the fixed distance from each other K A, they will assume different positions with regard to the observer looking down on them. In the position on the diagram, circle XIV. is below and to the right of

circle XII. and when K reaches K_1, XIV. will be to the left of
XII. and above it, so in the complete revolution, the two circles
XII. and XIV. will revolve about one another, and their relative
motion with regard to each other will be the same if one, say, XII.,
is fixed, and XIV. revolving round it at radius K A, and, taking
this to be the case, all the positions of the cut-off valve ports with
relation to those on the back of the main valve can be determined ;
and, further, the position of crank at admission by cut-off valve, at
cut-off, and at reopening of main valve ports, can be laid out in per-
centages of stroke or otherwise.

Describe the circle IV. on centre O at radius equal to K A, then,
taking radius of port circle XIV. in compasses, describe circle at H
on circle III. touching the line C D.   The radius K H will represent
position of cut-off eccentric radius when cut-off valve has closed
ports on back of main valve, that is, when steam is cut-off ; the distance A H will show the angular movement from beginning of stroke
to point of cut-off by cut-off valve.   Transfer this distance to circle
IV. and draw the radius O V cutting the circle VI. at V, drop a perpendicular from V on to R Q and read off percentage of stroke.   In
the present case of an expansion gear controlled by the stroke of the
cut-off valve being decreased or increased by the governor or other
means, this will be the latest cut-off corresponding here to the maximum stroke of the cut-off valve.   For the earliest cut-off, let circle
XIV. be moved along line O A and take the position B giving a
shorter stroke to cut-off eccentric, describe the circle VIII. with
radius K B on centre K, and describe a circle XI. with same radius
on centre O.   As before, take radius of port circle and describe circle
S with its centre on circle VIII. and touching the line C D ; the distance from B to S will give angular movement from beginning of
stroke to point of cut-off, transfer this movement to circle XI.   From
centre O to I draw radial line O I and drop perpendicular from I_1
to R Q and read off percentage of stroke.   In valve gears where the
cut-off is varied by shortening the stroke of cut-off valve eccentric,
there is a danger of the ports reopening too soon and admitting steam
again late in the stroke before the lap of the main valve has covered
the steam port.   To find where reopening occurs, describe port circle
S VIII. with centre on circle VIII. and touching line C D,
transfer the angular motion from B to S VIII. to circle XI. as
before, starting on line R Q and cutting the circle XI. at x_1.   Draw
radial line O x_1 cutting circle VI. in x_4, drop perpendicular on the line
R Q, note where it cuts at x_3, then if x_4 is on the right hand of L, the
point where the main valve closes the port, the reopening of cut-off

ports will then take place after the main valve has closed the steam port, and no second admission of steam will take place; if, however, x_3 is on the left hand side of L, second admission will take place, and the arrangement will have to be altered. Further, the bars of metal between cut-off ports can be taken from the greatest distance between the main and cut-off eccentric centres, that is, in this case, from K to B, so that the radius of circle VIII. will give the greatest relative movement of the valves on each other and the least possible distance between nearest edges of ports; about $\frac{1}{8}$th of an inch or more must be added in practice for safety.

Hand Adjustments for Meyer's Valve Gear.

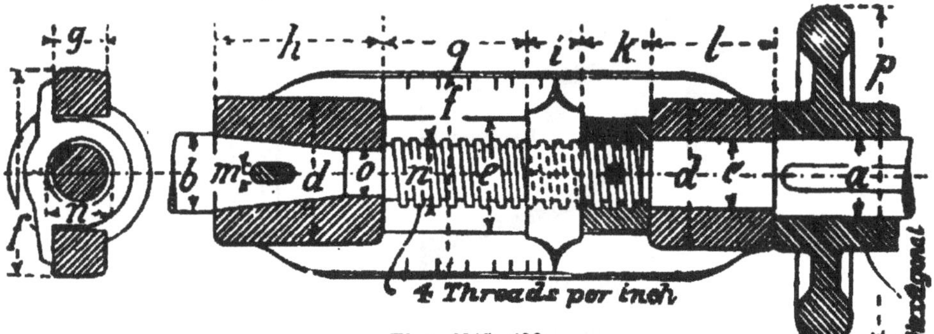

Figs. 601*, 602.

TABLE 59.—**Dimensions of Hand Adjustments for Meyer's Valve Gear** (Figs. 601*, 602).

H	D	*a*	*b*	*c*	*d*	*e*	*f*	*g*	*h*	*i*	*k*	*l*	*m*	*n*	*o*	*p*	*q**
16	8	1	1 1/8	1	1 7/8	1 1/2	2 3/4	3/4	2 3/8	3/4	1	1 5/8	1/4	1	11/16	4 7/8	1 1/8
20	10	1 1/8	1 1/4	1	2 1/8	1 1/2	3	3/4	2 1/2	3/4	1	1 3/4	1/4	1	3/4	5 1/4	1 3/8
24	12	1 1/4	1 5/16	1	2 1/4	1 5/8	3 1/4	7/8	2 1/2	3/4	1	2	5/16	1	3/4	5 1/2	1 3/4
28	14	1 1/4	1 3/8	1 1/8	2 3/8	1 3/4	3 3/8	1	2 5/8	7/8	1 1/8	2 1/8	3/8	1 1/8	3/4	5 3/4	2 1/16
32	16	1 3/8	1 1/2	1 1/4	2 1/2	2	3 5/8	1	2 7/8	1	1 1/4	2 1/4	3/8	1 1/4	1	6 3/8	2 5/8
36	18	1 3/8	1 1/2	1 3/8	2 5/8	2 1/8	3 3/4	1 1/8	3 1/4	1	1 3/8	2 3/8	3/8	1 1/4	1	6 3/4	2 1/2
40	20	1 1/2	1 5/8	1 3/8	2 3/4	2 1/4	4 1/4	1 1/4	3 5/8	1 1/8	1 3/8	2 1/2	7/16	1 3/8	1 1/8	7 1/8	2 5/8
44	22	1 5/8	1 3/4	1 1/2	2 7/8	2 3/8	4 1/2	1 1/4	4	1 1/4	1 1/2	2 3/4	1/2	1 3/8	1 1/4	7 3/8	3

All Dimensions are given in Inches.

In the above design (fig. 601*) the hand-wheel is rather small; the boss is therefore made hexagonal, so that a spanner may be used if required.

* *q* is for cut-off varying from 0 to ·73.

Hand Adjustment for Meyer's and Rider's Valve Gears.

Fig. 603.

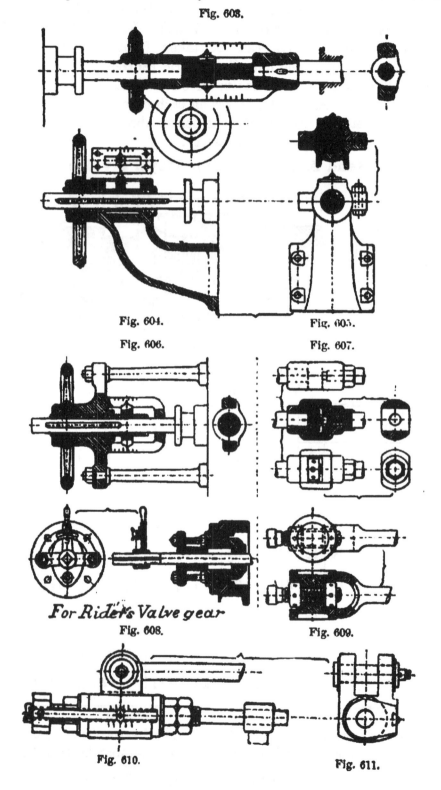

Fig. 604.

Fig. 605.

Fig. 606.

Fig. 607.

For Rider's Valve gear

Fig. 608.

Fig. 609.

Fig. 610.

Fig. 611.

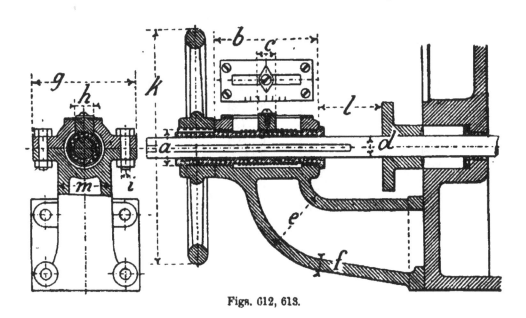

Figs. 612, 613.

TABLE 60.—Dimensions of Hand Adjustment for Meyer's Valve Gear (Figs. 612, 613).

H	D	d	a	b	c	e	f	g	h	i	k	l	m
20	10	$\frac{3}{4}$	$1\frac{1}{4}$	$3\frac{1}{4}$	$\frac{3}{4}$	2	$\frac{3}{8}$	4	1	$\frac{3}{8}$	6	2	$1\frac{1}{2}$
24	12	$\frac{7}{8}$	$1\frac{3}{8}$	$3\frac{3}{4}$	$\frac{7}{8}$	$2\frac{3}{8}$	$\frac{3}{8}$	$4\frac{3}{8}$	1	$\frac{1}{2}$	$7\frac{5}{8}$	$2\frac{3}{8}$	$1\frac{7}{8}$
28	14	1	$1\frac{1}{2}$	$4\frac{3}{8}$	1	$2\frac{3}{4}$	$\frac{3}{8}$	$4\frac{3}{4}$	$1\frac{1}{8}$	$\frac{1}{2}$	$9\frac{1}{4}$	$2\frac{3}{4}$	$2\frac{1}{4}$
32	16	$1\frac{1}{8}$	$1\frac{3}{4}$	5	$1\frac{1}{8}$	$3\frac{1}{4}$	$\frac{1}{2}$	$5\frac{1}{4}$	$1\frac{1}{4}$	$\frac{1}{2}$	$11\frac{1}{4}$	$3\frac{1}{4}$	$2\frac{1}{2}$
36	18	$1\frac{1}{4}$	$1\frac{7}{8}$	$5\frac{5}{8}$	$1\frac{1}{4}$	$3\frac{5}{8}$	$\frac{9}{16}$	$5\frac{5}{8}$	$1\frac{1}{4}$	$\frac{5}{8}$	$12\frac{3}{4}$	$3\frac{5}{8}$	$2\frac{7}{8}$
40	20	$1\frac{3}{8}$	$2\frac{1}{8}$	$6\frac{3}{8}$	$1\frac{1}{4}$	$4\frac{1}{4}$	$\frac{5}{8}$	6	$1\frac{3}{8}$	$\frac{5}{8}$	$14\frac{3}{8}$	4	$3\frac{1}{4}$
44	22	$1\frac{3}{8}$	$2\frac{1}{4}$	$7\frac{1}{4}$	$1\frac{3}{8}$	$4\frac{3}{8}$	$\frac{3}{4}$	$6\frac{3}{8}$	$1\frac{3}{8}$	$\frac{5}{8}$	16	$4\frac{3}{8}$	$3\frac{5}{8}$

All Dimensions are given in Inches.

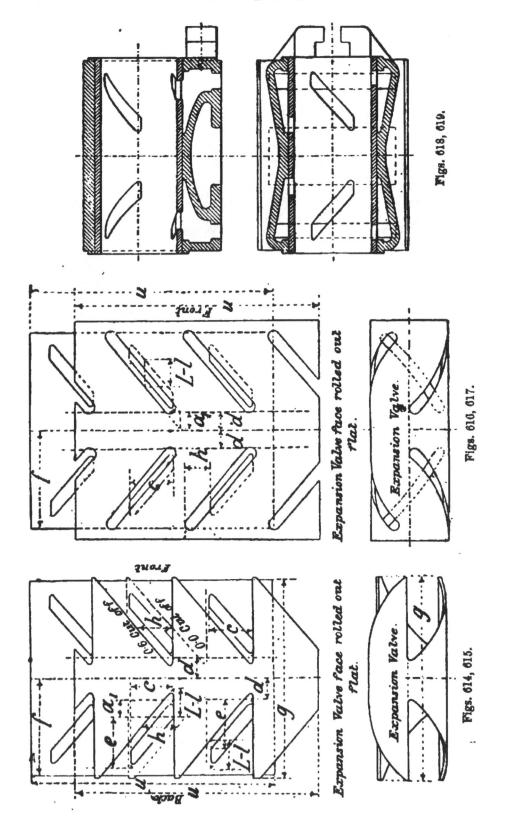

Figs. 618, 619.

Expansion Valve face rolled out Flat.

Figs. 616, 617.

Expansion Valve face rolled out Flat.

Figs. 614, 615.

TABLE 61.—Dimensions of Cut-off Valve Faces, &c., for Rider's Valve Gear (Figs. 614—619).

Stroke	H	20	24	28	32	36	40	44
Diameter of piston	D	10	12	14	16	18	20	22
Diameter of expansion valve	m	$3\frac{1}{4}$	4	$4\frac{3}{4}$	$5\frac{5}{8}$	$6\frac{5}{8}$	$7\frac{7}{8}$	$8\frac{7}{8}$
Circumference of expansion valve	u	$10\frac{3}{16}$	$12\frac{1}{2}$	$14\frac{7}{8}$	$17\frac{7}{8}$	$20\frac{3}{4}$	$23\frac{1}{16}$	$26\frac{3}{16}$
L−l for ·0 cut-off		$\frac{7}{16}$	$\frac{1}{2}$	$\frac{11}{16}$	$\frac{3}{4}$	1	$1\frac{1}{8}$	$1\frac{1}{4}$
L−l for ·6 cut-off		$\frac{7}{8}$	$1\frac{3}{16}$	$1\frac{5}{16}$	$1\frac{13}{16}$	$2\frac{1}{8}$	$2\frac{5}{16}$	$2\frac{5}{8}$
Width of port	a_1	$\frac{1}{2}$	$\frac{11}{16}$	$\frac{7}{8}$	1	$1\frac{1}{8}$	$1\frac{3}{8}$	$1\frac{1}{2}$
Width of port	b	$5\frac{5}{8}$	$6\frac{3}{4}$	$8\frac{3}{8}$	10	$11\frac{5}{8}$	$13\frac{1}{4}$	$14\frac{3}{4}$
Height of port (c=about ⅑)	c	$1\frac{3}{4}$	$2\frac{5}{16}$	$2\frac{3}{4}$	$3\frac{3}{8}$	4	$4\frac{3}{8}$	5
Dimension	d	1	$1\frac{1}{8}$	$1\frac{1}{4}$	$1\frac{3}{8}$	$1\frac{1}{2}$	$1\frac{5}{8}$	$1\frac{3}{4}$
Dimension	e	$2\frac{3}{8}$	$2\frac{5}{8}$	$3\frac{3}{4}$	4	$4\frac{5}{8}$	$5\frac{5}{8}$	$5\frac{3}{4}$
Half length of valve seat	f	$4\frac{1}{4}$	5	6	7	8	$8\frac{3}{4}$	$9\frac{1}{4}$
Length of cut-off valve	g	$8\frac{5}{8}$	$10\frac{3}{8}$	$12\frac{3}{8}$	$14\frac{3}{8}$	$16\frac{5}{8}$	$18\frac{5}{8}$	$20\frac{5}{8}$
Turning movement of valve	h	$1\frac{5}{8}$	$1\frac{5}{8}$	$1\frac{7}{8}$	$2\frac{1}{4}$	$2\frac{5}{8}$	3	$3\frac{3}{8}$
Cut-off at mean position of governor		·13	·13	·13	·13	·13	·13	·13

All Dimensions are given in Inches.

Rider's Valve Gear.

Rider's valves differ from Meyer's in having the working edges of the cut-off valve formed as a right and left hand screw, the valve itself being turned partially round in its seat, so as to give the same effect as the separate valves of Meyer moved further apart or nearer

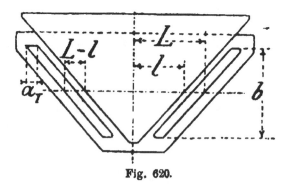

Fig. 620.

together by means of the right and left hand screws and nuts. The effect is the same if the valve is a flat plate with edges inclined right and left, fig. 620; if the plate be moved down the distance $L - l$ is decreased, and if the plate be moved upwards increased.

Fig. 621.   Fig. 622.

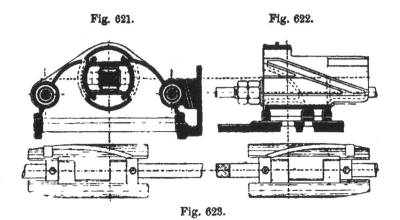

Fig. 623.

A modification of Rider's valve by Leutert of Halle is shown in figs. 621—626. The cut-off valve is in two parts, c and d, figs. 624—626, this giving short steam ports, and also rendering the necessary adjustment for variation of expansion of less range. On the back of the main valve are four ports, a_1, a_{11}, b_1, b_{11}; the first two unite into one port at the right hand end of the valve, and the two latter into one port at the left hand end of the valve; the cut-off valve has a square spindle by which it is turned in its seat to vary the cut-off. The two parts of the cut-off valve are kept up to their seat by springs, *h*.

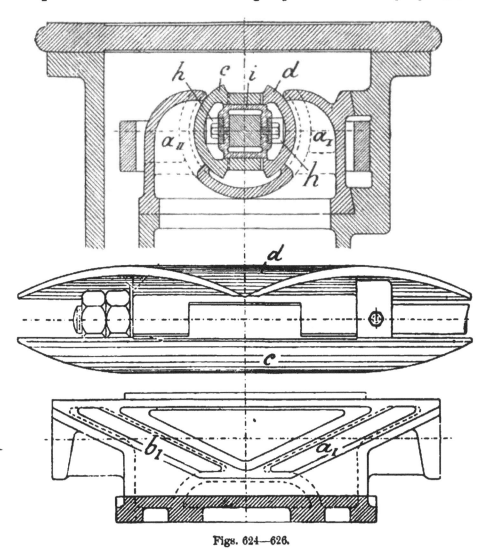

Figs. 624—626.

These valves are usually controlled by the governor. The two halves of the valve form a kind of piston valve, and should work with very little friction.

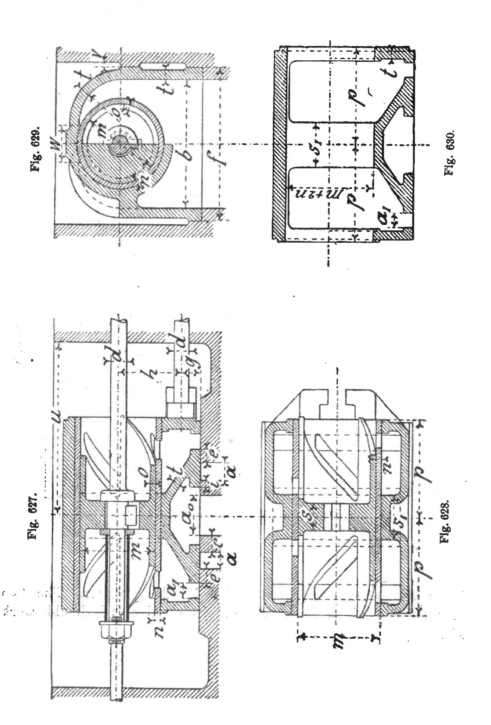

Fig. 629.

Fig. 630.

Fig. 627.

Fig. 628.

TABLE 62.—Dimensions of Rider's Closed Valves (Figs. 627—630).

H	D	a_0	a	a_1	b	c	d	e	f	g	h	i	m	n	o	p	q	s	s_1	t	u	v	w	$r=r_1$
20	10	$1\frac{3}{4}$	$\frac{5}{8}$	$\frac{1}{2}$	$5\frac{5}{8}$	$\frac{11}{16}$	$1\frac{1}{8}$	$\frac{1}{2}$	$6\frac{3}{4}$	$1\frac{1}{4}$	$3\frac{1}{4}$	$\frac{1}{4}$	$3\frac{1}{4}$	$\frac{5}{16}$	$\frac{5}{16}$	$4\frac{1}{4}$	$5\frac{13}{16}$	$1\frac{1}{8}$	$2\frac{3}{8}$	$\frac{1}{2}$	$7\frac{1}{4}$	$\frac{1}{4}$	$1\frac{1}{2}$	1
24	12	$1\frac{7}{8}$	$\frac{3}{4}$	$\frac{11}{16}$	$6\frac{3}{4}$	$\frac{3}{4}$	$1\frac{1}{4}$	$\frac{5}{8}$	$8\frac{3}{8}$	$1\frac{3}{8}$	$3\frac{3}{8}$	$\frac{5}{16}$	4	$\frac{3}{8}$	$\frac{3}{8}$	5	$6\frac{3}{4}$	$1\frac{1}{8}$	$2\frac{5}{8}$	$\frac{5}{8}$	$8\frac{5}{8}$	$\frac{3}{8}$	$1\frac{3}{4}$	$1\frac{5}{16}$
28	14	$2\frac{3}{8}$	1	$\frac{7}{8}$	$8\frac{3}{8}$	$\frac{7}{8}$	$1\frac{1}{4}$	$\frac{3}{4}$	10	$1\frac{5}{8}$	$4\frac{5}{8}$	$\frac{5}{16}$	$4\frac{3}{4}$	$\frac{1}{2}$	$\frac{1}{2}$	6	$7\frac{7}{8}$	$1\frac{3}{4}$	$2\frac{3}{4}$	$\frac{9}{16}$	$10\frac{1}{4}$	$\frac{3}{8}$	2	$1\frac{1}{8}$
32	16	$2\frac{3}{4}$	$1\frac{1}{8}$	1	10	1	$1\frac{3}{8}$	$\frac{7}{8}$	$11\frac{5}{8}$	$1\frac{3}{4}$	5	$\frac{3}{8}$	$5\frac{5}{8}$	$\frac{1}{2}$	$\frac{1}{2}$	7	$9\frac{5}{8}$	$1\frac{7}{8}$	3	$\frac{9}{16}$	$11\frac{5}{8}$	$\frac{3}{8}$	$2\frac{1}{4}$	$1\frac{7}{8}$
36	18	$3\frac{1}{8}$	$1\frac{1}{4}$	$1\frac{1}{8}$	$11\frac{5}{8}$	$1\frac{1}{8}$	$1\frac{3}{8}$	1	$13\frac{3}{8}$	$1\frac{3}{4}$	$5\frac{3}{4}$	$\frac{1}{2}$	$6\frac{5}{8}$	$\frac{1}{2}$	$\frac{1}{2}$	8	$10\frac{1}{4}$	2	$3\frac{1}{4}$	$\frac{5}{8}$	$13\frac{1}{4}$	$\frac{3}{8}$	$2\frac{3}{8}$	$2\frac{1}{8}$
40	20	$3\frac{3}{8}$	$1\frac{1}{2}$	$1\frac{3}{8}$	$13\frac{1}{4}$	$1\frac{1}{4}$	$1\frac{1}{2}$	$1\frac{1}{8}$	$15\frac{1}{4}$	2	$6\frac{3}{8}$	$\frac{1}{2}$	$7\frac{7}{8}$	$\frac{5}{8}$	$\frac{5}{8}$	$8\frac{3}{4}$	$11\frac{1}{4}$	$2\frac{1}{8}$	$3\frac{3}{8}$	$\frac{11}{16}$	$14\frac{3}{8}$	$\frac{3}{8}$	$2\frac{5}{8}$	$2\frac{1}{2}$
44	22	4	$1\frac{5}{8}$	$1\frac{1}{2}$	$14\frac{3}{4}$	$1\frac{1}{4}$	$1\frac{5}{8}$	$1\frac{1}{4}$	$16\frac{3}{4}$	$2\frac{1}{4}$	$7\frac{1}{4}$	$\frac{5}{8}$	$8\frac{5}{8}$	$\frac{5}{8}$	$\frac{5}{8}$	$9\frac{3}{4}$	$12\frac{1}{2}$	$2\frac{1}{4}$	$3\frac{5}{8}$	$\frac{3}{4}$	16	$\frac{3}{8}$	$2\frac{3}{4}$	$2\frac{3}{4}$

All Dimensions are given in Inches.

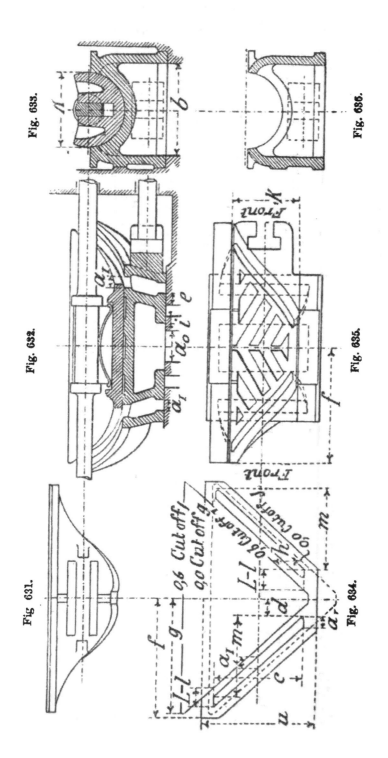

Fig. 633.

Fig. 636.

Fig. 632.

Fig. 635.

Fig. 631.

Fig. 634.

TABLE 63.—Dimensions of Rider's Open Valves (Figs. 631—636).

Stroke	H	16	20	24	28	32
Diameter of piston	D	8	10	12	14	16
Diameter of cut-off valve . .	k	$2\frac{3}{4}$	$3\frac{5}{8}$	$4\frac{5}{8}$	$5\frac{5}{8}$	$6\frac{5}{8}$
Half circumference . . .	u	$8\frac{5}{8}$	$11\frac{5}{16}$	$14\frac{1}{2}$	$17\frac{7}{8}$	$20\frac{3}{4}$
Width of port	a_1	$\frac{3}{8}$	$\frac{1}{2}$	$\frac{11}{16}$	$\frac{7}{8}$	1
$L-l$ for ·0 cut-off . . .		$-\frac{3}{8}$	$-\frac{7}{16}$	$-\frac{1}{8}$	$-\frac{11}{16}$	$-\frac{3}{4}$
$L-l$ for ·6 cut-off . . .		$\frac{11}{16}$	$\frac{7}{8}$	$1\frac{3}{16}$	$1\frac{5}{16}$	$1\frac{13}{16}$
Height of port c=about ·8 of h .	c	$3\frac{5}{8}$	$4\frac{3}{8}$	$5\frac{5}{8}$	$6\frac{3}{4}$	$8\frac{3}{8}$
Dimension	d	$\frac{2}{3}$	1	$1\frac{1}{4}$	$1\frac{1}{2}$	2
Dimension	m	$3\frac{3}{8}$	4	5	$6\frac{1}{8}$	$7\frac{1}{2}$
Half length of main valve . .	f	$4\frac{3}{4}$	6	$7\frac{7}{8}$	$9\frac{3}{8}$	$11\frac{3}{8}$
Half length of cut-off valve . .	g	$4\frac{5}{8}$	$5\frac{3}{4}$	7	9	11
Turning movement of cut-off valve .	h	$1\frac{1}{4}$	$1\frac{1}{2}$	$1\frac{7}{8}$	$2\frac{3}{8}$	$2\frac{3}{4}$
Cut-off with governor in mean position .		·13	·13	·13	·13	·13

All Dimensions are given in Inches

Connection between Rider's Valve Gear and the Governor.

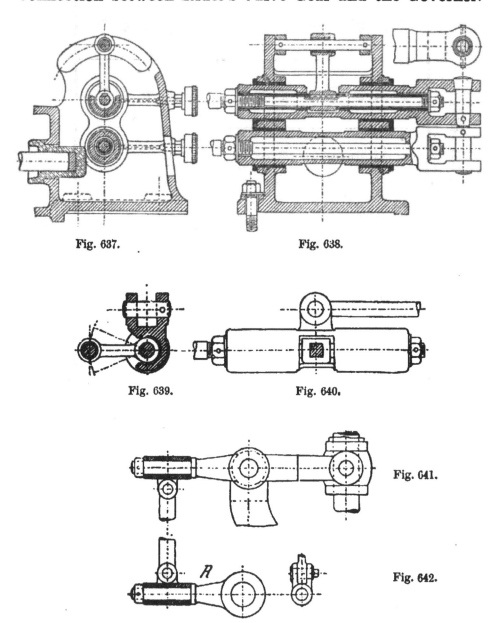

Fig. 637.   Fig. 638.

Fig. 639.   Fig. 640.

Fig. 641.

Fig. 642.

The connection between Rider's valve gear and the governor is shown in various ways in figs. 637—642. Figs. 637, 638, show a method by Starke and Hoffman, with cast-iron guides to the valve rods; figs. 639, 640, a method by Leutert; figs. 641, 642, a method of connection with a kind of universal joint, to allow for the backwards and forwards movement of the valve rod.

Connection between Rider's Valve Gear and Governor.

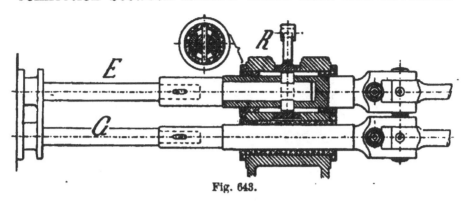

Fig. 643.

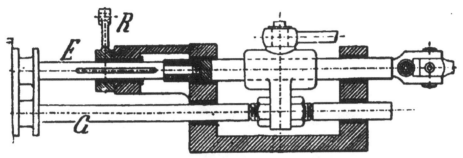

Fig. 644.

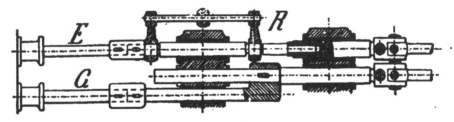

Fig. 645.

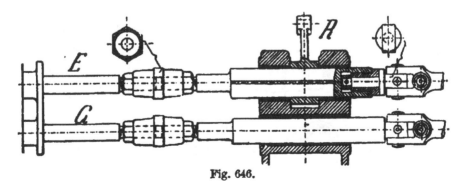

Fig. 646.

G, the main valve rod; E, the cut-off valve rod; R, the arm to which the governor rod is attached.

Connection between Rider's Valve Gear and Governor.

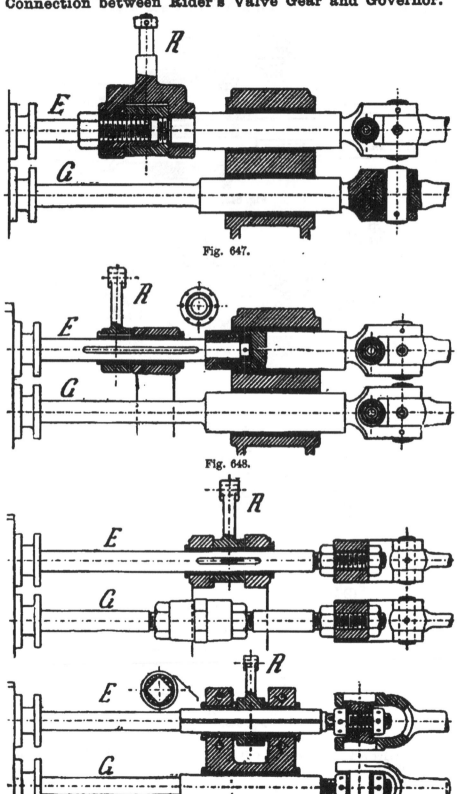

Fig. 647.

Fig. 648.

Remarks on the Governor Bracket (Figs. 651—663).

The combined governor bracket and valve rod guide on the next page may be taken as an example, a somewhat complicated piece of designing, but at the same time a substantial fixing for the governor, driving gear and guides. In engine design, especially with horizontal girder engines, it is well to have as few fixings on the girder as possible, for neatness and other obvious reasons. The whole of the governor gear and attachment to the valve rod, in this case, can be fitted up together, ready to bolt on the engine girder. In cases where a feed-pump is fitted to the engine, the barrel can often be made in the same casting as the valve-rod guides with the necessary valve boxes bolted on. This forms a very compact arrangement, and if, as may happen, the pump centre comes far out from the girder, a stay of wrought iron can be fitted from the pump casting to the slide valve chest to take the thrust of the pump.

By making the flanges at both ends of the pump barrel of the same size, the pump can be used for both right- and left-hand engines, a very important point in the economical manufacture of steam engines, and in many other machines.

In figs. 651—663 one of the valve-rod guides is shown bushed with brass or bronze. If both guide-plunger and guide are of cast iron, there is certainly no necessity for this, although it is often convenient for the owner of an engine to have such guides bushed, even if it is only with cast iron, in order that new bushes can be supplied by the maker, without having to supply a new bracket, with a risk of variation in the centres, causing trouble and delay.

Combined Bracket for carrying Governor and Valve-Rod Guides (Figs. 651—663).

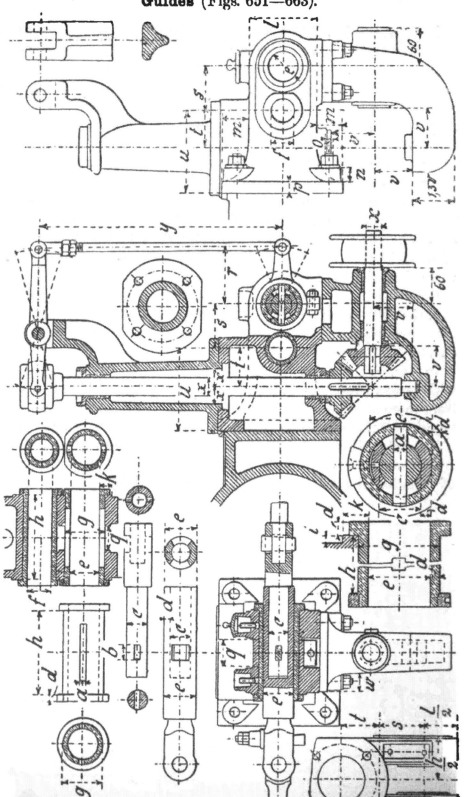

TABLE 64.—**Dimensions of Valve-Rod Guides and Governor Stands for Rider's Valve Gear**
(Figs. 651—663).

H	D	*a*	*b*	*c*	*d*	*e*	*f*	*g*	*h*	*i*	*k*	*l*	*m*	*n*	*o*	*p*	*q*	*r*	*s*	*t*	*u*	*v*	*w*	*x*	*y*
20	10	1/2	1	1 3/8	3/8	2 1/4	1 5/8	3	6 1/2	1/4	1	5	2	7/8	5/8	3/4	1 3/4	4	3 1/4	2 3/4	5 5/8	3	1 1/4	1 3/8	16
24	12	1/2	1	1 1/2	7/16	2 3/8	1 3/4	3 3/8	7	1/4	1 1/8	5 1/4	2 1/2	1	3/4	7/8	2	4 1/4	3 5/8	3	6 3/8	3 1/4	1 3/8	1 3/8	18
28	14	9/16	1 1/8	1 5/8	1/2	2 5/8	2	3 5/8	7 3/4	1/4	1 1/4	6	2 3/4	1	3/4	1	2 1/8	4 1/2	4 3/8	3 1/8	7 1/4	3 3/8	1 1/2	1 1/2	20
32	16	5/8	1 1/4	1 7/8	1/2	2 7/8	2 1/8	4	8 1/4	1/4	1 1/4	6 1/2	3 1/4	1 1/4	7/8	1	2 3/8	4 5/8	5	3 1/4	8	3 1/2	1 5/8	1 1/2	22
36	18	5/8	1 1/4	2	9/16	3 1/8	2 3/8	4 1/4	9 1/4	3/8	1 3/8	7	3 3/4	1 3/8	1	1 1/8	2 1/2	4 3/4	5 3/4	3 3/8	9	3 3/4	1 3/4	1 1/2	24
40	20	3/4	1 3/8	2 1/4	5/8	3 3/8	2 1/2	4 5/8	9 3/4	3/8	1 3/8	7 3/4	4	1 3/8	1	1 1/4	2 5/8	5 1/4	6 3/8	3 5/8	9	3 7/8	2	1 3/4	26
44	22	3/4	1 1/2	2 3/8	5/8	3 5/8	2 3/4	4 7/8	10	3/8	1 1/2	8	4 1/4	1 1/2	1 1/4	1 1/4	2 3/4	5 3/4	7 1/4	3 3/4	10	4	2 3/8	1 3/4	28

All Dimensions are given in Inches.

Valve Rod Guides and Joints.

Figs. 664—668.

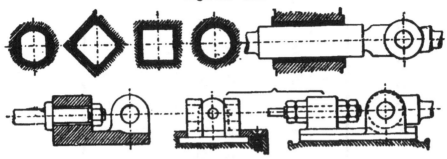

Figs. 669—671.

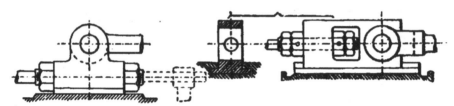

Figs. 672—675.

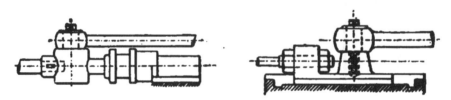

Figs. 676, 677.

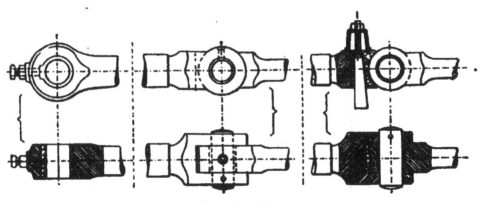

Figs. 678—681.

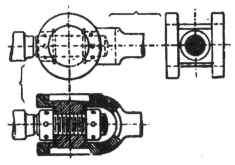

Figs. 682—684.

Figs. 664 to 685 show a variety of examples of valve-rod joints and guides. That shown in fig. 685, is a very useful form when the

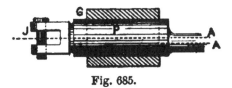

Fig. 685.

eccentric rod and valve rod are not in line, the guide plunger, P, valve rod and joint, J, being in one forging, and turned in the lathe on two centres, A, A; this form is used in locomotives.

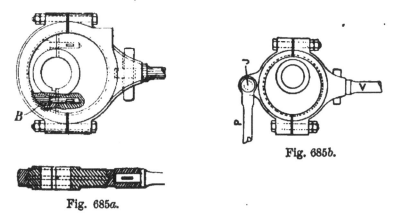

Fig. 685b.

Fig. 685a.

Fig. 585a shows an eccentric in halves joined by cottered bolts ; the head of the bolt B is turned with eccentric sheave when the two halves are bolted together. This method saves room, and is suitable for many small eccentrics where there is no space for bolts as in fig. 693. Fig. 685b shows an arrangement for working two rods off one strap, V and a. This is sometimes useful in small vertical engines, where the feed pump and slide valve have to be worked off one eccentric, the pump rod being jointed, as shown, to the outer end of the strap.

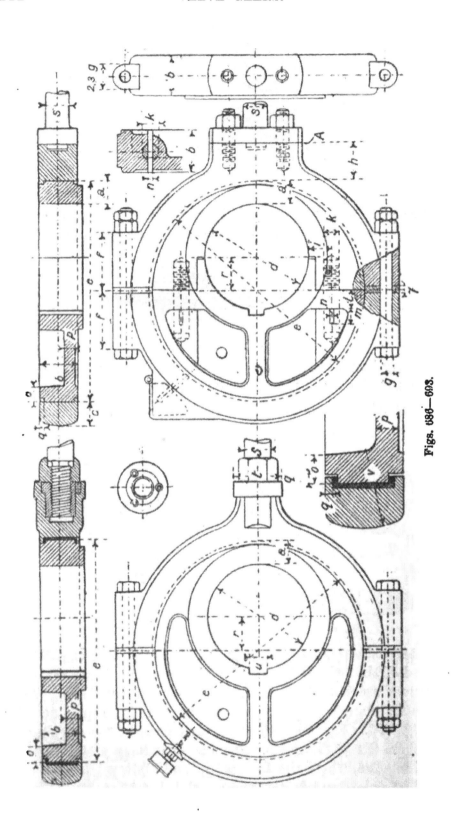

Figs. 686—693.

TABLE 65.—Dimensions of Eccentrics (Figs. 686—693).

H	D	*r*	*d*	*a*	*b*	*c*	*e*	*f*	*g*	*h*	*i*	*k*	*l*	*m*	*n*	*o*	*p*	*q*	*s*	*t*	*u*	*v*
12	6	—	—	—	1 1/2	7/8	—	2	1/2	1 1/2	—	—	—	—	—	3/4	1/2	1/4	1	2 5/8	1/2	1 1/2
16	8	—	—	—	1 3/4	1	—	2 3/8	1/2	1 3/4	—	—	—	—	—	7/8	1/2	1/4	1 1/4	2 3/4	5/8	2
20	10	1	5 1/4	7/8	2	1	9	2 3/4	5/8	2	1	7/8	3/4	3/4	1/4	1	5/8	1/4	1 3/8	3	5/8	2 1/2
24	12	1 5/16	6	1 1/8	2 1/4	1 1/8	10 7/8	3 1/4	3/4	2 1/4	1 1/4	1	7/8	3/4	1/4	1 1/8	5/8	5/16	1 1/2	3 1/4	5/8	2 1/2
28	14	1 5/8	7 3/8	1 1/4	2 1/2	1 1/4	13 1/8	3 5/8	3/4	2 1/2	1 3/8	1 1/8	1	3/4	5/16	1 1/4	5/8	5/16	1 5/8	3 3/8	3/4	2 3/4
32	16	1 7/8	8	1 3/8	2 3/4	1 1/4	14 1/2	4	7/8	2 1/2	1 1/2	1 1/4	1	7/8	3/8	1 3/8	3/4	5/16	1 3/4	3 5/8	3/4	3
36	18	2 1/8	8 5/8	1 3/8	3	1 3/8	15 5/8	4 5/8	7/8	2 3/4	1 3/4	1 1/4	1 1/8	7/8	3/8	1 3/8	3/4	5/16	2	4	3/4	3 1/4
40	20	2 1/2	10	1 1/2	3 1/4	1 1/2	18	4 3/4	1	3	2	1 3/8	1 1/4	7/8	3/8	1 1/2	3/4	3/8	2 1/8	4 1/2	3/4	3 1/2
44	22	2 3/4	11 1/4	1 5/8	3 1/2	1 1/2	20	5 1/4	1	3 1/4	2 1/4	1 3/8	1 1/4	1	3/8	1 1/2	7/8	3/8	2 1/4	4 1/2	7/8	3 1/2

All Dimensions are given in Inches.

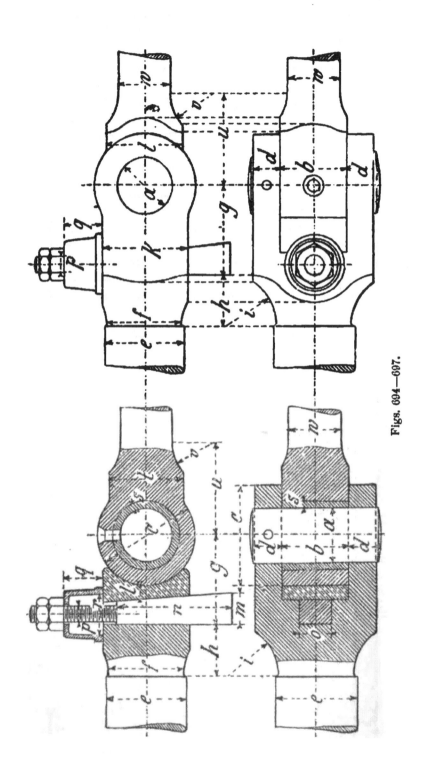

Figs. 694—697.

TABLE 66.—Dimensions of Valve and Eccentric Rod Joints (Figs. 694—697).

H	D	a	b	c	d	e	f	g	h	i	k	l	m	n	o	p	q	r	s	t	u	v	w
12	6	$\frac{7}{8}$	$1\frac{3}{8}$	$2\frac{1}{8}$	$\frac{1}{2}$	$1\frac{1}{2}$	$1\frac{1}{4}$	$1\frac{3}{4}$	$1\frac{1}{8}$	1	$1\frac{5}{8}$	$\frac{1}{4}$	$\frac{3}{4}$	$2\frac{3}{8}$	$\frac{5}{8}$	$\frac{3}{8}$	$\frac{7}{8}$	$\frac{7}{8}$	$\frac{1}{8}$	$1\frac{1}{4}$	$1\frac{5}{8}$	$\frac{3}{4}$	$\frac{3}{4}$
16	8	1	$1\frac{1}{2}$	$2\frac{1}{4}$	$\frac{5}{8}$	$1\frac{1}{2}$	$1\frac{3}{8}$	2	$1\frac{1}{4}$	$1\frac{1}{8}$	$1\frac{3}{4}$	$\frac{1}{4}$	$\frac{3}{4}$	$2\frac{1}{2}$	$\frac{3}{4}$	$\frac{3}{8}$	1	1	$\frac{3}{16}$	$1\frac{3}{8}$	$1\frac{3}{4}$	$\frac{3}{4}$	$\frac{7}{8}$
20	10	$1\frac{1}{8}$	$1\frac{1}{2}$	$2\frac{3}{8}$	$\frac{5}{8}$	$1\frac{5}{8}$	$1\frac{1}{2}$	$2\frac{1}{8}$	$1\frac{1}{4}$	$1\frac{1}{4}$	2	$\frac{3}{8}$	$\frac{3}{4}$	$2\frac{5}{8}$	$\frac{3}{4}$	$\frac{1}{2}$	1	1	$\frac{3}{16}$	$1\frac{1}{2}$	2	$\frac{7}{8}$	1
24	12	$1\frac{1}{4}$	$1\frac{5}{8}$	$2\frac{5}{8}$	$\frac{5}{8}$	$1\frac{7}{8}$	$1\frac{3}{4}$	$2\frac{1}{4}$	$1\frac{1}{4}$	$1\frac{1}{4}$	$2\frac{1}{8}$	$\frac{3}{8}$	$\frac{3}{4}$	$2\frac{3}{4}$	$\frac{3}{4}$	$\frac{1}{2}$	$1\frac{1}{8}$	1	$\frac{3}{16}$	$1\frac{3}{4}$	$2\frac{1}{8}$	1	$1\frac{1}{8}$
28	14	$1\frac{3}{8}$	$1\frac{3}{4}$	$2\frac{3}{4}$	$\frac{3}{4}$	2	$1\frac{7}{8}$	$2\frac{3}{8}$	$1\frac{3}{8}$	$1\frac{3}{8}$	$2\frac{1}{4}$	$\frac{3}{8}$	$\frac{7}{8}$	3	$\frac{7}{8}$	$\frac{1}{2}$	$1\frac{1}{4}$	$1\frac{1}{8}$	$\frac{3}{16}$	$1\frac{7}{8}$	$2\frac{1}{4}$	1	$1\frac{3}{8}$
32	16	$1\frac{3}{8}$	$1\frac{7}{8}$	$2\frac{3}{4}$	$\frac{3}{4}$	$2\frac{1}{8}$	2	$2\frac{1}{2}$	$1\frac{3}{8}$	$1\frac{3}{8}$	$2\frac{3}{8}$	$\frac{3}{8}$	$\frac{7}{8}$	$3\frac{1}{8}$	$\frac{7}{8}$	$\frac{1}{2}$	$1\frac{1}{4}$	$1\frac{1}{8}$	$\frac{1}{4}$	2	$2\frac{1}{2}$	$1\frac{1}{8}$	$1\frac{1}{2}$
36	18	$1\frac{1}{2}$	2	3	$\frac{3}{4}$	$2\frac{3}{8}$	$2\frac{1}{8}$	$2\frac{5}{8}$	$1\frac{1}{2}$	$1\frac{1}{2}$	$2\frac{1}{2}$	$\frac{3}{8}$	$\frac{7}{8}$	$3\frac{1}{4}$	1	$\frac{1}{2}$	$1\frac{3}{8}$	$1\frac{1}{4}$	$\frac{1}{4}$	$2\frac{1}{8}$	$2\frac{5}{8}$	$1\frac{1}{4}$	$1\frac{5}{8}$
40	20	$1\frac{1}{2}$	$2\frac{1}{8}$	$3\frac{1}{8}$	$\frac{7}{8}$	$2\frac{1}{2}$	$2\frac{3}{8}$	$2\frac{3}{4}$	$1\frac{1}{2}$	$1\frac{1}{2}$	$2\frac{3}{4}$	$\frac{3}{8}$	$\frac{7}{8}$	$3\frac{3}{8}$	1	$\frac{1}{2}$	$1\frac{3}{8}$	$1\frac{1}{4}$	$\frac{1}{4}$	$2\frac{3}{8}$	$2\frac{3}{4}$	$1\frac{3}{8}$	$1\frac{7}{8}$
44	22	$1\frac{5}{8}$	$2\frac{1}{4}$	$3\frac{1}{4}$	$\frac{7}{8}$	$2\frac{3}{4}$	$2\frac{3}{8}$	$2\frac{3}{4}$	$1\frac{5}{8}$	$1\frac{5}{8}$	$2\frac{7}{8}$	$\frac{3}{8}$	1	$3\frac{5}{8}$	1	$\frac{1}{2}$	$1\frac{1}{2}$	$1\frac{1}{4}$	$\frac{1}{4}$	$2\frac{3}{8}$	3	$1\frac{3}{8}$	2

All Dimensions are given in Inches.

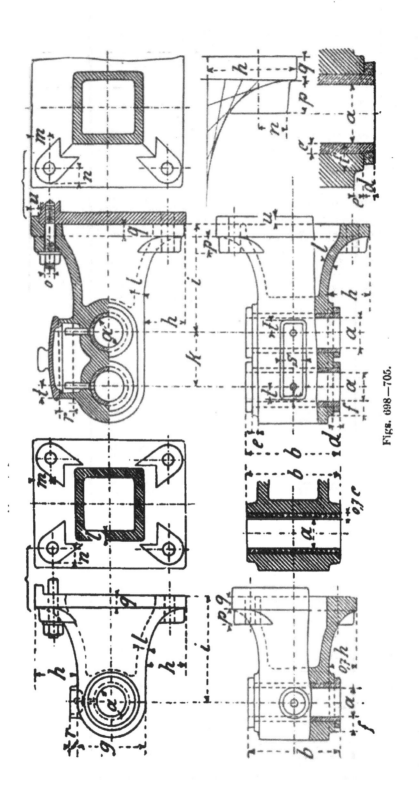

Figs. 698—705.

TABLE 67.—**Dimensions of Valve-Rod Guides for Simple and Meyer's Valve Gears** (Figs. 698—705).

H	D	*a*	*b*	*c*	*d*	*e*	*f*	*g*	*h*	*i*	*k*	*l*	*m*	*n*	*o*	*p*	*q*	*r*	*s*	*t*	*u*
12	6	1 1/2	2 3/4	1/4	5/16	1/4	5/8	3 5/8	—	—	—	—	—	—	—	—	—	—	—	—	—
16	8	1 1/2	3 1/2	1/4	5/16	1/4	5/8	3 3/4	—	—	—	—	—	—	—	—	—	—	—	—	—
20	10	1 5/8	4 1/2	5/16	3/8	1/4	3/4	4 1/4	2	4 3/4	3 1/4	1/2	1 1/4	1	5/8	3/4	3/4	3/4	1 1/4	3/4	3/8
24	12	1 3/4	5 1/4	5/16	3/8	1/4	7/8	4 5/8	2 3/8	5 3/4	3 3/8	9/16	1 1/4	1	5/8	7/8	3/4	3/4	1 1/4	3/4	3/8
28	14	2	6	3/8	1/2	3/8	1	5	2 3/4	6 3/4	3 5/8	9/16	1 3/8	1	3/4	1	7/8	1	1 1/2	3/4	1/2
32	16	2 1/8	6 3/4	3/8	1/2	3/8	1	5 1/4	3 1/4	8	3 7/8	5/8	1 1/2	1	3/4	1	1	1	2	7/8	1/2
36	18	2 3/8	7 3/4	3/8	1/2	3/8	1 1/8	5 5/8	3 5/8	9	4 1/4	11/16	1 1/2	1 1/4	7/8	1 1/8	1	1 1/4	2 1/2	7/8	5/8
40	20	2 1/2	8 1/2	3/8	1/2	3/8	1 1/4	6	4	10	4 3/8	3/4	1 5/8	1 1/4	7/8	1 1/4	1 1/8	1 3/8	2 3/4	1	5/8
44	22	2 3/4	8 3/4	3/8	1/2	3/8	1 1/4	6 3/8	4 1/4	10 1/2	4 5/8	3/4	1 3/4	1 1/4	1	1 1/4	1 1/4	1 3/8	3	1	3/4

All Dimensions are given in Inches.

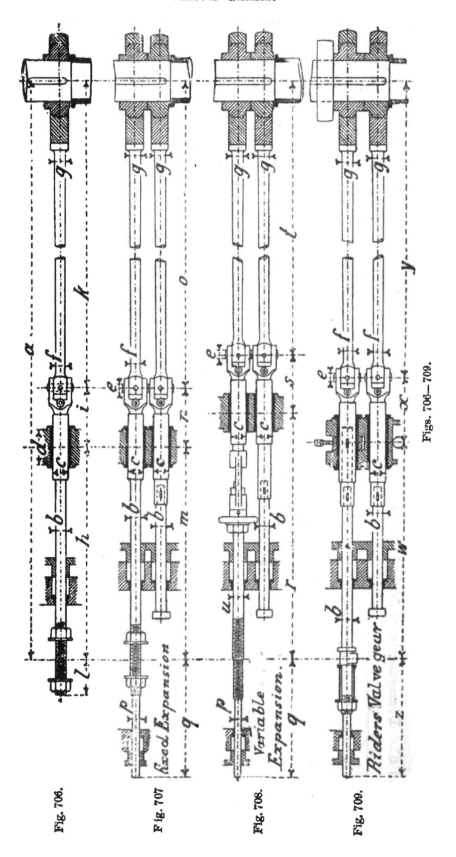

Fig. 706.

Fig. 707.   Fixed Expansion.

Fig. 708.   Variable Expansion.

Fig. 709.   Riders Valve gear.

Figs. 706—709.

TABLE 68.—Dimensions of Eccentric Rods and Valve Rods (Figs. 706—709).

H	D	Dimensions common to figs. 706—709.							Dimen. for fig. 708.				Dimensions for fig. 707.					Dimensions for fig. 708, for Meyer's valve gear adjusted by hand.					Dimensions for fig. 709, for Rider's valve gear adjusted by governor.			
		a	b	c	d	e	f	g	h	i	k	l	m	n	o	p	q	r	s	t	u	Threads per in.	w	x	y	z
12	6	58	$\frac{7}{8}$	$1\frac{1}{2}$	$2\frac{3}{4}$	$\frac{7}{8}$	$\frac{3}{4}$	1	30	5	23	$2\frac{5}{8}$	—	—	—	—	—	—	—	—	—	—	—	—	⋮	—
16	8	$74\frac{7}{8}$	1	$1\frac{1}{2}$	$3\frac{1}{2}$	1	$\frac{7}{8}$	$1\frac{1}{4}$	$33\frac{3}{4}$	$5\frac{7}{8}$	35	3	35	$5\frac{7}{8}$	33	$\frac{3}{4}$	$13\frac{1}{4}$	$41\frac{3}{4}$	$5\frac{7}{8}$	27	$1\frac{1}{4}$	4	—	—	—	—
20	10	90	$1\frac{1}{8}$	$1\frac{5}{8}$	$4\frac{1}{2}$	$1\frac{1}{8}$	1	$1\frac{3}{8}$	35	7	48	$3\frac{3}{8}$	$37\frac{3}{8}$	$6\frac{5}{8}$	46	$\frac{3}{4}$	15	$43\frac{3}{8}$	$6\frac{5}{8}$	40	$1\frac{3}{8}$	4	38	8	44	$14\frac{3}{8}$
24	12	$106\frac{1}{4}$	$1\frac{3}{16}$	$1\frac{3}{4}$	$5\frac{1}{4}$	$1\frac{1}{4}$	$1\frac{1}{8}$	$1\frac{1}{2}$	$38\frac{1}{4}$	8	60	$4\frac{3}{8}$	$42\frac{1}{4}$	$7\frac{1}{2}$	56	$\frac{7}{8}$	$16\frac{5}{8}$	$48\frac{3}{4}$	$7\frac{1}{2}$	50	$1\frac{1}{2}$	4	$42\frac{1}{4}$	9	55	17
28	14	122	$1\frac{1}{4}$	2	6	$1\frac{3}{8}$	$1\frac{3}{8}$	$1\frac{5}{8}$	43	9	70	$4\frac{7}{8}$	47	8	67	1	$18\frac{3}{4}$	53	8	61	$1\frac{5}{8}$	4	$46\frac{1}{4}$	$9\frac{3}{4}$	66	$19\frac{1}{4}$
32	16	138	$1\frac{3}{8}$	$2\frac{1}{8}$	$6\frac{3}{8}$	$1\frac{3}{8}$	$1\frac{1}{2}$	$1\frac{3}{4}$	—	—	—	—	49	9	80	$1\frac{1}{8}$	$20\frac{3}{4}$	57	9	72	$1\frac{3}{4}$	4	$50\frac{3}{8}$	$10\frac{1}{2}$	77	$21\frac{1}{8}$
36	18	154	$1\frac{3}{8}$	$2\frac{3}{8}$	$7\frac{1}{2}$	$1\frac{1}{2}$	$1\frac{5}{8}$	$1\frac{3}{4}$	—	—	—	—	54	10	90	$1\frac{1}{4}$	$23\frac{1}{4}$	63	10	81	$1\frac{7}{8}$	3	$56\frac{1}{2}$	$11\frac{1}{4}$	86	24
40	20	$169\frac{3}{4}$	$1\frac{1}{2}$	$2\frac{3}{8}$	$8\frac{1}{2}$	$1\frac{1}{2}$	$1\frac{7}{8}$	2	—	—	—	—	$59\frac{3}{4}$	11	100	$1\frac{3}{8}$	$24\frac{3}{4}$	$64\frac{3}{4}$	11	94	2	3	$60\frac{3}{4}$	12	97	$25\frac{5}{8}$
44	22	$186\frac{3}{4}$	$1\frac{5}{8}$	$2\frac{3}{4}$	$8\frac{3}{4}$	$1\frac{5}{8}$	2	$2\frac{1}{4}$	—	—	—	—	$61\frac{3}{4}$	12	113	$1\frac{3}{8}$	$26\frac{3}{4}$	$70\frac{3}{4}$	12	104	$2\frac{1}{8}$	3	$64\frac{3}{4}$	13	109	28

All Dimensions are given in Inches.

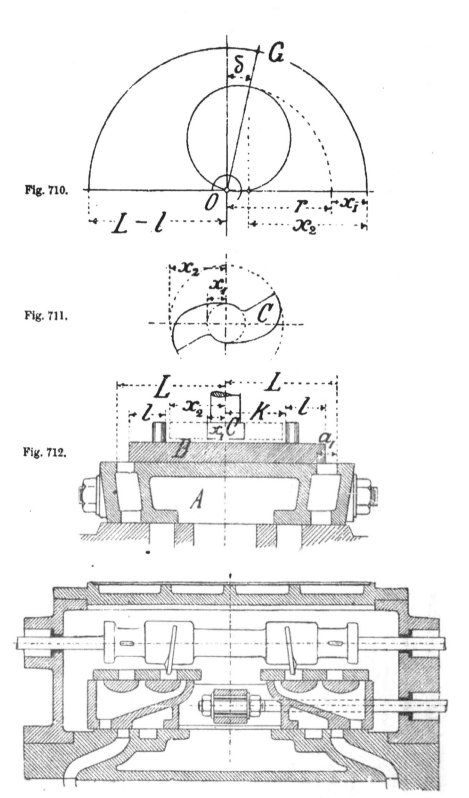

Fig. 710.

Fig. 711.

Fig. 712.

Fig. 713.

Farcot's Valve Gear.

The expansion valve B, fig. 712, is here loose on the back of the main valve A, and is dragged along by friction with the latter; the distance to which the expansion valve is carried is determined by the position of the cam C, figs. 711 and 712; the range of variation in this gear can be from ·0 to ·4. The limit of the latest cut-off is when the crank is at O G, fig. 710, and is dependent on the angle of advance. The valve diagram is constructed as follows :—

$\delta =$ the angle of advance of main valve eccentric ; $r =$ the radius of eccentricity of main valve eccentric ; $x =$ the smallest diameter of the cam, $\frac{3}{8}''$ to $1''$; $L - l = r + x_1$; then

$x_2 = L - l - r$ sin. $\delta =$ the greatest diameter of the cam.

$2k = 2 (L - l) - a_1.$

$a_1 = \; < 2 (L - l - x_2).$

When these equations are satisfied, the port, a_1, will be fully open when x is at its least value. The opening of a_1 is usually too small, so that two or more ports are required.

Guhrauer's valve gear is shown in fig. 713, and is, in effect, similar to that of Meyer.

Piston Valves.

Piston valves have been the subject of much ingenuity for many years, and at length are fairly well established in marine and other engines, where steam of very high pressure is used, especially for the high pressure cylinder of triple expansion engines.

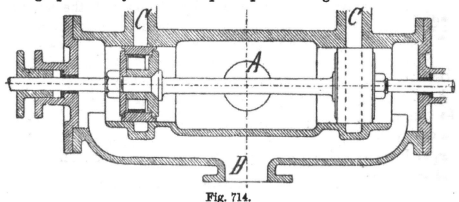

Fig. 714.

An example is shown in fig. 714 for a simple valve gear : C C are the steam ports, one at each end of the cylinder ; B, the steam

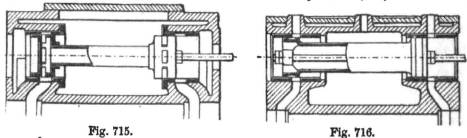

Fig. 715.   Fig. 716.

supply ; A, the exhaust.   Other examples are given in figs. 715, 716, and fig. 717 shows an outside view of the cylinder of an engine of 5′ 7″ stroke, with the piston-valve case bolted on by means of flanges.

Figs. 718 — 727 show an example of a piston valve for Rider's valve gear for an engine of 5′ 7″ stroke, 2′ 7″ diameter of piston, and 58 revs. per minute. The variation of cut-off is from ·0 to ·6, and the valve is turned through an angle of 36° by the governor.

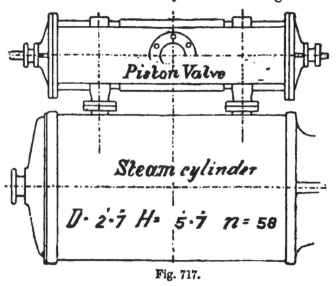

Fig. 717.

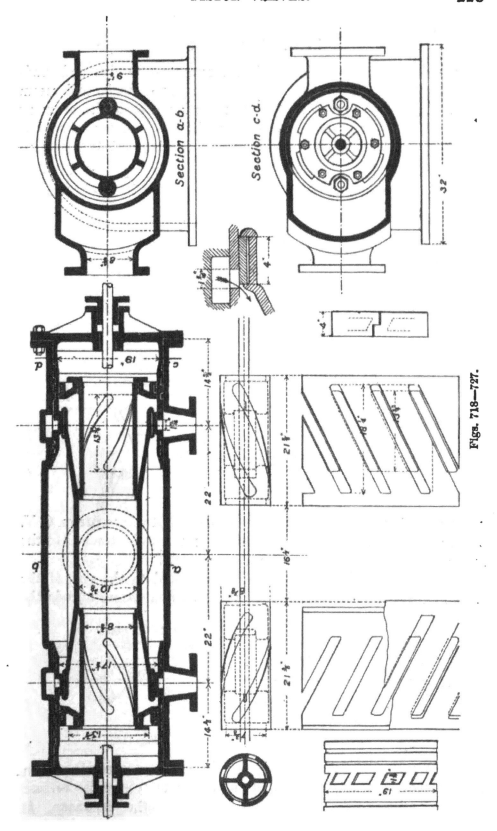

Figs. 718—727.

Reversing Gears.

Reversing gears are chiefly used on locomotives, marine and winding engines, also on traction engines for common roads and steam
road-rollers.   The prevailing type of reversing gear is the ordinary
link motion of Stephenson or some modification of the same, but
other types are used for special purposes.   Stephenson's link motion

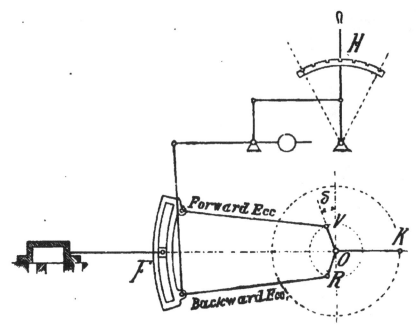

Fig. 728.

is shown in diagram in fig. 728 ; on the shaft, O, two eccentrics, O V,
O R, are keyed ; a rod from each of these eccentrics is attached to the
ends of the link or sector F, one rod to each end.

A block free to slide in the link F is attached to the end of the
valve rod.   By means of the hand lever, H, and a system of rods, the

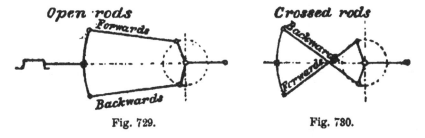

Fig. 729.   Fig. 730.

link can be raised or lowered, so as to bring either eccentric rod in
line with the block ; it will be seen that the two eccentrics are set
so that one will run the engine backwards, the other forwards.   If

the link is in its highest or lowest position, the valve will receive the full stroke of one of the eccentrics ; if the link is in any other position, the stroke of the valve will be reduced, if the link is in a mean position, then the valve will receive the minimum amount of stroke. There are two ways of setting this valve gear, one, with open rods, fig. 729, the other, with crossed rods, fig. 730 ; the angle of advance, δ, is usually made the same for both forward and backward eccentric. The effect of open and crossed rods on the distribution of steam is shown in the valve diagrams, figs. 732, 733.

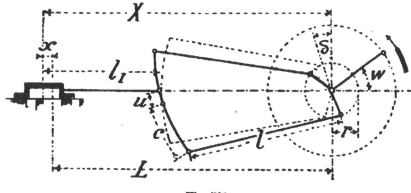

Fig. 731.

In fig. 731,

r = the radius or half stroke of both eccentrics.

δ = the angle of advance.

c = the half length of the link measured from the centre line to the point where the eccentric rod is attached.

u = the distance from the centre of the block to the centre of the link, u is positive when the link is down and negative when the link is up.

l = the length of the eccentric rod.

q = the radius of the link.

l_1 = the length of the valve rod.

for a chosen position of the crank corresponding to an angular movement W, gives for X_m (mean X)—

$$X_m = l + l_1 - \frac{r^2}{2\,l}\cos^2 \delta + (c^2 - u^2)\frac{l - q}{2\,l\,q} = L.$$

The link should be curved to a radius equal to the length of the eccentric rod.

Q

Stephenson's Link Motion with Open Rods.
($\frac{1}{2}$ natural size.)

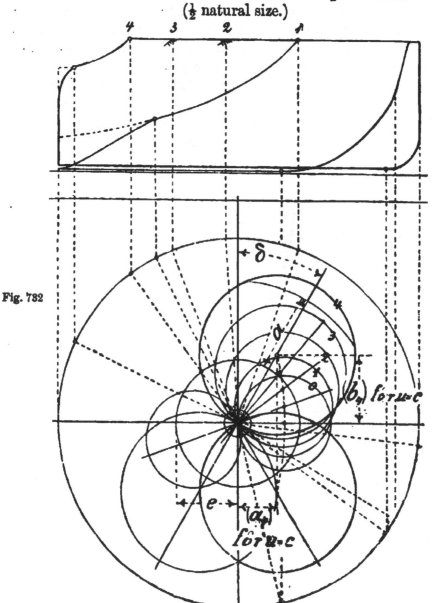

Fig. 732

($a = 1\cdot18$ ins. ; $r = 2\cdot36$ ins. ; $l = 55$ ins. ; $c = 5\cdot9$ ins. ; $e = \cdot95$ ins. ; $i = \cdot27$ ins.)

$$(a) = \tfrac{1}{2}\, r \left(\sin.\ \delta + \frac{c^2 - u^2}{c\, l} \cos.\ \delta\right) \qquad (b) = \tfrac{1}{2}\, r\, \frac{u}{c}\, \cos.\ \delta$$

For u max. $= c$, fig. 731 :—

Full gear forwards.	Mid gear.	Full gear backwards.
$(a_4) = \tfrac{1}{2}\, r \sin.\ \delta$	$(a_0) = \tfrac{1}{2}\, r \sin.\ \delta + \tfrac{1}{2}\, r\, \dfrac{c}{l}\, \cos.\ \delta$	$(a_4) = \tfrac{1}{2}\, r \sin.\ \delta$
$(b_4) = \tfrac{1}{2}\, r \cos.\ \delta$	$(b_0) = 0$	$(b_4) = -\tfrac{1}{2}\, r \cos.\ \delta$

Stephenson's Link Motion with Crossed Rods.
($\frac{1}{2}$ natural size.)

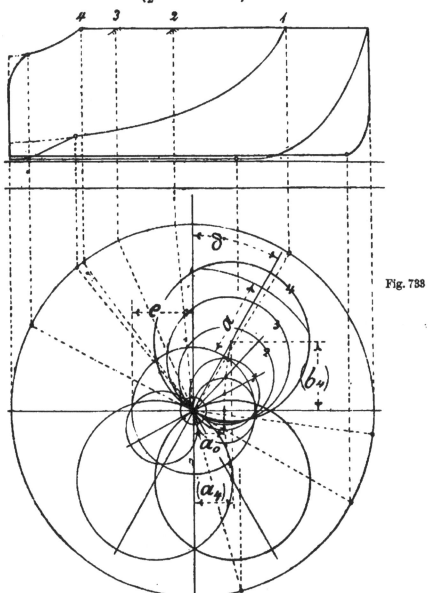

Fig. 733

($a = 1{\cdot}18$ ins.; $R = 2{\cdot}36$ ins.; $l = 55$ ins.; $c = 5{\cdot}9$ ins.; $e = {\cdot}95$ ins.; $i = {\cdot}27$ ins.)

$$(a) = \tfrac{1}{2} r \left(\sin. \delta - \frac{c^2 - u^2}{c\,l} \cos. \delta \right) \qquad (b) = \tfrac{1}{2} r \, \frac{u}{c} \cos. \delta$$

For u max. $= c$, fig. 731 :—

Full gear forwards.	Mid gear.	Full gear backwards.
$(a_4) = \tfrac{1}{2} r \sin. \delta$	$(a_0) = \tfrac{1}{2} r \sin. \delta - \tfrac{1}{2} r \dfrac{c}{l} \cos. \delta$	$(a_4) = \tfrac{1}{2} r \sin. \delta$
$(b_4) = \tfrac{1}{2} r \cos. \delta$	$(b_0) = 0$	$(b_4) = -\tfrac{1}{2} r \cos. \delta$

Q 2

For the distance, x, from the centre of the port face to the centre of the valve, fig. 731, we have the following approximate formulæ :—

For open rods,

$$x = r\left(\sin.\ \delta + \frac{c^2 - u^2}{c\,l}\ \cos.\ \delta\right)\cos.\ w + \frac{u\,r}{c}\ \cos.\ \delta\ \sin.\ w.$$

For crossed rods,

$$x = r\left(\sin.\ \delta - \frac{c^2 - u^2}{c\,l}\ \cos.\ \delta\right)\cos.\ w - \frac{u\,r}{c}\ \cos.\ \delta\ \sin.\ w.$$

These equations may be expressed for Polar co-ordinates :—

For open rods,

$$(a) = \tfrac{1}{2}\,r\left(\sin.\ \delta + \frac{c^2 - u^2}{c\,l}\ \cos.\ \delta\right);$$

$$(b) = \tfrac{1}{2}\,r\,\frac{u}{c}\ \cos.\ \delta.$$

For crossed rods,

$$(a) = \tfrac{1}{2}r\left(\sin.\ \delta - \frac{c^2 - u^2}{c\,l}\ \cos.\ \delta\right);$$

$$(b) = \tfrac{1}{2}\,r\,\frac{u}{c}\ \cos.\ \delta.$$

Thus we have the equation of a circle which passes through the centre point.

If we now take u max. $= C$, and have 9 equi-distant notches in the notch plate for the reversing lever, we have the following values of u for the nine different positions :—

With open rods.		With crossed rods.
$u = c$		$u = -c$
$u = \tfrac{3}{4}\,c$	Forwards	$u = -\tfrac{3}{4}\,c$
$u = \tfrac{1}{2}\,c$		$u = -\tfrac{1}{2}\,c$
$u = \tfrac{1}{4}\,c$		$u = -\tfrac{1}{4}\,c$
$u = 0$	Mid-gear	$u = 0$
$u = -\tfrac{1}{4}\,c$		$u = \tfrac{1}{4}\,c$
$u = -\tfrac{1}{2}\,c$	Backwards	$u = \tfrac{1}{2}\,c$
$u = -\tfrac{3}{4}\,c$		$u = \tfrac{3}{4}\,c$
$u = -c$		$u = c$

further these values give :—

With open rods.   With crossed rods.

Full gear forwards.

$(a) = \tfrac{1}{2}\,r\ \sin.\ \delta,$ $(a) = \tfrac{1}{2}\,r\ \sin.\ \delta,$

$(b) = \tfrac{1}{2}\,r\ \cos.\ \delta.$ $(b) = \tfrac{1}{2}\,r\ \cos.\ \delta.$

Mid gear.

$(a) = \tfrac{1}{2}\,r\ \sin.\ \delta + \tfrac{1}{2}\,r\,\dfrac{c}{l}\ \cos.\ \delta,$ $(a) = \tfrac{1}{2}\,r\ \sin.\ \delta - \tfrac{1}{2}\,r\,\dfrac{c}{l}\ \cos.\ \delta,$

$(b) = 0.$ $(b) = 0.$

Full gear backwards.

$(a) = \tfrac{1}{2}\,r\ \sin.\ \delta,$ $(a) = \tfrac{1}{2}\,r\ \sin.\ \delta,$

$(b) = -\tfrac{1}{2}\,r\ \cos.\ \delta.$ $(b) = -\tfrac{1}{2}\,r\ \cos.\ \delta.$

From the diagram fig. 732, it will be seen that the port is only full open to steam when the link is in either extreme position, in any intermediate position the port is only partially opened; on this account it is usual to make the ports very wide.*

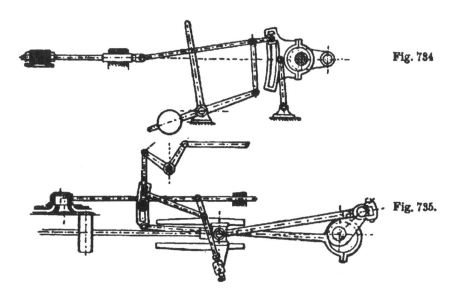

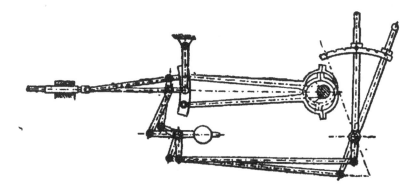

Fig. 734.—Link motion reversing gear, by Pius Fink, with one eccentric, one link, and one valve.

Fig. 735.—Link motion reversing gear, by Hensinger Von Waldegg, with one eccentric, one link, and one valve

Fig. 736.—Link motion reversing gear by Polonceau, with two links and two valves.

---

* A full description and analysis of these link motions will be found in Zeuner's "Treatise on Valve Gears," translated by Moritz Müller. London: Spon

Allan's Straight Link Motion.

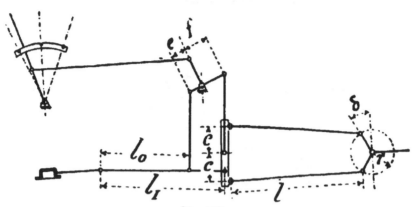

Fig. 737.

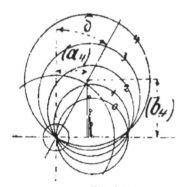

Fig. 738.

With open rods.

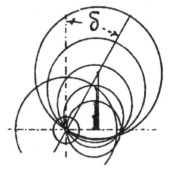

Fig. 739.

With crossed rods.

$$(a) = \tfrac{1}{2}\, r \left(\sin. \delta + \frac{nc^2 - u^2}{nc\,l} \cos. \delta \right) \qquad (a) = \tfrac{1}{2}\, r \left(\sin. \delta - \frac{nc^2 - u^2}{nc\,l} \cos. \delta \right)$$

$$(b) = \frac{r\,u}{2\,c} \left[\cos. \delta - c\frac{(n-1)}{n\,l} \sin. \delta \right] \qquad (b) = \frac{r\,u}{2\,c} \left[\cos. \delta + c\frac{(n-1)}{n\,l} \sin. \delta \right]$$

thus, $$\qquad\qquad\qquad n = 1 + \frac{l_1}{l_0}\frac{e}{f}$$

and therefore, $$\qquad \frac{e}{f} = \frac{l_0}{l}\left(1 + \sqrt{1 + \frac{l}{l_1}}\,\right).$$

The distinguishing feature of Allan's straight link motion reversing gear, fig. 737, is that the link is a straight bar, not a curved
sector, and that link is raised and the block lowered simultaneously
by a system of levers, the diagrams, fig. 738, 739, show that the distribution of steam is much the same as with the Stevenson's link
motion, but the lead is more nearly constant for all positions of the
link.

Gooch's Link Motion.

This link motion reversing gear, fig. 740, is sometimes called the "fixed link" motion, as the link is suspended from a fixed point, and is not moved up and down, the reversing action being obtained by moving the block up and down in the link.

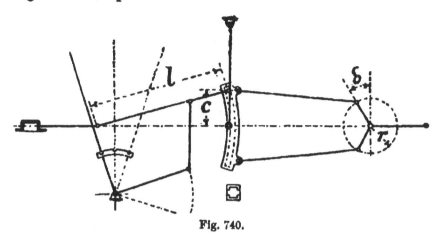

Fig. 740.

Crossed rods give the same distribution of steam, and are seldom used with this motion.

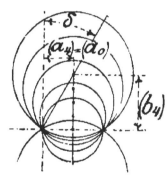

Fig. 741.

With open rods.	With crossed rods.

$$(a) = \tfrac{1}{2} r \left(\sin. \delta + \frac{c}{l} \cos. \delta \right), \qquad (a) = \tfrac{1}{2} r \left(\sin. \delta - \frac{c}{l} \cos. \delta \right),$$

$$(b) = \frac{r}{2} \frac{u}{c} \left(\cos. \delta - \frac{c}{l} \sin. \delta \right). \quad (b) = \frac{r}{2} \frac{u}{c} \left(\cos. \delta + \frac{c}{l} \sin. \delta \right)$$

$$u = + c \text{ Full gear forwards} \quad u = - c,$$
$$u = 0 \quad \text{Mid gear} \qquad\qquad u = 0,$$
$$u = - c \text{ Full gear backwards} \quad u = + c.$$

In the diagram, fig. 741, for open rods all the centres of the valve circles lie in a straight line, therefore the lead and cut-off are constant.

Reversing Gears.

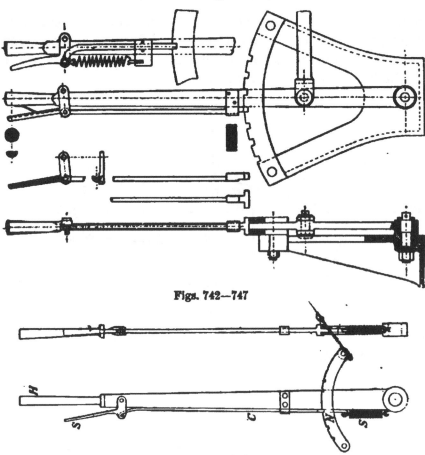

Figs. 742—747

Figs 748, 749.

Reversing levers are of various designs ; figs. 742 and 749 show two ordinary types, that in fig. 749, has the advantage of having the

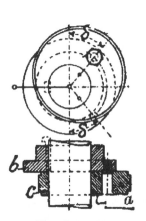

Figs. 750, 751.

spring, S, low down out of the way and also the hand lever, H, is carried up well above the handle of the catch, S, so that both hands may be used on the lever.

A simple arrangement for reversing the direction of running in small engines, such as agricultural engines, but one that requires the engine to be stopped to effect the reversal, is that of having a disc keyed on the shaft, *b*, fig. 751, and a bolt, *a*, to fix the eccentric to the disc ; a slot in the eccentric allows it to be put over in position for forward or backward running.

One form of reversing gear which has been used on small marine engines consists of a sleeve, *a*, fig. 752, loose on the crank shaft, the eccentric, *b*, is fixed on the sleeve, *a*, and a stud in *c* engages in a thread cut in the shaft, so that when *c* is slid along on the shaft it causes the eccentric to turn round sufficient to reverse the engine.

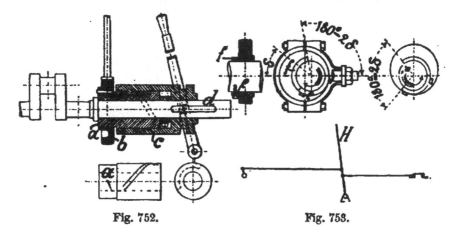

Fig. 752.   Fig. 753.

Another form of reversing gear with a loose eccentric, fig. 753, has been largely used in oscillating paddle engines.   The eccentric is free to revolve on the shaft between limits formed by a stop, *e*, the eccentric is moved for reversing by means of the lever, H, the valve rod being disengaged from the eccentric rod first by a device known as a "gab" and catch ; it is usual to balance the weight of the eccentric by a plate or disc on the opposite side of the shaft, in order to lessen the labour of reversing.

Valve Gears with Mushroom and Double-beat Valves.

These valve gears would seem to be elaborations of the original Cornish double-beat valve gears, they are usually rather complicated, and are therefore not very largely used ; the valves of this kind are used in large winding engines, and are capable of being controlled either automatically or by hand.   Sections of the valves and seats are given in figs. 754 to 761.

These valves were formerly made of gun metal, but now almost exclusively of cast iron ; the valve seating, also of cast iron, should be especially massive, to avoid the possibility of their getting out of truth.   The seatings are frequently cast in one with the cylinder, and require care in the disposition of the metal, in order to secure sound castings.   Some examples of the ordinary arrangements of these valves are shown by figs. 762—766 in outline.

Mushroom and Double-beat Valves.*

Schweiz Locomotive and Engine Works.   Socin and Wick, Basel.

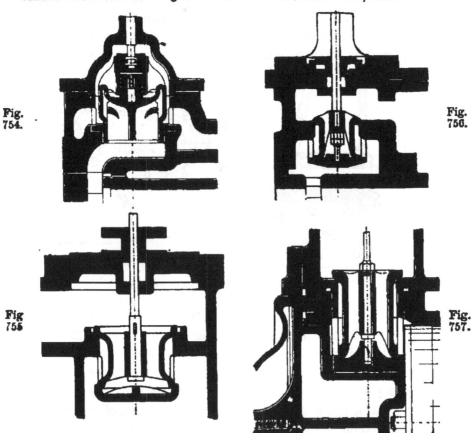

Fig.
754.

Fig.
756.

Fig
755

Fig.
757.

Société Anonyme de Marcinelle et Cowllet, Belgium.   Société de l'Home, St. Julien.

Görlitzer Engine Works.   C. Nolet, Ghent.

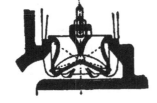

Fig 758.

Fig. 760

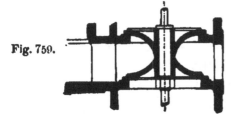

Fig. 759.

Fig. 761.

Pusey, Jones & Co., New York.   Görlitzer Engine Works.

* These sections are from Uhland's "Corliss Valve Engines."

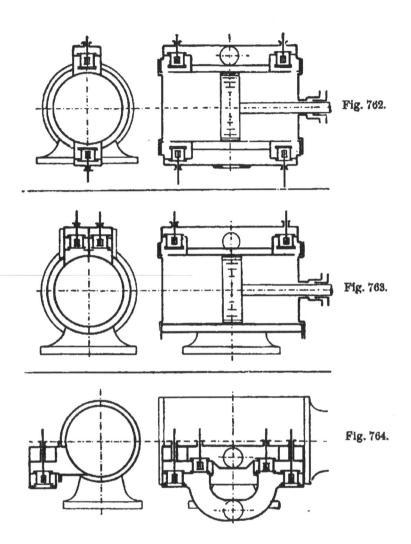

Fig. 762.

Fig. 763.

Fig. 764.

Fig. 762.—The two admission valves above, two exhaust valves below. A very common arrangement—for example, Görlitz, Sulzer, &c.

Fig. 763.—The two admission valves and the two exhaust valves on the top of the cylinder.

Fig. 764.—The case for the valves bolted on to the side of the cylinder.

Valve Gear, with Valves driven by an Eccentric
(Figs. 765, 766).

Fig. 765.

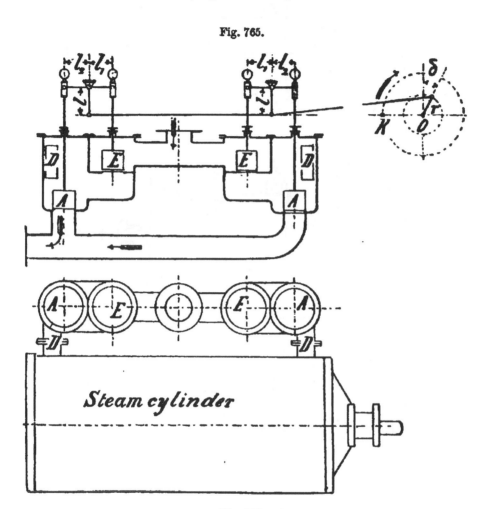

Fig. 766.

The above arrangement (figs. 765, 766) were much used in winding engines—

E E, the steam valves

D D, the steam ports.

The valve motion is obtained by means of an eccentric and bell crank levers. The valve spindles are fitted with weights on their upper ends, to ensure prompt closing. As this valve gear works exactly in the same manner as an ordinary slide valve gear, a link may be introduced, and the whole used as a reversing gear or for a variable cut-off.

In fig. 765,

h = the stroke of the valves.

v = the lead.

s = the amount of play between the end of the lever and the slot in the valve spindle when the eccentric is in the mean position.

d_1 = the diameter of the admission valve.

h_1 = stroke of admission valve.

l_1 = length of lever for admission valve.

l = length of lever, see fig. 765.

d_2 = diameter of the exhaust valve.

h_2 = stroke of exhaust valve.

l_2 = length of lever for exhaust valve.

then we have—

$$\frac{l_2}{l_1} = \frac{h_2}{h_1} \; ; \; r = \frac{l}{l_1}(h+s) \; ; \; r \sin. \delta = \frac{l}{l_1}(s+v) \; ; \; \sin. \delta = \frac{l}{l_1}\frac{(s+v)}{r}.$$

Valve Gear with Cam Motion.

Fig 767.

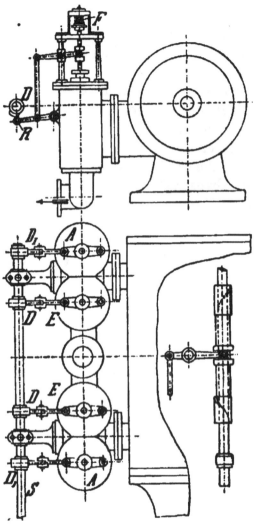

Fig. 768.

In figs. 767, 768,

A A, are the exhaust valves.

E E, the admission valves.

$D_1 D_1$, the cams for the exhaust valves.

D D, the cams for the admission valves.

S, the cam spindle.

R, the rollers at end of valve levers and resting on the cams.

F, the springs for closing the valves.

Construction of the Cams (Figs. 769—773).

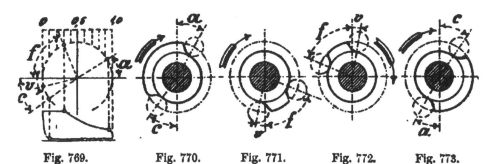

| Fig. 769. | Fig. 770. | Fig. 771. | Fig. 772. | Fig. 773. |

Fig. 769.—Diagram.
Fig. 770.—Exhaust at left hand.
Fig. 771.—Admission at left hand.

Fig. 772.—Admission at right hand.
Fig. 773.—Exhaust at right hand.

In the diagram fig. 769, the cut-off is taken at ·3 then let

v = the angle for lead. f = the angle for cut-off.
a = the angle for exhaust. c = the angle for compression.

The cam spindle is shown in section, and the circle giving the position of rest and the half circle of the roller are drawn in. If the cut-off is to be varied either by hand or by the governor, both admission cams are made of screw form, and the cam spindle is moved lengthways to alter the cut-off.

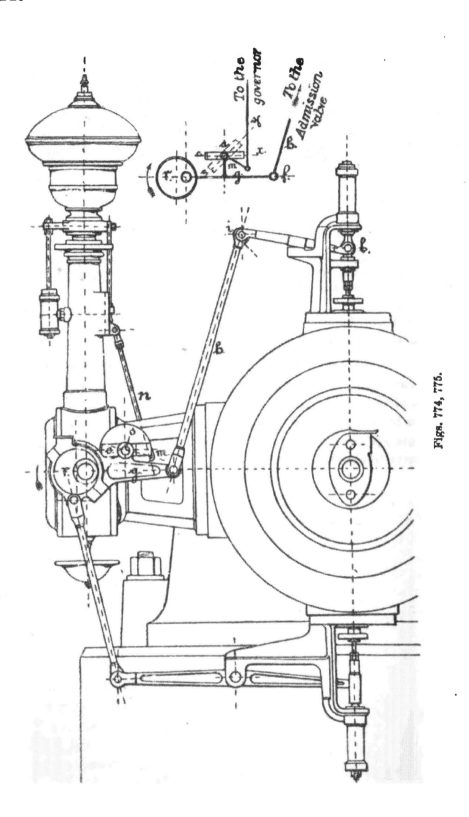

Figs. 774, 775.

Mushroom Valve Gear with Positive Motion to the Valves.

Hartung's Patent, made by the Harzer Co., Nordhausen, and the Buckau engine works, Magdeburg. Fig. 775.

The arrangement of this valve gear is as follows : an eccentric, *r*, with an elongated ring, *g*, is keyed on the valve shaft ; on the elongation of the eccentric ring is a pin, *s*, with a block which slides in the link, *c*, this link is moved as shown in dotted lines, figs. 774, 775, by means of the rod, *n*, in connection with the governor ; at the end of *g* is a pin, *f*, to which the rod, *b*, is attached ; the upper end of the rod, *b*, is attached to the lever, *i*, *h*, this lever being connected to the admission valve spindle, but resting only on the fulcrum bracket. In fig. 775, the engine is supposed to be at the dead point, and the valve open only to the extent of the lead, and the governor is at its lowest position corresponding to the latest cut-off, ·9 of the stroke ; the pin, *s*, is so arranged that the link may be moved without affecting the lead.

By the motion of the valve shaft when the engine is running, the eccentric moves in the direction of the arrow, and causes the end with the pin, *f*, to move up and down, thus opening and closing the valve by means of the rod, *b*, and lever, *i*, *h*. By this motion the pin, *s*, slides in the link, *c*, and if the governor rises, the link is turned from right to left, by means of the rod, *n*, and then the pin, *s*, is no longer guided in a horizontal but in an inclined direction, causing the path of the point, *f*, to be altered, and not to extend so far below the horizontal line during the opening of the valve ; this difference causes the valve to close sooner, and to give an earlier cut-off; when the governor is at its highest position, the point, *f*, does not go below the horizontal line, and consequently there is no admission of steam.

Widnmann's Patent Mushroom Valve Gear with Positive Motion to the Valves.

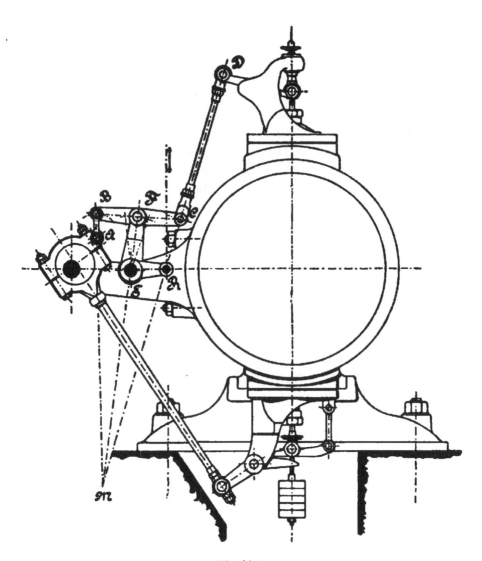

Fig. 776.

Mushroom Valve Gear with Positive Motion to Valves.

H. Widnmann's Patent, Munich.   Fig. 776.

The eccentric for giving motion to the valves in this gear is keyed on a side shaft, and has a long rod connected to a lever turning on a fixed point for working the exhaust valve; this renders any motion taken from the eccentric ring to be definite; a short pair of links, A B, fig. 776, are jointed to the upper side of the eccentric ring, and to the lever, B F C, and the rod, C D, gives motion to the admission valve through a rod and lever.   The lever arm, E F, is keyed on a spindle, and this spindle is turned by the governor.   By turning the spindle, E, a varying inclination is given to the arm, E F, and therefore also to the links, A B, and by this means the period during which the valve is open is altered, and an earlier or later cut-off obtained.

In order that the lead may be as nearly constant for all variations in the cut-off; the centre of the spindle, E, should be the centre of a circle, which approximately represents the path of the point, F.

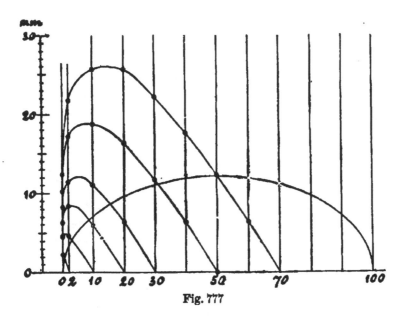

Fig. 777

O. Recke's Patent Valve Gear.

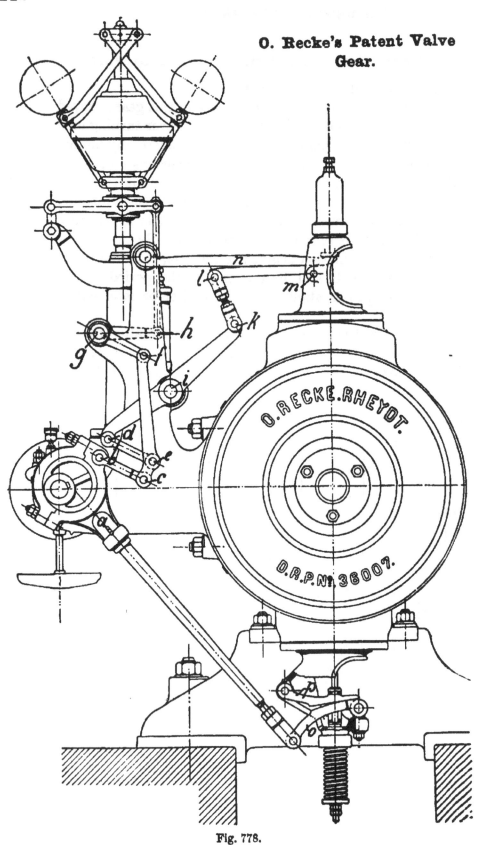

Fig. 778.

Mushroom Valve Gear with Positive Motion to the Valves.

The eccentric, *a*, fig. 778, O. Recke's Patent, moves the exhaust valve by means of the roller levers, *o* and *p*, and the admission valve through the pin, *b*.

The governor lever, *g h*, turns on the pin, *g*, which also carries the lever, *g f*, the point *f* forms a turning point for the lever, *f e c*, connected to eccentric ring at *b*, by the rod *b c*, and also connected by *d e* to the lever *d i k*; at *k* this lever is connected with the upper lever, *l m n*, which moves the admission valve; *g f*, *d e*, and *b c*, are of equal length, and in the opening position of the valve parallel to one another.

This valve gear gives a very nearly constant lead, and a sufficient opening of the valves for the normal cut-off without excessive opening for the early cut-off, and very little back pressure on the governor.

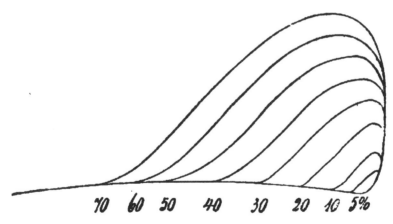

Fig 779.—Valve diagram, drawn by a model of the valve gear.

Kuchenbecker's Valve Gear.

Figs. 780, 781.

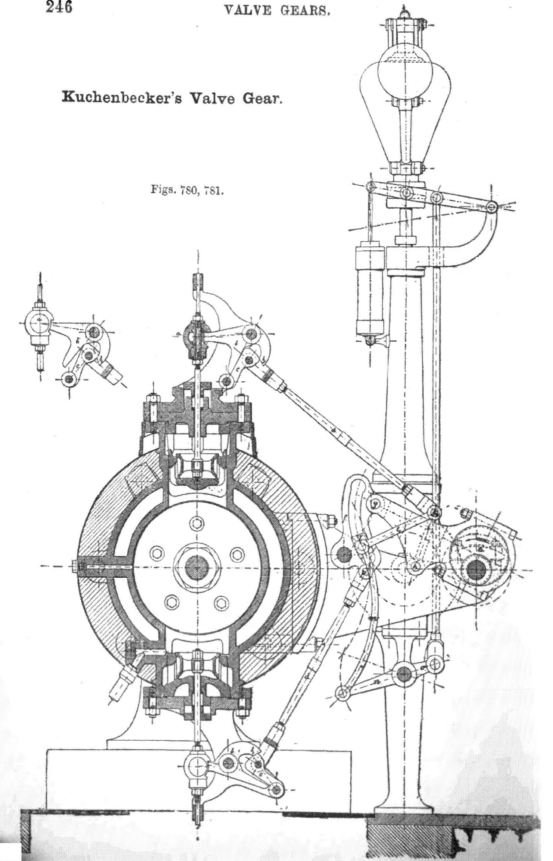

Kuchenbecker's Patent Mushroom Valve Gear with Positive Motion to the Valves.

The shaft, e, fig. 780, is turned in the direction of the arrow by gearing from the crank shaft, and carries an eccentric which gives a vibrating motion to the link, f. The sliding block, l, in this link, by means of the rods, i_1, i, and d, gives the necessary motion to the admission valve.

The double lever, b, b_1, communicates the motion by means of the arm, c, which is connected to the rod, d; the arm, c, acting against b, opens the valve, and acting against b_1, closes the valve; fig. 781 shows the position of the levers with the valve open, fig. 782 with the valve closed. The rod, d, is connected to the link at p, for opening and closing the exhaust valve.

The governor alters the position of the block in the link, f, by means of the lever, n o, and the rod, m, and varies the cut-off.

The movement of the valves is very quick, and is positive, without the aid of dash pots or springs for either opening or closing.

Proell's Patent Mushroom Valve Gear with Positive Motion to the Valves.

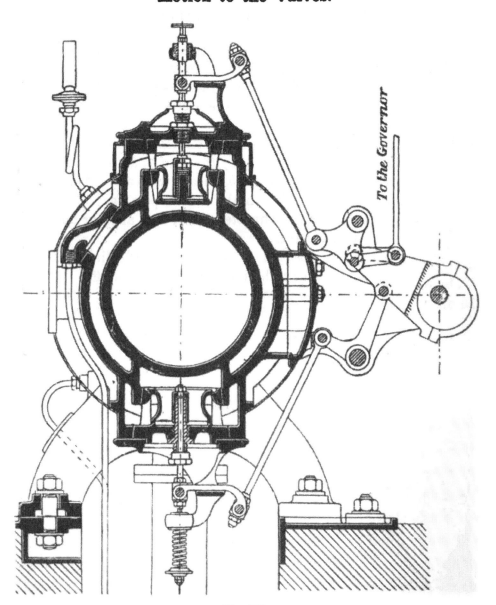

Fig. 782.

This gear consists essentially of valves driven by an eccentric; a point in the eccentric ring moves in a closed curve, and by means of an adjustable lever connected to the governor the cut-off is varied; by this peculiar motion the valves move with varying speed to and from their seatings, and open and close quietly. The exhaust valve is by levers attached to the eccentric ring, as shown in fig. 782.

E. König's Mushroom Valve Gear, with Positive Motion to the Valves.*

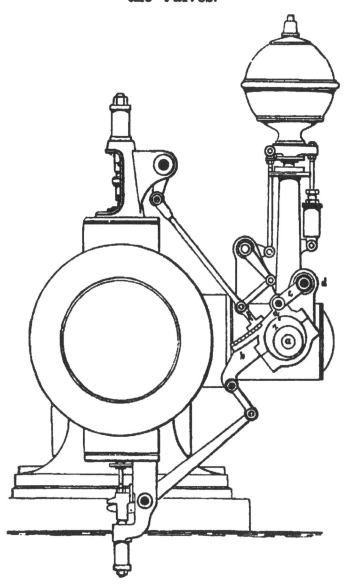

Fig. 788.

The eccentric ring in fig. 783 is made with a projection, b, and is jointed at g to an arm, c, which swings on a fixed point, d; the admission valve is moved by the rod, f, resting against the eccentric ring, b, the position of f is altered by the governor, and varies the cut-off

* Dingler's " Polytechnic Journal," No. 3, 1888.

Gamerith's Patent Valve Gear, with Trip Arrangement by Stark & Hoffman, of Hirschberg.

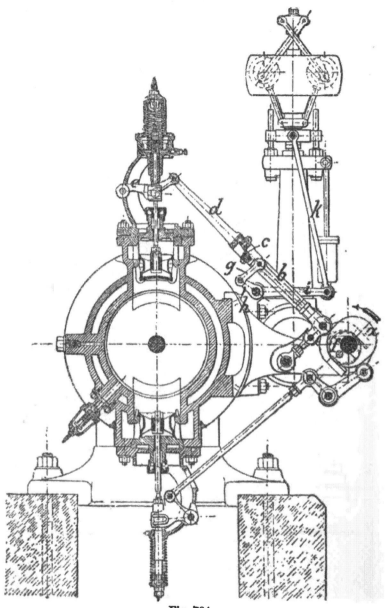

Fig. 784.

The valves in fig. 784 are worked by the cam, *a*, the admission valve is lifted by means of the catch, *c*, this slides away and allows the valve to fall at different positions determined by the governor, which raises the piece on which the catch acts by means of the rods *g*, *i* and *k*, and thus alters the cut-off. The exhaust valve is worked by the same cam, *a*.

Sulzer's Valve Gear, with Trip Arrangement
(Sulzer Bros., Winterthur).

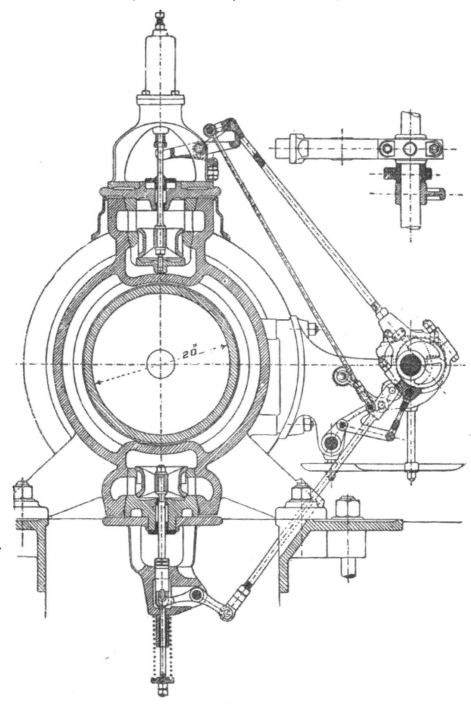

Fig. 785.

Fig. 785 shows the arrangement of valve gear by Sulzer, in which the valves are opened by an eccentric, and provided with trip gear, by which they are allowed to close by means of a spring.

Corliss Valve Gear.

The characteristics of the Corliss valve gear are, 1st, that there are two separate admission valves and two separate exhaust valves; 2ndly, that the admission valves are opened by an eccentric, then

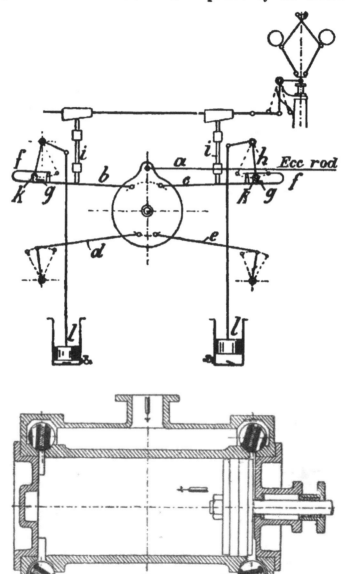

Figs. 786, 787.

released and suddenly closed by either weights, springs, or dash pots; 3rdly, that the valves are cylindrical, and have a partial rotatory movement imparted to them.

The connection between the eccentric and the admission valve is generally in two parts, one being connected with the valve, the other with the wrist plate, which receives its motion from the eccentric rod ; during the opening of the valves the two parts are coupled, but to allow the valve to close the two parts are suddenly uncoupled.

The general action of the Corliss valve gear is shown in diagram in figs. 786, 787. The centre disc, or "wrist plate," receives an oscillating motion from the eccentric rod, a, the two rods, b and c, are formed into springs at f, f. The lever, h, is connected to the valve, the connection between the lever, h, and the rod, c, is by means of a kind of catch or detent arrangement, k, g, the governor acts by the rods, i, i ; when the governor rises, the rods, i, i, are pushed down, and cause the catch to slip, leaving the lever, h, disconnected, and allowing the valve to be closed suddenly by dash pots, l, or by weights. The position of the governor determines the time of release.

Harris' Corliss Valve Gear (Figs. 788, 789).

This is an arrangement very much the same as above, but modified in the details, the rod, a, receives motion from the wrist plate, the short arm is free to turn on the valve spindle, d, at g is a small projection against which the curved arm, f, rests ; the backward and forward motion of the rod, a, causes the f to slide against g, and according to the position of g (determined by the governor) depresses f and

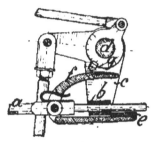

Fig. 788.

releases the catch, e, and thus allows the valve to be closed by the dash pot or weights.

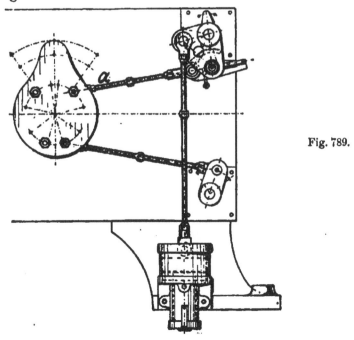

Fig. 789.

Reynold's Corliss Valve Gear (Fig. 790).

The arrangement is the same with respect to the general features as the original Corliss gear, the wrist plate receiving its motion from

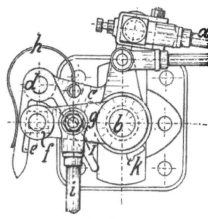

an eccentric. The lever, *c*, fig. 790, is loose on the valve spindle, *b*, and, together with *d*, is moved by the rod, *a*; from the wrist plate on *d* is a piece of steel, *e*, and on *e* the block *f* rests, this block is on lever *g*, the latter being fast on the valve spindle, *b*. The spring, *h*, serves to keep the forked lever, *d*, pressed up against *f*. Again, on the valve spindle, *b*, is the governor lever with the projection, I, against which by the motion the bell crank lever presses and thus

Fig. 790.

releases the catch; if the governor ceases to act by the strap breaking, then the projection, *k*, releases the valve, and no more steam can enter the cylinder; the usual dash pot, or weight, for closing the valve is attached by the rod, *i*.

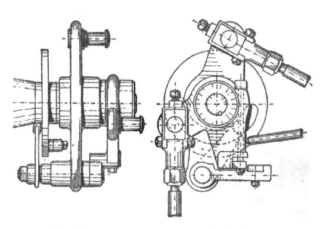

Fig. 791.   Fig. 792.

Figs. 791, 792 show an arrangement for obtaining the release of the valve without the use of springs. The releasing lever has a pin working in a groove on a disc adjustable by the governor.

Wheelock Corliss Valve Gear (Figs. 793, 794).

In this arrangement all the four ports are brought to the ends of the cylinder, the exhaust valves are driven direct from the wrist

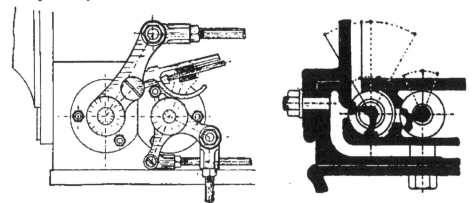

Fig. 793.   Fig. 794.

plate and are hollow, fig. 794. The admission valves act as expansion valves.

Corliss Valve Gear, by J. R. Frikart, Paris * (Fig. 795).

The exhaust valves are worked by the eccentric and levers as in fig. 795, and a five-armed lever takes the place of the wrist plate

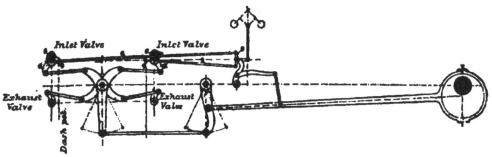

Fig. 795.

in other types of Corliss gear. The upper arms of this lever work on the double arms, A, A, these are free to turn on the bush which forms the bearing of the valve spindle, C, fig. 796. On C the tappet lever, D, D, is firmly fixed ; this lever, D, D, has on one side a plate of hardened steel, and on the other a joint and rod connected to the dash pot piston for closing the valve.

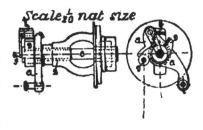

Fig. 796.

* " Zeitschrift der Verein deutsch. Ingenieur," 1890, page 917.

Another tappet, E, is fixed to the short arm, F, fig. 796, which is free to turn on a pin fixed to A; a small rod connects the angle

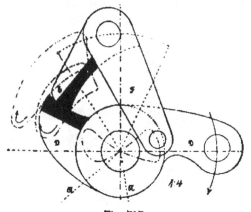

Fig. 797.

lever, H, with the eccentric rod, and at the upper end of H a small three-armed lever, I, is jointed; the rods, G, G, convey the motion from H to the arm F, which carries the tappet, E; by this motion E comes in contact with D, and opens the valve; the duration of the opening lasts until the inner edge of E escapes from the tappet D, then the valve closes. The governor is connected to the three-armed lever, I, and it will be seen from fig. 797 that the release will take place earlier or later according to the position of the lever, F, and with it the tappet, E, the alteration of position for the variation of cut-off being effected by the governor. The curves in chain dotted lines show the movement for the earliest and latest cut-off.

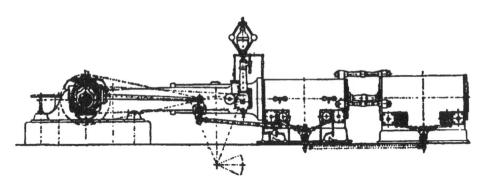

Fig. 798. —Corliss Engine by Thomas Powell, Rouen.*

Figures 798, 799, and 800, give examples of the general arrangement of Corliss gear by American and French engineers. With Corliss valves the length of the ports is very nearly equal to the diameter of the cylinder. The area of the ports is about ·07 of the piston area for the admission, and ·10 for the exhaust. The diameter of the valves is from ·25 to ·32 of the cylinder diameter.

---

* "Zeitschrift der Verein deutsch. Ingenieur," 1890, page 924.

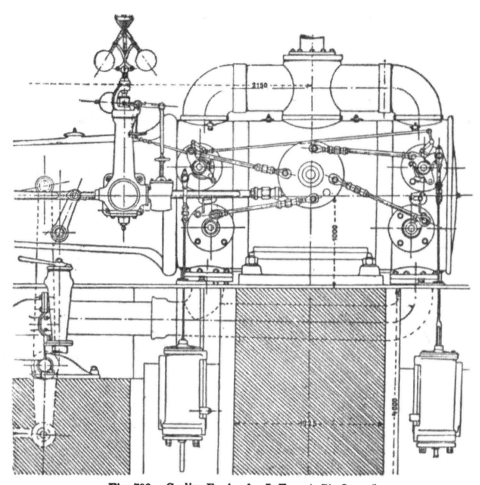

Fig. 799.—Corliss Engine by J. Farcot, St. Ouen.*

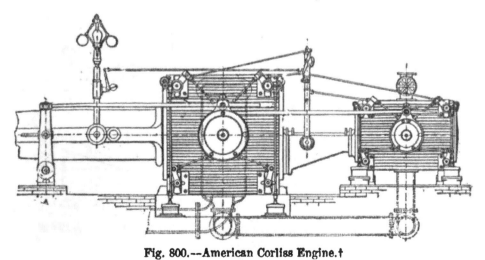

Fig. 800.--American Corliss Engine.†

* "Zeitschrift der Verein deutsch. Ingenieur," 1890, page 924.
† *Engineering*, 1891, page 750.

The valve spindles either pass through as in fig. 801, or are merely

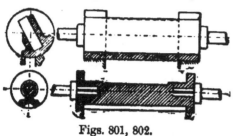

gudgeons as in fig. 802 ; the ends of the rods are provided with adjustments to take up wear.

The dash pots, figs. 803, 804, have working cylinders about ·6 to ·5 of the diameter of the engine cylinder, and the dash pot proper about ·4 to ·3 of the cylinder

Figs. 801, 802.

diameter. Small adjustable valves are provided at a and b, to regulate the action of both pistons ; the arrangement shown in fig. 804 has

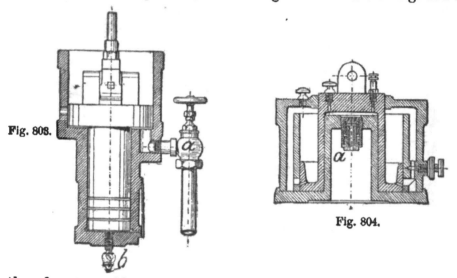

Fig. 803.

Fig. 804.

the advantage of being noiseless in action, but is not so cheap to make as that shown in fig. 803.

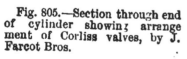

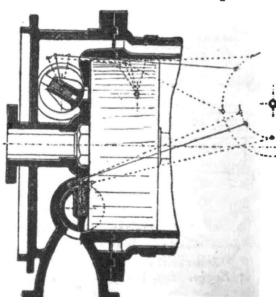

Fig. 805.—Section through end of cylinder showing arrangement of Corliss valves, by J. Farcot Bros.

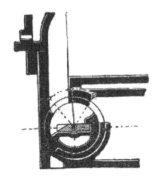

Fig. 806.—Section of Corliss valve, by
Douglas & Grant, Kirkcaldy.

Fig. 807.—Section of Corliss valve,
by the Sangerhauser Engine Works.

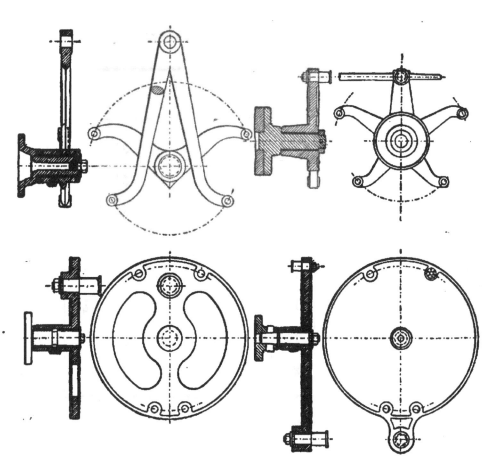

Figs. 808—815.—Various designs for wrist-plates and multiple-armed levers for Corliss
gear.

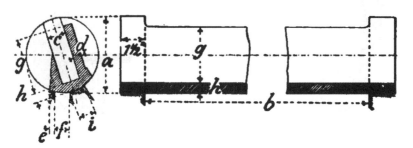

Figs. 816, 817.—Sections of Corliss Valves.

TABLE 69.—**Dimensions of Corliss Valves** (Figs. 816, 817).

H	D	a	b	c	d	e		g	h	i
48	16	$4\frac{1}{2}$	$14\frac{1}{2}$	$1\frac{1}{8}$	$\frac{5}{8}$	$\frac{5}{16}$	$\frac{7}{8}$	$3\frac{1}{4}$	$\frac{3}{4}$	1
48	18	5	$16\frac{1}{2}$	$1\frac{1}{4}$	$\frac{5}{8}$	$\frac{3}{8}$	$\frac{15}{16}$	$3\frac{7}{8}$	$\frac{3}{4}$	$1\frac{1}{8}$
48	20	$5\frac{1}{2}$	$18\frac{1}{2}$	$1\frac{3}{8}$	$\frac{3}{4}$	$\frac{7}{16}$	$1\frac{1}{16}$	$4\frac{1}{4}$	$\frac{3}{4}$	$1\frac{1}{4}$
54	22	6	21	$1\frac{1}{2}$	$\frac{3}{4}$	$\frac{7}{16}$	$1\frac{1}{8}$	$4\frac{5}{8}$	$\frac{7}{8}$	$1\frac{3}{8}$
54	24	$6\frac{1}{2}$	23	$1\frac{5}{8}$	$\frac{7}{8}$	$\frac{1}{2}$	$1\frac{3}{16}$	5	$\frac{7}{8}$	$1\frac{1}{2}$
54	26	7	25	$1\frac{3}{4}$	$\frac{7}{8}$	$\frac{9}{16}$	$1\frac{3}{8}$	$5\frac{3}{8}$	$\frac{7}{8}$	$1\frac{5}{8}$
60	28	$7\frac{1}{2}$	27	$1\frac{7}{8}$	1	$\frac{5}{8}$	$1\frac{1}{2}$	$5\frac{3}{4}$	1	$1\frac{3}{4}$
60	30	$8\frac{1}{2}$	29	2	1	$\frac{3}{4}$	$1\frac{15}{16}$	$6\frac{3}{8}$	1	$1\frac{7}{8}$

All Dimensions are given in Inches.

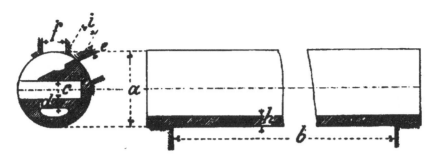

Figs. 818, 819.—Section of Corliss Valve.

TABLE 70.—**Dimensions of Corliss Valves** (Figs. 818, 819).

H	D	a	b	c	d	e	f	h	i
48	16	$4\frac{1}{2}$	$14\frac{1}{2}$	$1\frac{1}{8}$	$\frac{5}{8}$	$\frac{1}{8}$	$1\frac{7}{16}$	$\frac{3}{4}$	1
48	18	5	$16\frac{1}{2}$	$1\frac{1}{4}$	$\frac{5}{8}$	$\frac{3}{16}$	$1\frac{9}{16}$	$\frac{3}{4}$	$1\frac{1}{8}$
48	20	$5\frac{1}{2}$	$18\frac{1}{2}$	$1\frac{3}{8}$	$\frac{3}{4}$	$\frac{3}{16}$	$1\frac{3}{4}$	$\frac{3}{4}$	$1\frac{1}{4}$
54	22	6	21	$1\frac{1}{2}$	$\frac{3}{4}$	$\frac{3}{16}$	$1\frac{7}{8}$	$\frac{7}{8}$	$1\frac{3}{8}$
54	24	$6\frac{1}{2}$	23	$1\frac{5}{8}$	$\frac{7}{8}$	$\frac{1}{4}$	2	$\frac{7}{8}$	$1\frac{1}{2}$
54	26	7	25	$1\frac{3}{4}$	$\frac{7}{8}$	$\frac{1}{4}$	$2\frac{1}{8}$	$\frac{7}{8}$	$1\frac{5}{8}$
60	28	$7\frac{1}{2}$	27	$1\frac{7}{8}$	1	$\frac{1}{4}$	$2\frac{5}{16}$	1	$1\frac{3}{4}$
60	30	$8\frac{1}{2}$	29	2	1	$\frac{5}{16}$	$2\frac{1}{2}$	1	$1\frac{7}{8}$

All Dimensions are given in Inches.

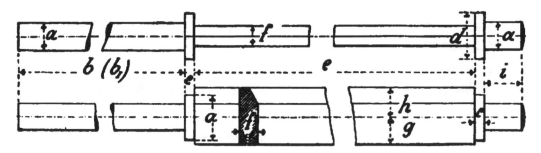

Figs. 820, 821.—Corliss Valve Spindles.

TABLE 71.—Dimensions of Corliss Valve Spindles
(Figs. 820, 821).

H	D	a	b	b_1	c	d	e	f	g	h	i
48	16	$1\frac{1}{2}$	$15\frac{7}{8}$	$11\frac{3}{8}$	$\frac{1}{2}$	$2\frac{5}{8}$	$17\frac{1}{2}$	$1\frac{1}{8}$	$1\frac{3}{8}$	$1\frac{7}{8}$	$2\frac{1}{4}$
48	18	$1\frac{5}{8}$	$17\frac{1}{8}$	$12\frac{1}{8}$	$\frac{5}{8}$	$2\frac{3}{4}$	$19\frac{1}{2}$	$1\frac{1}{4}$	$1\frac{5}{8}$	$2\frac{1}{4}$	$2\frac{1}{2}$
48	20	$1\frac{3}{4}$	$18\frac{3}{4}$	$13\frac{1}{4}$	$\frac{5}{8}$	$2\frac{7}{8}$	$21\frac{1}{2}$	$1\frac{3}{8}$	$1\frac{7}{8}$	$2\frac{3}{8}$	$2\frac{3}{4}$
54	22	$1\frac{7}{8}$	$19\frac{3}{4}$	14	$\frac{3}{4}$	3	24	$1\frac{1}{2}$	2	$2\frac{5}{8}$	3
54	24	2	$20\frac{3}{4}$	$14\frac{3}{4}$	$\frac{3}{4}$	$3\frac{1}{4}$	26	$1\frac{5}{8}$	$2\frac{1}{4}$	$2\frac{3}{4}$	$3\frac{1}{4}$
54	26	$2\frac{1}{8}$	$21\frac{3}{4}$	$15\frac{1}{2}$	$\frac{7}{8}$	$3\frac{1}{2}$	28	$1\frac{3}{4}$	$2\frac{1}{2}$	$2\frac{7}{8}$	$3\frac{1}{2}$
60	28	$2\frac{1}{4}$	$22\frac{3}{4}$	$16\frac{1}{4}$	$\frac{7}{8}$	$3\frac{5}{8}$	30	$1\frac{7}{8}$	$2\frac{5}{8}$	$3\frac{1}{8}$	$3\frac{7}{8}$
60	30	$2\frac{3}{8}$	24	17	1	$3\frac{3}{4}$	32	2	$3\frac{1}{8}$	$3\frac{1}{4}$	$4\frac{1}{4}$

All Dimensions are given in Inches.

b for admission valves.
b_1 for exhaust valves.

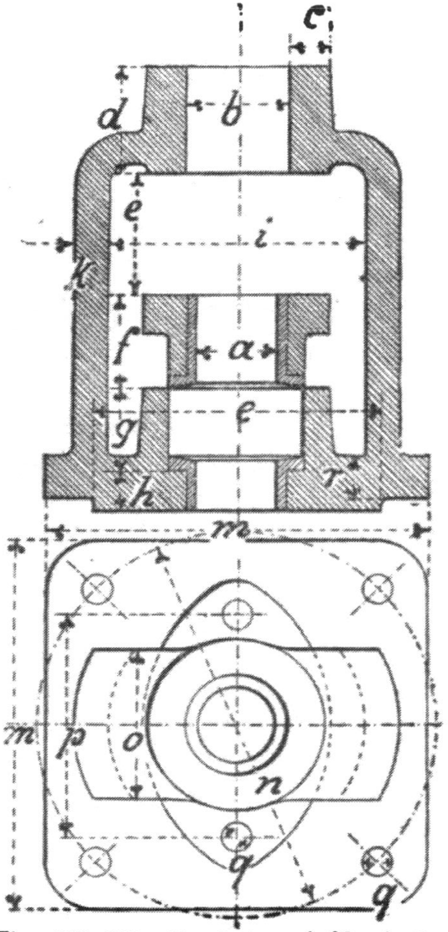

Figs. 822, 823.—Brackets and Glands for Corliss Valve Spindles.

Table 72.—Dimensions of Glands and Brackets for Corliss Valve Spindles.

H	D	a	b	c	d	e	f	g	h	i	k	l	m	n	o	p	q	r
48	16	$1\frac{1}{2}$	$1\frac{7}{8}$	$\frac{13}{16}$	$1\frac{7}{8}$	$3\frac{1}{2}$	$1\frac{1}{2}$	$1\frac{1}{2}$	$\frac{3}{4}$	$5\frac{1}{2}$	$\frac{9}{16}$	$4\frac{7}{8}$	7	$7\frac{7}{8}$	$2\frac{7}{8}$	$4\frac{1}{2}$	$\frac{5}{8}$	$\frac{3}{4}$
48	18	$1\frac{5}{8}$	2	$\frac{7}{8}$	2	$3\frac{1}{2}$	$1\frac{3}{4}$	$1\frac{5}{8}$	$\frac{3}{4}$	6	$\frac{5}{8}$	$5\frac{3}{8}$	$7\frac{1}{2}$	$7\frac{5}{8}$	3	$5\frac{1}{4}$	$\frac{5}{8}$	$\frac{13}{16}$
48	20	$1\frac{3}{4}$	$2\frac{1}{4}$	$\frac{15}{16}$	$2\frac{1}{4}$	$3\frac{5}{8}$	$1\frac{3}{4}$	$1\frac{7}{8}$	$\frac{7}{8}$	$6\frac{1}{4}$	$\frac{11}{16}$	$5\frac{7}{8}$	8	$8\frac{1}{4}$	$3\frac{1}{4}$	$5\frac{3}{8}$	$\frac{3}{4}$	$\frac{15}{16}$
54	22	$1\frac{7}{8}$	$2\frac{3}{8}$	1	$2\frac{1}{8}$	$3\frac{5}{8}$	2	2	1	$6\frac{3}{4}$	$\frac{3}{4}$	$6\frac{3}{8}$	$8\frac{1}{2}$	$8\frac{7}{8}$	$3\frac{1}{2}$	$5\frac{1}{2}$	$\frac{3}{4}$	1
54	24	2	$2\frac{5}{8}$	$1\frac{1}{16}$	$2\frac{3}{8}$	$3\frac{3}{8}$	$2\frac{1}{4}$	$2\frac{1}{8}$	1	7	$\frac{13}{16}$	$6\frac{7}{8}$	$9\frac{1}{4}$	$9\frac{1}{8}$	$3\frac{3}{4}$	$5\frac{3}{4}$	$\frac{3}{4}$	$1\frac{1}{8}$
54	26	$2\frac{1}{8}$	$2\frac{3}{4}$	$1\frac{1}{8}$	$2\frac{7}{8}$	$3\frac{3}{4}$	$2\frac{3}{8}$	$2\frac{1}{4}$	$1\frac{1}{8}$	$7\frac{1}{4}$	$\frac{7}{8}$	$7\frac{1}{8}$	10	$10\frac{1}{4}$	4	6	$\frac{7}{8}$	$1\frac{1}{8}$
60	28	$2\frac{1}{4}$	3	$1\frac{3}{16}$	$2\frac{7}{8}$	$3\frac{3}{4}$	$2\frac{3}{8}$	$2\frac{3}{8}$	$1\frac{1}{4}$	$7\frac{1}{2}$	$\frac{15}{16}$	$7\frac{7}{8}$	$10\frac{5}{8}$	11	$4\frac{1}{4}$	$6\frac{1}{4}$	$\frac{7}{8}$	$1\frac{1}{4}$
60	30	$2\frac{3}{8}$	$3\frac{1}{8}$	$1\frac{1}{4}$	$3\frac{1}{4}$	$3\frac{3}{4}$	$2\frac{1}{4}$	$2\frac{1}{2}$	$1\frac{1}{4}$	$7\frac{3}{4}$	1	$8\frac{7}{8}$	$11\frac{1}{4}$	$11\frac{3}{4}$	$4\frac{1}{2}$	$6\frac{1}{2}$	$\frac{7}{8}$	$1\frac{5}{16}$

All Dimensions are given in Inches.

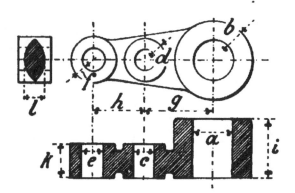

Figs. 824—826.—Lever Arms for Corliss Valves.

TABLE 73.—Dimensions of Lever Arms for Corliss Valves (Figs. 824—826).

H	D	a	b	c	d	e	f	g	h	i	k	l
48	16	$1\frac{1}{2}$	$\frac{3}{4}$	$\frac{11}{16}$	$\frac{3}{8}$	$\frac{15}{16}$	$\frac{7}{16}$	$2\frac{3}{4}$	2	$2\frac{1}{4}$	$1\frac{1}{4}$	$\frac{13}{16}$
48	18	$1\frac{5}{8}$	$\frac{3}{4}$	$\frac{13}{16}$	$\frac{7}{16}$	1	$\frac{1}{2}$	3	$2\frac{1}{8}$	$2\frac{1}{2}$	$1\frac{3}{8}$	$\frac{7}{8}$
48	20	$1\frac{3}{4}$	$\frac{13}{16}$	$\frac{7}{8}$	$\frac{1}{2}$	$1\frac{1}{16}$	$\frac{9}{16}$	$3\frac{1}{8}$	$2\frac{3}{8}$	$2\frac{3}{4}$	$1\frac{1}{2}$	$\frac{15}{16}$
54	22	$1\frac{7}{8}$	$\frac{7}{8}$	$\frac{7}{8}$	$\frac{1}{2}$	$1\frac{1}{8}$	$\frac{9}{16}$	$3\frac{3}{8}$	$2\frac{1}{2}$	$2\frac{7}{8}$	$1\frac{5}{8}$	1
54	24	2	$\frac{15}{16}$	$\frac{15}{16}$	$\frac{9}{16}$	$1\frac{3}{16}$	$\frac{5}{8}$	$3\frac{1}{2}$	$2\frac{5}{8}$	3	$1\frac{3}{4}$	$1\frac{1}{16}$
54	26	$2\frac{1}{8}$	1	1	$\frac{9}{16}$	$1\frac{1}{4}$	$\frac{5}{8}$	$3\frac{3}{4}$	$2\frac{3}{4}$	$3\frac{1}{8}$	$1\frac{3}{4}$	$1\frac{1}{8}$
60	28	$2\frac{1}{4}$	$1\frac{1}{16}$	$1\frac{1}{16}$	$\frac{5}{8}$	$1\frac{5}{16}$	$\frac{11}{16}$	4	3	$3\frac{1}{4}$	$1\frac{7}{8}$	$1\frac{3}{16}$
60	30	$2\frac{3}{8}$	$1\frac{1}{8}$	$1\frac{1}{8}$	$\frac{5}{8}$	$1\frac{3}{8}$	$\frac{11}{16}$	$4\frac{1}{8}$	$3\frac{1}{8}$	$3\frac{1}{2}$	2	$1\frac{1}{4}$

All Dimensions are given in Inches.

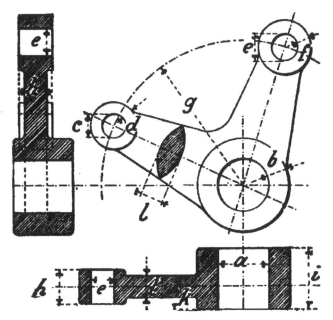

Figs. 827—829.—Levers for Corliss Valves.

TABLE 74.—Dimensions of Levers for Corliss Valves
(Figs. 827—829).

H	D	a	b	c	d	e	f	g	h	i	k	l
48	16	$1\frac{7}{8}$	$\frac{13}{16}$	$\frac{13}{16}$	$\frac{7}{16}$	$\frac{15}{16}$	$\frac{1}{2}$	$5\frac{1}{4}$	$1\frac{1}{8}$	$2\frac{1}{4}$	$\frac{3}{4}$	$\frac{13}{16}$
48	18	2	$\frac{7}{8}$	$\frac{7}{8}$	$\frac{7}{16}$	1	$\frac{1}{2}$	$5\frac{1}{2}$	$1\frac{1}{4}$	$2\frac{1}{2}$	$\frac{7}{8}$	$\frac{7}{8}$
48	20	$2\frac{1}{4}$	$\frac{15}{16}$	$\frac{15}{16}$	$\frac{1}{2}$	$1\frac{1}{8}$	$\frac{9}{16}$	6	$1\frac{3}{8}$	$2\frac{3}{4}$	$\frac{7}{8}$	$\frac{15}{16}$
54	22	$2\frac{3}{8}$	1	1	$\frac{1}{2}$	$1\frac{1}{8}$	$\frac{9}{16}$	$6\frac{1}{2}$	$1\frac{1}{2}$	$2\frac{7}{8}$	1	1
54	24	$2\frac{5}{8}$	$1\frac{1}{16}$	1	$\frac{1}{2}$	$1\frac{1}{4}$	$\frac{5}{8}$	7	$1\frac{5}{8}$	3	$1\frac{1}{8}$	$1\frac{1}{16}$
54	26	$2\frac{3}{4}$	$1\frac{1}{8}$	$1\frac{1}{8}$	$\frac{9}{16}$	$1\frac{5}{16}$	$\frac{5}{8}$	$7\frac{1}{2}$	$1\frac{3}{4}$	$3\frac{1}{8}$	$1\frac{1}{8}$	$1\frac{1}{8}$
60	28	3	$1\frac{3}{16}$	$1\frac{3}{16}$	$\frac{5}{8}$	$1\frac{3}{8}$	$\frac{11}{16}$	8	$1\frac{7}{8}$	$3\frac{1}{4}$	$1\frac{1}{4}$	$1\frac{13}{16}$
60	30	$3\frac{1}{8}$	$1\frac{1}{4}$	$1\frac{1}{4}$	$\frac{5}{8}$	$1\frac{1}{2}$	$\frac{3}{4}$	$8\frac{1}{2}$	2	$3\frac{1}{2}$	$1\frac{3}{8}$	$1\frac{1}{4}$

All Dimensions are given in Inches.

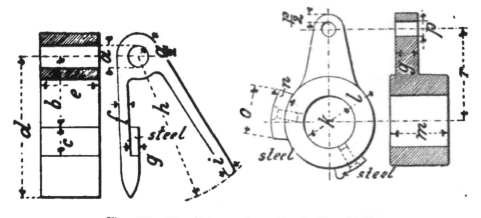

Figs. 830—833.—Trip gear levers for Corliss valves.

TABLE 75.—Dimensions of Trip-gear Levers for Corliss Valves (Figs. 830—833).

H	D	a	b	c	d	e	f	g	h	i	k	l	m	n	p	q	r
48	16	$\frac{7}{8}$	$2\frac{5}{8}$	1	$5\frac{1}{8}$	$2\frac{1}{4}$	$\frac{7}{16}$	$\frac{5}{16}$	$5\frac{5}{8}$	$\frac{5}{16}$	$1\frac{7}{8}$	$1\frac{11}{16}$	$2\frac{1}{4}$	$\frac{5}{8}$	$\frac{5}{8}$	$\frac{7}{8}$	$3\frac{1}{2}$
48	18	$\frac{15}{16}$	$2\frac{7}{8}$	$1\frac{1}{8}$	$5\frac{5}{8}$	$2\frac{1}{2}$	$\frac{7}{16}$	$\frac{5}{16}$	$6\frac{1}{8}$	$\frac{5}{16}$	2	$\frac{7}{8}$	$2\frac{1}{2}$	$\frac{5}{8}$	$\frac{5}{8}$	1	$3\frac{3}{4}$
48	20	1	$3\frac{1}{8}$	$1\frac{1}{4}$	6	$2\frac{3}{4}$	$\frac{1}{2}$	$\frac{3}{8}$	$6\frac{5}{8}$	$\frac{3}{8}$	$2\frac{1}{4}$	$\frac{5}{16}$	$2\frac{3}{4}$	$\frac{11}{16}$	$\frac{3}{4}$	1	4
54	22	$1\frac{1}{16}$	$3\frac{3}{8}$	$1\frac{1}{4}$	$6\frac{1}{2}$	$2\frac{3}{4}$	$\frac{1}{2}$	$\frac{3}{8}$	7	$\frac{3}{8}$	$2\frac{3}{8}$	1	$2\frac{7}{8}$	$\frac{11}{16}$	$\frac{3}{4}$	$1\frac{1}{16}$	$4\frac{1}{4}$
54	24	$1\frac{1}{8}$	$3\frac{5}{8}$	$1\frac{3}{8}$	$6\frac{7}{8}$	3	$\frac{9}{16}$	$\frac{7}{16}$	$7\frac{1}{2}$	$\frac{7}{16}$	$2\frac{5}{8}$	$1\frac{1}{16}$	3	$\frac{3}{4}$	$\frac{3}{4}$	$1\frac{1}{8}$	$4\frac{1}{2}$
54	26	$1\frac{1}{8}$	$3\frac{3}{4}$	$1\frac{3}{8}$	$7\frac{1}{4}$	$3\frac{1}{4}$	$\frac{9}{16}$	$\frac{7}{16}$	8	$\frac{7}{16}$	$2\frac{3}{4}$	$1\frac{1}{8}$	$3\frac{1}{8}$	$\frac{3}{4}$	$\frac{7}{8}$	$1\frac{1}{8}$	$4\frac{3}{4}$
60	28	$1\frac{6}{16}$	4	$1\frac{1}{2}$	$7\frac{3}{4}$	$3\frac{1}{4}$	$\frac{5}{8}$	$\frac{1}{2}$	$8\frac{1}{2}$	$\frac{1}{2}$	3	$1\frac{3}{16}$	$3\frac{1}{4}$	$\frac{7}{8}$	$\frac{7}{8}$	$1\frac{3}{16}$	5
60	30	$1\frac{3}{8}$	$4\frac{1}{4}$	$1\frac{1}{2}$	$8\frac{1}{4}$	$3\frac{1}{2}$	$\frac{5}{8}$	$\frac{1}{2}$	9	$\frac{1}{2}$	$3\frac{1}{4}$	$1\frac{1}{4}$	$3\frac{1}{2}$	$\frac{7}{8}$	$\frac{7}{8}$	$1\frac{1}{4}$	$5\frac{1}{2}$

All Dimensions are given in Inches.

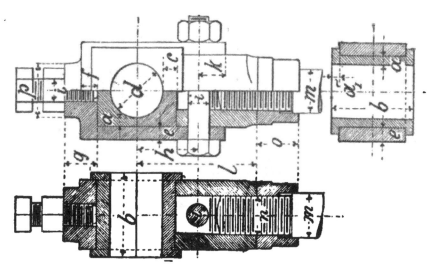

Figs. 834—836.—Valve Rod-End for Corliss Valves.

TABLE 76.—Dimensions of Valve Rod-Ends for Corliss Valves (Figs. 834—836).

d	b	a	a_1	c	e	f	g	h	i	k	l	m	n	o	p
1	$1\frac{1}{2}$	$\frac{1}{8}$	$\frac{3}{16}$	$\frac{3}{16}$	$\frac{1}{4}$	$\frac{5}{16}$	$\frac{5}{8}$	$1\frac{1}{4}$	$\frac{1}{2}$	$\frac{5}{8}$	$2\frac{3}{8}$	$\frac{3}{4}$	$\frac{5}{8}$	$\frac{3}{4}$	$1\frac{1}{4}$
$1\frac{1}{16}$	$1\frac{5}{8}$	$\frac{1}{8}$	$\frac{3}{16}$	$\frac{3}{16}$	$\frac{1}{4}$	$\frac{5}{16}$	$\frac{3}{4}$	$1\frac{3}{8}$	$\frac{1}{2}$	$\frac{5}{8}$	$2\frac{5}{8}$	$\frac{7}{8}$	$\frac{3}{4}$	$\frac{7}{8}$	$1\frac{1}{4}$
$1\frac{3}{16}$	$1\frac{3}{4}$	$\frac{3}{16}$	$\frac{3}{16}$	$\frac{5}{16}$	$\frac{5}{16}$	$\frac{7}{16}$	$\frac{3}{4}$	$1\frac{7}{16}$	$\frac{1}{2}$	$\frac{5}{8}$	$2\frac{3}{4}$	1	$\frac{7}{8}$	1	$1\frac{1}{4}$
$1\frac{1}{4}$	$1\frac{7}{8}$	$\frac{3}{16}$	$\frac{3}{16}$	$\frac{5}{16}$	$\frac{5}{16}$	$\frac{7}{16}$	$\frac{3}{4}$	$1\frac{1}{2}$	$\frac{1}{2}$	$\frac{5}{8}$	$2\frac{7}{8}$	1	$\frac{7}{8}$	1	$1\frac{1}{4}$
$1\frac{3}{8}$	2	$\frac{3}{16}$	$\frac{3}{16}$	$\frac{5}{16}$	$\frac{5}{16}$	$\frac{7}{16}$	$\frac{3}{4}$	$1\frac{5}{8}$	$\frac{5}{8}$	$\frac{3}{4}$	$3\frac{1}{8}$	$1\frac{1}{8}$	1	$1\frac{1}{8}$	$1\frac{1}{2}$
$1\frac{7}{16}$	$2\frac{1}{8}$	$\frac{1}{4}$	$\frac{1}{4}$	$\frac{3}{8}$	$\frac{3}{8}$	$\frac{1}{2}$	$\frac{7}{8}$	$1\frac{3}{4}$	$\frac{5}{8}$	$\frac{3}{4}$	$3\frac{1}{4}$	$1\frac{1}{8}$	1	$1\frac{1}{8}$	$1\frac{1}{2}$
$1\frac{1}{2}$	$2\frac{1}{4}$	$\frac{1}{4}$	$\frac{1}{4}$	$\frac{3}{8}$	$\frac{3}{8}$	$\frac{1}{2}$	$\frac{7}{8}$	$1\frac{3}{4}$	$\frac{5}{8}$	$\frac{3}{4}$	$3\frac{3}{8}$	$1\frac{1}{4}$	$1\frac{1}{8}$	$1\frac{1}{4}$	$1\frac{1}{2}$
$1\frac{5}{8}$	$2\frac{1}{2}$	$\frac{1}{4}$	$\frac{1}{4}$	$\frac{3}{8}$	$\frac{3}{8}$	$\frac{1}{2}$	1	$1\frac{7}{8}$	$\frac{5}{8}$	$\frac{3}{4}$	$3\frac{5}{8}$	$1\frac{1}{4}$	$1\frac{1}{8}$	$1\frac{1}{4}$	$1\frac{1}{2}$

All Dimensions are given in Inches.

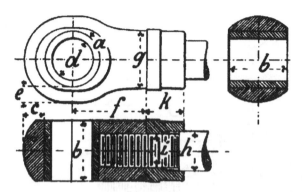

Figs. 837—839.—Valve Rod-End for Corliss Valves.

TABLE 77.—Dimensions of Valve Rod-Ends for Corliss Valves (Figs. 837—839).

d	b	a	c	e	f	g	h	i	k
$\frac{3}{4}$	$1\frac{1}{8}$	$\frac{1}{8}$	$\frac{3}{8}$	$\frac{1}{4}$	$1\frac{3}{8}$	$1\frac{1}{16}$	$\frac{5}{8}$	$\frac{1}{2}$	$\frac{5}{8}$
$\frac{7}{8}$	$1\frac{1}{8}$	$\frac{1}{8}$	$\frac{3}{8}$	$\frac{1}{4}$	$1\frac{1}{2}$	$1\frac{1}{16}$	$\frac{3}{4}$	$\frac{5}{8}$	$\frac{3}{4}$
$\frac{15}{16}$	$1\frac{1}{4}$	$\frac{1}{8}$	$\frac{7}{16}$	$\frac{5}{16}$	$1\frac{3}{8}$	$1\frac{1}{8}$	$\frac{3}{4}$	$\frac{5}{8}$	$\frac{3}{4}$
1	$1\frac{7}{16}$	$\frac{1}{8}$	$\frac{7}{16}$	$\frac{3}{8}$	$1\frac{3}{4}$	$1\frac{3}{8}$	$\frac{7}{8}$	$\frac{3}{4}$	$\frac{7}{8}$
$1\frac{1}{16}$	$1\frac{1}{2}$	$\frac{5}{32}$	$\frac{1}{2}$	$\frac{3}{8}$	$1\frac{7}{8}$	$1\frac{3}{8}$	$\frac{7}{8}$	$\frac{3}{4}$	$\frac{7}{8}$
$1\frac{1}{8}$	$1\frac{1}{2}$	$\frac{3}{16}$	$\frac{1}{2}$	$\frac{3}{8}$	2	$1\frac{3}{8}$	$\frac{7}{8}$	$\frac{3}{4}$	$\frac{7}{8}$
$1\frac{3}{16}$	$1\frac{3}{4}$	$\frac{3}{16}$	$\frac{9}{16}$	$\frac{7}{16}$	$2\frac{1}{4}$	$1\frac{5}{8}$	1	$\frac{7}{8}$	1
$1\frac{1}{4}$	$1\frac{3}{4}$	$\frac{3}{16}$	$\frac{5}{8}$	$\frac{7}{16}$	$2\frac{3}{8}$	$1\frac{5}{8}$	1	$\frac{7}{8}$	1

All Dimensions are given in Inches.

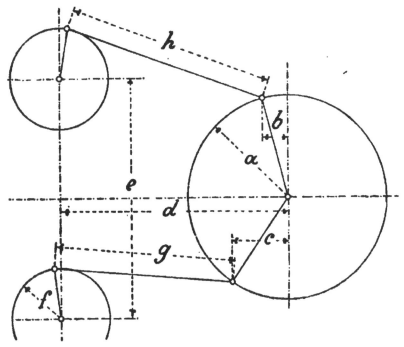

Fig. 840.—Diagram showing Centres of Valve Rods for Corliss Valve Gear.

TABLE 78.—**Dimensions of Centres of Valve Rods for Corliss Valve Gear** (Fig. 840).

H	D	a	b	c	d	e	f	g	h
48	16	10	$3\frac{1}{4}$	$4\frac{1}{4}$	27	$23\frac{1}{2}$	$5\frac{1}{4}$	$23\frac{1}{2}$	$23\frac{3}{4}$
48	18	11	$3\frac{1}{4}$	$4\frac{1}{2}$	$27\frac{1}{4}$	$25\frac{1}{2}$	$5\frac{1}{2}$	$23\frac{1}{2}$	$24\frac{1}{2}$
48	20	12	$3\frac{3}{8}$	$4\frac{3}{4}$	$27\frac{1}{2}$	$28\frac{1}{4}$	6	$21\frac{1}{2}$	25
54	22	13	$3\frac{1}{2}$	5	$30\frac{3}{4}$	$30\frac{1}{2}$	$6\frac{1}{2}$	$28\frac{1}{4}$	27
54	24	14	$3\frac{7}{8}$	$5\frac{3}{8}$	31	$33\frac{1}{2}$	7	$26\frac{1}{4}$	$27\frac{5}{8}$
54	26	15	4	$5\frac{3}{4}$	$31\frac{1}{2}$	$36\frac{1}{4}$	$7\frac{1}{2}$	$26\frac{1}{2}$	28
60	28	16	$4\frac{1}{4}$	$6\frac{1}{4}$	$34\frac{1}{2}$	$38\frac{3}{4}$	8	29	$30\frac{3}{4}$
60	30	17	$4\frac{1}{2}$	$6\frac{1}{2}$	$35\frac{1}{4}$	$41\frac{3}{4}$	$8\frac{1}{2}$	30	$31\frac{3}{4}$

All Dimensions are given in Inches.

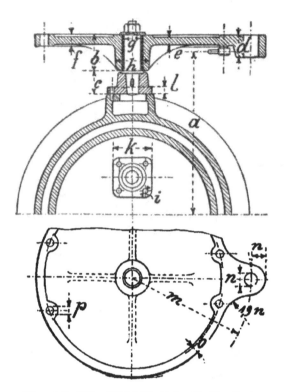

Figs. 841, 842.—Wrist Plate for Corliss Gear.

TABLE 79.—Dimensions of Wrist Plate for Corliss Valve Gear (Figs. 841, 842).

H	D	a	b	c	d	e	f	g	h	i	k	l	m	n	o	p
54	24	$25\frac{1}{2}$	$4\frac{7}{8}$	$4\frac{1}{4}$	$3\frac{3}{8}$	$1\frac{1}{8}$	$1\frac{5}{8}$	$2\frac{1}{2}$	$5\frac{1}{4}$	$\frac{3}{4}$	$6\frac{3}{4}$	1	$19\frac{1}{2}$	$2\frac{3}{8}$	$1\frac{3}{4}$	$1\frac{5}{16}$
54	26	$27\frac{5}{16}$	$5\frac{5}{8}$	$4\frac{1}{2}$	$3\frac{3}{4}$	$1\frac{1}{8}$	$1\frac{3}{4}$	$2\frac{3}{4}$	$5\frac{1}{2}$	$\frac{7}{8}$	7	$1\frac{1}{8}$	$20\frac{1}{2}$	$2\frac{1}{2}$	2	$1\frac{5}{16}$
60	28	$28\frac{7}{8}$	$5\frac{5}{8}$	$4\frac{3}{4}$	4	$1\frac{1}{4}$	$1\frac{7}{8}$	$2\frac{7}{8}$	$5\frac{3}{4}$	$\frac{7}{8}$	7	$1\frac{1}{8}$	$21\frac{1}{2}$	$2\frac{5}{8}$	$2\frac{1}{4}$	$1\frac{3}{8}$
60	30	$30\frac{1}{2}$	6	$4\frac{3}{4}$	$4\frac{1}{4}$	$1\frac{3}{5}$	2	3	6	$\frac{7}{8}$	7	$1\frac{1}{8}$	$23\frac{1}{2}$	$2\frac{3}{4}$	$2\frac{1}{2}$	$1\frac{3}{4}$

All Dimensions are given in Inches.

SECTION V.

CONDENSERS, AIR-PUMPS, AND FEED-PUMPS.

Condensers are divided into two principal classes : (*a*) *Injection Condensers*, where the condensing water acts in direct contact with the steam, and therefore mixes with the water from the condensed

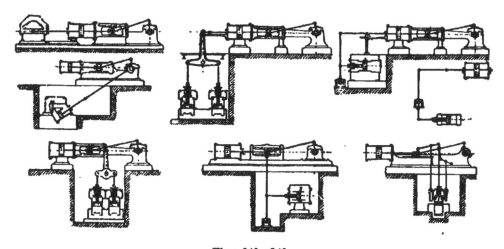

Figs. 843—849.

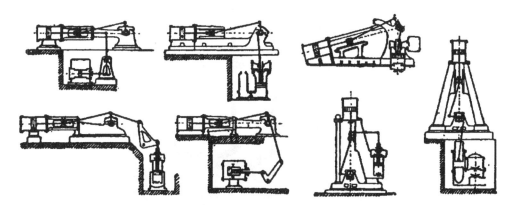

Figs. 850—856.

steam ; (*b*) *Surface Condensers*, where the condensing water acts on one side of a thin wall of metal, the steam being in contact with the other, and thus the water from the condensed steam is kept separate from the condensing water ; these are the two varieties most in use.

A few special methods of condensing steam are occasionally used ; of these some may be said to belong to the class (*a*), others to the class (*b*).

The earliest examples of condensers and air-pumps were vertical and single-acting, and were generally applied to beam engines. When horizontal engines came into fashion, the air-pumps were often vertical, worked by means of a bell-crank lever ; but owing to the number of parts required to drive a vertical air-pump from a horizontal engine, the simpler method of putting the air-pump surrounded by the condenser horizontal, and in the same line as the piston-rod, and driving direct from the tail rod, has come into use to a large extent.

An objection to horizontal air-pumps driven in this way, has often been urged against their use, namely, that with high piston-speed engines, the speed of air-pump bucket, necessarily the same, is too high for efficiency. By good proportions this objection can be removed, and even speeds of 800 feet per minute have been used with good results, especially with plunger air-pumps like that shown in fig. 876, taken from the Allen engine made by Whitworth & Co.

Figs. 843 to 856 show in diagram several methods of driving air-pumps from both horizontal and vertical engines.

(a.) Injector Condensers with Air-Pumps.

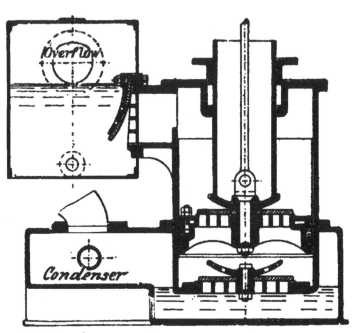

Fig. 857.—Vertical Bucket and Plunger Air-Pump of ordinary type.

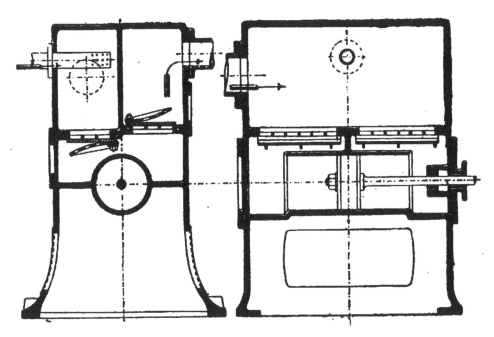

Figs. 858, 859.— Horizontal Air Pump and Condenser with Rectangular Valves.

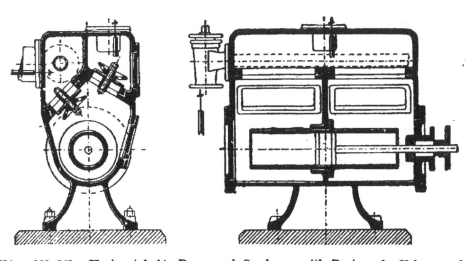

Figs. 860, 861.—Horizontal Air Pump and Condenser with Rectangular Valves, made by the Prince Rudolf Iron Works, Dülmen.

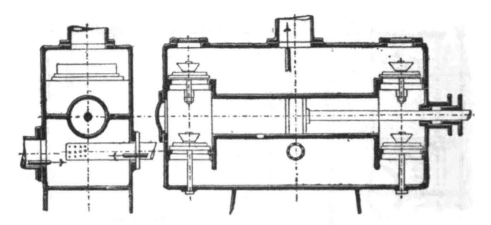

Figs. 862, 863.—Horizontal Air Pump and Condenser, with Rectangular Valves and Injection Nozzle, and Exhaust Inlet below the Barrel.

Horn's patent air pump and condenser, made by G. Brinkman & Co. of Witten, is shown in section, figs. 864—867 and 870—872 ; the air pump piston or bucket is shown at the right hand end of the barrel and is just starting back to the left, at this moment the space between the suction and delivery valves and piston is full of water, as the piston continues to move to the left the water level sinks, (whilst the delivery valve remains closed by the external atmospheric pressure,) and maintains a vacuum in the space between the surface of the water and delivery valve ; as the water level sinks it allows the small air valves, L L, to open, and any air in the condensing chamber passes through into the space left by the movement of the piston, without having to pass through the suction valve below, whilst the water from the condensing chamber passes through the suction valve. The water and air are thus kept separate, and also the air is drawn out of the condensing chamber through the small valves, L L, at the beginning of the piston stroke, and not, as is usually the case with horizontal air pumps, at the end of the stroke through the suction valves, which are necessarily placed low down. This construction should get over the difficulty which often occurs of getting rid of the air quietly, and should secure the prompt closing of the delivery valves.

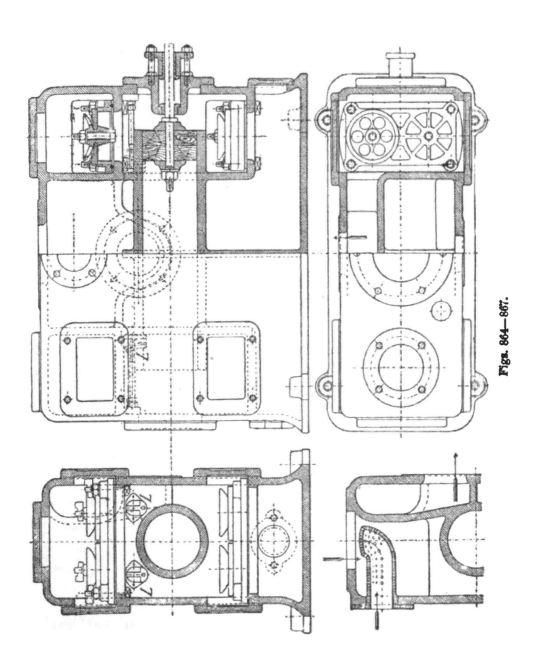

Figs. 864—867.

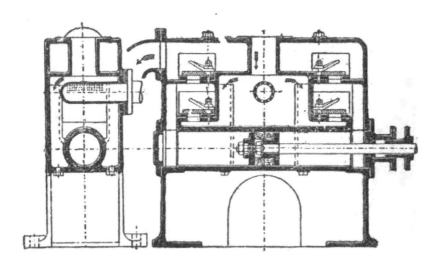

Figs. 868, 869.—Ed. König's Patent Air Pump and Condenser, with Suction and
Delivery Valves above Barrel.

In Ed. König's air pump made by the Chemnitz Steam Engine and
Spinning Machine Works, both the suction and delivery valves are
above the barrel, figs. 868, 869.

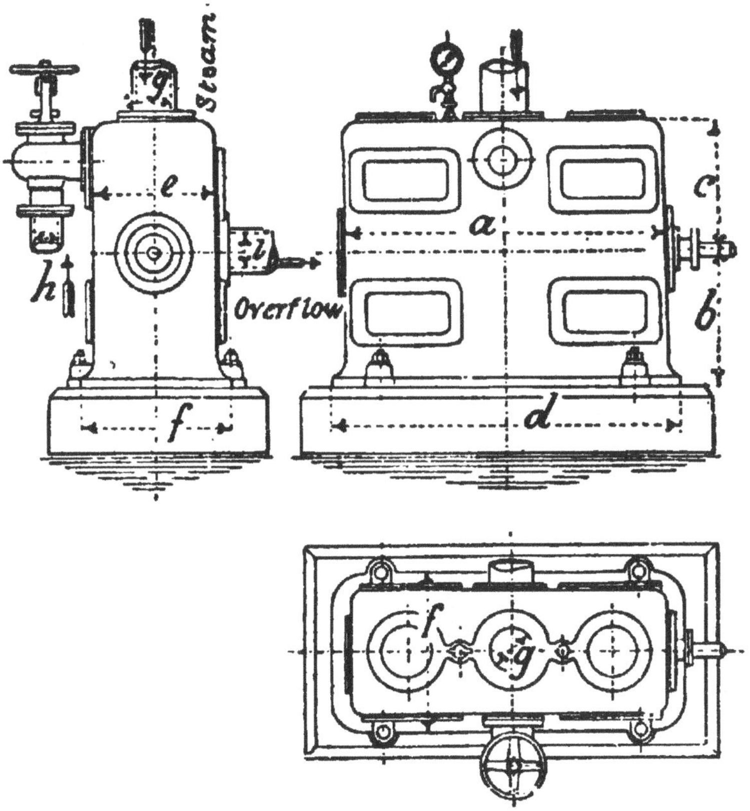

Figs. 870—872.—Outside Views of Horn's Patent Air Pump and Condenser.

TABLE 80.—**Dimensions of Horn's Patent Air Pump and Condenser** (Figs. 864—867 and 870—872).

Engine.		Air Pump and Condenser.								Pipes.		
H	D	H	D	*a*	*b*	*c*	*d*	*e*	*f*	Exhaust. *g*	Injection. *h*	Overflow. *i*
19⅝	11¾	19⅝	5	33½	15¾	15¾	37½	13¾	17⅝	3½	2⅜	4
23⅝	13¾	23⅝	6¼	39½	16½	17	43½	15	19	4⅜	3	4¾
27½	15¾	27½	7	47¼	17⅝	17⅝	51¼	16	20	5	4	5½
31½	17⅝	31½	7¾	49¼	19⅝	19⅝	54¼	19⅝	23⅝	5½	4¾	6¼
35½	19⅝	35½	8¾	65	19⅝	20½	69¼	22½	27½	6¼	5½	7
39½	21⅝	39½	9¾	65	27½	25½	71	27½	35½	7	6¼	8

All Dimensions are given in Inches.

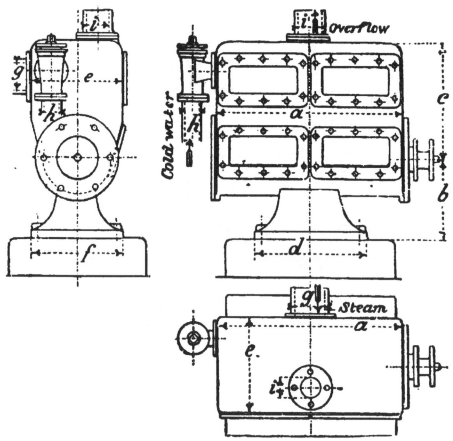

Figs. 873—875.—Outside Views of the Dülmen Air Pump and Condense

TABLE 81.—Dimensions of Air Pump and Condenser
(Figs. 873—875 and 860, 861).

Engine.		Air Pump and Condenser.								Pipes.		
H	D	H	D	a	b	c	d	e	f	Exhaust. g	Injection. h	Overflow. i
$19\frac{5}{8}$	$11\frac{3}{4}$	$19\frac{5}{8}$	$4\frac{3}{8}$	$33\frac{1}{2}$	$13\frac{3}{4}$	$19\frac{5}{8}$	$23\frac{5}{8}$	$16\frac{1}{2}$	$15\frac{3}{4}$	$3\frac{1}{2}$	$2\frac{3}{8}$	$2\frac{3}{4}$
$23\frac{5}{8}$	$13\frac{3}{4}$	$23\frac{5}{8}$	5	$37\frac{3}{8}$	$15\frac{3}{4}$	$20\frac{5}{8}$	$27\frac{1}{2}$	$16\frac{1}{2}$	$17\frac{5}{8}$	4	$2\frac{3}{8}$	$3\frac{1}{4}$
$27\frac{1}{2}$	$15\frac{3}{4}$	$27\frac{1}{2}$	$5\frac{1}{2}$	$43\frac{3}{8}$	$19\frac{5}{8}$	$23\frac{5}{8}$	$33\frac{1}{2}$	$19\frac{3}{4}$	$21\frac{5}{8}$	5	$2\frac{3}{8}$	$3\frac{1}{2}$
$31\frac{1}{2}$	$17\frac{5}{8}$	$31\frac{1}{2}$	$6\frac{1}{4}$	49	$23\frac{5}{8}$	$24\frac{5}{8}$	$39\frac{3}{8}$	$19\frac{3}{4}$	$27\frac{1}{2}$	6	$3\frac{1}{4}$	4
$35\frac{1}{2}$	$19\frac{5}{8}$	$35\frac{1}{2}$	7	55	$23\frac{5}{8}$	$26\frac{1}{2}$	$43\frac{3}{8}$	$19\frac{3}{4}$	$31\frac{1}{2}$	6	$3\frac{1}{2}$	5
$39\frac{1}{2}$	$21\frac{5}{8}$	$39\frac{1}{2}$	8	59	$27\frac{1}{2}$	$28\frac{1}{2}$	$47\frac{1}{4}$	$21\frac{5}{8}$	$31\frac{1}{2}$	7	4	5

All Dimensions are given in Inches.

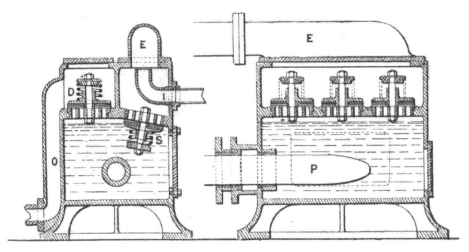

Figs. 876, 877.—Plunger Air Pump and Condenser from the Allen Engine.

E, exhaust pipe.

P, plunger.

O, overflow pipe.

Diameter of engine piston, 12″.

Stroke, 24″.

Revs. per minute, 200.

Diameter of air pump piston, 5″.

A full account of this engine will be found in Proceedings of Inst. Mech. Engineers for 1868.

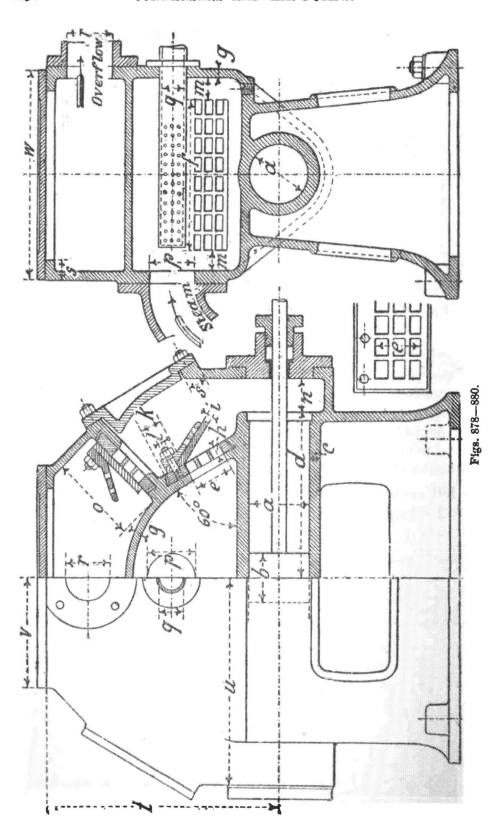

Figs. 878—880.

TABLE 82.—**Dimensions of Air Pump and Condenser** (Figs. 878—880).

H	D	*a*	*b*	*c*	*d*	*e*	*f*	*g*	*h*	*i*	*k*	*l*	*m*	*n*	*o*	*p*	*q*	*r*	*s*	*t*	*u*	*v*	*w*
24	12	$4\frac{3}{4}$	4	$\frac{7}{8}$	$12\frac{5}{8}$	$3\frac{1}{4}$	$11\frac{5}{8}$	$\frac{5}{8}$	$\frac{3}{4}$	$\frac{1}{2}$	$1\frac{3}{4}$	$\frac{5}{8}$	$1\frac{1}{2}$	$2\frac{5}{8}$	$6\frac{3}{4}$	$3\frac{5}{8}$	$2\frac{3}{8}$	$3\frac{1}{4}$	$1\frac{1}{2}$	18	16	$8\frac{3}{8}$	16
28	14	$5\frac{5}{8}$	$4\frac{3}{8}$	$\frac{7}{8}$	$14\frac{3}{4}$	$3\frac{5}{8}$	$12\frac{3}{4}$	$\frac{5}{8}$	$\frac{3}{4}$	$\frac{1}{2}$	$1\frac{3}{4}$	$\frac{5}{8}$	$1\frac{3}{4}$	3	8	$4\frac{3}{8}$	3	$3\frac{3}{4}$	$1\frac{1}{2}$	$20\frac{3}{4}$	$18\frac{5}{8}$	$9\frac{3}{4}$	$17\frac{5}{8}$
32	16	$6\frac{3}{8}$	$4\frac{3}{4}$	$\frac{7}{8}$	17	4	14	$\frac{5}{8}$	$\frac{7}{8}$	$\frac{5}{8}$	2	$\frac{3}{4}$	$2\frac{1}{8}$	$3\frac{3}{8}$	9	5	$3\frac{5}{8}$	$4\frac{3}{8}$	$1\frac{1}{2}$	$22\frac{3}{4}$	$21\frac{1}{4}$	$11\frac{1}{4}$	$19\frac{5}{8}$
36	18	$6\frac{3}{4}$	$5\frac{1}{4}$	1	$19\frac{3}{8}$	$4\frac{3}{4}$	$15\frac{1}{4}$	$\frac{3}{4}$	$\frac{7}{8}$	$\frac{5}{8}$	2	$\frac{3}{4}$	$2\frac{1}{2}$	4	10	$5\frac{5}{8}$	$4\frac{1}{4}$	5	$1\frac{1}{2}$	$25\frac{1}{4}$	$23\frac{3}{4}$	$12\frac{3}{4}$	$21\frac{5}{8}$
40	20	8	$5\frac{5}{8}$	1	$21\frac{5}{8}$	$5\frac{5}{8}$	$16\frac{3}{4}$	$\frac{3}{4}$	1	$\frac{5}{8}$	2	$\frac{3}{4}$	$2\frac{3}{4}$	$4\frac{3}{8}$	11	$6\frac{3}{4}$	$4\frac{3}{4}$	$5\frac{5}{8}$	$1\frac{3}{4}$	$27\frac{5}{8}$	$26\frac{3}{4}$	$14\frac{3}{8}$	24
44	22	$8\frac{3}{4}$	6	1	24	$6\frac{3}{8}$	$18\frac{3}{8}$	$\frac{3}{4}$	1	$\frac{5}{8}$	2	$\frac{3}{4}$	3	$4\frac{3}{4}$	12	$7\frac{1}{4}$	$5\frac{1}{4}$	6	$1\frac{3}{4}$	30	$29\frac{5}{8}$	16	26

All Dimensions are given in Inches.

The quantity of condensing water required depends in some measure upon the temperature, but a rule which will serve as a basis upon which to judge of the amount required is from 20 to 30 times the amount of feed water used; an actual example taken by measuring the overflow water as it left the condenser gave from 61 to 80 gallons per indicated HP per hour; the temperature of the injection water was 56°, and that of the overflow 100°; the engine had a 12″ piston and 15″ stroke, the boiler pressure being 55 lbs., and at the time when the water was measured indicated from 20 to 24 HP; the air pump was a vertical plunger pump.

(b.) Surface Condensers.

Surface condensers are now almost exclusively used in marine work, and enable the boilers to be worked at much higher pressures

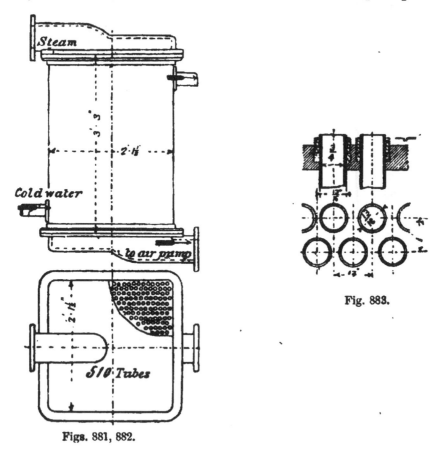

Fig. 883.

Figs. 881, 882.

on account of the purity of the feed water, only a small amount of auxiliary feed being used direct from the sea; they are also increasing in use on land, especially where water is plentiful but bad; their

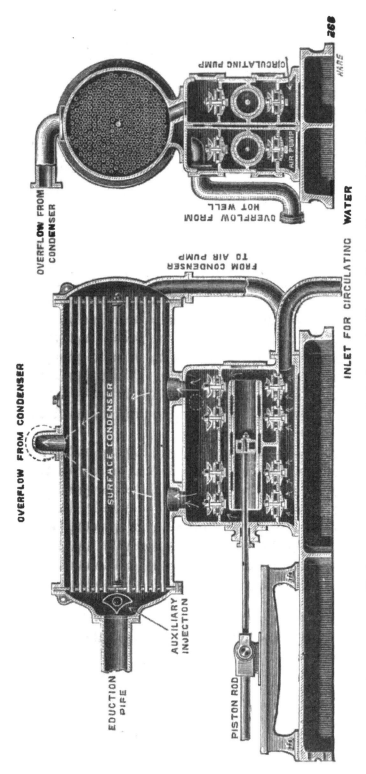

Figs. 884, 885.—Horizontal Surface Condenser and Air Pump, by Messrs. Ruston, Proctor & Co., Lincoln.

first cost is much greater than an ordinary jet condenser, but there is much to be said as to their suitability for special positions, such as by the side of brackish rivers, or rivers where the water has a bad action on boiler plates. An outside view of one form is shown in figs. 881, 882, and fig. 883 shows one method of fixing the tubes. The tubes are usually of solid drawn brass of $\frac{5}{8}''$ or $\frac{3}{4}''$ or $\frac{13}{16}''$ diameter, the tube plates of brass or copper. $\frac{5}{8}''$ tubes run $10\frac{3}{4}''$ to the lb., $\frac{3}{4}''$ tubes, $9\frac{1}{2}''$ to the lb., the thickness being 18 B W G.

The method shown in fig. 883, of fixing the tubes by small screwed glands and packing allows of free expansion and contraction, and also admits of a tube being drawn for examination. In marine surface condensers the cooling surface is about 3 square feet per indicated HP. A surface condenser combined with air and circulating pumps, by Messrs. Ruston & Proctor of Lincoln, is shown in figs. 884, 885, arranged for placing behind the cylinder of a horizontal engine, on an extension of the bed plate; in this example the exhaust steam is passed through the tubes, the circulating water being pumped through the chamber containing them, and thus coming in contact with the outside of the tubes; many surface condensers are made so that the circulating water is pumped through the tubes, the exhaust steam passing through the chamber, and coming into contact with the outside of the tubes.

The quantity of circulating water required varies from 55 to 90 gallons per indicated HP per hour.

In places where the quantity of condensing water available is small, various devices have been made use of to cool the water, so that it may be used over and over again; shallow ponds answer very well and are largely used. An ingenious device by Theisen,* of the Engine Works, Grevenbroich, is shown in fig. 886, here the water from the condenser is cooled down by a series of metal discs dipping partly in water and kept slowly revolving, a fan draws dry air through the spaces between the discs, and cools them by evaporation.

---

* A full account of this cooling arrangement appeared in Dingler's Journal, Vol. 267, Part 13, page 586.

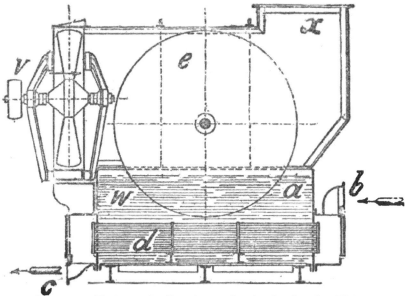

Fig. 886.—Theisen's Cooling Apparatus for Condensing Water.

The cold water reservoir *a*, with surface condenser tubes immersed : *b*, inlet for exhaust steam ; *e*, a series of metal discs partially immersed in the condensing water, as they revolve a current of air is forced over them by the fan, V, fig. 886 ; *x*, outlet for vapour and air from fan.

Other special varieties of condenser are known as Ejector condensers, and have no air pump or moving parts ; they are almost the same in construction as the Giffards Injector, and are kept at work by a stream of cold water from a tank overhead ; their action is continuous, and they keep a fair vacuum.

The economy obtained by using a condenser varies too much in practice to allow of a definite figure being given, but it may be taken as from 15 per.cent. upwards.

(c.) Feed Pumps.

Feed pumps are made in endless variety, according to their position on the engine or boiler; formerly all engines had a feed pump attached to some part of the frame or bed, now the tendency is to have a separate feed system, worked by its own donkey engine, placed close to the boilers. Locomotives depend upon some form of injector, and very often on large portable or under-type engines an auxiliary feed by injector or donkey pump is provided. When a

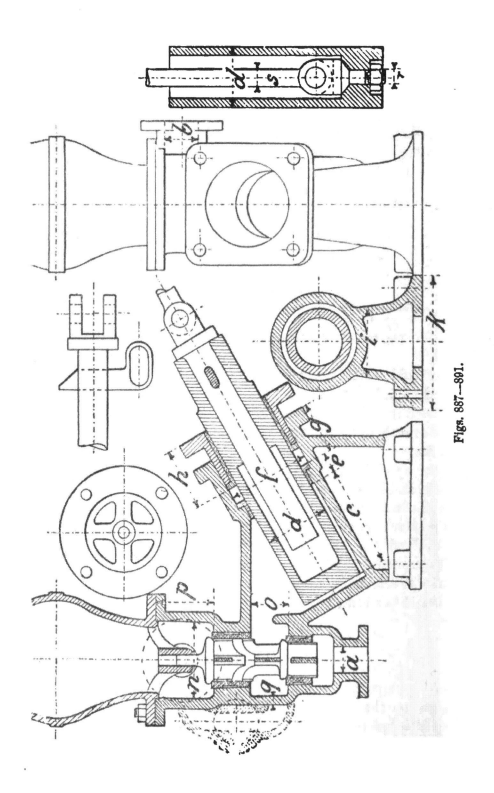

Figs. 887—891.

TABLE 83.—**Dimensions of Feed Pump** (Figs. 887—891).

Engine.		Feed-pump.																		
H	D	*d*	H	*a*	*b*	*c*	*e*	*f*	*g*	*h*	*i*	*k*	*l*	*m*	*n*	*o*	*p*	*q*	*r*	*s*
12	6	1¼	1¾	¾	¾	1¾	1	2¼	2	2⅜	1¼	5¼	1	1¼	2	1⅝	2⅜	½	—	—
16	8	1⅝	2	1¼	1	1⅞	1¼	2¾	2⅝	2¾	1⅝	5⅝	1⅜	1¾	2⅜	2	2¾	½	—	—
20	10	2	2⅝	1⅜	1¼	2½	1¼	2⅜	3¼	3⅜	2	6⅜	1½	2	2¾	2	3¼	½	—	—
24	12	2¾	3¼	1½	1⅜	3⅛	1⅜	4¼	3¾	4	2¾	7¼	2	2⅜	3⅜	2¾	3⅝	½	1	1¼
28	14	3¼	3⅝	1¾	1¾	3⅝	1½	4¾	4⅜	4⅜	3¼	8	2¼	2⅝	4	3	4	½	1¼	1⅜
32	16	3⅝	4	2	2	4	1¾	5¼	5	4¾	3⅝	8⅜	2⅜	2⅞	4⅜	3¼	4⅜	½	1¼	1⅝
36	18	4	4⅜	2⅜	2⅜	4⅜	2	5⅝	5⅝	5¼	4	9¼	2¾	3⅜	4¾	3⅜	4¾	½	1⅜	1¾
40	20	4⅜	5	2¾	2¾	4¾	2⅜	6	6	5⅜	4⅝	10	3¼	3¾	5⅜	3⅝	5¼	½	1⅜	1¾
44	22	4¾	5⅝	3¼	3¼	5⅜	2¾	6⅜	6⅜	5⅝	5¼	10¾	3⅝	4¼	6	4	5⅝	⅝	1⅜	2

range of boilers is fed from one pump, there must be a feed escape
valve, placed so as to command the whole feed system, and loaded so
as to blow off a little above the boiler pressure, and this valve should
be in a conspicuous position ; if any obstruction occur this valve
will blow off and show that there is something resisting the flow of
the water.

An ordinary feed pump for bolting down to the engine foundation,
and worked by an eccentric, is shown in fig. 887. A method of
disengaging the plunger, is shown in upper fig., this method is often

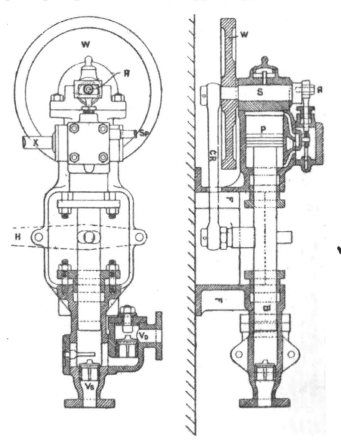

Fig. 892.　　　　Fig. 893.

used in slow moving pumps when required to do intermittent work,
but is not often applied to boiler feed pumps.

Figs. 892—893, show a simple boiler feeding donkey pump.

F F, the frame by which the pump is bolted to the wall ; W, the
fly wheel ; S, the crank shaft ; R, a small crank pin for working the
slide valve ; P, the steam piston ; B, the pump plunger ; V d, the
delivery valve ; V s, the suction valve ; H, a hand lever for working
the pump by hand when required.

(d.) Feed-Water Heaters.

Feed-water heaters are extensively used, and effect great economy in fuel. They may be considered as a reversed surface condenser, the exhaust steam being used to warm the water as it passes from the

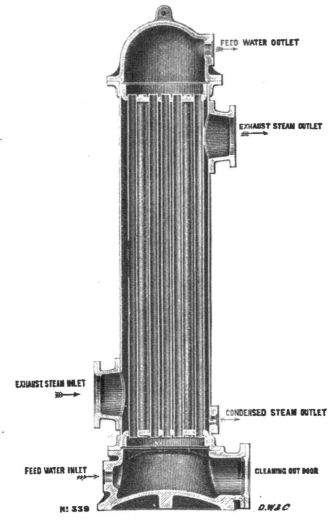

Fig. 894.—Feed-Water Heater, by Messrs. Marshall Sons & Co. Ltd., Gainsboro.

pump to the boiler, two examples are shown in figs. 894—895. Feed-water heaters of this type are sometimes placed horizontally. If pure water could be used, the heaters would work efficiently for long periods, but as water always contains mineral matters which are partially precipitated when the water is warmed, the heater tubes become coated with scale, and have to be cleaned. Occasionally, the feed water seems to select certain tubes for its flow, and not infre-

U

quently, if the heaters have been neglected, only some of the tubes are deeply scaled,* the rest being comparatively free; baffle plates, to ensure good distribution of the water, would possibly prevent this

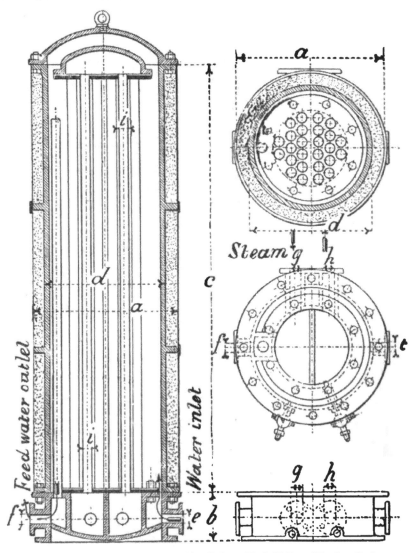

Figs. 895—898.—Feed-heater, by the Prince Rudolf Iron Works, Dülmen.

selection. From the scaling it is obvious that feed-water heaters are to a certain extent feed-water purifiers, and if of ample size, must act beneficially in this direction. In some feed-heaters, the tubes are re-

---

* An instance of this occurred in practice where a vertical heater of the above type, with about 65 tubes, had been in use for a long time without cleaning, upwards of 50 of the tubes were totally blocked up, and the remainder comparatively clear.

placed by an arched branch of exhaust pipe, surrounded by a chamber through which the feed is pumped. Such heaters are fairly efficient, more so than would be supposed from the small heating surface, and can be readily cleaned.

Other types of heaters depend on a small jet of water from the pump, carrying the exhaust steam with it into a tank, and thus heating the water.

The maximum speed of the feed water in any part of the feed system, should not exceed from 3 to 4 feet per second.

TABLE 84.—**Dimensions of Feed-Water Heater**
(Figs. 895—898).

Nominal H.P.	Heating-surface in sq. ft.	a	b	c	d	Feed-water.		Steam.		Tubes	
						Inlet	Outlet	Inlet	Outlet	No.	i
10	7·53	17¾	11¾	42	13¾	1¼	1¼	2⅜	2⅜	4	2
15	10·76	17¾	11¾	61	13¾	1⅝	1⅝	2¾	2¾	4	2
25	16·14	19¾	13¾	59	15¾	2	2	3⅛	3⅛	6	2
40	26·90	26	13¾	67	21⅝	2	2	3½	3½	10	2
60	37·66	28	13¾	67	23⅝	2	2	4	4	14	2
80	64·56	28	13¾	86½	23⅝	2⅜	2⅜	5	5	18	2
100	91·46	34¼	15¾	74½	29½	2⅜	2⅜	6	6	30	2
125	107·6	34¼	15¾	86½	29½	2¾	2¾	6	6	30	2
150	177·5	44½	17¾	71	39⅜	3⅛	3⅛	7	7	6	2

All Dimensions are given in Inches except the Heating-surface.

SECTION VI.

EXAMPLES OF VARIOUS TYPES OF HORIZONTAL AND VERTICAL ENGINES FROM ACTUAL PRACTICE.

With Tables of Dimensions, Weights, &c.

Horizontal Engines of the more usual Types.

Fig. 899.

Engine with forked or **Y** frame, bent or slotted out crank shaft, arranged to carry the fly-wheel outside the bearings on either side of the engine, frequently known as "self-contained" horizontal engines. These engines are usually made with cylinders from 5 to 12 inches diameter, the stroke being from $1\frac{1}{4}$ to $1\frac{1}{2}$ times the diameter.

Fig. 900.

Girder or "Corliss" Frame Engines, with cylinder bolted on to end of, and overhanging the girder. Frame unsupported except by a foot at each end. Crosshead guides cast in the frame for small and medium-sized engines, and either bored or with planed flat surfaces.

Fig. 901.

Girder type of engine supported by feet on cylinder, and at end of frame under crank shaft bearings. Piston rod extended and guided through back cylinder cover. Crosshead guides cast in one with frame in small and medium-sized engines.

Fig. 902.

Girder type of engine with extra supporting foot under centre of frame.

Fig. 903.

Semi-Girder type of engine, with half the length of frame bolted down to foundation, and with support under cylinder.

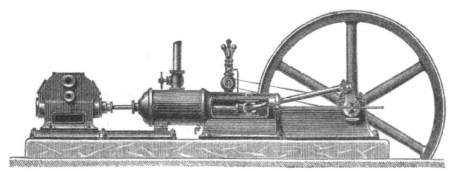

Fig. 904.

Condensing engine, with air-pump at back of cylinder and worked by tail rod.

TABLE 85.—Dimensions of Horizontal Steam Engines.

Stroke . . . H	16		20		24		28		32		36		40		44		48	
Diameter of cylinder . D	8	9	10	11	12	13	14	15	16	17	18	19	20	21	22	23	24	25
Ratio . . . H : D	2	1·78	2	1·82	2	1·85	2	1·87	2	1·88	2	1·89	2	1·90	2	1·91	2	1·92
Revolutions per minute n	110		100		90		85		80		78		75		72		70	
Piston speed in feet per minute .	283		334		360		396		426		468		500		528		560	
Diameter of fly-wheel .	66		84		96		120		138		156		180		192		216	

All Dimensions are given in Inches.

TABLE 86.—Dimensions of Horizontal Corliss Engines.

Stroke . . H	30	36	42	48	54	60	66
Diameter of cylinder . . D	10, 12	12, 14	14, 16, 18	16, 18, 20	22, 24, 26	28, 30	32, 34
Ratio . . H : D (n)	3, 2·67	3, 2·57	3, 2·62, 2·33	3, 2·66, 2·40	2·45, 2·25, 2·07	2·15, 2·00	2·06, 1·97
Revolutions per minute . n	80	75	72, 70	68	65	60	55
Piston speed in feet per minute	400, 375	465, 432	505, 490	544	585	600	605
Diameter of fly-wheel . .	108, 120	120, 132	144, 156, 168	168, 180, 192	204, 216, 240	264, 288	312, 336

All Dimensions are given in Inches.

TABLE 87.—Dimensions of Vertical Steam Engines.

Stroke . . H	6	8	10	12	16	20	24	30	36	42
Diameter of cylinder . D $\big\}$ n $\big\}$	4 5	6 7	8 9	10 12	14 16	18 20	22 24	28 30	34 38	42 46
Ratio . H:D	1·5 1·2	1·33 1·14	1·25 1·11	1·20 1·00	1·14 1·00	1·11 1·00	1·09 1·00	1·07 1·00	1·06 ·95	1·00 ·91
Revolutions per minute . n	300	280	260	245	210	180	160	130	110	100
Piston speed in feet per minute .	300	374	434	490	560	600	640	650	660	700
Diameter of fly-wheel . .	42	48	54	60	72	84	96	120	144	168

All Dimensions are given in Inches.

TABLE 88.—Dimensions of Compound Engines.

Stroke H	20		24		28		32		36		40		44		48	
Diameter of high pressure cylinder	10	11	12	13	14	15	16	17	18	19	20	21	22	23	24	25
Diameter of low pressure cylinder	16	17½	19	20½	22	24	25	27	29	30	32	33	35	37	38	40
Ratio of capacities	2·56	2·53	2·51	2·49	2·46	2·56	2·44	2·52	2·60	2·49	2·56	2·46	2·46	2·58	2·51	2·56
Revolutions per minute	90		80		75		70		68		65		62		60	
Piston speed in feet per minute	300		320		350		373		408		433		455		480	
Diameter of fly-wheel	78		96		120		138		162		180		198		216	

All Dimensions are given in Inches.

TABLE 89.—Dimensions of Compound Corliss Engines.

Stroke . . . H	30	36	42	48	54	60
Diam. of high-pressure cylinder	10, 12	12, 14	14, 16	18, 20	22, 24, 26	28, 30
Diam. of low-pressure cylinder	16, 19	19, 22	22, 25	29, 32	35, 38, 42	44, 48
Ratio of capacities	2·56, 2·51	2·51, 2·46	2·46, 2·44	2·60, 2·56	2·46, 2·51, 2·60	2·46, 2·56
Revolutions per minute	80, 75	72	70	68	65	60
Piston speed in feet per minute	400, 375	465, 432	505, 490	490, 544	585	600
Diameter of fly-wheel	108, 120	132, 144	156, 168	180, 192	204, 216, 240, 264	288, 312

All Dimensions are given in Inches.

Leading Dimensions of Single Cylinder Horizontal Engines, with and without Condensers.

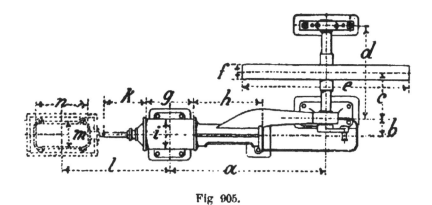

Fig 905.

TABLE 90.—Overall Dimensions of Horizontal Engines (Fig. 905).

H	a	b	c	d	e	f	g	h	i	k	l	m	n
16	75	9	$27\frac{3}{4}$	51	75	8	22	$36\frac{1}{2}$	$15\frac{3}{4}$	—	—	—	—
20	90	$10\frac{3}{4}$	$29\frac{3}{4}$	57	93	10	$26\frac{3}{4}$	42	$18\frac{1}{2}$	$30\frac{1}{2}$	71	$17\frac{3}{4}$	$33\frac{1}{2}$
24	105	$12\frac{1}{2}$	$31\frac{1}{2}$	63	110	12	$31\frac{1}{2}$	48	$21\frac{1}{4}$	36	77	19	39
28	122	14	34	69	130	$14\frac{3}{4}$	$36\frac{1}{2}$	$54\frac{1}{2}$	$23\frac{3}{4}$	$40\frac{1}{2}$	82	20	47
32	136	$15\frac{1}{2}$	$35\frac{1}{2}$	75	150	17	41	60	26	45	98	$23\frac{3}{4}$	49
36	151	17	$39\frac{1}{2}$	83	165	20	$45\frac{1}{2}$	66	$28\frac{3}{4}$	50	108	$27\frac{1}{2}$	65
40	168	$18\frac{1}{2}$	$43\frac{1}{2}$	90	185	$21\frac{3}{4}$	50	$73\frac{1}{2}$	$30\frac{3}{4}$	$55\frac{1}{2}$	118	36	65

All Dimensions are given in Inches.

Floor Space required for Single Cylinder Horizontal Engines, with and without Condensers.

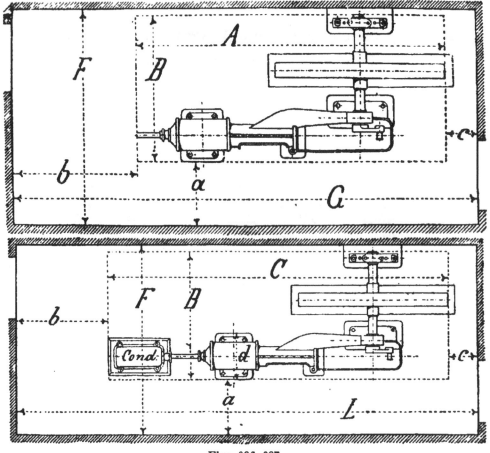

Figs. 906, 907.

TABLE 91.—Floor Space Dimensions for Horizontal Engines (Figs. 906, 907).

H	Without condenser, fig. 906.								With condenser fig. 907.	
	A	B	a	b	c	d	F	G	C	L
16	126	40	32	63	20	24	110	209	—	—
20	181	50	36	67	20	28	130	268	231	318
24	196	60	$39\frac{1}{2}$	71	24	32	144	291	264	359
28	245	69	$43\frac{1}{2}$	75	24	36	160	344	300	399
32	277	119	47	79	28	40	173	384	342	449
36	307	130	51	83	28	44	189	418	384	495
40	333	142	55	87	28	48	205	448	420	535

All Dimensions are given in Inches.

Floor Space required, Horizontal Coupled Engines, with and without Condensers.

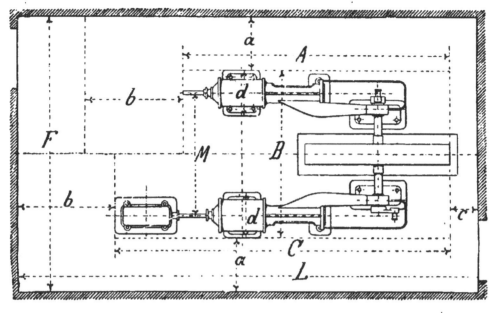

Fig. 908.

TABLE 92.—**Floor Space Dimensions for Horizontal Coupled Engines** (Fig. 908).

H	A	B	M	a	b	c	d	F	C	L
16	—	106	82	32	63	20	24	169	—	—
20	181	118	90	36	67	20	28	189	231	318
24	196	130	96	39½	71	24	32	209	264	359
28	245	142	104	43½	75	24	36	228	300	399
32	277	152	112	47	79	28	40	246	342	449
36	307	169	118	51	83	28	44	274	384	495
40	333	173	126	55	87	28	48	283	420	535

All Dimensions are given in Inches.

Weights of Engines in Detail.

In the following tables—

CI = Cast iron.	St = Mild steel.
WI = Wrought iron.	CS = Cast steel.
M = White metal.	G = Gun metal.
B = Bolts.	

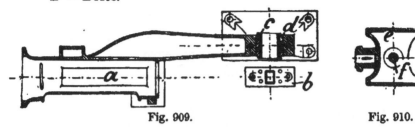

Fig. 909.   Fig. 910.

TABLE 93.—Weights of Engine Frames and Crossheads.

Engine.		Frame (Fig. 909).									Crosshead (Fig. 910).		
Stroke.	Diameter of Piston.	Frame.	Bearing Cap.	Brasses.	Wedges.	Frame complete with Bearing Cap.					Crosshead.	Pin.	Total.
H	D	a	b	c	d	CI	G	WI	B	Total.	e	f	
		CI	CI	G	WI						CI	St.	
12	6	700	—	—	—	700	—	—	—	700	15	2	17
16	8	830	30	13	—	860	12	—	8	880	24	2	26
20	10	1060	57	18	11	1117	18	11	11	1157	42	4	46
24	12	1540	90	26	15	1630	26	15	15	1685	64	7	71
28	14	2100	140	37	17	2240	37	17	17	2310	90	11	101
32	16	2816	220	53	19	3036	53	19	18	3125	120	15	135
36	18	3740	290	70	22	4030	70	22	23	4145	155	19	174
40	20	5060	370	88	24	5430	88	24	23	5565	194	24	218
44	22	6600	470	110	28	7070	110	28	26	7234	234	31	265

Dimensions in Inches, Weights in Pounds.

Weights of Engines.

Pistons, and Piston Rods.

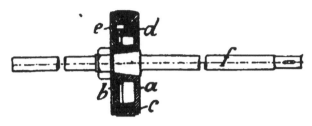

Fig. 911.

TABLE 94.—Weights of Pistons and Piston Rods.

Engine.		Piston body. a	Cover. b	Inner ring. c	Nuts. d	Screws. e	Piston rod. f	Piston complete with rod. a to f			
Stroke.	Diameter of piston.										
H	D	CI	CI	CI	G	St	St	CI	G	St	Total.
12	6	15	4	9	—	—	7	28	—	7	35
16	8	20	7	13	—	—	13	40	—	13	53
20	10	26	10	18	—	—	24	55	—	24	79
24	12	33	18	24	—	—	57	75	—	57	132
28	14	44	26	30	4	4	88	100	4	92	196
32	16	66	40	40	4	4	121	146	4	125	275
36	18	92	57	57	7	7	154	206	7	161	374
40	20	121	73	68	7	7	200	262	7	207	476
44	22	179	95	92	9	9	286	366	9	295	570
48	24	220	128	125	11	11	396	473	11	407	891
—	28	330	187	191	13	15	726	708	13	741	1462
—	32	450	253	260	18	20	1188	963	18	1208	2189
—	36	572	330	338	22	23	1738	1240	22	1764	3026
—	40	720	418	429	26	33	2420	1567	26	2453	4046

Dimensions in Inches, Weights in Pounds.

Weights of Engines.

Crank Shafts, Fly Wheels and Outside Bearing.

Fig. 912.   Fig. 913.   Fig. 914.

TABLE 95.—Weights, Crank Shafts, Fly Wheels and Outside Bearings.

Engine.		Crank Shaft (Fig. 912).				Fly Wheel (Fig. 913).			Outside Bearing (Fig. 914).			
Stroke.	Diameter of Piston.	Shaft.	Key.	Governor Pulley.	$a+b+c$.	Fly Whee'.	Bolts and Rings.	$d+e$	Block and Cap.	Brasses.	Bolts.	$f+g+h$.
		a	b	c		d	e		f	g	h	
H	D	St	St	CI	Total.	CI	WI	Total.	CI	G	WI	Total.
12	6	—	—	—	—	385	—	385	—	—	—	—
16	8	—	—	—	—	1045	—	1045	—	—	—	—
20	10	325	5·5	27·5	358	1650	—	1650	110	14	11	135
24	12	528	8	39	575	2530	—	2530	242	24	18	284
28	14	836	10	54	900	3520	44	3564	352	35	23	410
32	16	1255	14	66	1335	5012	48	5060	462	48	32	542
36	18	1760	15	80	1855	6548	52	6600	554	62	44	660
40	20	2244	18	92	2354	8963	57	9020	660	77	55	792
44	22	3256	24	110	3390	13138	62	13200	770	88	66	824

Dimensions in Inches, Weight in Pounds.

Weights of Engines.

Rider's Valves and Valve Rods.

Fig. 915.

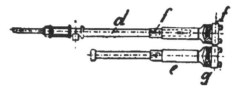

Fig. 916.

TABLE 96.—Weight of Rider's Valves and Valve Rods.

Engine.		Rider's valve, fig. 915.				Valve rods, fig. 916.				
Stroke.	Diameter of piston.	Main valve.	Case.	Expansion valve.	$a+b+c$.	Valve rod.	Guide piece.	Cotters and bolts.	Adjusting pieces.	$d+e+f+g$.
		a	b	c		d	e	f	g	
H	D	CI	CI	CI	Total.	St	WI	St	G	Total.
12	6	—	—	—	—	7	9	1	1	18
16	8	—	—	—	—	9	13	1	1	24
20	10	42	6·6	4·4	53	13	22	2	1	38
24	12	66	13	9	88	18	35	2	1	56
28	14	100	22	15	137	24	52	3	3	82
32	16	145	33	26	204	31	70	4	5	110
36	18	194	46	35	275	40	88	7	5	140
40	20	242	62	48	352	48	105	7	5	165
44	22	290	84	66	440	57	123	8	5	193

Dimensions in Inches, Weights in Pounds.

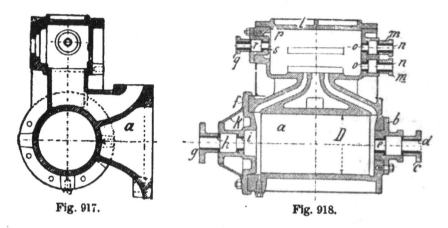

Fig. 917.   Fig. 918.

TABLE 97.—**Weights of Cylinders with**

Engine.		Cylinder.	Front cover.	Gland.	Bush.	Bush.	Back cover.	Gland.	Bush.	Bush.	Casing.	Valve chest covers.
Stroke.	Diameter of piston.	a	b	c	d	e	f	g	h	i	k	l
H	D	CI	CI	CI	G	G	CI	CI	G	G	CI	CI
12	6	286	13	4	0·7	0·4	22	—	—	—	—	13
16	8	475	22	7	1·2	0·7	40	—	—	—	—	28
20	10	690	35	9	1·5	1·2	59	—	—	—	—	72
24	12	1090	48	11	2·2	1·5	90	11	2·5	1·1	22	75
28	14	1540	64	14	2·8	2·2	143	15	3·5	1·5	26	134
32	16	2125	80	15	3·5	2·6	200	19	4	1·9	40	194
36	18	2860	94	18	4·2	3·3	308	24	4·5	2·4	48	275
40	20	3520	112	22	4·8	3·7	440	30	5	3·0	57	335
44	22	4225	132	26	5·5	4·4	572	37	5·5	3·7	66	400

Dimensions in Inches, Weights in Pounds.

Weights of Cylinders, Covers and Stuffing Boxes.

Note : in Table 97, Cylinders from 12″ to 16″ stroke have simple valve gear ; those from 20″ to 44″ stroke have Rider's valve gear with closed valves.

Covers and Stuffing Boxes (Figs. 917, 918).

Gland. m	Bush. n	Bush. o	Stuffing-box. p	Gland. q	Bush. r	Bush. s	Casing. t	Cylinder complete with covers and glands. $a+\&c.+t$				
CI	G	G	CI	GI	G	G	WI	CI	G	WI	B	Total.
—	—	—	—	—	—	—	7	338	1·1	7	11	357
—	—	—	—	—	—	—	13	572	1·9	13	22	608
7	1·3	0·9	15	3	0·4	0·4	22	860	5·7	22	31	919
7	1·5	1·1	24	4	0·4	0·4	40	1382	11	40	42	1475
9	1·8	1·1	30	5	0·7	0·4	57	1980	14	57	55	2106
11	2·0	1·3	37	6	0·9	0·4	81	2727	17	81	70	2895
13	2·2	1·3	46	7	0·9	0·7	105	3693	19	105	88	3905
15	2·4	1·5	52	8	1·1	0·7	132	4591	22	132	102	4847
18	2·6	1·5	62	9	1·1	0·9	160	5547	25	160	119	5851

Note.—Cylinders with jackets weigh 18 per cent. more.

Weights of Engines.

Connecting Rods, Cranks, and Crank Pins.

Fig. 919.

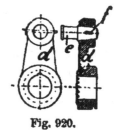

Fig. 920.

TABLE 98.—Weights of Connecting Rods, Cranks, and Crank Pins.

Engine.		Connecting-rods, fig. 919.				Cranks and crank-pins, fig. 920.			
Stroke.	Diameter of piston.	Connecting-rod. a	Cotter. b	Brasses. c	a+b+c.	Crank. d	Crank-pin. e	Cotter. f	d+e+f.
H	D	WI	St	G	Total.	WI	St	St	Total.
12	6	24	3	3	30	—	—	—	—
16	8	42	3	5	50	—	—	—	—
20	10	66	7	9	82	70	12	2	84
24	12	100	7	11	118	119	17	2	138
28	14	142	9	13	164	176	23	4	203
32	16	187	11	18	216	238	34	6	278
36	18	265	13	24	302	308	52	6	366
40	20	319	15	33	367	376	55	9	440
44	22	385	15	44	444	462	70	11	543

Note.—Cast-iron cranks are about 20% heavier.
Dimensions in Inches, Weights in Pounds.

Weights of Engines.

Eccentrics and Eccentric Rods.

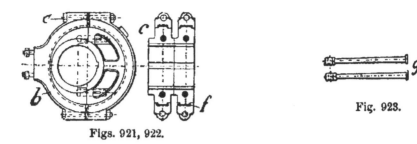

Figs. 921, 922.

Fig. 923.

TABLE 99.—Weights of Two Eccentrics and Rods.

Engine.		Two eccentrics, figs. 921, 922.							Two eccentric rods, fig. 923.
Stroke.	Diameter of piston.	Eccentric sheaves. *a*	Eccentric rings. *b*	Bolts. *c*	Packings. *d*	Bolts. *e*	Linings. *f*	Two eccentrics complete *a* to *f*	*g*
H	D	CI	CI	WI	G	WI	M	Total.	WI
12	6	10	19	—	0·4	1·1	—	30·5	9
16	8	12	25	—	0·4	2·6	—	40	15
20	10	18	35	1·5	0·7	3	6·6	64·8	22
24	12	31	64	2	0·9	4	13	115	38
28	14	44	109	2	1	5	20	172	60
32	16	62	145	3	1	7	26	244	92
36	18	77	202	4	1	7	30	321	125
40	20	97	257	5	1·4	7·6	40	408	158
44	22	121	320	5	1·5	8·5	44	500	194

Dimensions in Inches, Weights in Pounds.

Weights of Engines.

Valve Rod Guides, with Governor Bracket, Bevel Wheels, Spindles, and Levers, exclusive of Governor and Spindle.

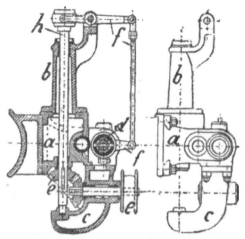

Figs. 921, 925.

TABLE 100.—Weights of Governor Bracket, &c.
(Figs. 924, 925).

Engine.		Valve-rod guides. a	Governor bracket. b	Bracket for footstep. c	Bevel wheels and pulley. e	Lever. f	Spindle. g	Bushes. d	Weight complete, as in figs. 924, 925. a to g					
Stroke.	Diameter of piston.													
H	D	CI	CI	CI	CI	WI	St	G	CI	G	WI	St	B	Total.
20	10	70	26	33	18	31	11	7	160	18	11	7	4	200
24	12	121	40	40	24	37	15	7	238	24	15	7	7	291
28	14	165	50	46	33	44	22	9	305	33	22	9	9	378
32	16	215	66	53	40	53	26	9	387	40	26	9	11	473
36	18	268	84	62	46	59	33	11	473	46	33	11	13	576
40	20	325	103	68	53	64	37	11	560	53	37	11	15	676
44	22	375	121	77	62	70	44	13	643	62	44	13	18	780

Dimensions in Inches, Weights in Pounds.

Weights of Engines.

Foundation Bolts and Plates, Guard Rail, and Barring Apparatus.

Fig. 926.

Fig. 927.

Fig. 928.

TABLE 101.—Weights of Foundation Bolts, &c.

Engine.		Foundation bolts and plates, fig. 926.			Guard rail, fig. 927.	Barring apparatus, fig. 928.			
Stroke.	Diameter of piston.	Plates.	Bolts.			Bracket.	Lever.	Lewis bolts.	Barring apparatus complete.
		b	a	$b+a$	c	d	e	f	$d+e+f$
		CI	WI	Total.	WI	CI	WI	WI	Total.
12	6	44	35	79	—	—	—	—	—
16	8	44	48	92	—	—	—	—	—
20	10	140	66	206	11	44	22	13	79
24	12	176	132	308	15	44	22	13	79
28	14	330	198	528	22	55	26	18	99
32	16	396	264	660	29	55	26	18	99
36	18	616	352	968	35	77	35	26	158
40	20	616	440	1056	44	77	35	26	158
44	22	748	550	1290	55	77	35	26	158

Dimensions in Inches, Weights in Pounds.

TABLE 102.—Summary of the Tables of Weights, 92 to 101.

Engine Stroke. H	Diameter of piston. D	Cast-iron. CI	Gun metal. G	Wrought-iron. WI	Steel. St	Bolts. WI	Weight without fly-wheel or governor. lbs.	Governor. lbs.	Fly-wheel. lbs.	Sundry fittings, valves, &c. lbs.	Weight with Rider's valve gear without condenser. lbs.	Condenser. lbs.	Weight with Condenser. lbs.	Feed-pump with eccentric. lbs.
20	10	2663	66	326	405	75	3535	110	1650	66	5361	—	—	88
24	12	4073	97	532	651	100	5453	176	2530	88	8247	1760	10007	110
28	14	5787	140	774	1020	125	7846	242	3564	110	11762	3080	14642	155
32	16	7806	185	1038	1502	158	10689	308	5060	155	16212	3520	19732	220
36	18	10428	233	1355	2075	200	14291	374	6600	176	21441	4400	25841	308
40	20	13188	287	1676	2625	230	18006	462	9020	198	27686	5500	33186	418
44	22	16380	343	2045	3782	264	22814	550	13200	220	36734	6600	43384	528
Per cent. of material		75·5	1·8	9·2	11·4	2·1	100							
		71·9	1·5	8·9	16·5	1·2	100							

Without fly-wheel for engines up to 20″ stroke.

,,   ,,   ,,   44″ stroke.

Dimensions in Inches, Weights in Pounds.

TABLE 103.—Cost of Patterns, complete with Core Boxes. For Engines of 20 to 44 Inches stroke, with Rider's Valve Gear.

Stroke .	20	24	28	32	36	40	44
Diameter of piston .	10	12	14	16	18	20	22
Frame with bearing cap and brasses .	250	264	285	300	320	350	390
Crosshead .	25	30	38	44	50	60	65
Connecting-rod brasses .	5	6	7	8	9	10	12
Cylinder with cover and glands .	195	210	220	240	260	280	300
Piston with rings and cover .	24	26	29	31	35	40	45
Outside main bearing .	33	36	41	46	55	60	70
Rider's valve .	70	75	80	85	95	105	115
Adjusting nuts for valve gear .	1	1	1	2	2	2	2
Eccentrics with rings .	30	35	40	45	50	57	65
Valve rod guides with governor bracket, bevel wheels and pulley .	70	80	90	105	115	130	150
Foundation plates .	3	3	3·5	3·5	3·5	3·5	3·5
Barring apparatus .	9	9	10·5	10·5	12·5	12·5	12·5
Feed pump .	120	130	140	150	160	170	185
Total cost of patterns	835	905	985	1070	1165	1280	1415

The dimensions are given in inches, the cost in marks, the value of a mark being about 11¾ English pence.
The patterns admit of the engine being built either right or left-handed.

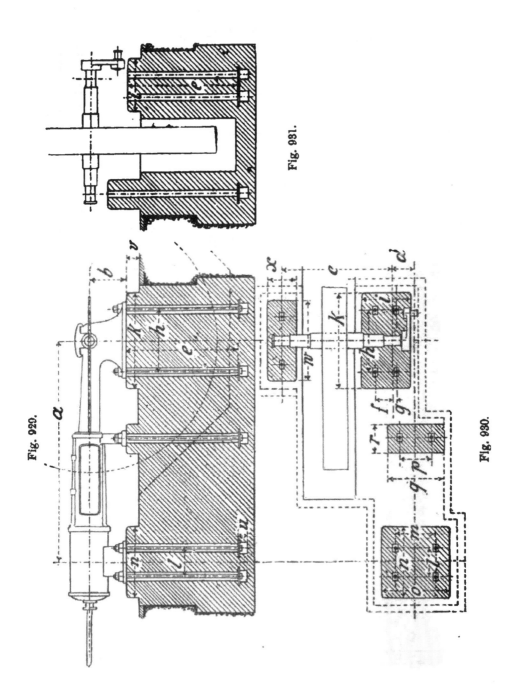

Fig. 931.

Fig. 929.

Fig. 930.

TABLE 104.—**Dimensions of Engine Foundations for Horizontal Engines** (Figs. 929—931).

H	D	*a*	*b*	*c*	*d*	*e*	*f*	*g*	*h*	*i*	*k*	*l*	*m*	*n*	*o*	*p*	*q*	*r*	*s*	*t*	*u*	*v*	*w*	*x*	M*
20	10	76	14½	51	9	55	7	2	22	20½	36¼	—	15½	23⅝	23⅝	—	—	—	2⅜	4⅜	4	15¾	39½	15¾	6·5
24	12	90	18	57	10⅝	63	8	2¼	25⅝	20½	41	13¾	17¾	27¾	27¾	—	—	—	2⅜	4⅜	4¾	14¾	43½	16¾	10·5
28	14	106	20	63	12½	71	9	2¾	30	26	46½	15¾	20½	31½	31½	—	—	—	2¾	4¾	5½	13¾	47½	17¾	14·4
32	16	121½	22	70	14	75	10¼	3⅜	34	31	52	17¾	22¾	35½	35½	20½	35½	20	2¾	5	6¼	12¾	52	18¾	19·6
36	18	135	24	75	15½	79	11¾	4	37	31	57	18¾	25¼	39½	39½	22¼	38⅝	20¾	3⅛	5½	7	11¾	55	19¾	26
40	20	151	26	82	17	84	12½	4⅜	40½	36⅝	62	20	27¾	43½	43½	22¾	42	22¼	3⅛	6	8	10¾	60	20¾	32·7
44	22	168	28	90	18½	90	14	5	44½	36⅝	69	21¾	29½	47½	47½	25¼	46	23⅝	3⅛	6⅜	8	9¾	64	21¾	39·3

* (M), the contents of Foundations in Cubic Yards; all other Dimensions in Inches.

Engine Foundations.

The depth of is in some measure determined by the nature of the ground. It may be necessary to go down a great depth to reach a solid basis whereon to build, and to fill up with coarse concrete up to the level of the foundation bolts and then begin the foundation proper. The material depends on the district; in some districts concrete is the most ready material, in others brick or masonry. In cases where a building for manufacturing purposes has to be erected on very loose ground and where concrete is easily obtained, it is a good plan to floor the whole area occupied by factory, engine and boiler house with a bed of concrete of sufficient thickness, and to build all structures on this bed. Settlement is very unlikely to take place with such a system, as the weight is distributed over the largest possible area of the loose ground.

For brick foundations each course should be grouted in thoroughly with good cement, and all bolt holes formed by inserting wood bars about 3″ to 4″ square, the lower end of these resting in the foundation plates, and the upper ends in a template fixed in places; the wood bars are afterwards withdrawn and the bolts inserted. When the engine is in place and bolted down, the spaces round the bolts may be filled in with cement grout. In concrete the same plan with regard to the bolt holes may be used.

With masonry foundations the holes are usually cut through. A top course of stone is very good on brick foundations, but is expensive in districts far from the quarries.

When the first motion drive from the engine is through spur or bevel wheels, great care should be taken with the foundations, and if of concrete as much time as possible should be allowed after building before the engine is started. The most convenient form of foundation bolt is perhaps the cottar bolt, as it can be passed down the hole in the foundation without trouble, and should such an accident happen as a defective bolt, it can be replaced. In small work ordinary bolts with heads and nuts are much used, being built in the foundation.

Note.—The particulars given in Tables 85 to 104, and the corresponding illustrations, are from engines of continental make, and are given exactly as they appear in the 3rd edition of M. Haeder's book, "Die Dampfmaschine," except that the dimensions are converted into English measures.

SECTION VII.

PARTICULARS OF STANDARD ENGINES BY ENGLISH MAKERS.

The following Tables, 105 to 129, give the particulars of small and medium-sized engines by English makers who manufacture large numbers of these engines, and have given every attention to details of construction and design ; they may therefore be taken as examples of best English practice in the various types of which tables and illustrations are given.

Descriptions of some of the special valve gears applied to these engines are given in the Section on Valve Gears, and examples of indicator diagrams from actual practice are given in the Section on Indicator Diagrams.

The particulars in each table were supplied by the makers themselves.

Fig. 932.

TABLE 105.—Particulars of Messrs. Ransomes, Sims & Jefferies' Long-Stroke Horizontal Engine without Condenser (Fig. 932).

Diameter of cylinder	10	11	12	13	14	15	16	17	18	19
Length of stroke	20	20	24	24	28	28	32	32	36	36
Revolutions per minute	110	110	90	90	80	80	70	70	60	60
Boiler-pressure per $\square$"	80	80	80	80	80	80	80	80	80	80
Best average H.P.	30	40	45	55	65	75	85	95	100	115
Diameter of crank-shaft	4	4¼	4¾	5	5⅝	5⅞	6¼	6¾	7¼	7½
Diameter of fly-wheel	84	84	96	96	108	108	120	120	144	144
Width of fly-wheel	8	8	10	10	12	12	14	14	16	16
Weight of fly-wheel, cwts.	24	24	46	46	60	60	90	90	110	110
Height to centre of cylinder	16½	16½	19	19	22	22	23	23	30	30
Total length, including fly-wheel	153	153	181	181	210	210	238	238	281	281
Total width to outer bearing	74	74	82½	82½	96	96	107	107	131	131
Approx. weight packed, cwts.	72	76	106	112	163	172	218	230	291	307

All Dimensions are given in Inches.

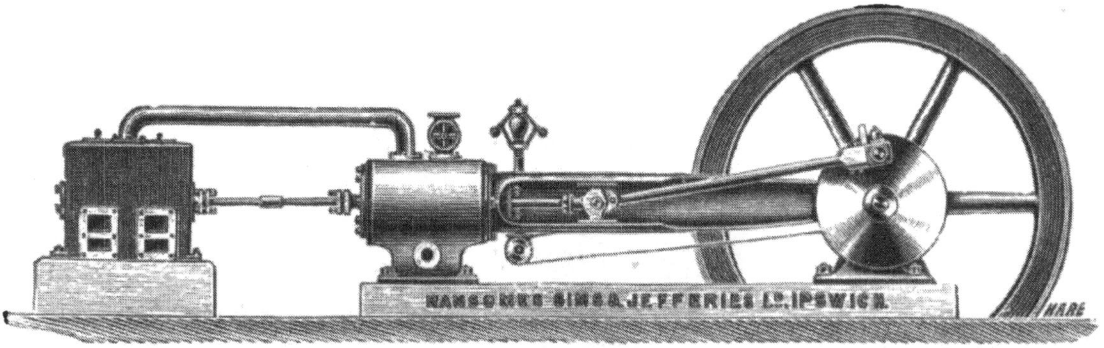

Fig. 933

TABLE 106.—Particulars of Messrs. Ransomes, Sims & Jefferies' Long-Stroke Engine with Condenser (Fig. 933).

Diameter of cylinder	10	11	12	13	14	15	16	17	18	19
Length of stroke	20	20	24	24	28	28	32	32	36	36
Revolutions per minute	110	110	90	90	80	80	70	70	60	60
Boiler pressure	80	80	80	80	80	80	80	80	80	80
Best average H.P.	40	50	55	65	80	90	105	115	125	140
Diameter of fly-wheel	84	84	96	96	108	108	120	120	144	144
Width of fly-wheel	8	8	10	10	12	12	14	14	16	16
Weight of fly-wheel, cwts.	24	24	46	46	60	60	90	90	110	110
Diameter of crank-shaft	4	4¼	4¾	5	5⅝	5⅞	6½	6¾	7¼	7½
Diameter of air-pump bucket	4	4	4	4	5½	5½	5½	5½	7	7
Height to centre of cylinder	16½	16½	19	19	22	22	23	23	30	30
Total length, including fly-wheel	241	241	272	272	313	313	345	345	420	420
Width to outer bearing	78½	78½	87	87	102	102	111	111	135	135
Approx. weight packed, cwts.	89	93	126	132	188	197	257	269	348	364

All Dimensions are given in Inches.

Fig. 934.

TABLE 107.—**Particulars of Messrs. Marshall's Vertical Short-Stroke Engines** (Fig. 934).

Diameter of cylinder	$4\frac{1}{2}$	$5\frac{1}{2}$	$6\frac{1}{2}$	$7\frac{1}{2}$	8	9	10	11	12	13
Stroke	8	8	10	10	12	12	14	14	16	16
Revolutions per minute	260	260	210	210	175	175	150	150	130	130
Boiler-pressure, lbs. per □″	100	100	100	100	100	100	100	100	100	100
Best average H.P.*	5	$7\frac{1}{2}$	$10\frac{1}{2}$	$13\frac{3}{4}$	16	20	25	$30\frac{1}{2}$	36	42
Diameter of fly-wheel	32	32	$41\frac{1}{2}$	$41\frac{1}{2}$	$52\frac{1}{2}$	$52\frac{1}{2}$	60	60	66	66
Width of fly-wheel	5	5	6	6	$7\frac{1}{2}$	$7\frac{1}{2}$	$9\frac{1}{2}$	$9\frac{1}{2}$	$11\frac{1}{4}$	$11\frac{1}{4}$
Weight of fly-wheel, cwts.	$2\frac{1}{4}$	$2\frac{1}{4}$	$4\frac{3}{4}$	$4\frac{3}{4}$	$7\frac{3}{4}$	$7\frac{3}{4}$	11	11	17	17
Diameter of crank-shaft	$2\frac{1}{2}$	$2\frac{1}{2}$	$2\frac{3}{4}$	$2\frac{3}{4}$	$3\frac{1}{4}$	$3\frac{1}{4}$	$3\frac{3}{4}$	$3\frac{3}{4}$	$4\frac{1}{2}$	$4\frac{1}{2}$
Total height of engine	$55\frac{5}{16}$	$55\frac{5}{16}$	$66\frac{1}{4}$	$66\frac{1}{4}$	$78\frac{1}{8}$	$78\frac{1}{8}$	$89\frac{1}{4}$	$89\frac{1}{4}$	$105\frac{1}{8}$	$105\frac{1}{8}$
Floor space, width†	32	32	$41\frac{1}{2}$	$41\frac{1}{2}$	$52\frac{1}{2}$	$52\frac{1}{2}$	60	60	66	66
Floor space, length†	$43\frac{1}{2}$	$43\frac{1}{2}$	52	52	63	63	70	70	70	70
Height of centre from ground	$8\frac{1}{2}$	$8\frac{1}{2}$	10	10	$11\frac{1}{2}$	$11\frac{1}{2}$	$13\frac{1}{2}$	$13\frac{1}{2}$	15	15

* Effective H.P. † Including space for fly-wheel.

All Dimensions are given in Inches.

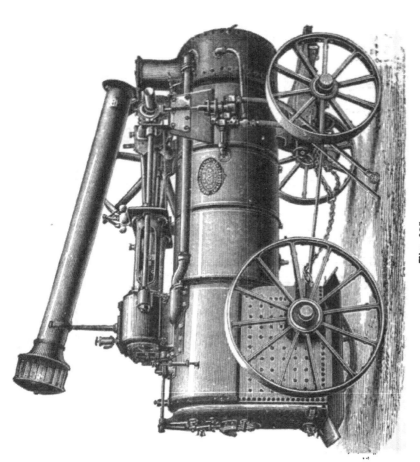

Fig. 985.

Table 108.—Particulars of Messrs. Marshall's Double Cylinder Portable Engines (Fig. 935).

Nominal horse-power	14	16	20	25	30	35	40
Diameter of cylinders (each)	9	10	11	12	13	13¾	14½
Length of stroke	14	14	16	16	18	18	20
Revolutions per minute	115	115	95	95	85	85	80
Boiler pressure per □″	90	90	90	90	90	90	90
Best average H.P.	35	40	50	63	75	88	100
Diameter of crank-shaft	4	4	4¾	5	5½	6	6¼
Diameter of fly-wheel	67	67	72	72	79	79	99
Width of fly-wheel	9½	9½	13	13	15	15	15
Weight of fly-wheel in cwts.	11	11	15¼	15¼	19	19	30
Total heating-surface of boiler, ordinary, sq. feet	280·52	314·59	389·81	422·62	471·092	560·907	622·685
Total heating-surface of boiler, colonial, sq. feet	285·73	321·94	395·32	429·241	479·177	569·114	633·683
Area of grate, ordinary	9·04	9·68	12·69	13·810	15·265	17·747	20·035
Area of grate, colonial	10·74	11·93	14·34	15·910	17·747	20·285	23·411
Diameter of boiler barrel	40¾	42¾	45	49⅛	51	51	55
Total length of boiler, ordinary	150	158	174¼	178	189	203	211
Total length of boiler, colonial	157	167	180	185	197	211	221
Length of boiler barrel	91½	94	100¼	100	105	111	115

All Dimensions are given in Inches.

Fig. 986.

TABLE 109.—**Particulars of Messrs. Ruston & Proctor's Horizontal Self-Contained Short-Stroke Engines** (Fig. 936).

Diameter of cylinder	5½	6½	7¼	8	8¾	9½	10½	11½
Length of stroke	8	10	10	12	12	14	14	16
Revolutions per minute	190	160	160	140	140	125	125	110
Boiler pressure, lbs. per square inch	80	80	80	80	80	80	80	80
Best average H.P.	7	11	13	17	20	24	30	36
Diameter of crank-shaft	2	2¼	2½	2¾	3	3¼	3½	3¾
Diameter of fly-wheel	33	36	39	40	45	48	54	60
Width of fly-wheel	4½	4½	5	5	6	6	7	7½
Weight in cwts.	2	2½	3	3½	4¼	5¼	6¾	8
Height to centre	17	18	18	28	28	30	30	30
Total length	64	74	76	88	89	100	103	116
Total width	32	36	36	42	44	50	52	60
Approx. weight unpacked, cwts.	7	9	11	15	17	24	27	35

All Dimensions are given in Inches.

Fig. 937.

TABLE 110.—Particulars of Messrs. Buston & Proctor's Vertical Short-Stroke Engines (Fig. 937).

	Engine 1	Engine 2	Engine 3	Engine 4	Engine 5	Engine 6
Diameter of cylinder	6	6¾	7½	8¼	9½	10½
Length of stroke	6	6	8	8	10	10
Revolutions per minute	150 / 200 / 250	150 / 200 / 250	150 / 200 / 250	150 / 200 / 250	150 / 200 / 250	150 / 200 / 250
Best average H.P.	5 / 7 / 9	7 / 9 / 11	10 / 14 / 18	14 / 18 / 23	22 / 29 / 36	27 / 35 / 44
Boiler pressure, lbs. per sq. in.	80	80	80	80	80	80
Diameter of fly-wheel	30	30	33	33	42	42
Width of fly-wheel	4	5	4½	6	6	8
Weight of fly-wheel in cwts.	2	3½	5	6	7½	9
Diameter of crank-shaft	2¼	2⅝	3	3¼	3½	3¾
Total width of engine	30	30	33	33	42	42
Total height from ground	57	57	66	66	78	78
Total length	34	34	40	40	48	48
Approx. weight in cwts.	12	14	16	17	20	22

All Dimensions are given in Inches.

Fig. 988.

TABLE 111.—**Particulars of Messrs. Ruston & Proctor's Long-Stroke Horizontal Engines** (Fig. 938).

Diameter of cylinder	8	9	10	11	12	13	14	15	16	17	18	19	20	21	22	23	26	27
Length of stroke . .	16	16	20	20	24	24	28	28	32	32	36	36	40	40	44	44	52	52
Revs. per minute .	135	135	110	110	90	90	80	80	70	70	65	65	60	60	60	60	60	60
Boiler press., lbs. per square inch	80	80	80	80	80	80	80	80	80	80	80	80	80	80	80	80	80	80
Best average H.P. .	15	20	25	30	35	40	48	55	65	75	85	95	110	120	140	160	230	250
Diam. of fly-wheel .	62	66	85	87	99	101	116	116	120	120	144	144	146	146	168	168	177	177
Width of fly-wheel .	7	9	8	8	10	10	12	14	14	16	16	18	20	22	22	24	28	30
Weight of fly-wheel, cwts. . .	10	12½	21½	21½	29½	29½	48	54	66	74	89½	105	130	—	—	—	—	—
Diam. of crank-shaft	3	3	3¾	3¾	4½	4½	5¼	5¼	6	6	6¾	6¾	7½	7½	8¼	8¼	9¾	9¾
Total length . .	142	142	160	160	188	188	218	218	240	240	274	274	294	294	335	335	378	378
Total width . .	75	75	84	84	93	93	102	102	114	114	123	123	132	132	141	141	150	150
Approx. weight, cwts.	48	50	76	80	106	112	156	162	204	214	310	323	338	358	473	493	700	720
Height to centre . .	36	36	36	36	36	36	36	36	36	36	36	36	36	36	36	36	36	36

All Dimensions are given in Inches.

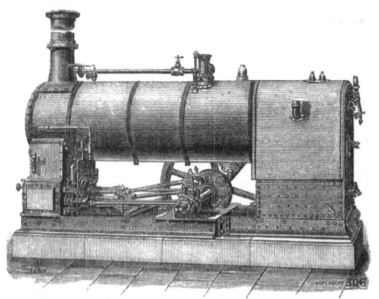

Fig. 939.

TABLE 112.—Particulars of Compound Under-type Engines by Messrs. E. R. & F. Turner (Fig. 939).

Diameter of small cylinder . .	7	8	9	10
Diameter of large cylinder . . .	11¼	12¾	14	16
Length of stroke	12	14	16	18
Revolutions per minute . . .	180	155	135	120
Piston speed in feet per minute .	360	360	360	360
Best average indicated horse-power .	38	50	63	78
Diameter of crank-shaft . . .	3½	3¾	4¼	5
Diameter of fly-wheel	60	72	72	84
Width of fly-wheel	8	9	10½	12
Weight of fly-wheel, cwt. . . .	8	13	16	22
Height to centre of boiler . .	42½	49	58	66¼
Height to centre of crank-shaft . .	13	14½	17	19⅝
Diameter of boiler-barrel . . .	34½	36¾	40½	47
Length of boiler-barrel . . .	112	121½	132	142
Heating-surface in square feet .	187·5	250	312·8	390
Area of fire-grate in square feet .	5·06	6·6	8·2	10·25
Width over all	86	91	102	116
Working pressure in lbs. per sq. in. .	140	140	140	140

All Dimensions in Inches.

N.B.—The heating-surfaces and boiler dimensions in the table are given for ordinary English coal; for inferior and colonial coal, about 25 per cent. should be added to grate area and fire-box heating surface.

Fig. 940.

TABLE 113.—Particulars of Compound Portable Engines by Messrs. E. R. & F. Turner (Fig. 940).

Diameter of small cylinder . .	7	8	9
Diameter of large cylinder . . .	$11\frac{1}{4}$	$12\frac{3}{4}$	14
Length of stroke	12	14	16
Revolutions per minute . .	180	155	135
Piston speed in feet per minute .	360	360	360
Best average indicated horse-power .	36	48	60
Diameter of crank-shaft . . .	$3\frac{3}{4}$	$3\frac{3}{4}$	$4\frac{1}{4}$
Diameter of fly-wheel	60	72	72
Width of fly-wheel	8	9	$10\frac{1}{2}$
Weight of fly-wheel in cwt. . . .	8	13	16
Diameter of boiler-barrel . . .	$34\frac{1}{2}$	$36\frac{3}{4}$	$40\frac{1}{2}$
Length of boiler over all . . .	147	$161\frac{1}{2}$	179
Heating-surface in square feet . .	187·5	250	312·8
Area of grate in square feet . .	5·06	6·6	8·2
Length over all	158	173	192
Width over axles	87	89	93
Height to top of boiler . . .	109	118	126
Working-pressure in lbs. per sq. in. .	140	140	140

Dimensions in Inches.

See remarks as to heating-surface in Table 112.

Fig. 941.

TABLE 114.—Particulars of Single-Cylinder Portable Engines by Messrs. E. R. & F. Turner (Fig. 941).

Diameter of cylinder .	6	$6\frac{3}{4}$	$7\frac{1}{2}$	$8\frac{1}{2}$	9	$9\frac{1}{2}$	$10\frac{1}{2}$
Length of stroke . .	9	$10\frac{1}{2}$	$10\frac{1}{2}$	12	12	12	12
Revs. per minute .	180	150	150	130	130	130	130
Piston speed in feet per minute . .	270	263	263	260	260	260	260
Best aver. indic. H.P.	6	8	10	12	14	16	20
Diam. of crank-shaft .	$2\frac{1}{8}$	$2\frac{3}{8}$	$2\frac{1}{2}$	$2\frac{3}{4}$	3	3	$3\frac{1}{4}$
Diam. of fly-wheel .	45	52	52	60	60	60	60
Width of fly-wheel .	$4\frac{1}{2}$	5	5	6	6	6	7
Weight of do. cwt.	3	$3\frac{1}{2}$	$3\frac{1}{2}$	$6\frac{1}{2}$	$6\frac{3}{4}$	$6\frac{3}{4}$	$7\frac{1}{2}$
Diam. of boiler-barrel	24	29	29	$30\frac{3}{8}$	$33\frac{1}{2}$	$33\frac{1}{2}$	$34\frac{1}{2}$
Length of do. . .	62	67	81	83	$80\frac{5}{8}$	$85\frac{5}{8}$	$95\frac{1}{4}$
Heating-surface, sq. ft.	59·4	78·36	96·37	109·03	128	144·27	172·29
Area of fire-grate, sq. ft.	2·02	2·38	2·96	3·27	3·61	4·12	5·01
Approx. weight, cwt.	40	50	57	65	74	82	95
Length over all . .	96	112	120	126	126	132	138
Width over axles . .	58	66	66	73	77	79	82
Height to top fly-wheel	75	93	93	99	104	106	110
Working-pressure in lbs. per sq. inch .	80	80	80	80	80	80	80

Dimensions in Inches.

See remarks as to heating-surface, &c., in Table 112.

Portable engines have been and are still manufactured in large numbers in England, and have settled down into few varieties. In the first portable engines, pressures were low and there was no objection to throwing the whole strain of the working on to the barrel plates of the boiler. Now, however, with higher pressures the tendency has been to relieve the boiler as much as possible of the working strain due to the pressure of steam on the piston, by adding stay bars between the cylinder and the crank shaft bearings, or in some cases of mounting the engine on a frame of its own which is then bolted to stools rivetted on the boiler ; this would seem to commend itself on account of the facilities of packing for export, and facility of carriage up difficult countries.

From the portable engine the road locomotive or traction engine has been developed, and the number of these for farm purposes increases every year ; they do not differ greatly from the portable engine as far as the engine itself is concerned, but have the addition of gearing and travelling wheels of various designs.

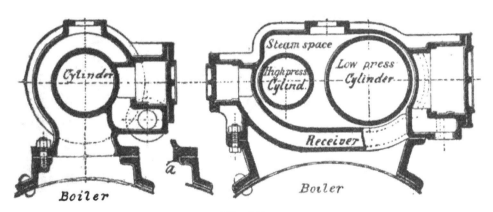

Fig. 941A.

Compound portable engines have come into favour for the larger sizes ; the cylinders of these are usually arranged side by side, Fig. 941A, and the cranks at right angles, the receiver taking the form of a pipe under the cylinders and concealed in the casing so that the receiver has the advantage of being well protected from cold air, and from its position close to the boiler top is kept in a hot atmosphere. The steam pipe in portable engines is reduced to a minimum in length and the steam jacket can be readily drained direct into the boiler ; these are great advantages and no doubt contribute to the very economical results which are obtained from portable engines.

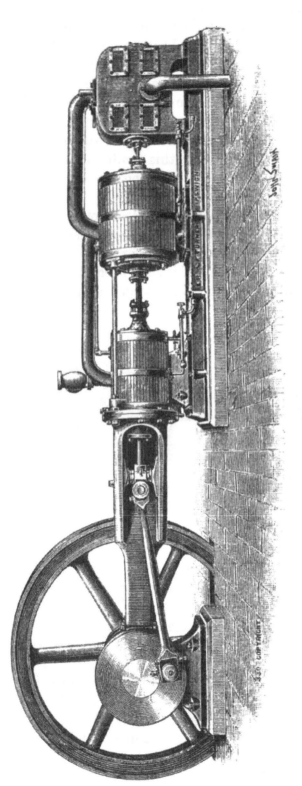

Fig. 942.

TABLE 115.—**Particulars of Tandem Compound Engines by Messrs. E. R. & F. Turner** (Fig. 942).

Best average indicated H.P.	44	55	68	82	96	110	124	140
Diameter of small cylinder	9	10	11	12	13	14	15	16
Diameter of large cylinder	14	16	18	20	21	23	25	26
Length of stroke	16	20	20	24	24	28	28	36
Revolutions per minute	150	120	120	100	100	86	86	70
Diameter of fly-wheel	84	96	96	114	114	129	129	144
Width of fly-wheel	8	9	9	11	11	12	12	14
Weight of fly-wheel in cwts.	30	50	50	62	62	80	80	100
Diameter of crank-shaft at journal	$4\frac{1}{4}$	5	5	6	6	$6\frac{1}{2}$	$6\frac{1}{2}$	$7\frac{1}{2}$
Diameter of crank-shaft at fly-wheel	$5\frac{1}{2}$	$6\frac{3}{8}$	$6\frac{3}{8}$	$7\frac{1}{2}$	$7\frac{1}{2}$	$8\frac{1}{4}$	$8\frac{1}{4}$	$9\frac{1}{2}$
Height of centre from ground	28	30	30	32	32	34	34	36

Dimensions are given in Inches.

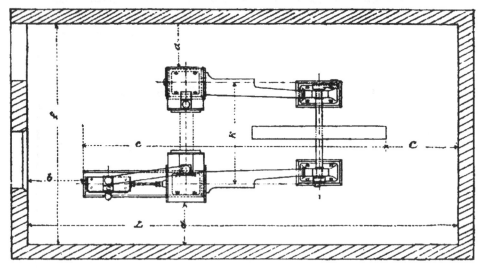

Fig. 943.

TABLE 116.—Particulars of Floor-Space occupied by Coupled Compound Condensing Engines by Messrs. E. R. & F. Turner (Fig. 943).

	9 & 14	10 & 16	11 & 18	12 & 20	13 & 21	14 & 23	15 & 25	16 & 26
Diameter of cylinders . .								
Length of stroke . .	16	20	20	24	24	28	28	36
Distance from cyls. to wall a	30	30	30	30	30	30	30	30
„ „ „ b	36	36	36	36	36	36	36	36
„ „ „ c	12	12	12	18	18	18	18	18
Total length of engine C	—	201	201	237	237	272	272	342
Total width of engine room f	173	176	176	188	190	199	202	210
Distance between centres of cylinders . . K	78	78	78	84	84	90	90	96
Total length of engine room L	—	249	249	285	285	320	320	390

Dimensions are given in Inches.

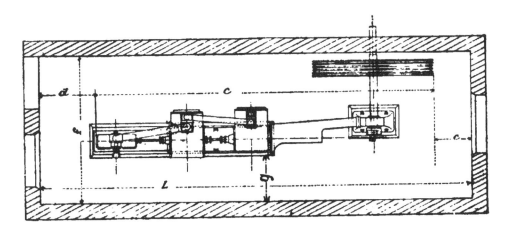

Fig. 944.

TABLE 117.—Particulars of Floor-Space Occupied by Tandem
  Compound Condensing Engines by Messrs. E. R. &
  F. Turner (Fig. 944).

	9 & 14	10 & 16	11 & 18	12 & 20	13 & 21	14 & 23	15 & 25	16 & 26
Diameter of cylinders . .								
Stroke of piston . . .	16	20	20	24	24	28	28	36
Total length of engine-room L	—	327	327	381	381	—	—	—
Total width of engine-room F	—	107	107	121	121	—	—	—
Distance from engine to wall c	15	15	15	15	15	15	15	15
,, ,, ,, d	36	36	36	42	42	42	42	48
,, ,, ,, g	30	30	30	30	30	30	30	30
Length over all of engine C	—	276	276	324	324	—	—	—

Dimensions are given in Inches.

z

TABLE 118.—Particulars of Compound Coupled Condensing Engines by Messrs. E. R. & F. Turner (see also Table 116).

Best average indicated H.P.	44	55	68	82	96	110	124	140
Diameter of small cylinder	9	10	11	12	13	14	15	16
Diameter of large cylinder	14	16	18	20	21	23	25	26
Length of stroke	16	20	20	24	24	28	28	36
Revolutions per minute	150	120	120	100	100	86	86	70
Diameter of fly-wheel	84	96	96	114	114	129	129	144
Width of fly-wheel	8	9	9	11	11	12	12	14
Weight of fly-wheel in cwts.	25	40	40	50	50	64	64	80
Height of centre from ground	24	24	24	26	26	27	27	33
Diameter of crank-shaft at journal	3¼	3¾	3¾	4¼	4¼	5	5	6
Diameter of crank-shaft at fly-wheel	4¼	4¾	4¾	5¾	5¾	6½	6½	7½

Dimensions are given in Inches.

Fig. 945.

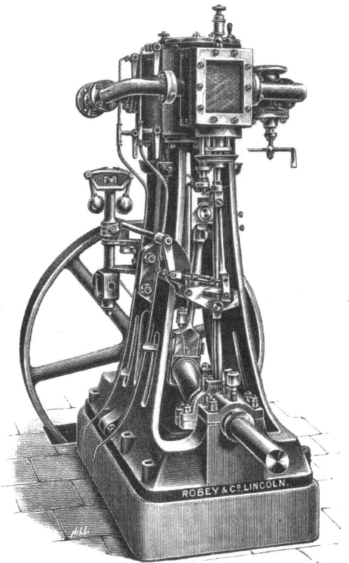

TABLE 119.—Particulars of a Double Cylinder Vertical
Engine * by Messrs. Robey & Co. (Fig. 945).

Nominal horse-power .	16	Width of fly-wheel . .	11
Diameter of cylinders, each	9½	Height to centre of crank from under side of standard . . .	11
Length of stroke . .	12		
Revolutions per minute .	140		
Best average I.H.P. . .	32	Total height . . .	79
Diameter of crank-shaft .	4	,, width	60
Diameter of fly-wheel . .	60	,, length . . .	80
Weight of fly-wheel, cwt. .	15	Approx. weight in cwt. .	54

* For 80 lbs. boiler pressure.   Dimensions are given in Inches.

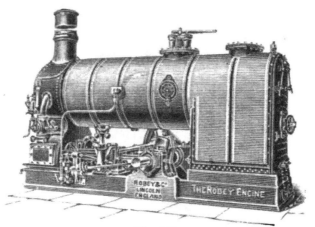

Fig. 946.

TABLE 120.—Particulars of Compound Undertype Engines by Messrs. Robey & Co. (Fig. 946).

Nominal H.P.	8	50
Diameter of H.P. cylinder	$5\frac{1}{2}$	$13\frac{1}{4}$
Diameter of L.P. cylinder	$9\frac{1}{2}$	23
Length of stroke	12	24
Revolutions per minute	200	100
Best average I.H.P.	24	150
Diameter of crank-shaft	$3\frac{1}{4}$	8
Diameter of fly-wheel	58	96
Width of fly-wheel	$7\frac{1}{2}$	23
Weight of fly-wheel in cwts.	$8\frac{1}{4}$	96
Height to centre of boiler	46	$94\frac{1}{2}$
Height to centre of engine	$15\frac{1}{2}$	$33\frac{1}{2}$
Diameter of boiler	$31\frac{3}{8}$	61
Length of boiler	128	231
Heating-surface in square feet	169·4	757·7
Grate area in square feet	5·8	21·8
Width over all	63	126
Approx. weight, cwts.	50	380
Boiler-pressure	140	140

Dimensions are given in Inches.

ROBEY & C° LINCOLN

Fig. 947.

TABLE 121.—Particulars of Horizontal Girder Engines by Messrs. Robey & Co. (Fig. 947).

Nominal H.P.	8	30
Diameter of cylinder	9	18
Length of stroke	18	36
Revolutions per minute	116	75
Best average I.H.P.	20	100
Diameter of crank-shaft	4	8
Diameter of fly-wheel	66	144
Width of fly-wheel	8	17
Weight of fly-wheel, cwts.	18	90
Height to centre of cylinder . . .	15	28
Total length over all	125	247
Total width over all	65	134
Total weight, approx. in cwts. . .	48	270
Boiler-pressure	80	80

Dimensions are given in Inches.

Fig. 948.

TABLE 122.—Particulars of Compound Coupled Non-condensing Engine by Messrs. John Fowler & Co.

Diameter of high pressure cylinder	10	11	13	15	$17\frac{1}{2}$
Diameter of low pressure cylinder	16	$17\frac{1}{2}$	23	24	$27\frac{1}{2}$
Length of stroke . .	20	20	24	30	36

Dimensions are given in Inches.

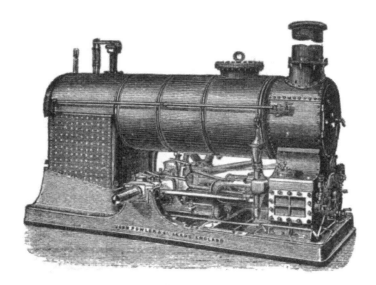

Fig. 940.

TABLE 123.—Particulars of Compound Undertype Engines by Messrs. John Fowler & Co.

Diameter of high pressure cylinder . . }	$5\frac{3}{4}$	$6\frac{5}{8}$	$7\frac{1}{4}$	8	9	10	11	12	13	17	18
Diameter of low pressure cylinder . . }	9	$10\frac{1}{2}$	$11\frac{1}{4}$	$12\frac{3}{4}$	14	16	$17\frac{1}{2}$	21	23	27	29
Length of stroke .	12	14	14	15	16	18	18	24	24	30	30

Dimensions are given in Inches.

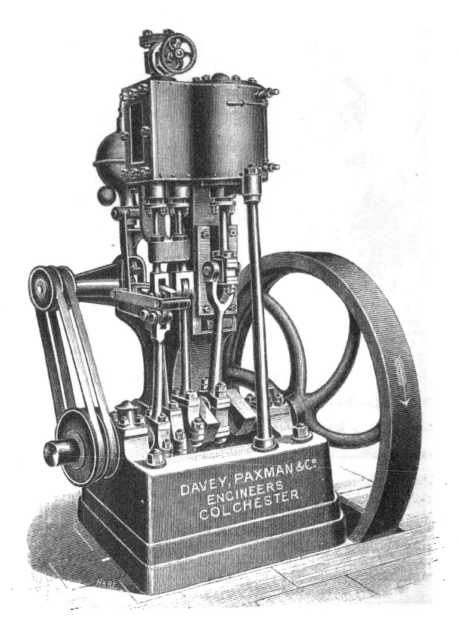

Fig. 950.

TABLE 124.—**Single Cylinder Vertical Engines** (Fig. 950) **by Davey, Paxman & Co.**

Nominal H.P.	2	3	4	5	6	8	10	12
Diameter of cylinder	$4\frac{1}{2}$	$5\frac{1}{2}$	$6\frac{1}{2}$	$7\frac{1}{4}$	$8\frac{1}{4}$	$9\frac{1}{2}$	$10\frac{1}{2}$	12
Length of stroke	6	7	7	8	8	9	10	12
Revolutions per minute	300 400	260 350	260 350	225 300	225 300	200 260	180 250	160 220
Best average I.H.P.	5	$7\frac{1}{2}$	10	$12\frac{1}{2}$	15	20	25	30
Diameter of fly-wheel	42	42	42	48	48	48	54	54
Width of fly-wheel	$3\frac{1}{2}$	4	5	5	6	7	8	8

TABLE 125.—**Double Cylinder Vertical Engines by Davey, Paxman & Co.**

Nominal H.P.	4	6	8	10	12	16	20	25
Diameter of cylinders	$4\frac{1}{2}$	$5\frac{1}{2}$	$6\frac{1}{2}$	$7\frac{1}{4}$	$8\frac{1}{4}$	$9\frac{1}{2}$	$10\frac{1}{2}$	12
Length of stroke	6	7	7	8	8	9	10	12
Revolutions per minute	300 400	260 350	260 350	225 300	225 300	200 260	180 250	160 220
Best average I.H.P.	10	15	20	25	30	40	50	62
Diameter of fly-wheel	42	42	42	48	48	48	54	60
Width of fly-wheel	5	6	7	8	9	10	11	12

All Dimensions are given in Inches.

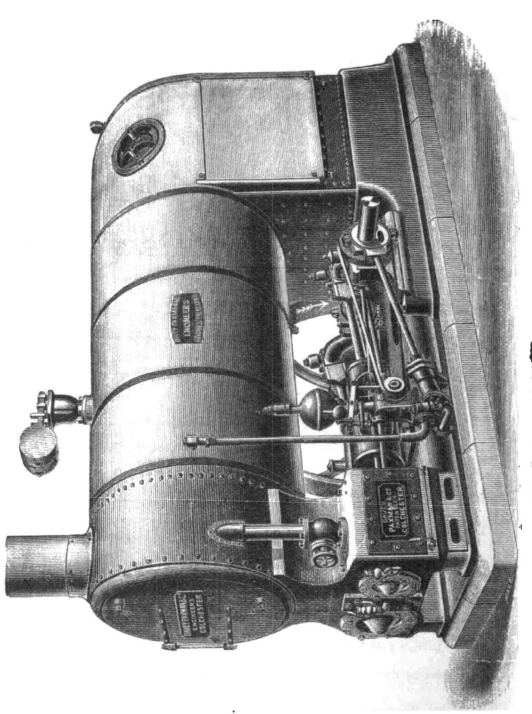

Fig. 951.

Undertype Engines by Messrs. Davey, Paxman & Co.

TABLE 126.—Compound Engines (Fig. 951).

Nominal H.P.	8	10	12	16	20	25	30	35	40	50	60
Diameter of high pressure cylinder	5½	6½	7	8	9	10	11	12	12¾	14	16
Diameter of low pressure cylinder	9	10½	11¼	13	14¼	16	17½	18¾	20	22½	25
Length of stroke	14	14	14	14	14	18	18	24	24	24	24
Revolutions per minute	155	155	155	155	155	120	120	90	90	90	90
Best average I.H.P.	20	25	30	40	50	62	75	80	100	125	150
Diameter of fly-wheel	60	60	60	66	66	84	84	102	102	102	102
Width of fly-wheel	7	8	9	10	11	12	14	15	17	20	22

TABLE 127.—Single Cylinder.

Nominal H.P.	4	5	6	8	10	12
Diameter of cylinder	6½	7¼	8¼	9½	10½	12
Length of stroke	12	12	12	12	14	14
Revolutions per minute	125	125	125	125	115	115
Best average I.H.P.	6	12½	15	20	25	30
Diameter of fly-wheel	52	60	60	60	66	66
Width of fly-wheel	5	5	6	7	8	9

All Dimensions are given in Inches.

TABLE 128.—**Particulars of Willan's Central Valve Engines with Two and Three Cranks** (Fig. 952).

Number of cranks	2	2	2	2	2	2	3	2	3	2	3
Diameter of low pressure cylinder	8½	10	12	14	17	20	20	28	28	34	34
Effective area of piston □″	102	143	206	282	416	580	870	1120	1680	1660	2490
Stroke	5	5	6	6	8	9	9	13½	13½	18	18
Revolutions per minute	550	520	470	460	380	350	350	260	260	200	200
Boiler pressure	90	90	90	90	90	90	90	90	90	90	90
Indicated H.P.	28	38	60	80	135	200	300	400	600	600	900
Diameter of fly-wheel	21½	23½	33	36	—	—	—	—	—	—	—
Width of fly-wheel	4	4	4½	5	—	—	—	—	—	—	—
Height to top of cylinder, simple	45⅜	47⅝	55	56	—	—	—	—	—	—	—
" " compound	55½	57½	66⅞	68⅝	—	—	—	—	—	—	—
" " triple expansion	—	66¼	78⅛	79⅜	—	—	—	—	—	—	—

All Dimensions are given in Inches.

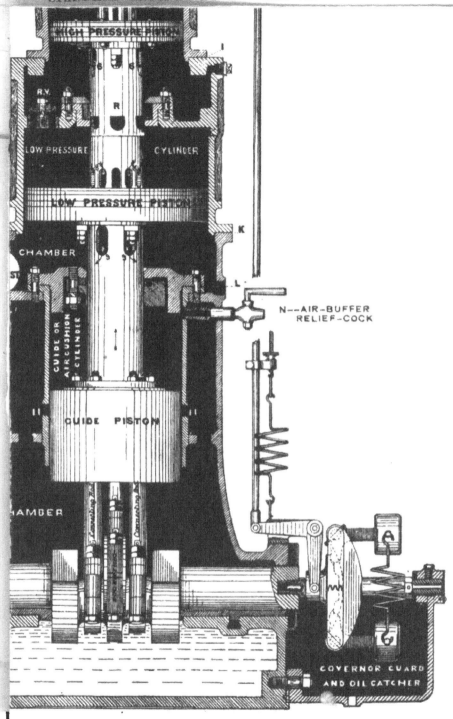

HIGH PRESSURE PISTON

R.V.

LOW PRESSURE   CYLINDER

LOW PRESSURE PISTON

CHAMBER

GUIDE OR AIRCUSHION B CYLINDER

GUIDE   PISTON

CHAMBER

N--AIR-BUFFER
RELIEF-COCK

GOVERNOR GUARD
AND OIL CATCHER

PLUG
DRAW

PISTONS ON UP STROKE, ONE-FOURTH
OF STROKE COMPLETED: STEAM EX-
HAUSTING AS SHOWN BY ARROWS;
PISTONS AND PISTON-ROD IN
ELEVATION.

[To face p. 348.

TABLE 129.—Particulars of Willan's Central Valve Engines with Single Cranks.

Diameter of low pressure cylinder	5	6	7	8½	10
Stroke	3	4	4	5	5
Effective area of piston ☐″	16·8	25	34·5	51	71·5
Revolutions per minute	700	600	600	550	520
Boiler pressure	90	90	90	90	90
Indicated H.P.	3½	6	8½	14	19

All Dimensions are given in Inches.

SECTION VIII.

COMPOUND ENGINES.

THE early compound engines by Woolf had no intermediate receiver, and the passage of the steam was direct from the high to the low pressure cylinder. In some cases, as in figs. 953, 954, both pistons moved together in the same direction. A form of valve suitable for this kind of engine is shown in fig. 954, which also gives a section

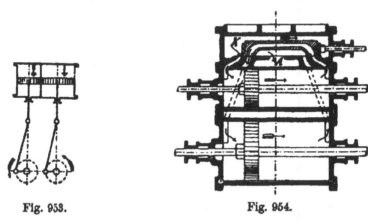

Fig. 953.   Fig. 954.

through the cylinders with arrows to indicate the course of the steam through the ports and passages. In this arrangement the passages

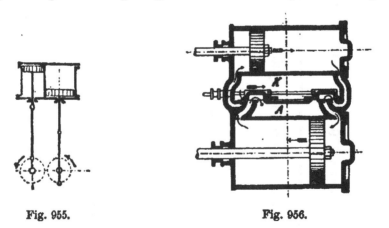

Fig. 955.   Fig. 956.

to the low pressure cylinder are long and thus give a large clearance space.

In the arrangement shewn in figs. 955, 956, the pistons move in opposite directions. The clearance space here is less than in the former example, figs. 953, 954.

The indicator diagram, fig. 957, is from an arrangement like fig. 956, with cut-off at ·4 in the high, and at ·8 in the low pressure cylinder.

In these types of compound engines, it is a good plan to have the cut-off in the high pressure cylinder controlled by the governor, and

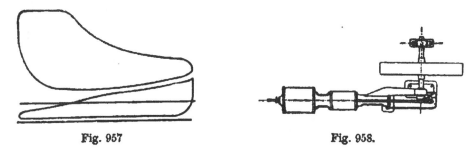

Fig. 957   Fig. 958.

that of the low variable by hand. The side-by-side cylinders, with pistons moving together as fig. 954, have been much used for beam pumping engines.

Tandem Compound Engine.

The tandem horizontal engines, as fig. 958, often have a receiver even if it only takes the form of a large connecting pipe. These engines take up but little room in the width, but are rather long.

Examples of the various methods of connecting the high and low pressure cylinders of tandem compound engines are shewn in figs. 959—963.

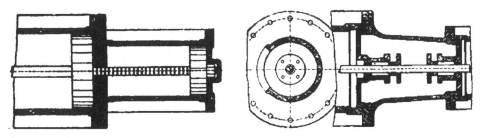

Fig. 959.—High and low-pressure cylinders for tandem engine by Simpson, of Dartmouth.*

Fig. 960. — Connecting - piece for tandem cylinders used for vertical engines.

* For performance of a small engine of this type, see reports of judges of Royal Agricultural Society's meeting at Plymouth, 1890.

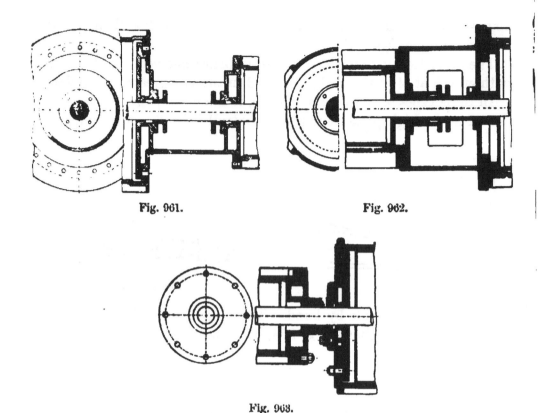

Fig. 961.   Fig. 962.

Fig. 963.

Figs. 961—963.—Various methods of arranging the connecting-piece and glands for tandem cylinder.

Compound Engines with the Cranks at 90°.

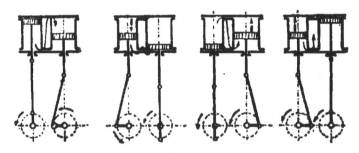

Fig. 964.

The outline diagrams, fig. 964, shew the different positions of cranks and pistons in a compound engine with two cranks at right angles to each other, and fig. 965 shews the indicator diagrams corresponding to the two cylinders. H in fig. 965 gives the position of the high pressure crank, and N that of the low.

In compound engines of this kind, the cut-off in the high pressure cylinder is usually controlled by the governor, and that of the low is either fixed or better varied by hand.

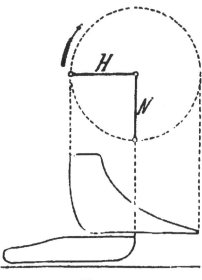

Fig. 965.

Ratio of Cylinder Volumes of Compound Engines.

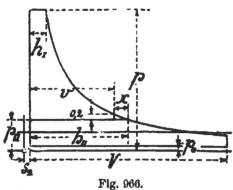

Fig. 966.

From the theoretical diagram, fig. 966, the ratio of the cylinder volumes can be determined :

t = the temperature of the entering steam.

p = pressure of the entering steam.

t_0 = the temperature of the exhaust steam.

p_0 = pressure of the exhaust steam.

The mean temperature of the cylinders should be equal to half the total fall of temperature. Let the range of temperature difference in the two cylinders be taken as nearly equal as possible, then

$$t_\mu = \frac{t + t_0}{2}$$

A A

From this temperature and corresponding pressure p, the line passing through the point in the curve at the height p_u, will be the division line between the two cylinder diagrams, and b_u as the admission line of the low pressure cylinder diagram, an allowance of about 3 lbs. pressure (·2 atmosphere) being made for the drop between

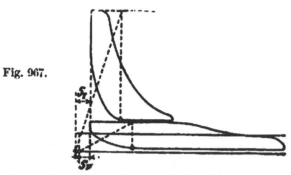

Fig. 967.

the cylinders, then the volume of the high pressure cylinder r will be a little less than b_u. The diagram can be then rounded off and corrected, when it will appear as in fig. 967. Sometimes the endeavour is made to exactly equalize the work in the two cylinders, but although for many reasons it is good practice, the equality can only happen at certain loads unless the low pressure cylinder is provided with a variable expansion gear worked by hand.

Receivers for Compound Engines.

The receiver was formerly merely a large pipe between the cylinders of compound engines, or in some cases a wrought-iron barrel lagged and cased, but now they are often steam jacketed, and sometimes constructed as in fig. 968 with tubes. An ordinary form is that shewn in fig. 970, which is simple and cheap to make.

One of the most important points to note is that the receiver and jacket should be efficiently drained.

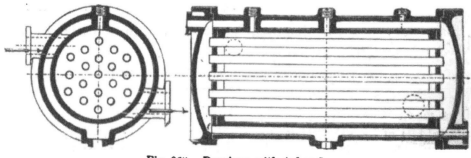

Fig. 968.—Receiver with tubes.*

---

* "Zeitschrift d. Verein Deutsch Ingenieur," 1888, plate 15.

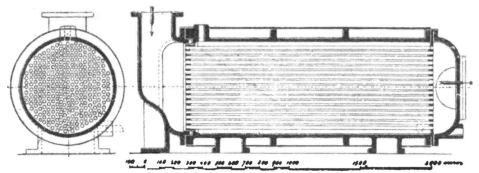

Fig. 969.—Receiver with tubes for tandem engine.*

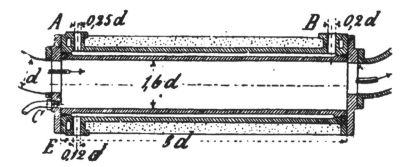

Fig. 970.—Ordinary jacketed receiver.

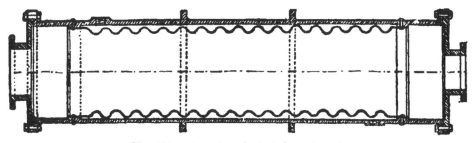

Fig. 971.--American jacketed receiver.†

Triple Expansion Engines.

a. Marine Engines.

The number of triple expansion engines built increases every year, and it is now the recognized type for marine engines with boiler pressure of about 160 lbs. per square inch. Four different arrangements are in use.‡

---

* "Zeitschrift d. Verein Deutsch Ingenieur," 1890, plate 22.

† *Engineering*, 1891, p. 750.

‡ These arrangements are from a paper by Otto J. Müller, jun., "Zeitschrift d. deutsches Verein Ingenieur," 1887, page 445. See also "Proceedings of the Institution of Mechanical Engineers," July, 1891.

(1.) In fig. 972 there are cranks at right angles, and No. I. cylinder is placed tandem fashion on the top of No. II. A special variety with No. II. cylinder annular, and placed round No. I., see fig. 973.

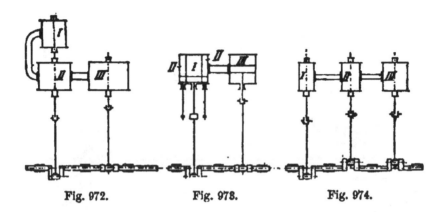

Fig. 972.   Fig. 973.   Fig. 974.

(2.) Fig. 974 shews the very usual arrangement with three cranks at 120° to each other, the three cylinders side by side.

(3.) In fig. 975, there are two high pressure cylinders, Nos. I.

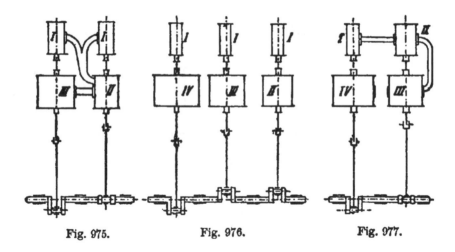

Fig. 975.   Fig. 976.   Fig. 977.

I. placed over Nos. II. and III.; in this arrangement there are two cranks at right angles to each other. An elaboration of this arrangement for quadruple expansion is given in fig. 976.

(4.) A better arrangement for quadruple expansion is shewn in fig. 977.

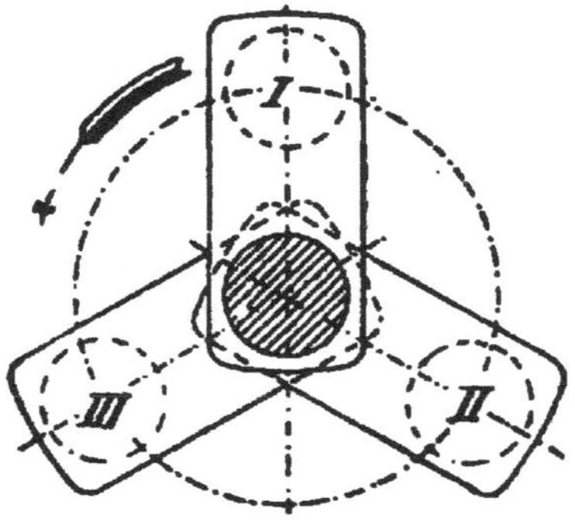

TABLE 130.—Leading Particulars of Triple-Expansion Condensing Engines, for 150 lbs. working pressure.

Stroke of all three cranks H	16	24	32	40	48	56	64	72	80
I. Diameter of high pressure cylinder . d_1	9	13¼	18	22½	27	32	36	40	44
II. Diam. of intermediate pressure cylinder . d_2	14¼	21¾	29	36	44	52	59	66	72
III. Diameter of low pressure cylinder . d_3	24	36	48	60	72	84	96	108	118
Proportion of cylinder volumes (in round numbers) { II. : I.	2·5	2·6	2·6	2·6	2·7	2·6	2·7	2·7	2·7
III. : II.	2·8	2·8	2·8	2·8	2·7	2·6	2·6	2·7	2·7
III. : I.	7·1	7·1	7·1	7·1	7·1	7·0	7·1	7·3	7·2
Revolutions per minute n	200	140	120	100	85	77	70	66	60
Piston speed in feet per minute . }	530	560	640	660	680	710	740	790	800
N, with 150 lbs. pressure N	250	600	1200	2000	2800	4000	5600	7400	9300
Steam used in lbs. per indicated H.P. per hour . }	16·1	15·63	15·63	15·00	14·6	14·1	13·7	13·45	13·23

All Dimensions are given in Inches.

Fig. 978.

The cranks of the triple expansion marine engines may be arranged in order I., II., III., as in fig. 978, with the ship going ahead, so that the steam continuously expands in the shortest possible time while doing its work.*

* "Zeitschrift d. Verein Deutsch Ingenieur," 1886, No. 24.

Stationary Triple-Expansion Engines.

The triple-expansion engine does not offer such great advantages for use on land as for use at sea. The amount of steam used per HP is no doubt less, especially when pressures up to 160 lbs. per square inch are employed, than with simple or compound engines using lower pressures. The disadvantages of triple-expansion engines consist of an increased number of moving parts, by about one-third, and the cost of maintenance and repairs are increased. The high pressures render it less easy to keep the steam pipes and joints steam tight. The power absorbed with the engine running empty is greater than with simple and compound engines.

Professor Schöter gives an interesting account of experiments with a triple-expansion engine built by the Augsburger Engine Company in the Zeitschift d. Verein deutsches Ingenieur, 1890, No. 1.

The engine had two cranks at 90°; the (I) high and (II) intermediate cylinders were placed tandem with one piston rod common to the two, and the (III) low-pressure cylinder on the other side of the fly-wheel.

The working pressure was 150 lbs. per square inch, and the engine condensing; the normal HP at 70 revolutions per minute was 200. For the leading dimensions, see Table 131.

TABLE 131.—**Leading Particulars of Triple-Expansion Engine.**

	High Pressure Cylinder I.		Intermediate Pressure Cylinder II.		Low Pressure Cylinder III.	
	Front.	Back.	Front.	Back.	Front.	Back.
Diameter of pistons .	11·102		17·75		27·61	
Diameter of piston rods	2·95	3·35	3·35	0	3·35	3·35
Stroke	39·37		39·37		39·39	
Ratio of cylinder vols.	1		2·73		6·63	
Ratio of cylinder vols.	—		1		2·34	
P_m in lbs. per square inch . . .	48·36	46·65	12·83	13·11	12·40	12·30

Dimensions in Inches.

The values of P_m are from the mean of five different experiments.

A set of indicator diagrams to a reduced scale with pressures in atmospheres is given in fig. 979.

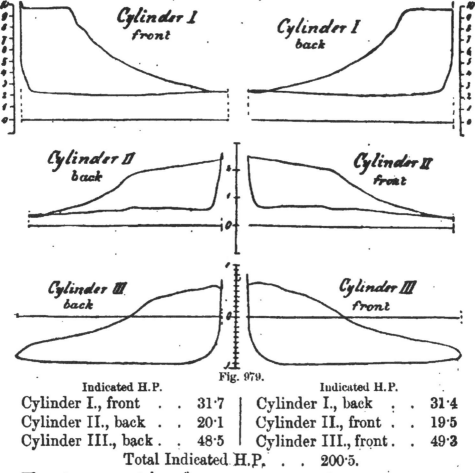

Fig. 979.

Indicated H.P.		Indicated H.P.	
Cylinder I., front	31·7	Cylinder I., back	31·4
Cylinder II., back	20·1	Cylinder II., front	19·5
Cylinder III., back	48·5	Cylinder III., front	49·3
		Total Indicated H.P.	200·5

The steam was taken from a water tube boiler by Dürr & Co., Ratinger, Düsseldorf, with a permitted pressure of 190 lbs. per sq. inch, 150 lbs. only being used during the trials. The heating surface of the boiler was 1722 square feet. The steam used per I.H.P. per hour was 12·52.

From diagrams taken with the engine running light, gave 23·8 I.H.P., about 11·5 per cent. of the normal power.

In the next table the performance of some examples of triple expansion engines is given from actual practice.

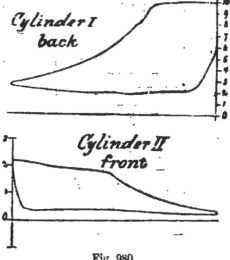

Fig. 980.

TABLE 132.—**Particulars of Triple-Expansion Engines from Actual Practice.**

Horizontal Type.

Cylinder Diam. High.	Cylinder Diam. Intermediate.	Cylinder Diam. Low.	Stroke.	Revolutions per Minute. *n*	Steam Pressure.	Indicated H.P. *Ni*	Steam in lbs. per I.H.P. per Hour. Guaranteed	Steam in lbs. per I.H.P. per Hour. Attained	Heating Surface of Boiler in square feet.	Builder of Engine.	User of Engine.
23⅝	35½	53¼	63	65	150	1000	12·13	11·62	—	Sulzer Bros.	Brunswick Flax Works.
21⅝	33½	48⅛	47¼	68	150	700	12·13	11·80	—	Sulzer	H. Haggemacher, Buda Pesth.
19¾	29½	47¼	55¼	65	150	700	13·78	12·45	6264	Augsburg Engine Co.	Thread Works, Göggingen.
18¾	29½	43½	41½	70	150	450	13·23	12·01	—	Sulzer Bros.	Kinkindaer Steam Mill.
14¼	22⅝	35½	43½	70	150	400	13·23	—	—	Görlitz Engine Works	L. Loewe & Co., Berlin.
13½	21⅝	33⅝	39⅜	70	170	330	13·00	—	—	Görlitz Engine Works	Hansa Mill, Bremen.
14¾	21⅝	31½	39⅜	70	150	240	13·23	—	—	Görlitz Engine Works	Ammunition Works, Spandau.
11	15¾	23⅝	27½	85	205	225	14·33	13·44	1614	Nuremberg Engine Works	N. Wiederer, Fürth.
9¾	15	22½	31½	85	175	200	14·33	13·44	1280	Nuremberg Engine Works	C. Sclenk, Rotha, S.
11	17¾	27½	39⅜	70	150	200	—	12·4 12·0	1764	Augsburg Engine Co.	Augsburg Engine Co.

Vertical Type.

Cylinder Diam. High.	Cylinder Diam. Intermediate.	Cylinder Diam. Low.	Stroke.	Revolutions per Minute. *n*	Steam Pressure.	Indicated H.P. *Ni*	Steam in lbs. per I.H.P. per Hour. Guaranteed	Steam in lbs. per I.H.P. per Hour. Attained	Heating Surface of Boiler in square feet.	Builder of Engine.	User of Engine.
21⅝	35	55¼	35½	85	150	825	12·7	—	6963	Sächs Engine Works	Steam Mill, Wansbeck.
23⅝	37¾	53¼	23⅝	90	157	700	13·0	—	—	G. Luther, Brunswick	Dietrich Bros., Weissenfels.
23⅝	37¾	53¼	23⅝	90	157	480	13·0	—	—	G. Luther, Brunswick	Wittener Rolling Mills, Duisburg.

Dimensions in Inches.

Proportions of Cylinder Volumes with equal strokes for Triple-Expansion Engines.

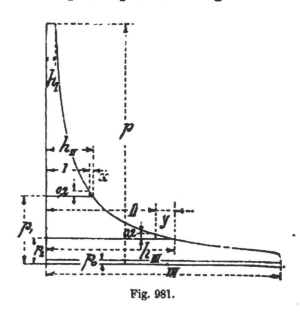

Fig. 981.

From the diagram fig 981, the proportions of cylinder volumes can be determined :

t = temperature of entering steam.

p = pressure of the same.

t_1 = temperature of steam in inter. cylinder.

p_1 = pressure of steam in inter. cylinder.

t_2 = temperature of steam in LP cylinder.

p_2 = pressure of steam in LP cylinder.

t_0 = temperature of exhaust steam.

p_0 = pressure of exhaust steam.

Taking the mean temperature to be half the extreme difference,

$$t_1 = \frac{2t + t_0}{3}$$

$$t_2 = \frac{t + 2t_0}{3}.$$

Then taken the corresponding pressures p_1 and p_2, the diagram can be divided as with the one for compound engines, a drop being allowed of 3 lbs. per square inch. h_{II} and h_{III} will be respectively the points of cut-off from the inter. and LP cylinders; the diagram may then be corrected for compression and losses.

Figs. 982, 983, shew the pistons and cranks of triple-expansion engines in various positions.

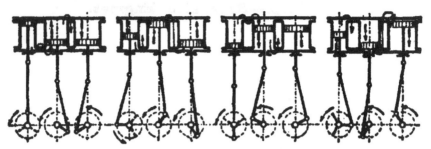

Fig. 982.—Triple-expansion engine with two receivers.

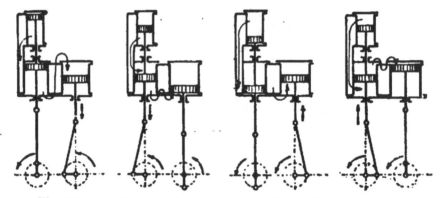

Fig. 983.—Semi-tandem triple-expansion engine with two receivers.

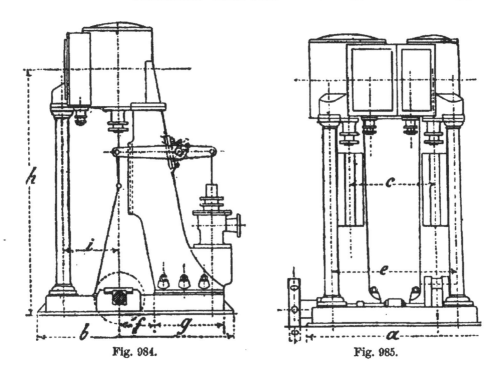

Fig. 984.

Fig. 985.

TABLE 133.—Compound Engine for Screw Steamers
(Figs. 984, 985).

		$7\frac{7}{8}$	$9\frac{1}{4}$	$11\frac{3}{4}$	$13\frac{3}{4}$	$15\frac{1}{4}$	$19\frac{1}{4}$	$23\frac{1}{4}$
Stroke of both pistons . .	H							
Diam. of high-press. piston	d	$5\frac{3}{8}$	$6\frac{3}{4}$	$7\frac{7}{8}$	$9\frac{1}{4}$	$11\frac{1}{4}$	$13\frac{3}{4}$	17
Diam. of low-press. piston .	D	$8\frac{1}{4}$	$10\frac{5}{8}$	$12\frac{1}{4}$	$14\frac{5}{8}$	$17\frac{3}{4}$	$21\frac{3}{4}$	$26\frac{1}{2}$
Proportion of cylinder vols.	$\frac{v}{d}$	2·5	2·5	2·5	2·5	2·5	2·5	2·5
Proportion of H : d . .		1·5	1·5	1·5	1·5	1·4	1·4	1·4
Revolutions per minute .	n	280	260	245	230	210	180	150
Piston speed in ft. per min.	c	365	420	470	515	530	590	590
I.H.P. with 105 lbs. boiler press.		25	50	80	120	180	270	400
Dimension	a	$23\frac{5}{8}$	$29\frac{1}{2}$	$37\frac{1}{2}$	$45\frac{1}{2}$	55	73	90
„	b	$23\frac{5}{8}$	$29\frac{1}{2}$	$37\frac{1}{2}$	$45\frac{1}{2}$	55	73	90
„	c	$9\frac{1}{2}$	$11\frac{3}{4}$	$16\frac{1}{2}$	$19\frac{3}{4}$	$23\frac{5}{8}$	$37\frac{1}{2}$	$47\frac{1}{2}$
„	e	$19\frac{3}{4}$	$24\frac{5}{8}$	$29\frac{1}{2}$	$34\frac{1}{2}$	$41\frac{1}{2}$	55	$70\frac{3}{4}$
„	f	$5\frac{1}{2}$	7	$8\frac{1}{4}$	$9\frac{3}{4}$	11	$13\frac{3}{4}$	$16\frac{1}{2}$
„	g	$10\frac{1}{4}$	$12\frac{5}{8}$	$15\frac{1}{2}$	$17\frac{3}{4}$	$20\frac{1}{2}$	$25\frac{5}{8}$	$30\frac{3}{4}$
„	h	$41\frac{1}{2}$	51	59	$70\frac{3}{4}$	$78\frac{3}{4}$	98	118
„	i	$7\frac{7}{8}$	$9\frac{3}{4}$	$12\frac{5}{8}$	15	17	$21\frac{5}{8}$	26
Weight in cwts. . . .	G	$15\frac{3}{4}$	$31\frac{1}{2}$	55	$88\frac{1}{2}$	137	236	452

All Dimensions are given in Inches.

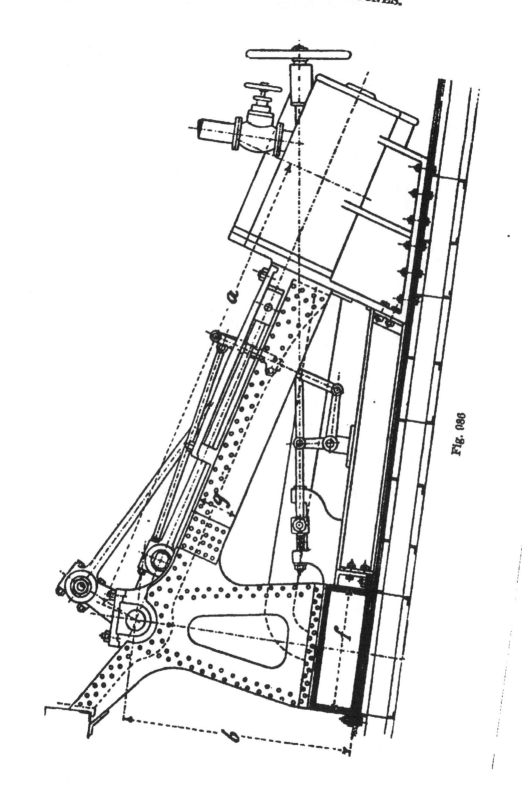

Fig. 086

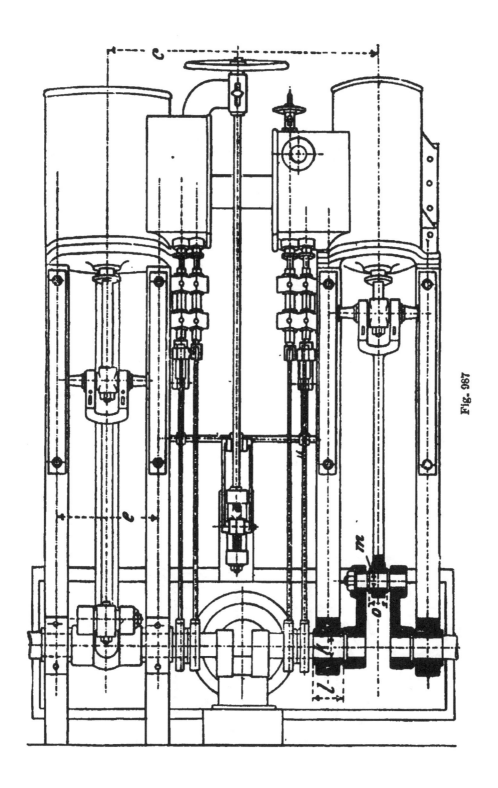

Fig. 987

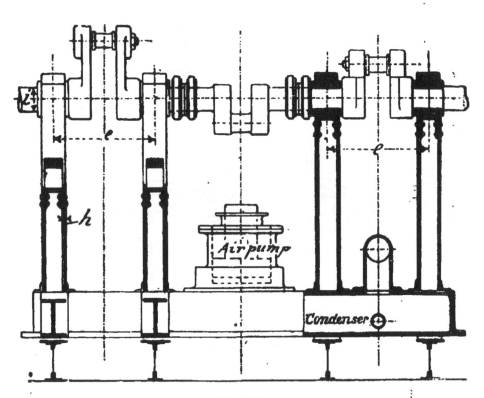

Fig. 988.

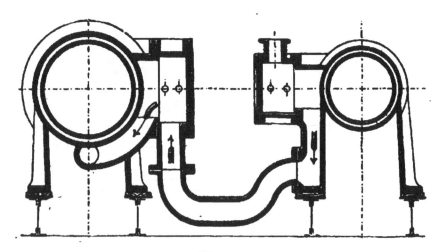

Fig. 989.

TABLE 134.—**Compound Engines for Paddle Steamers, 105 lbs. Boiler Pressure** (Figs. 986—989).

					lbs. pressure.									Dia. of paddle-shaft.	Bearings.		Crank-pin.		Weight in cwts.
H	d*	D*	V†/v	n	p	H.P.	a	b	c	e	f	g	h	i	k	l	m	o	G
19¾	12¼	19¾	2·5	50	120	40	86⅝	47¼	51	19¾	23¾	7	5/16	5⅞	5⅛	7⅞	3½	6¾	79
23¾	14½	23¾	2·5	46	120	60	102⅜	51	63	23¾	29½	9½	11/32	6½	5¾	8⅝	4⅛	7½	128
31½	18	31½	2·5	40	120	125	134	57	78¾	29½	33½	11¾	11/32	7⅞	6¾	9½	5⅛	8⅝	295
39½	21¾	39½	2·5	38	120	210	165½	63	94½	36¼	39½	15¾	3/8	9½	8¼	11½	6½	10¼	551
47	25¾	47	2·5	35	120	350	197	67	110	43¼	43¼	19¾	7/16	11¾	9¾	13½	7⅞	12⅝	925
55	29½	55	2·5	32	120	500	232	71	126	51	47¼	25⅝	15/16	13¾	11¾	15¾	9½	15	1377
63	34¾	63	2·5	30	120	700	268	75	141	59	51	31½	½	15¾	13¾	18	11	17	1968

* D = Diameter of low-pressure piston; d = Diameter of high-pressure piston.
H = Stroke of both pistons.
† V = Volume of low-pressure cylinder; v = Volume of high-pressure cylinder.

All Dimensions are given in Inches.

SECTION IX.

INDICATOR AND INDICATOR DIAGRAMS.

In the beginning of section IV. on Valve gears, page 151, indicator diagrams have been mentioned, and a method of drawing an approximate expansion curve has been given; in this section the subject is given in more detail, with examples of diagrams from actual practice.

The Indicator.

The original indicator, as invented and made by James Watt, has been since improved in detail although the principle remains the same. The object of the improvements has been to decrease the weight of the moving parts and to make the stroke of the piston as short as possible.

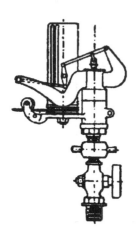 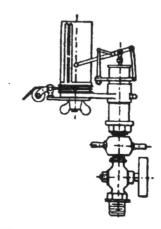

Fig. 990.—Richards' Indicator.   Fig. 991.—Thompson's Indicator.

Amongst the earliest improvements was that of Richards, fig. 990, who reduced the stroke of the piston but retained the longer stroke of the pencil by introducing a system of light levers which also formed a parallel motion for the same. This indicator is perhaps the most largely used, and with ordinary speeds gives very good results. The union or coupling by which this indicator is attached ᴏ the cock, is cut with threads of different pitches in the two parts, hat which screws on to the indicator itself having a fine thread, and 'ᴀat part which screws on to the cock has a coarse thread ; the part oᶠ ᴌᴇ cock is conical and fits a corresponding taper on the indicator ; ᴊis makes a very neat arrangement, and easy to take on and off.

Fig. 991 shews a modification of Richards' indicator by Thompson.

further modification by Crosby, fig. 992, has many points of ᴈerest, the spring fixed rigidly only to the cylinder cover, and is attached to the piston by a ball and socket joint ; the spring is also double wound, right and left hand, an arrangement intended to do away with any tendency to twist as the spring compresses. The whole indicator is much smaller than Richards', and better adapted

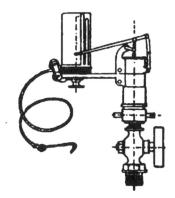

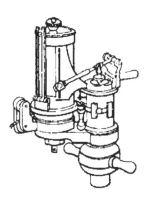

Fig. 992.—Crosby's Indicator.   Fig. 993.—Darke's Indicator.

for very high speeds. The coupling for attaching the indicator is like that of Richards, but has a right and left hand screw instead of two right hand threads of different pitch ; this makes it much less easy to take on and off. A still smaller indicator is that of Darke, fig. 993, where the pencil is guided by a loose slide in a slot ; the coupling is the same as that of Richards, and is interchangeable with it. This indicator is arranged for very high speeds, and is fitted with a dentent or catch to hold the paper drum whilst string is being hooked on.

The stroke of the paper drums in all these indicators is necessarily much less than that of the engine. To reduce the stroke a moving lever is generally used, and care should be taken in leading the string to the indicator that its motion is always truly in the direction of the axis of the string.

A segment of wood fitted to the lever of correct proportion to give the right stroke will, if of sufficient extent, always ensure the string moving correctly. The levers may be made of wood, or better of iron. Figs. 994—997 shew an example of levers. The choice of arrangement of indicator gear necessarily depends on the style and

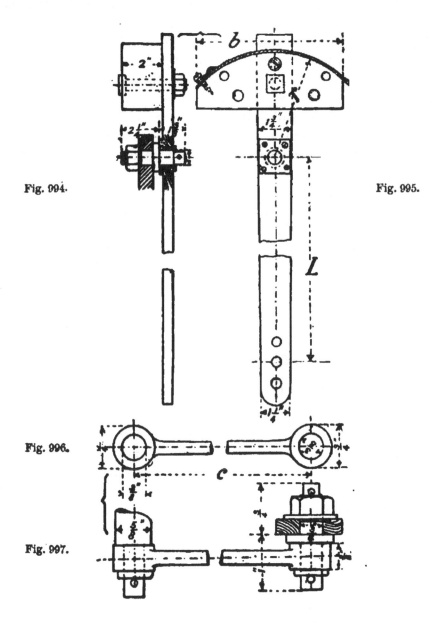

Fig. 994.

Fig. 995.

Fig. 996.

Fig. 997.

position of the engine to be indicated ; sometimes the lever may have to be attached to the walls or roof of the engine-room, but now the best makers will supply self-contained indicator gear with the engines they make.

Fig. 998 shews in outline an indicator gear of the ordinary lever kind, fitted to a horizontal girder engine. Fig. 999, a reducing gear with different sized drums pulled round by a string from an arm fixed to the cross head ; these arrangements are not so simple as the

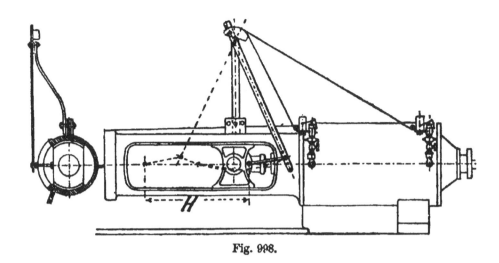

Fig. 998.

ordinary lever ; the lower end of the lever should be connected to a pin in the crosshead by a link and not, as is often done, by a slot in

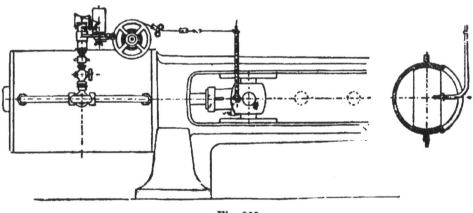

Fig. 999.

the end of the lever which gives more error to the motion of the paper due to the arc described by the end of the lever.

The practice of putting the indicator on a system of pipes from both ends of the cylinder, fig. 999, to which is fitted a 3-way cock, gives very pretty results (fig. 1000) by enabling diagrams from both ends of the cylinder to be produced on one card, but is not to be re-

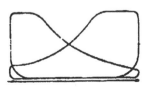

Fig. 1000.

B B 2

commended, as elements of inaccuracy are thus introduced. For very exact work two indicators should be used, one for each end, and occasionally they should be changed over from one end to the other to eliminate a possible chance of error. An example of an extreme case of error from long pipes is given on page 378, fig. 1017 ; here the pipes were lead to the centre, and a cock fixed at each end, not even with a 3-way cock in the middle.

Fig. 1018 shews diagram taken from same engine with same load on with indicator fixed direct on each end of cylinder, the pipes having been removed.*

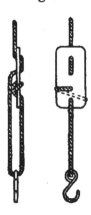

Fig. 1001.

Some operators prefer to have a sliding joint in the string by using a piece of wood or metal as in fig. 1001 ; this may be of use with slow speeds, but with high speeds a dead length string with a small ring at the end, and a hook on the indicator strings or *vice versa*, is the best, or the string can be arranged to pull through the edge of the wood segment on the lever and up to a knot, and can be held whilst taking the diagram, and thus the hook need not be used.

It is good before starting to indicate an engine to put the string on stretch in the engine-room, so as to get it to the same temperature and dryness as the surrounding air ; if this be done, very little trouble will occur with the string whilst in use. In indicating the pencil should be pressed to the paper very gently, and if the engine has only been running for a few days or hours, that is, if the engine is new, the piston of the indicator should be taken out very frequently and the cylinder sponged out ; the lower limits of a diagram are very liable to error from dirt accumulated in the cylinder, and an old indicator should always be used on a new engine ; no instrument regarded as a standard should be applied to any engine which has not run itself clean from sand and dirt off the steam ports and passages. If after having taken a few diagrams the atmospheric line appears to be a trifle higher than on the first diagram it is a sure sign that the cylinder is foul, and it should be sponged out before any more diagrams are taken.

---

* Mr. Haeder says that the bosses for indicator corks are tapped with 1" English thread. In England the custom is to tap with $\frac{3}{4}$" Whitworth thread.

To calculate the power from an indicator diagram, the average or mean pressure on the piston is found either by using a planimeter or more conveniently by the method of equidistant ordinates. The diagram is divided into ten equal parts, figs. 1002, 1003, and the mean height of each part is measured by the scale corresponding to the spring used in the indicator; the ten mean heights are then added together and divided by ten; this gives the mean pressure on the piston with fair accuracy. A quick and accurate way of measuring the added lengths or heights of the ordinates

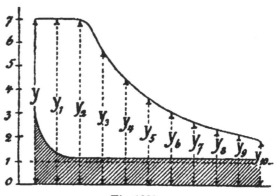

Fig. 1002

is to take a narrow strip of paper and to mark off with a sharp pencil the length of the first division, then run the strip to the next and make a mark, and so on to the tenth, then measure the total length between the first and last mark and point off for dividing by ten; this gives the mean pressure, which multiplied by the area of the piston in square inches by twice the stroke in feet, and by the number of revolutions per minute, and divided by 33,000, gives the indicated horse-power. If diagrams be taken with a load on the engine and then with the load off, the difference

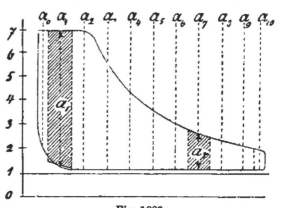

Fig. 1003.

between the two results will give the useful or effective horse power. It is not easy to get accurate measurements of power from a large engine when running without load, and therefore it is seldom possible to get the true effective load by this means; but a fairly accurate idea of the power taken by individual machines out of a large number driven by one engine may be obtained by indicating the engine with the particular machine on and then with it off, and taking the difference for the power required for driving the machine.

Indicator Diagrams.
Combined Diagrams from Compound Engines.

The proportion of the area of the combined diagrams to the area of the figure A, B, C, D, E, gives approximately the efficiency of the proportion of the efficiency of the engine.   To combine the diagrams from the two cylinders of a compound engine they may be laid out

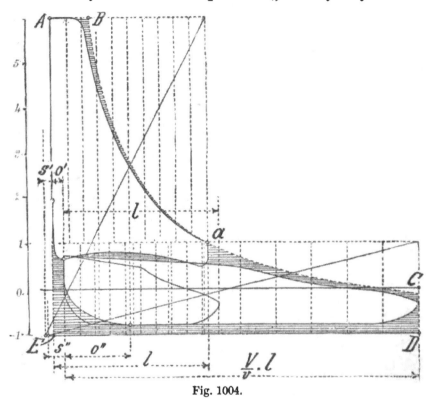

Fig. 1004.

to the same scale and length, l, so that the admission line of the low pressure diagram comes just to the beginning of the compression o^1 of high pressure diagram ; the low pressure diagram is then laid out to a length equal to the proportion of the cylinder volumes $\dfrac{V}{v} \times l$.

The theoretical expansion curve is drawn through the point a, and the shaded portion will show the theoretical loss, fig. 1004.

s' = the clearance of the high-pressure cylinder.
s'' = the clearance of the low-pressure cylinder.
o' = the compression in high-pressure cylinder.
o'' = the compression in low-pressure cylinder.

The effect of laying out combined diagrams, is to produce a diagram which should represent what would take place in one cylinder of the volume of the low-pressure cylinder of the compound engine.

Indicator Diagrams

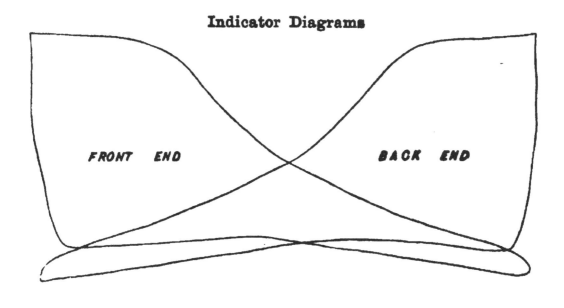

Scale $\frac{1}{64}$

HIGH PRESSURE CYLINDER
Fig. 1005.

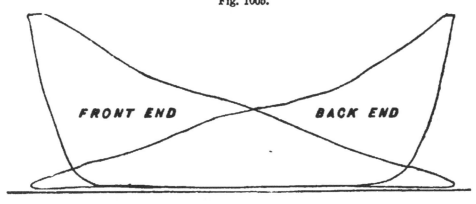

Scale $\frac{1}{32}$

LOW PRESSURE CYLINDER
Fig. 1006.

Diagrams* from compound engine with Davey Paxman's valve gear controlled by the governor. The two valves are driven by separate eccentrics, and the cut-off valve works on a false port face between the main and cut-off valves.

---

* See Royal Agricultural Society's report of Newcastle meeting, 1887,

Diagrams from Actual Practice.

Scales of all are given in fractions of an inch to one pound per square inch.

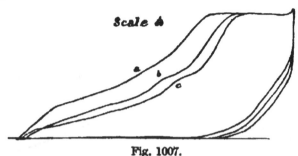

Fig. 1007.

*Diagrams from a portable engine fitted with single valve controlled by Hartnell's crank-shaft governor. Cylinder $8\frac{1}{2}''$ diameter, stroke $12''$.

    a. 127 revolutions per minute 13·9 indicated HP.
    b. 129 revolutions per minute 10·8 indicated HP.
    c. 130 revolutions per minute 10·1 indicated HP.

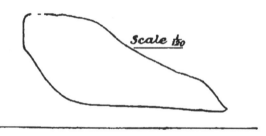

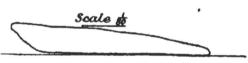

Figs. 1008, 1009.

Diagrams from compound undertype engine with high-pressure cylinder valve controlled by Hartnell's governor low-pressure valve by simple eccentric.

       High-pressure cylinder $8''$ diameter.
       Low-pressure cylinder $12\frac{3}{4}''$ diameter.
       Stroke of both, $14''$.
       Revolutions per minute, 155.

---

* See reports of Cardiff meeting of the Royal Agricultural Society.

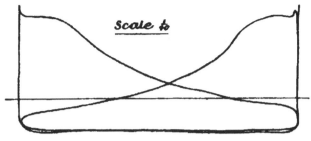

Fig. 1010.

Diagrams from condensing engine with Meyer valve gear and throttle valve. Cylinder 18″ diameter; 30″ stroke. Revolutions per minute, 60.

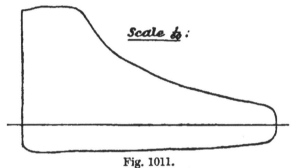

Fig. 1011.

Diagram from condensing engine with cut-off valve controlled by Hartnell governor. Cylinder $16\frac{1}{8}$″ diameter; 36″ stroke. Revolutions per minute, 63.

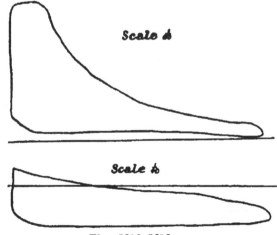

Figs. 1012, 1013.

Diagrams from a compound horizontal engine, cranks at 90°, cut-off valve of high-pressure cylinder controlled by Hartnell's governor the valve of low-pressure cylinder worked by simple eccentric.

Diameter of high-pressure cylinder, 16″; low-pressure cylinder, 26″ Stroke of both, 36″. Revolutions per minute, 67.

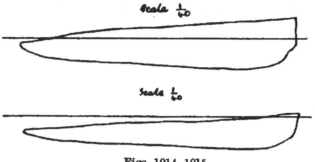

Figs. 1014, 1015.

Diagrams from a side lever marine engine by Miller & Ravenhill, dated 1839, used as a stationary engine.

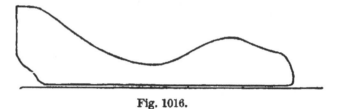

Fig. 1016.

Diagram shewing a case of accidental re-admission by main valve over-running port face. Cylinder $11\frac{1}{4}''$ diameter, 24″ stroke.

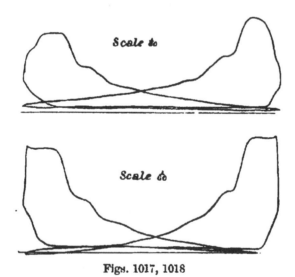

Figs. 1017, 1018

Fig. 1017 shews the effect of long pipes between cylinder and indicator.

Fig. 1018 from same engine with same load, the indicator being fixed direct on cylinder without any pipes. Cylinder $13\frac{1}{4}''$ diameter, 24″ stroke, 100 revolutions per minute.

Diagrams shewing the Defects in Valve Gears which may often be met with in Practice.

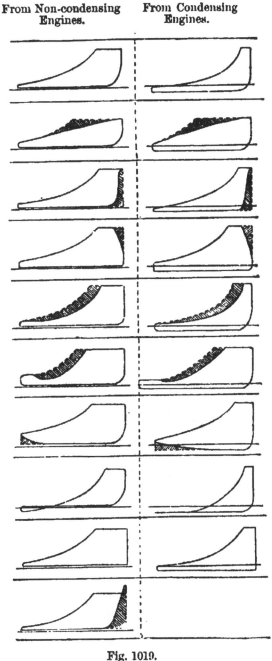

	From Non-condensing Engines.	From Condensing Engines.

Example of a normal indicator diagram, from an engine with good expansion gear.

Diagram shewing the effect of throttling.

Too early admission, with light fly-wheel.

Too late admission.

Leaking valves, allowing steam to pass after cut-off.

Re-admission after cut-off, caused by re-opening cut-off ports before main valve has closed the steam-port. See page 192.

Too late opening of exhaust, or may be caused by exhaust being too small.

Load too light for size of engine.

Too little compression.

Too much compression.

Fig. 1019.

The shaded parts in the above diagrams shew the losses.

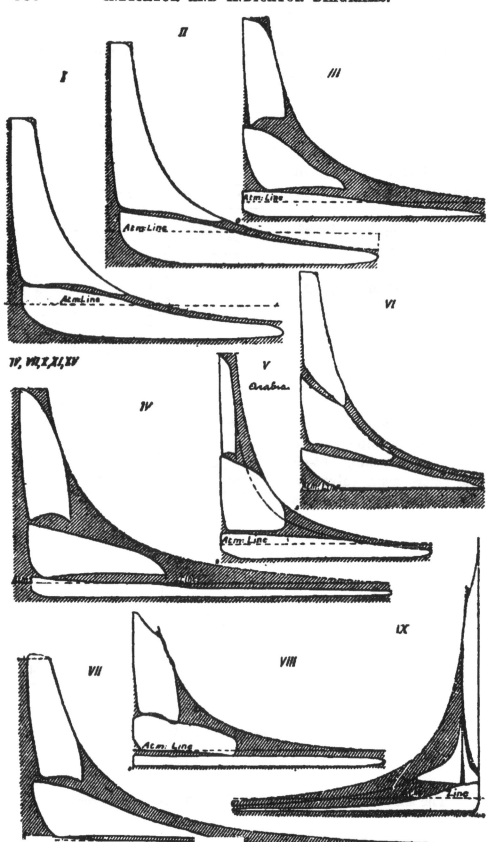

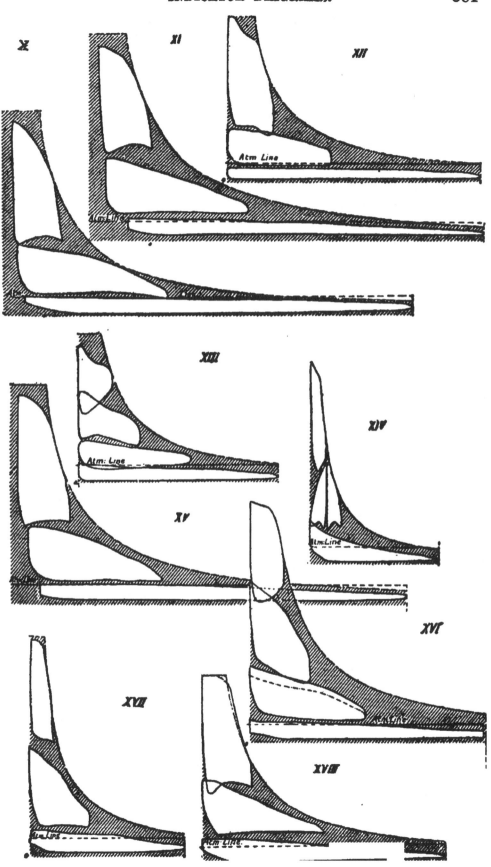

Diagrams from Triple-Expansion and Compound Engines, pages 380, 381.

Nos. I. & II., S.S. Bachheibel.
  III., S.S. Falkenburg.
  IV., S.S. African.
  V., S.S. Arabia.
  VI., Stülchen's 3-cylinder compound.
  VII., S.S. Para.
  VIII., S.S. Aberdeen, with superheater efficiency ·67.
  IX., S.S. Wanderer.
  X., S.S. Stella.
  XI., S.S. Lusitania.
  XII., S.S. Aberdeen, with superheater efficiency ·65.
  XIII., Adamson's quadruple-expansion efficiency ·71.
  XIV., S.S. Isle of Dursey.
  XV., S.S. Jungfrau.
  XVI., S.S. Rimnag na Maia.
  XVII., S.S. Sobraleuse.
  XVIII., S.S. Nierstein.

The above diagrams are from a paper by Otto H. Müller, " Zeitschrift der Verein Deutsch. Ingenieur," 1887, page 445, and shew different ways of combining diagrams from compound engines.

SECTION X.

CALCULATIONS FOR POWER AND STEAM CONSUMPTION.

THE following terms and letters are used in these calculations :—

N_i = the indicated horse-power.

N_e = the effective horse-power.

Q = the effective surface of the piston in square inches.

H = the stroke in inches.

n = the revolutions per minute.

c = the piston speed in feet per minute.

h = the admission or cut-off when H = 1.

P = the initial pressure in lbs. per square inch.

k = expansion coefficient dependent upon the admission h, and the clearance s, see Table 135.

s = the clearance space in terms of piston area, so that the length of the line s on the diagrams, figs. 1022, 1023, represents the volume of the clearance space when H = 1.

P_m = the mean pressure on the piston in lbs. per square inch.

P_o = the back pressure in lbs. per square inch.

σ = the sum of the losses of work by wire-drawing, compression, early opening of exhaust, back pressure, etc.

$$\text{then } c = 2Hn.$$

$$N_i = \frac{Q\,c\,P_m}{33,000}.$$

The mean pressure $P_m = kp - (P_e + \sigma)$.

The expansion coefficient $k = h + (h + p)\,log_\epsilon\,\dfrac{1+s}{h+s}$; see Tables 135 and 169.

The back pressure P_e of the exhaust steam is dependent on the terminal pressure ω, and the size of the exhaust passages.

Table 137 gives the value of the back pressure for usual proportions, and for a speed of about 100 feet per second of the steam in the passages, allowance also being made for the sum of the losses σ.

TABLE 135.—**Value of the Expansion Coefficient** *k*.

h	Clearance space *s*.								
	2%	3%	4%	5%	6%	7%	8%	9%	10%
0·00	0·079	0·107	0·130	0·152	0·172	0·191	0·210	0·226	0·240
0·02	0·151	0·173	0·190	0·210	0·230	0·250	0·263	0·276	0·289
0·04	0·204	0·232	0·250	0·268	0·280	0·292	0·302	0·314	0·328
0·06	0·255	0·273	0·292	0·303	0·321	0·332	0·343	0·353	0·366
0·08	0·305	0·321	0·337	0·348	0·363	0·371	0·383	0·392	0·403
0·10	0·356	0·369	0·381	0·392	0·403	0·412	0·422	0·432	0·440
0·12	0·394	0·406	0·417	0·427	0·437	0·446	0·455	0·464	0·472
0·14	0·431	0·442	0·452	0·462	0·470	0·479	0·487	0·495	0·503
0·16	0·467	0·477	0·486	0·496	0·502	0·511	0·518	0·525	0·533
0·18	0·502	0·513	0·519	0·529	0·533	0·542	0·548	0·554	0·562
0·20	0·535	0·545	0·552	0·559	0·565	0·571	0·577	0·584	0·590
0·22	0·564	0·573	0·578	0·586	0·592	0·597	0·603	0·609	0·615
0·24	0·592	0·600	0·606	0·612	0·615	0·622	0·628	0·633	0·639
0·26	0·619	0·626	0·631	0·637	0·643	0·646	0·652	0·656	0·662
0·28	0·645	0·651	0·655	0·661	0·667	0·671	0·675	0·678	0·683
0·30	0·670	0·675	0·680	0·685	0·689	0·692	0·696	0·700	0·704
0·32	0·693	0·697	0·702	0·706	0·710	0·714	0·718	0·721	0·725
0·34	0·715	0·718	0·723	0·726	0·730	0·734	0·738	0·741	0·745
0·36	0 736	0·738	0·743	0·745	0·749	0·753	0·757	0·760	0·764
0·38	0·756	0·757	0·762	0·763	0·767	0·772	0·775	0·778	0·782
0·40	0·773	0·775	0·779	0·781	0·784	0·787	0·794	0·797	0·800
0·42	0·791	0·792	0·794	0·798	0·801	0·803	0·810	0·812	0·815
0·44	0·808	0·809	0·810	0·814	0·817	0·818	0·824	0·826	0·829
0·46	0·824	0·825	0·827	0·829	0·832	0·831	0·837	0·839	0·842
0·48	0·838	0·839	0·841	0·843	0·845	0·847	0·849	0·851	0·854
0·50	0·850	0·852	0·854	0·856	0·857	0·858	0·862	0·864	0·866
0·55	0·879	0·881	0·883	0·885	0·886	0·887	0·889	0·890	0·891
0·60	0·906	0·908	0·910	0·912	0·913	0·913	0·914	0·915	0·916
0·65	0·927	0·929	0·931	0·932	0·933	0·934	0·935	0·935	0·936
0·70	0·947	0·949	0·951	0·952	0·953	0·953	0·954	0·954	0·955
0·75	0·962	0·964	0·966	0·967	0·968	0·968	0·968	0·968	0·973
0·80	0·976	0·978	0·980	0·980	0·981	0·981	0·981	0·981	0·981
0·90	0·994	0·995	0·995	0·995	0·996	0·997	0·997	0·998	0·998

Example.—Given the cut-off *h* = ·2, the clearance space *s* = 7 per cent., the expansion coefficient *k* = ·571.

The losses of power from wiredrawing, &c., as shown in diagrams, figs. 1022, 1023, are represented by σ, expressed in

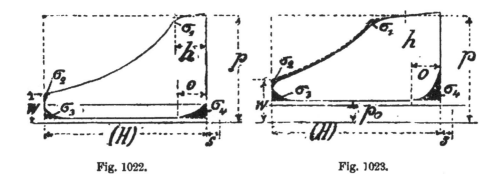

Fig. 1022.   Fig. 1023.

pressure on the piston area during the whole stroke in lbs. per square inch.

σ_1 the loss due to wiredrawing or throttling the steam during admission.

σ_2 the loss due to early opening of the exhaust.

σ_3 the loss due to the back pressure of the exhaust steam.

σ_4 the loss due to compression.

σ_5 the loss due to the drop in pressure in compound engines.

$\sigma = \sigma_1 + \sigma_2 + \sigma_3 + \sigma_4 + \sigma_5 =$ the sum of all these losses.

The loss σ, by wiredrawing increases with the lateness of the cut-off h for engines with the usual valve-gears, Meyer's, Rider's, &c., and is given in Table 136.

TABLE 136.—**Values of σ_1.**

Cut-off h . .	·05	·10	·15	·20	·30	·40	·50	·60	·70
Without jacket .	1·14	1·42	1·70	2·15	2·56	2·84	3·41	3·70	4·00
With jacket .	·43	·57	·71	1·00	1·14	1·42	1·70	2·00	2·13

TABLE 137.—Values of σ_2 in lbs. per Square Inch.

Percentage of exhaust opening before end of stroke.	Without condenser. Final pressure w in lbs. per sq. in.				With condenser. Final press. in lbs. per sq. in.		
	17·64	29·4	44·1	58·8	14·7	29·4	44·1
·02	·000	·000	·000	·000	·000	·000	·000
·05	·000	·073	·147	·220	·073	·117	·147
·10	·043	·220	·430	·588	·294	·357	·430
·20	—	1·17	1·32	1·47	·882	1·17	1·32
·30	—	1·47	1·91	2·20	—	—	—

If the exhaust opens up 2 per cent. or less before the end of the stroke the loss is very small, some valve gears, however, will not allow of the exhaust being kept closed later than from 20 to 30 per cent. before the end of the stroke.

The values of σ_2 are given in Table 137.

TABLE 138.—Values of Back Pressure σ_3.

Exhaust lead. V_0	Without condenser. Final pressure w in lbs. per sq. in.				With condenser. Final press. in lbs. per sq. in.		
	18·37	29·4	44·1	58·8	14·7	29·4	44·1
$V_0 = a$	·000	·043	·147	·430	·073	·147	·294
$V_0 = 0·5\,a$	·073	·117	·220	·588	·147	·730	1·17
$V_0 = 0·2\,a$	·294	·430	·588	1·03	·588	1·17	1·76
$V_0 = 0$	·588	1·32	1·47	1·76	1·17	1·47	2·64

The values of σ_3, the back pressure or exhaust resistance caused by early closing, are dependent on the inside or exhaust lead, and the final pressure w, and are given in Table 138.

Values of Compression σ_4.

TABLE 139.—**Without Condenser** ($\rho_s = 16\cdot4$ lbs. per sq. in.).

Com-pression 0	Clearance space in per cent. of stroke s.								
	2%	3%	4%	5%	6%	7%	8%	9%	10%
0·00	0	0	0	0	0	0	—	—	—
0·025	·228	·214	·209	·185	·171	·128	·114	·085	·071
0·050	·626	·551	·485	·415	·341	·271	·228	·185	·142
0·075	·925	·855	·782	·712	·640	·571	·485	·385	·285
0·10	1·550	1·38	1·14	·891	·792	·732	·700	·685	·670
0·15	—	2·70	2·34	1·96	1·71	1·44	1·26	1·06	·99
0·20	—	—	3·47	3·25	2·90	2·56	2·28	2·09	1·71
0·25	—	—	—	4·45	4·10	3·76	3·51	3·28	2·98
0·30	—	—	—	—	5·32	5·00	4·75	4·46	3·75

TABLE 140.—**With Condenser** ($\rho_s = 3\cdot13$ lbs. per sq. in.).

0·00	0	0	0	0	0	0	0	0	0
0·025	·028	·028	·028	·028	·014	·014	·014	·014	·014
0·050	·071	·057	·043	·043	·028	·014	·014	·014	·014
0·075	·142	·128	·114	·081	·057	·043	·028	·014	·014
0·10	·284	·256	·214	·157	·128	·100	·071	·043	·028
0·15	·525	·470	·412	·341	·285	·256	·228	·209	·171
0·20	·821	·770	·670	·570	·512	·455	·400	·341	·314
0·25	1·10	1·01	·925	·810	·770	·728	·640	·527	·485
0·30	1·54	1·41	1·24	1·03	·970	·855	·810	·770	·728

Table 141.—Values of the Cut-off h with a given Final Pressure, w, for Clearance Spaces of 3 to 7 per cent.

At ab.	$p=8$ Atmos. Absolute.			$p=7$ Atmos. Absolute.			$p=6$ Atmos. Absolute.			$p=5$ Atmos. Absolute.			$p=4$ Atmos. Absolute.		
w	$s=3\%$	5%	7%	3%	5%	7%	3%	5%	7%	3%	5%	7%	3%	5%	7%
0·6	0·047	0·027	0·012	0·058	0·040	0·021	0·073	0·055	0·037	0·093	0·076	0·059	0·124	0·106	0·090
0·7	0·061	0·042	0·023	0·073	0·055	0·037	0·090	0·072	0·054	0·114	0·097	0·080	0·150	0·134	0·118
0·8	0·073	0·055	0·037	0·088	0·070	0·052	0·107	0·090	0·072	0·135	0·118	0·101	0·176	0·160	0·144
0·9	0·086	0·068	0·053	0·103	0·085	0·067	0·124	0·107	0·096	0·155	0·139	0·123	0·202	0·186	0·171
1·0	0·098	0·081	0·064	0·117	0·100	0·083	0·141	0·125	0·108	0·176	0·160	0·144	0·229	0·212	0·197
1·2	0·127	0·107	0·095	0·147	0·130	0·113	0·174	0·160	0·144	0·217	0·202	0·183	0·279	0·265	0·251
1·4	0·150	0·133	0·117	0·176	0·160	0·144	0·210	0·195	0·179	0·255	0·244	0·229	0·337	0·318	0·305
1·6	0·178	0·160	0·144	0·205	0·190	0·174	0·244	0·230	0·215	0·299	0·286	0·272	0·389	0·370	0·358
1·8	0·202	0·186	0·171	0·234	0·220	0·205	0·279	0·265	0·251	0·340	0·328	0·315	0·434	0·422	0·412
2·0	0·227	0·212	0·197	0·265	0·250	0·235	0·313	0·300	0·287	0·382	0·370	0·358	0·485	0·475	0·465
2·5	0·292	0·278	0·264	0·337	0·325	0·312	0·399	0·387	0·375	0·485	0·475	0·465	0·614	0·606	0·600
3·0	0·356	0·343	0·331	0·411	0·400	0·390	0·485	0·475	0·465	0·588	0·580	0·572	0·742	0·737	0·732
3·5	0·420	0·409	0·398	0·485	0·475	0·405	0·571	0·562	0·554	0·693	0·685	0·679	0·871	0·868	0·862
4·0	0·485	0·475	0·465	0·558	0·550	0·541	0·656	0·650	0·643	0·794	0·790	0·786	1·000	1·000	1·000
4·5	0·549	0·540	0·531	0·632	0·625	0·617	0·742	0·737	0·731	0·897	0·893	0·890	—	—	—
5·0	0·610	0·600	0·599	0·705	0·700	0·695	0·830	0·821	0·811	1·000	1·000	1·000	—	—	—

Pressures in Atmospheres Absolute.

Example.—Given the final pressure $w=1.2$ atmospheres absolute, the clearance $s=5$ per cent., and the initial pressure $p=7$ atmospheres absolute, then the cut-off h will=0·13.

Values of the Final Pressure w in Atmospheres Absolute for the most Economical Normal Horse-power.

TABLE 142.—Simple Engine.

N_i.	Non-condensing.				Condensing.			
	Initial pressure p in Atmospheres Absolute.							
	4—5·5	6—7·5	8—9	10	4—5·5	6—7·5	8—9	10
2—5	2·0	2·0	2·1	2·2	—	—	—	—
5—10	1·8	1·8	1·9	2·1	—	—	—	—
10—50	1·6	1·7	1·8	2·0	0·8	0·9	1·0	1·1
50—100	1·5	1·6	1·7	1·9	0·8	0·9	1·0	1·1
100—200	1·4	1·5	1·6	1·8	0·7	0·8	0·9	1·0
200 and upwards.	1·3	1·4	1·5	1·7	0·7	0·8	0·9	1·0

TABLE 142A.—Compound Engine.

10—50	—	—	1·6	1·7	0·7	0·8	0·9	1·9
50—100	—	—	1·5	1·6	0·7	0·8	0·8	0·9
100—500	—	—	1·4	1·5	0·6	0·7	0·8	0·9
500 and upwards.	—	—	1·3	1·4	0·5	0·6	0·7	0·8

Example.—The best final pressure w for a simple condensing engine with N_i = 150 H.P., and 7 atmospheres absolute is from the Table ·8 atmospheres absolute, the corresponding cut-off from Table 133, with 7 per cent. clearance space, gives ·052.

The losses σ_4 by compression given in Tables 139, 140, are dependent on the length of the compression period o, and the back pressure P_r. The clearance space depends on the kind of valve-gear used. See Table **33**.

Clearance space s expressed in terms of length of stroke, for $H = 1$.

TABLE 143.

Kind of valve-gear used.			
Ordinary valve-gear.	Divided valves and piston valves.	Mushroom valves.	Corliss valves.
0·06 — 0·08	0·03 — 0·06	0·04	0·025

The above values for s are for ordinary piston speeds. For very quick running engines with higher piston speed, the clearance space may be double the value given above.

A coefficient approximately proportional to the efficiency of an engine may be found by dividing the mean pressure (taken from the indicator diagram) by the final pressure (absolute) $\frac{P_m}{w}$. For example, an engine giving a mean pressure of 31·25, and a final pressure absolute of 23·7, gives this coefficient $\frac{31 \cdot 25}{23 \cdot 7} = 1 \cdot 56$. In many engines this coefficient is greater than 2, but has hardly reached 3.

The water per IHP per hour, can be approximated from the coefficient thus obtained. Divide the undermentioned constants by the coefficient, and the quotient will give the water per IHP per hour, in lbs.

When the final pressure is about 5 lbs. *below* the atmosphere, the constant = 36 ; with a final pressure 15 lbs. *above* the atmosphere, the constant = 34 ; when final pressure is 45 lbs. above atmosphere the constant = 32.

Either of these divided by the coefficient will give the quantity of water per IHP per hour, very nearly, *exclusive* of the losses by clearance and condensation, jacket, &c., and the gain by compression.

Take as an example the engine before referred to which had a final pressure of 9 lbs. above the atmosphere, and use corresponding constant 34. $\frac{34}{1\cdot56}$ = 21·7 lbs., add $\frac{1}{10}$ for clearance and loss exclusive of jacket = 23·87 lbs. per 1 H.P. per hour. The water measured was 24·1 lbs. per 1 H.P. per hour, which shows how near the formula is.

Let $l = l' + l''$ resistance in non-condensing engine running light ;
  $l = l'_c + l''_c$,,   condensing   ,,   ,,
  μ coefficient of additional friction for single cylinder engine.
  μ_s ,,   ,,   ,,   for double   ,,   ,,

The effective power for single cylinder $\dfrac{Qc\,(P_m - l)}{33000\,(l + \mu)}$.

    ,,   ,, for double cylinder $\dfrac{Qc\,(P_m - l)}{33000\,(1 + \mu_s)}$.

TABLE 144.

D	8	16	24	32	14
l''	1·86	1·00	·571	·428	·285
l''_c	3·14	1·57	1·00	·715	·571
μ	·18	·14	·12	·10	·08
μ_s	·20	·16	·13	·11	·10

TABLE 145.

p	59	88	118
l'	1·14	1·43	1·71
l'	1·71	2·00	2·28

p = pressure in lbs. per sq. inch.

By very careful management the coefficient μ may be reduced by 30%.

Calculation of the Power of Compound Engines.

The power of a compound engine should be the same as if the total expansion had been carried out in one large cylinder, the expression for the total expansion being

$$\frac{\text{initial absolute pressure}}{\text{final absolute pressure}} = \frac{P}{w}.$$

In figures 1024, 1025,

$h =$ the period of admission.
$s =$ the clearance.
$w =$ the final pressure.
$d =$ the diameter of the high-pressure cylinder.
$h', s', w', =$ as above for the high-pressure cylinder.
$D =$ diameter of low-pressure cylinder.
$h'', s'', w'' =$ as above for the low-pressure cylinder.
$\dfrac{V}{v} =$ the ratio of the cylinder volumes.
$Q =$ the surface of the low-pressure piston.
$h_4 =$ the ideal admission reduced the low-pressure cylinder volume corresponding to the total expansion.
$s = \dfrac{s''}{\dfrac{V}{v}}$ for determining the mean pressure for the ideal value of the clearance space.

Then, taking the stroke of both cylinders to be the same,

Taking no account of the clearance space.

$$\frac{V}{v \times h'} = \frac{P}{W''} = \frac{1}{h'} \times \frac{1}{h''}.$$

Allowing for the clearance space.

$$\frac{V \times (l + s'')}{v \times (h' + s')} = \frac{P}{W''} = \frac{1}{h' + s'} \times \frac{1}{h'' + s''}$$

Example.—To calculate the nominal power of a compound condensing engine.

Diameter of high-pressure cylinder . . d $15\frac{3}{4}''$.
Diameter of low-pressure cylinder . D $24''$.
Stroke of both .   .   .   .   . . H $27\frac{1}{2}''$.

Ratio of cylinder volumes . . . $\dfrac{V}{v}$ = 2·35.

Revolutions per minute . . . . n = 75.

Initial pressure absolute . .. . P = 103.

Clearance space of low-pressure cylinder s'' = about 5 per cent.

Final pressure $w = w''$ from Table 142A, w = 11·76. ·

Ideal clearance space $s_i = \dfrac{0·05}{2·35}$ . . s_i = 0·02.

Ideal admission from Table 141 . . h_i = 0·1.

Coefficient of expansion from Table 135 . k = 0·356.

Back pressure and loss of work . $P_e + \sigma$ = 7.

Then the mean pressure $P_m = kp - (P_e + \sigma) = ·356 \times 103 - 7 = 30·7$ lbs. per square inch.

The piston speed in feet per minute, c = 344.

the effective area of the piston, Q = 446 square inches ;

the ideal indicated horse-power N_{i},

$$= \frac{Qc\, P_m}{33000} = \frac{446 \times 344 \times 30·7}{33000} = \text{approximately } 140.$$

The friction coefficient μ_s = 0·16 (Table 144).

The resistance of the engine when running empty (see Tables 144, 145). $l = l'_e = 2·14 + 1·56 = 3·7$;

then the effective horse-power N_e

$$= \frac{Qc\, (P_m - l)}{33000\, (1 + \mu_s)} = \frac{446 \times 344\, (3017 - 3·7)}{33000\, (1 + 0·16)} = \text{nearly } 103.$$

The admission or cut-off in the high-pressure cylinder is determined as follows :—

The total expansion being $\dfrac{P}{w''} = \dfrac{103}{11·76} = 8·75.$

If now $s' = s'' = 0·05,$

then $\qquad \dfrac{V\, (1 + s'')}{v\, (h' + s')} = \dfrac{2·35 \times 1·05}{h' + 0·05} = 8·75 ;$

therefore $\qquad h' = \dfrac{2·35 \times 1·05}{8·75} - 0·05 = 0·23.$

The final pressure in the high-pressure cylinder will be

$$w' = \frac{(h' + s')\,P}{1 + s'} = \frac{(0{\cdot}23 + 0{\cdot}05) \times 103}{1{\cdot}05} = 27{\cdot}4$$

and we shall have the mean pressure in the low-pressure cylinder, taking the drop of pressure as 5·88,

$$p'' = 27{\cdot}4 - 5{\cdot}88 = 21{\cdot}52$$

then it follows that

$$h'' = \frac{w''\,(1 + s'')}{p''} - s'' = \frac{11{\cdot}76 \times 1{\cdot}05}{21{\cdot}52} - 0{\cdot}05 = {\cdot}525 \text{ sq. } {\cdot}55.$$

If the horse-power is given, and the diameter of the low-pressure cylinder is required, it can be approximated in the following manner:

From Table 142, p is selected, P_m from Table 146, and c from Table 147,

$$\text{then } Q = \frac{33000 \times N_i}{c\,P_m}.$$

Table 146.

		Initial pressure in lbs. per square inch.						
$P_m =$		59	74	88	103	118	132	147
		23·5	26·5	31	35·2	38·2	41	45·2

Indicator Diagrams for the Normal Horse-Power for the Compound Engines given in Table 147.

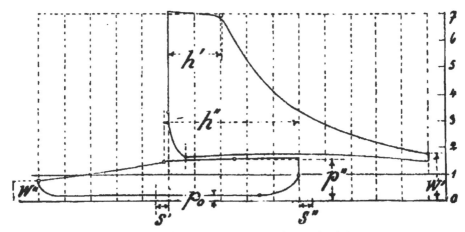

Fig. 1024.—Pressures in atmospheres absolute.

$$w' = \frac{(h' + s')\,p}{1 + s'}\;; \quad w'' = \frac{(h'' + s'')\,p''}{1 + s''}\;;$$

$$h' = \frac{w'\,(1 + s')}{p} - s'\;; \quad h'' = \frac{w''\,(1 + s'')}{p''} - s''\;;$$

$$w' - p'' = \text{the drop in the pressure.}$$

The power in both cylinders is nearly equal.

Indicator Diagram for the Maximum Horse-Power for the Compound Engines given in Table 147.

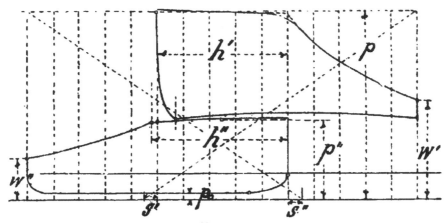

Fig. 1025.

TABLE 147.—Compound Condensing Engines, 108 lbs. Absolute Pressure per square inch.

Stroke. H	High-Pressure Cylinder d	Low-Pressure Cylinder D	$\frac{V}{v}$	n	c	Q	w	N_i	k	P_o	O	P_m	N	$N.$	N_e	Per I.H.P. per hour Water in lbs.	Per I.H.P. per hour Coal in lbs.	Injection Water in gals. per hour.	Maximum power effective $N.$	Maximum power effective Water per $N.$ per I.H.P. per hour in lbs.
20	11¾	18	2·3	90	300	254	11·76	·10	·356	3·1	2·7	30·7	65	47	45	18·66	2·86	2500	68	25·2
24	13¾	21	2·3	80	320	346	11·76	·10	·356	3·1	2·7	30·7	96	71	70	18·07	2·77	3525	107	23·8
28	15¾	24	2·3	75	350	452	11·76	·10	·356	3·1	2·7	30·7	140	106	100	17·62	2·64	5000	151	22·5
32	17½	27	2·35	70	370	572	11	·09	·33	3·1	2·7	28·1	174	132	130	16·95	2·40	6025	208	21·2
36	20	30½	2·35	67	400	730	11	·09	·33	3·1	2·7	28·1	235	179	175	16·29	2·20	7700	280	19·8
40	21¾	33½	2·37	65	430	881	11	·09	·33	3·1	2·7	28·1	308	237	230	15·63	2·09	9500	374	18·7

The high-pressure cylinder has variable cut-off from ·0 to ·5, compression $0' = 1$.

The low-pressure cylinder has fixed cut-off at ·5, compression $0'' = 2·56$.

$\frac{V}{v}$ = ratio of the cylinder volumes; Q = surface of low-pressure piston in square inches.

$s_i = \dfrac{g'}{\frac{V}{v}}$ = ideal clearance space; h_i = ideal cut-off; w = final pressure absolute.

SECTION XI.

THE EFFECT OF THE INERTIA OF THE RECIPROCATING PARTS OF A STEAM ENGINE.

THE effect of the inertia of the reciprocating parts of an engine especially with high speeds may have a great influence on the smoothness of the running.* The effect of inertia has been ignored by engine makers, it was pointed out in a paper on the Allen engine by Mr. C. T. Porter in 1868,† with special reference to the change in direction of the pressure on the crank-pins of steam engines at certain parts of the stroke.

Let P = the weight of the reciprocating mass in lbs.

f = the surface of the piston in square inches.

The approximate proportion of weight to piston surface will be $\dfrac{P}{f}$ = 3·98 for horizontal non-condensing engines, $\dfrac{P}{f}$ = 4·27 for horizontal condensing engines. In the Allen engine above alluded to, the weight of the reciprocating parts was 470 lbs., and the piston surface 113 square inches; this gives the proportion P to f as 4·16 to 1).

H = stroke in feet.

r = Crank radius in feet.

n = Revolutions per minute.

$v = \dfrac{2\, r\, \pi\, n}{60}$ = the average speed of the crank pin in feet per second.

(a.) The Connecting-Rod of Infinite Length.

The pull on the connecting-rod necessary to overcome the inertia of the reciprocating parts is equal to the horizontal component of the acceleration of the crank pin multiplied by the mass moved; at the dead point this component is equal to the total acceleration of the crank pin towards the centre of the crank shaft, i.e., to $\dfrac{v^2}{r}$.

---

* Radinger Maschinen mit höher Kolbengeschwindigkeit.
† Institution of Mechanical Engineers' Proceedings, April, 1868.

The total drag on the connecting-rod at the beginning of the stroke is therefore $\dfrac{Pv^2}{gr}$, hence the pressure on unit surface of the face of the piston necessary to neutralize this $-\dfrac{Pv^2}{grf} = q1$. At the highest point of the crank $q = 0$, since at that point there will be no further pressure expended in producing acceleration of the reciprocating parts, as the piston has attained the same speed as the crank pin. At intermediate points $q = q_1 \cos. \omega$, where $\omega =$ the angle swept out by the crank pin from the dead point.

It is easy to represent graphically the retarding or accelerating forces acting on the piston due to the inertia of the reciprocating parts, as in this case the motion of the piston is simple harmonic, i.e.,

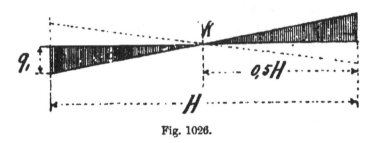

Fig. 1026.

the acceleration and therefore the accelerating force is proportional to the distance of the face of the piston from the centre of its path. If we plot out a curve where the ordinates are pressures and the abscissæ the corresponding position of the piston, we get a straight line which cuts the axis of abscissæ at the point k where $q = 0$.

Example. To determine the effect of the inertia of the moving parts of an engine where the diameter of the piston $D = 16''$ and the stroke $H = 28''$, $n = 100$.

$$\text{By our formula } \frac{P}{f} = 3\cdot98.$$

$$\therefore P = 3\cdot98 \times 16^2 \, \frac{\pi}{4}$$

$$= 798 \text{ lbs.}$$

$$\nu = \frac{2\pi \times 100 \times \frac{7}{6}}{60}$$

$$= 12\cdot2 \text{ feet per second.}$$

The pressure per square inch on the face of the piston necessary to move the reciprocating masses at the beginning of the stroke

$$= \frac{Pv^2}{grf} = \frac{798 \times (12\cdot2)^2}{32\cdot2 \times \frac{7}{6} \times 16^2 \times \frac{\pi}{4}} = 49\cdot4 \text{ lbs.}$$

The pressure diminishes towards the middle of the stroke, where it vanishes, the inertia of the reciprocating masses then assists the steam pressure, at the end of the stroke this pressure is 49·4 lbs. per square inch.

In order, therefore, that the pressure on the crank pin may be constant, we must have high pressure at the beginning of the stroke, and low pressure at the end of the stroke. The expansion of the steam does this, and compensates to a great extent for the forces introduced by the inertia of the reciprocating parts. If the compensation is not sufficient the momentum of the fly-wheel must help to drag the piston to its full speed at the beginning of the stroke, and oppose its motion at the end. Consequently, there is a change from extension to compression in the connecting-rod and a knock ensues which if neglected soon causes trouble. To remedy this, the steam must be cushioned at the end of the stroke by closing the exhaust early. The energy possessed by the moving reciprocating masses is thus employed in compressing the steam, and is restored at the beginning of the stroke where it is wanted.

(b.) With Connecting-Rod of Finite Length.

Let L = the length of the connecting-rod.

$\dfrac{r}{L}$ = ratio of crank radius to length of connecting-rod.

q = accelerating pressure in lbs. per square inch of the piston face necessary to overcome or retard the inertia of the moving parts.

ω = the angle swept out by the crank arm.

Then $q = \dfrac{Pv^2}{grf} \left(\cos. \omega + \dfrac{r}{L} \cos. 2\omega \right)$ approximately. At the dead point for the outstroke $q_1 = \dfrac{Pv^2}{grf} \left(1 + \dfrac{r}{L} \right)$ and opposes the steam pressure at the dead point at the end of the stroke $q_2 = \dfrac{Pv^2}{grf} \left(1 - \dfrac{r}{L} \right)$ and assists the steam pressure. The space S, travelled by the piston when the crank arm has turned through an angle ω is given by

$$S = r \left(1 - \cos. \omega + \dfrac{1}{2} \dfrac{r}{L} \sin.^2 \omega \right) \text{ approximately.}$$

This distance S is best calculated by graphical construction.

The case of $\dfrac{r}{L} = \dfrac{1}{5}$ is shown in fig. 1027.

For all values of S the ordinates are plotted out.

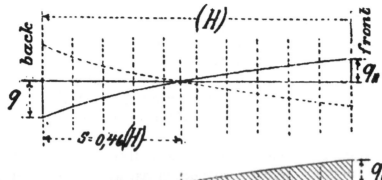

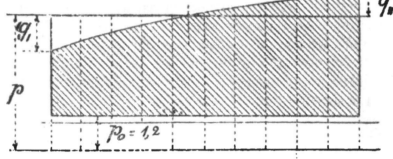

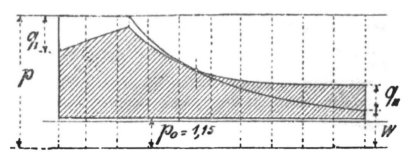

Figs. 1027—1029.

Outstroke—

$$\omega = 0 ; \qquad q_1 = \frac{6}{5} \frac{Pv^2}{grf} ;$$

$$\omega = 180° ; \quad q_2 = - \frac{4}{5} \frac{Pv^2}{grf}.$$

Return stroke (steam pressure acting in opposite direction)—

$$\omega = 180° ; \qquad q_1 = \frac{4}{5} \frac{Pv^2}{grf} ;$$

$$\omega = 360° ; \quad q_2 = - \frac{6}{5} \frac{Pv^2}{grf} ;$$

when
$$\omega = 79° \; ; \quad s = 0.46 \, H \; ; \quad q = 0.$$
$$\omega = 259° \; ; \quad s = 0.54 \, H \; ; \quad q = 0.$$

Example.—Take an engine where $D = 16''$, $H = 28''$, $n = 100$; $L = 5\,r$.

Then as in preceding example—
$$P = 798 \text{ lbs. } v = 12.2 \text{ feet per sec.}$$
$$q_1 = \frac{6}{5} \times 49.4 = 59.3.$$
$$q_2 = \frac{4}{5} \times 49.4 = 39.5.$$

Suppose the steam pressure to be 140 lbs. per square inch at the beginning of the stroke and to be expanded five times ; the pressure at the end of the stroke would be $\dfrac{140 + 15}{5} - 15 = 16$ lbs. per square inch approximately.

The pressure on the crank pin at the beginning of the stroke would be $= (140 - 59.3)f = 80.7f$, and at the end of the stroke it would be $= (16 + 39.5)f = 55.5f$. If the steam had been expanded 2.8 times, the pressure at the end of the stroke would equal the pressure at the beginning of the stroke. Had there been no expansion, the pressures would have been $80.7f$ at the beginning and $179.5f$ at the end of the stroke. The pressure on the crank pin at the end of the stroke would thus have been more than double the pressure at the beginning.

The values of q are plotted out in fig. 1027. In fig. 1028 the pressure on the crank pin is represented graphically when the steam pressure is maintained constant throughout the stroke. The shaded area above the line is exactly equal in area to the unshaded area below the line which could have been predicted since the energy communicated to the reciprocating masses at the beginning of the stroke is equal to the energy given up by them at the end of the stroke.

In fig. 1029, we see the influence of the reciprocating masses on the pressure on the crank pin for the same engine when the cut-off is at 0.4 of the stroke. From the diagram it is apparent that with quick-running engines working with late cut-off, the pressure on the crank pin due to the inertia of the reciprocating masses, and the pressure of the steam combined at the end of the stroke far exceeds the admission pressure. Cushioning the steam gets over this, and it seems at first sight to be most advantageous to have the compression at the dead point = the final steam pressure + the pressure due to

D D

the reciprocating masses; *i.e.*, $c = w + q_s$ (fig. 1030). Thus the admission pressure can be easily calculated.

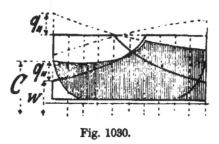

Fig. 1030.

In order to carry out a high degree of expansion, a high speed of piston is necessary, for the inertia of the reciprocating parts in this case compensates for the extreme variation in steam pressure consequent upon an early cut-off. If we consider smoothness of running only, the engine should be run so fast that the driving force produced by the highest pressure of the steam cannot exceed the inertia of the reciprocating parts, then a knock upon the centres becomes impossible.

The usual small compression given in slow-going engines causes nearly the whole of the initial pressure to act suddenly on the piston, and this makes the connecting-rod knock on the crank pin.

The author holds that it is of the very greatest importance to have smooth and noiseless running, and this is only possible with the help of compression. In engines with double valve gear and large clearance spaces, it is difficult to obtain sufficient compression, most makers avoiding the large valves and eccentrics necessarily required.

As a general rule, *always endeavour to have the compression in a non-condensing engine at least equal to half the admission pressure and in a condensing engine as much as possible.*

We can employ the standard proportions given on page 181. The valve gear, page 184, can only be used with divided valves (*i.e.*, in two short valves, one at each end of the cylinder for short ports) with small clearance space. The end pressure due to compression $C = \dfrac{(o + s)}{s} \ P_0$ can be determined by the use of the Tables 148 and 149, when the valve s of the clearance space, and the portion of the stroke during which compression takes place, are known. The pressures in the Tables are given in atmospheres. Non-condensing engines [$P_0 = 1\cdot15$], condensing engines [$P_0 = 0\cdot2$].

$$\text{Value of } q = \frac{Pv^2}{grf} \text{ (atmos.)}$$

TABLE 148.—**Pressure due to Compression in Absolute Atmospheres for Non-Condensing Engines, $P_0 = 1\cdot15$ At. Abs.**

Compression period. 0	Clearance space s in per cent.								
	2	3	4	5	6	7	8	9	10
·00	1·15	1·15	1·15	1·15	1·15	1·15	1·15	1·15	1·15
·025	2·55	2·10	1·87	1·73	1·63	1·56	1·50	1·47	1·44
·050	4·00	3·06	2·59	2·30	2·11	1·97	1·87	1·78	1·72
·075	5·46	4·03	3·31	2·87	2·57	2·38	2·28	2·11	2·01
·100	6·90	4·90	4·03	3·45	3·07	2·79	2·59	2·42	2·30
·150	—	6·90	5·46	4·60	4·00	3·60	3·31	3·06	2·87
·200	—	—	6·90	5·75	4·98	4·43	4·03	3·70	3·45
·250	—	—	—	6·90	5·95	5·29	4·74	4·34	4·02
·300	—	—	—	—	6·90	6·07	5·46	4·98	4·60

TABLE 149.—**For Condensing Engines $P_0 = \cdot2$.**

·00	·20	·20	·20	·20	·20	·20	·20	·20	·20
·025	·45	·37	·33	·30	·28	·27	·26	·26	·25
·050	·70	·53	·45	·40	·37	·34	·33	·31	·30
·075	·95	·70	·57	·50	·45	·41	·38	·37	·35
·100	1·20	·86	·70	·60	·53	·48	·45	·42	·40
·150	1·70	1·20	·95	·80	·70	·63	·57	·53	·50
·200	2·20	1·53	1·20	1·00	·86	·77	·70	·64	·60
·250	2·70	1·86	1·45	1·20	1·03	·97	·82	·75	·70
·300	3·20	2·20	1·70	1·40	1·20	1·05	·95	·86	·80

The pressure of the compression C rises to a height which may be obtained by the formula

$$C = \frac{(o + s)}{s} P_0$$

and can be taken from the above tables for any given per-centage of clearance.

TABLE 150.—Values of $\dfrac{Pv^2}{rgf}$ in Atmospheres.

Stroke in inches.	Diam. of piston in inches.	Revolutions per minute n.							
H	D	50	75	100	150	200	300	400	500
6	4	·04	·08	·15	·35	·60	1·40	2·50	4·00
12	8	·10	·21	·40	·90	1·60	3·50	—	—
20	12	·18	·42	·70	1·50	3·00	—	—	—
28	16	·27	·60	1·00	2·50	4·30	—	—	—
36	20	·34	·75	1·30	3·00	5·40	—	—	—
44	24	·40	·90	1·60	3·50	—	—	—	—
48	28	·45	1·05	1·80	4·00	—	—	—	—
56	32	·50	1·20	2·10	4·70	—	—	—	—
64	36	·60	1·35	2·40	5·40	—	—	—	—
72	40	·70	1·50	2·70	6·00	—	—	—	—

Unit to calculate with $\dfrac{Pv^2}{grf} \times \dfrac{1}{14\cdot7} = \dfrac{4\pi^2 n^2 H}{180 \times 32\cdot2 \times 14\cdot7} =$
·0000463 n^2 H in atmospheres.

·0000463 × 14·7 n^2 H = ·000681 n^2 H in lbs. per square inch.

Example.

$$\text{Let } H = 48'',$$
$$D = 28'',$$
$$n = 150, \quad \frac{r}{L} = \frac{1}{5}.$$

By the table
$$\frac{Pv^2}{grf} = 4\text{·}15 \text{ atmos.}$$

Thus
$$q_1 = 4\text{·}15 \times \frac{6}{5} = 4\text{·}98,$$

$$q_2 = 4\text{·}15 \times \frac{4}{5} = 3\text{·}32.$$

Initial pressure
$$p = 7 \text{ atmos.}$$
$$h = \text{cut-off at } 0\text{·}2.$$
$$s = 6\% \text{ clearance.}$$

This gives the pressure diagram, fig. 1031. The part shaded

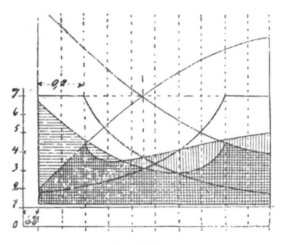

Fig. 1031.

vertically for the outstroke, and that shaded horizontally for the back-stroke.

SECTION XII.

FRICTION BRAKE, DYNAMOMETER.

In making trials of small engines, a friction brake is used to absorb the power during the trial. The original friction brake, fig. 1032, is due to Prony. A pair of wooden clamps, to one of which a lever l is fixed, are bolted together, fig. 1032, and nip the shaft to

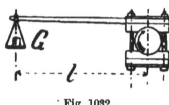

· Fig. 1032.

which they are applied with more or less pressure according to the tightness of the bolts; the shaft being run in the direction of the arrow, tends by friction between the clamps and shaft to raise the weight G; if the shaft runs uniformly and the belts are adjusted so as just to keep the weight balanced, the effect is very nearly the same as if the work done was that of raising the weight continuously at the speed G would move if allowed to run with the shaft.

Let G = the weight required in lbs.
  l = the length of the lever in feet.
  n = the revolutions per minute, so the "brake horse power" given out by the machine will be

$$B\,HP = G \times \frac{2\pi \times n \times l}{33000}$$

and G for any required load will $= \dfrac{33000\,(B\,HP)}{2\pi \times n \times l}$.

This form of brake is still used in special cases, but the more modern form of rope brake, fig. 1033, is now much used. The rope R is spliced or seized together at one end, and passed through the "bight" as in the figure; to the upper a spring balance is hooked, the balance itself being hung from a firm support; to the other end are attached the weights necessary to give the required load. The rope is kept in its place by blocks of wood b,b; a small block of wood c, is inserted to keep the rope from nipping the other part which is on the wheel. If required for long runs, the wheel is made with deep flanges P, and water is run in to keep it cool. The calculation is the same as for the Prony brake, taking the length of l from the centre of the shaft S to the centre of the rope ; but in measuring the

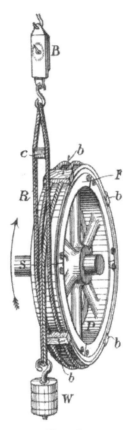

Fig. 1033.

work done, frequent readings of the spring balance must be taken and subtracted from the weight to give the time load lifted. These brakes work very well, require but little attention and are fairly reliable.

SECTION XIII.

SUNDRY DETAILS.

Diagrams of Special Reversing Gears.

In addition to those already shown on page 224, the diagrams below show the principle of some special reversing gears that are sometimes used for marine and other engines.*

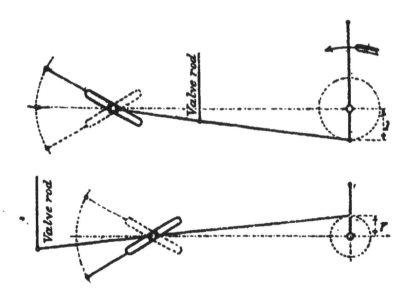

Figs. 1034, 1035.—Reversing gear by Hackworth.

--- --- --- --- --- --- --- --- --- --- ---

* "Zeitschrift der deutsch Ingenieur," 1885, page 949.

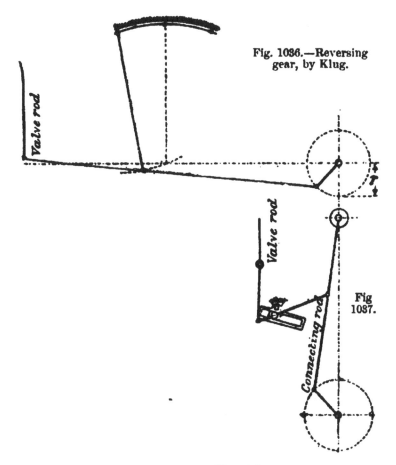

Fig. 1036.—Reversing gear, by Klug.

Fig 1037.

Fig. 1037.—Reversing gear, by Joy.

Barring Apparatus.

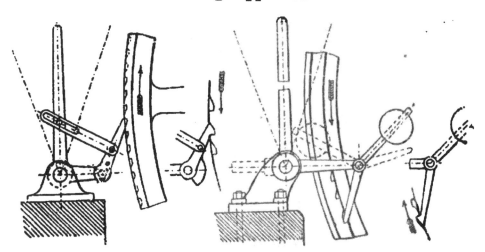

Figs. 1039, 1040.—Simple lever action.

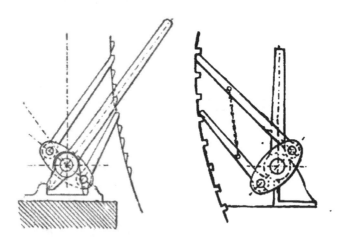

Figs. 1041, 1042.—Double lever action.

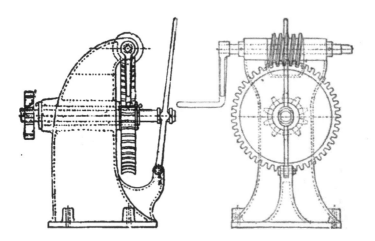

Figs. 1043, 1044.—Worm and worm-wheel.

TABLE 151.—Strength of Bolts.

Diameter of bolts.	No. of threads per inch.	Diameter at bottom of thread.	Area at bottom of thread in sq. inches.	Load on bolt in lbs. when stress on metal is 1 ton per sq. inch.
$\frac{3}{8}$	16	·295	·0683	153
$\frac{7}{16}$	14	·346	·0942	211
$\frac{1}{2}$	12	·393	·1213	272
$\frac{5}{8}$	11	·508	·2027	454
$\frac{3}{4}$	10	·622	·3039	681
$\frac{7}{8}$	9	·733	·4230	945
1	8	·840	·5542	1241
$1\frac{1}{8}$	7	·942	·6969	1561
$1\frac{1}{4}$	7	1·070	·8992	2014
$1\frac{3}{8}$	6	1·161	1·0569	2368
$1\frac{1}{2}$	6	1·287	1·2999	2910
$1\frac{5}{8}$	5	1·369	1·4210	3193
$1\frac{3}{4}$	5	1·494	1·7530	3927
2	$4\frac{1}{2}$	1·715	2·3087	5172
$2\frac{1}{4}$	4	1·930	2·9241	6550
$2\frac{1}{2}$	4	2·180	3·7311	8358

All Dimensions are given in Inches.

SECTION XIV.

BOILERS.

In the following pages (412 to 429), particulars of the most usual types of boilers will be found, together with figures showing their general construction.

Elephant or French Boiler.

Figs. 1045, 1046, show this type of boiler, which has been largely used in France and occasionally in England; the table gives the general proportions.

TABLE 152.—**Dimensions of Elephant Boilers.**

Nominal H.P.	10	·12	·15	·20	·25	·30
Length of boiler in feet . . .	14	16	18	23½	28	30
Diameter of heaters, or "bouilleurs," in inches	18	19	20½	21½	23	24
Diameter of shell in inches . .	30	32	34	36	38	40
Approximate heating surface in sq. ft.	169	203	254	338	422	507

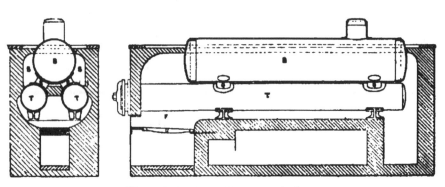

Figs. 1045, 1046.—Elephant Boiler.

Cornish Boilers.

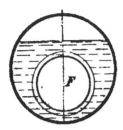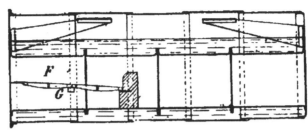

Figs. 1047, 1048.

This type, together with the double flued or Lancashire boiler, fig. 1053, is perhaps more largely used on land than any other type for supplying steam for steam-engines, or general manufacturing purposes.

The Tables 153 to 166, with the exception of table 161, give the dimensions of these boilers by different English makers.

TABLE 153.—Dimensions of Cornish Boilers made by Messrs. Marshall, Sons & Co. Limited.

Nominal H.P.	4	6	8	10	12	14	16	20	25
Dia. of boiler .	3' 10"	4' 5"	4' 5"	4' 9"	5' 3"	5' 4"	5' 9"	6' 2"	6' 2"
Length ,, .	9' 0"	10' 1"	13' 2"	14' 6"	14' 9"	17' 6"	19' 4"	21' 0"	26' 3"
Dia. of flue .	24	28	29	31	34	34	36	39	39
No. of Galloway tubes }	—	—	—	—	2	3	3	4	4
Weight in cwts.	44	67	77	104	110	139	153	180	215

TABLE 154.—Cornish Boilers made by Messrs. Davey, Paxman & Co.

Nom. H.P.	4	6	8	10	12	14	16	20	25	30
Dia., boiler	3' 6"	3' 8"	4' 6"	4' 6"	4' 9"	4' 9"	5' 0"	5' 6"	5' 6"	5' 9"
Length ,,	9' 0"	12' 0"	12' 0"	15' 0"	15' 0"	18' 0"	20' 0"	21' 0"	24' 0"	26' 0"
Dia. of flue, ins. }	24	24	30	30	32	32	33	36	38	38

Seating for Cornish Boilers (Figs. 1049—1051).

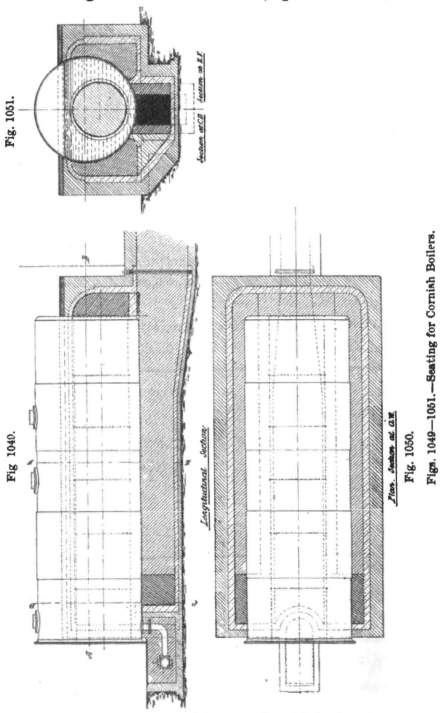

Fig. 1051.

Section on E F

Section at C D

Fig. 1049.

Longitudinal Section

Fig. 1050.

Plan. Section at A B.

Figs. 1049—1051.—Seating for Cornish Boilers.

The ordinary arrangement of flues for Cornish boilers is shown in the above figures, 1049, 1051 ; in all cases where possible, the flues should be made large enough to admit of thorough inspection being made.

TABLE 155.—Cornish Boilers made by Messrs. Ruston, Proctor, Limited.

Nominal H.P. . .	3	4	6	8	10	12	14	16	20
Diam. of boiler.	3' 0"	3' 6"	4' 0"	4' 6"	4' 6"	5' 0"	5' 0"	5' 6"	6' 0"
Length of boiler	8' 0"	9' 0"	10' 0"	12' 0"	15' 0"	16' 0"	18' 0"	19' 0"	20' 0"
Diam. of flue .	20	22	24	28	28	32	32	38	40
No. Galloway cross tubes .	1	2	2	2	3	3	3	4	4

TABLE 156.—Cornish Boilers made by Messrs. Ransomes, Sims & Jefferies, Limited.

Nom. H.P.	4	6	8	10	12	14	16	20	25	30
Dia., boiler	3' 6"	4' 0"	4' 6"	4' 6"	5' 0"	5' 0"	5' 6"	5' 6"	6' 0"	6' 0"
Length „	9' 0"	10' 0"	12' 0"	15' 0"	16' 0"	19' 0"	20' 0"	23' 0"	24' 0"	27' 0"
Dia. of flue	24	24	28	28	32	32	36	36	40	40
No. Gallo. cross-tubes	1	1	2	2	2	3	3	4	4	6

Double-Flued or Lancashire Boiler (Figs. 1052, 1053).

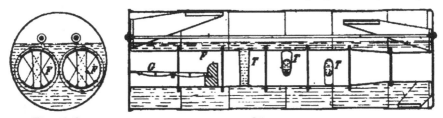

Fig. 1052.   Fig. 1053.

This type is generally used for large boilers on land, and is very efficient and durable. Below are tables of dimensions of these boilers by the same English makers as those given of Cornish boilers, and in the same order.

TABLE 157.—Dimensions of Lancashire Boilers.

Nominal H.P. . . .	20	25	30	35	40
Diameter of boiler . .	6' 2"	6' 6"	6' 8"	6' 8"	7' 0"
Length	19' 0"	22' 0"	24' 0"	27' 0"	28' 0"
Diameter of flues . .	28"	30"	30"	30"	32"
Weight in cwts. . . .	200	235	250	276	300

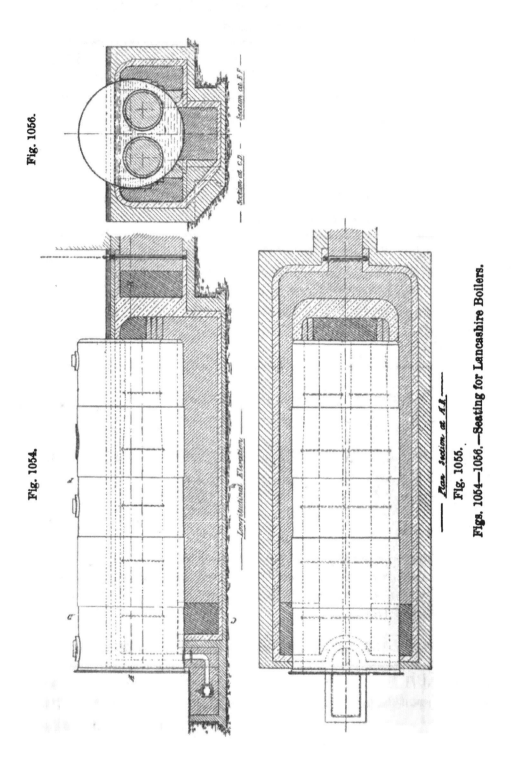

Fig. 1056.

Fig. 1054.

Section at C,D. Section at E,F.

Longitudinal Elevation.

Plan Section at A,B.

Fig. 1055.

Figs. 1054—1056.—Seating for Lancashire Boilers.

TABLE 158.

Nominal H.P.	20	25	30	35	40	45	50	55
Diameter of boiler	5' 6"	5' 6"	6' 0"	6' 3"	6' 6"	6' 9"	7' 0"	7' 6"
Length of boiler	19' 0"	21' 0"	22' 6"	24' 0"	26' 0"	28' 0"	30' 0"	30' 0"
Diameter of flues	24	24	27	28	30	31½	33	36

TABLE 159.

Nominal H.P.	18	22	25	28	30	35	40	50
Diameter of boiler	5' 6"	6' 0"	6' 0"	6' 6"	6' 6"	6' 6"	7' 0"	7' 0"
Length of boiler	19' 0"	20' 0"	24' 0"	24' 0"	26' 0"	28' 0"	28' 0"	30' 0"
Diameter of flues	22	26	26	29	29	29	31	31
No. of Galloway cross-tubes	6	6	6	6	6	8	8	10

TABLE 160.

Nominal H.P.	16	20	25	30	35	40	45	50
Diameter of boiler	6' 0"	6' 0"	6' 6"	6' 6"	7' 0"	7' 0"	7' 6"	7' 6"
Length of boiler	19' 0"	22' 0"	23' 0"	26' 0"	28' 0"	30' 0"	28' 0"	30' 0"
Diameter of flues	28	28	28	28	32	32	36	36
No. of Galloway cross-tubes	4	4	6	6	8	8	8	8

Seating for Lancashire Boilers (Figs. 1054—1056).

The flues in the above figs. (1054—1056), are shown arranged for the hot gases to pass through the flues, then down underneath the boiler, then round the sides, and finally to the chimney. With Cornish boilers the flues are usually arranged to take the hot gases round the sides first, and then along underneath the boiler. Each method has its advocates, but it is generally held that in Lancashire boilers the hottest possible gases should pass underneath, in order to act on the body of water between and below the flues; in Cornish boilers there is less water under the flue.

E E

Cornish Boilers of German Type, with Flue on one side.

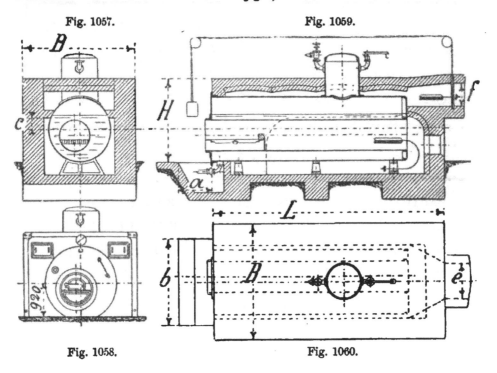

Fig. 1057.   Fig. 1059.

Fig. 1058.   Fig. 1060.

TABLE 161.—Dimensions of German Cornish Boiler Seating
(Figs. 1057—1060).

Horse-power.	Heating-surface sq. feet.	L	B	H	a	b	c	e	f
2	54	95	77½	70	18	32	6	20	20
4	97	136	82	75	20	36	7	20	20
6	140	173	85	77	22	39	7¾	20	20
8	172	198	87	78	24	43	8	24	24
10	215	220	92	81	26	47	9	24	24
15	300	228	98	90	28	51	10	24	24
25	430	285	110	94	30	55	11	28	23
40	690	340	118	94	32	59	12	28	28
50	860	427	138	96	34	63	13½	28	28

All dimensions in Inches except heating-surface, which is given in square feet.

Cylindrical Multitubular Boilers.

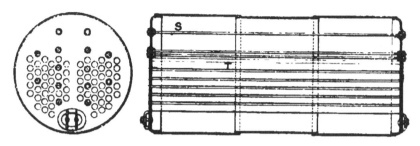

Figs. 1061, 1062.

TABLE 162.—Dimensions of Multitubular Cylindrical Boiler (Figs. 1061, 1062).

Nominal H.P. .	6	8	10	12	14	16	20	25	30	35	40	50
Dia. of boiler .	3½	3½	4	4	4½	4½	5	5	6	6	6½	6½
Length „	6	7½	8	9	9½	10½	11½	12½	12½	13½	13½	15
No. of tubes .	22	22	28	28	32	32	38	44	40	52	60	60
Dia. of tubes .	—	—	—	—	—	—	—	—	—	—	—	—
Heating-surface	—	—	—	—	—	—	—	—	—	—	—	—

This type of boiler is set in brickwork, the furnace and flue doors being also built in.

The boiler is fired from below, and the gases pass along underneath the boiler and through the tubes, returning back by the sides to the chimney. The tubes are easily got at for cleaning, and almost any description of fuel may be used. These boilers are suitable for export, owing to their small size in proportion to their heating surface, and are convenient for export.

Multitubular Loco-Type Boilers.

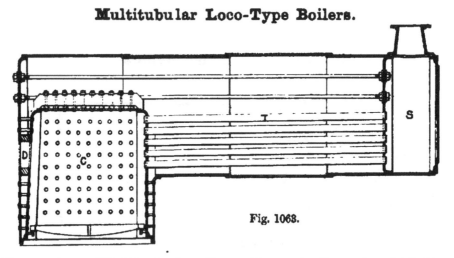

Fig. 1063.

TABLE 163.—**Multitubular Loco-Type Boilers for 140 lbs. working pressure.**

Nominal Horse-power.	8	10	12	16	20	25	30	40
Diameter of boiler .	$31\frac{1}{2}$	$33\frac{1}{2}$	$35\frac{1}{2}$	39	$41\frac{1}{2}$	$47\frac{1}{2}$	50	52
Length of boiler . .	135	146	148	162	172	$187\frac{1}{2}$	$189\frac{1}{2}$	$235\frac{1}{2}$
Number of tubes .	31	38	34	36	43	58	64	73
Length of tubes . .	$77\frac{1}{4}$	81	81	96	102	108	108	123
Diameter of tubes .	$2\frac{1}{4}$	$2\frac{1}{2}$	$2\frac{1}{2}$	$2\frac{1}{2}$	$2\frac{1}{2}$	$2\frac{1}{2}$	$2\frac{1}{2}$	$2\frac{1}{2}$
Heating surface . .	144·2	158·3	189·7	230·2	285·5	398·0	439·5	618·4
Length of fire-box .	31	35	35	37	38	$43\frac{1}{2}$	$45\frac{3}{4}$	$56\frac{3}{4}$
Grate area, sq. ft. .	5	6·5	7·3	7·8	9·0	12·1	13·6	17·7
Thickness of plates, tube . . .	$\frac{5}{8}$	$\frac{5}{8}$	$\frac{5}{8}$	$\frac{5}{8}$	$\frac{5}{8}$	$\frac{3}{4}$	$\frac{3}{4}$	$\frac{3}{4}$
Thickness of fire-box, top and sides	$\frac{7}{16}$	$\frac{7}{16}$	$\frac{7}{16}$	$\frac{1}{2}$	$\frac{1}{2}$	$\frac{1}{2}$	$\frac{1}{2}$	$\frac{1}{2}$
Thickness of front plate, fire-box .	$\frac{7}{16}$	$\frac{7}{16}$	$\frac{7}{16}$	$\frac{7}{16}$	$\frac{1}{2}$	$\frac{1}{2}$	$\frac{1}{2}$	$\frac{1}{2}$
Thickness of front tube plate, fire-box	$\frac{5}{8}$	$\frac{5}{8}$	$\frac{5}{8}$	$\frac{11}{16}$	$\frac{3}{4}$	$\frac{3}{4}$	$\frac{3}{4}$	$\frac{3}{4}$
Thickness of barrel .	$\frac{3}{8}$	$\frac{3}{8}$	$\frac{3}{8}$	$\frac{7}{16}$	$\frac{7}{16}$	$\frac{7}{16}$	$\frac{1}{2}$	$\frac{1}{2}$
Diameter of chimney	12	15	15	15	18	18	20	26
Length of smoke-box	$24\frac{1}{2}$	25	25	25	$26\frac{1}{2}$	$31\frac{1}{2}$	$31\frac{1}{2}$	$40\frac{1}{2}$

Dimensions in Inches, except heating surface which is in sq. feet.

This is a well-tried type of boiler, and is universally used for locomotives, and portable and traction engines.

Multitubular Loco-Type Boilers.

These boilers are similar to those shown, fig. 1063, Table 163, but for smaller powers ; and are for 80 to 90 lbs. working pressure.

TABLE 164.—Dimensions of Loco-Type Boilers.

Horse-power.	3	4	5	6	7	8	9	10	12
Dia. of boiler .	28½	31½	33½	35½	37½	39	39	41½	43½
Length ,, . .	102½	115	115½	117	125	129	133	139	146½
No. of tubes .	15	19	21	25	27	31	33	36	39
Length ,, . .	57	66	67	67	72½	76	78	78¾	87¾
Dia. ,, .	2½	2½	2½	2½	2½	2½	2½	2½	2½
Total heating-surface of boiler }	66·9	94·5	105·5	122·0	140·7	165·5	179·5	197·8	234·9
Length of fire-box	22½	24½	25	25¼	26¼	27¼	29½	32¼	32¼
Grate area, sq. ft.	3·37	4·59	4·67	5·07	5·51	6·16	6·59	7·83	8·28
Thickness of front tube }	$\frac{1}{2}$	$\frac{1}{2}$	$\frac{1}{2}$	$\frac{9}{16}$	$\frac{9}{16}$	$\frac{9}{16}$	$\frac{9}{16}$	$\frac{9}{16}$	$\frac{5}{8}$
,, fire-box side & top plates }	$\frac{5}{16}$	$\frac{5}{16}$	$\frac{5}{16}$	$\frac{5}{16}$	$\frac{3}{8}$	$\frac{3}{8}$	$\frac{3}{8}$	$\frac{3}{8}$	$\frac{3}{8}$
Thickness of fire box front plate }	$\frac{5}{16}$	$\frac{5}{16}$	$\frac{5}{16}$	$\frac{5}{16}$	$\frac{3}{8}$	$\frac{3}{8}$	$\frac{3}{8}$	$\frac{3}{8}$	$\frac{3}{8}$
Thickness of fire box tube plate }	$\frac{1}{2}$	$\frac{1}{2}$	$\frac{1}{2}$	$\frac{9}{16}$	$\frac{9}{16}$	$\frac{9}{16}$	$\frac{9}{16}$	$\frac{9}{16}$	$\frac{5}{8}$
Thickness of barrel plates }	$\frac{1}{4}$	$\frac{1}{4}$	$\frac{1}{4}$	$\frac{5}{16}$	$\frac{5}{16}$	$\frac{5}{16}$	$\frac{5}{16}$	$\frac{3}{8}$	$\frac{3}{8}$
Dia. of chimney .	8	9	10	12	12	12	12	15	15
Length of smoke-box . }	17	19	19	19¾	20¾	20¾	20	20	21½

Dimensions in Inches, except heating surface which is given in sq. feet.

Vertical Boilers.

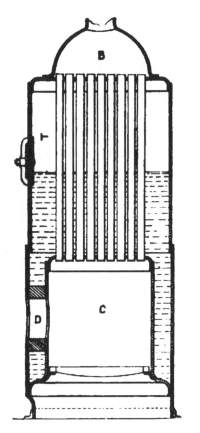

Fig. 1064.

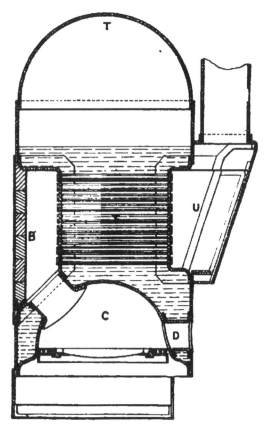

Fig. 1065.

Owing to the comparatively small space which vertical boilers occupy, and their convenient shape, they are largely used, notwithstanding the fact that their efficiency does not approach to either Cornish, Lancashire, or multitubular boilers. The form shown on fig. 1067, is in most general use, owing to its simplicity and cheapness; it is at the same time perhaps the most wasteful of fuel, to do away with which defect many other forms of vertical boilers have been constructed, to give increased heating surface and greater economy. Fig. 1064 shows one of these arrangements, in which the uptake is dispensed with, the gases, &c., from the fire-box passing through vertical tubes to the chimney. Fig. 1065 shows a vertical boiler constructed by Messrs. Cochrane, of Birkenhead. In this case the gases are conducted up one side of the boiler, and then pass through a number of horizontal tubes to the uptake ; the tubes being

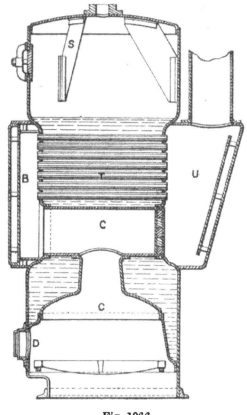

Fig. 1066.

arranged to give easy access for cleaning. Fig. 1066 shows a good form of vertical boiler by Messrs. Tinker, Shenton & Co.

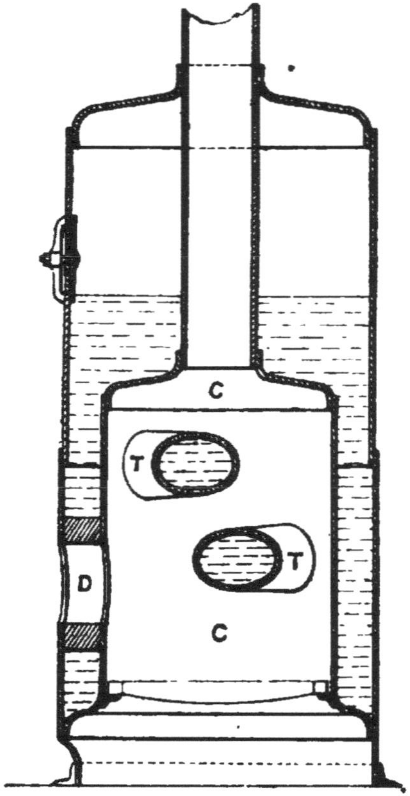

Fig. 1067.—Vertical Cross-Tube Boiler.

TABLE 165.—**Dimensions of Vertical Cross-Tube Boilers** (Fig. 1067).

Nominal horse-power	3	4	5	6	7	8	10	12	14	16
Diameter of boiler	30	33	36	39	39	42	48	48	51	57
Height of boiler	72	78	84	90	102	102	114	144	144	150
Approx. heating surface in sq. ft.	$28\frac{1}{2}$	$38\frac{1}{2}$	50	60	69	80	100	120	130	150
Grate area, sq. ft.	$3\frac{1}{2}$	$4\frac{1}{4}$	$5\frac{1}{4}$	$6\frac{1}{4}$	$6\frac{1}{4}$	$7\frac{1}{2}$	$10\frac{1}{4}$	$10\frac{1}{4}$	$11\frac{1}{2}$	15
Number of cross-tubes	2	2	2	3	3	3	3	4	4	4
Shell plates, thickness	$\frac{1}{4}$	$\frac{1}{4}$	$\frac{5}{16}$	$\frac{5}{16}$	$\frac{5}{16}$	$\frac{5}{16}$	$\frac{3}{8}$	$\frac{3}{8}$	$\frac{3}{8}$	$\frac{3}{8}$
Fire-box, thickness	$\frac{5}{16}$	$\frac{5}{16}$	$\frac{5}{16}$	$\frac{3}{8}$	$\frac{3}{8}$	$\frac{3}{8}$	$\frac{3}{8}$	$\frac{3}{8}$	$\frac{3}{8}$	$\frac{7}{16}$
Cross-tube, thickness	$\frac{1}{4}$	$\frac{1}{4}$	$\frac{5}{16}$	$\frac{5}{16}$	$\frac{5}{16}$	$\frac{5}{16}$	$\frac{5}{16}$	$\frac{5}{16}$	$\frac{5}{16}$	$\frac{5}{16}$
Uptake, thickness	$\frac{1}{4}$	$\frac{1}{4}$	$\frac{1}{4}$	$\frac{1}{4}$	$\frac{1}{4}$	$\frac{1}{4}$	$\frac{3}{8}$	$\frac{3}{8}$	$\frac{3}{8}$	$\frac{3}{8}$
Crown, thickness	$\frac{5}{16}$	$\frac{5}{16}$	$\frac{5}{16}$	$\frac{3}{8}$	$\frac{3}{8}$	$\frac{3}{8}$	$\frac{1}{2}$	$\frac{1}{2}$	$\frac{1}{2}$	$\frac{1}{2}$
Diameter of cross-tubes	7	8	8	8	8	9	9	9	9	10
Height to top of fire-box	41	44	48	51	57	57	64	81	81	84
Diameter of fire-box	26	—	—	—	—	—	—	—	—	—

Dimensions in Inches, except heating surface.

These vertical boilers are extensively used on board ship as donkey boilers, and also for working steam cranes.

TABLE 166.—Dimensions of Hopwood's Vertical Boilers (Fig. 1068).

Nominal horse-power	2	3	4	5	6	8	10	12
Diameter of boiler	27½	33	36	38½	41	43	48¾	52
Height of boiler	66	77	81	90	91	96	111	117
Height to uptake (B)	41¾	47½	52	54¾	60	64	76	79
No. of tubes	12	20	28	24	28	26	36	36
Diameter of tubes	2½	2½	2½	2½	2½	2½	2½	2½
Length of tubes	16	20¾	20¾	26½	27	28¼	34½	34½
Heating-surface (total) sq. feet	25	47·7	55·1	64·6	75·8	90·1	121·2	141·8
Grate-area	2·94	4·31	5·24	5·62	6·89	7·56	9·05	11·7

These boilers have manholes at D for access to tubes. The tubes are higher at one end than at the other. Vertical stays are used in the larger sizes, placed round the uptake, and connecting top of fire-box to crown of boiler.

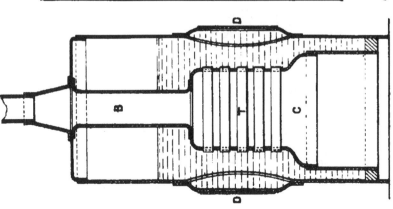

Fig 1068.

Small vertical boilers are used for steam fire-engines where steam has to be raised in the very shortest possible time. They have a

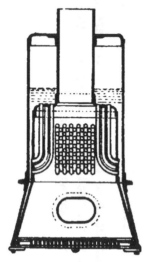

Fig. 1069.—Fire-engine boiler with cross and vertical tubes.

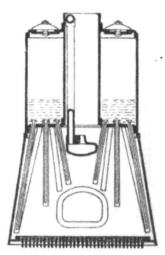

Fig. 1070.—Fire-engine boiler with Field tubes.

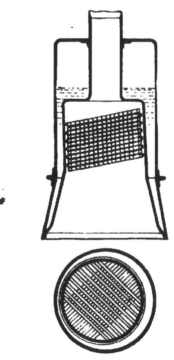

Fig. 1071.—Fire-engine boiler with cross-tubes.

very small water capacity, and are made to take to pieces for cleaning. Figs. 1069 to 1071, show in diagram types of these boilers.

Marine Boilers.

The type of marine boiler has gradually settled down, after many modifications, into an internally fired flue and tube boiler, and has

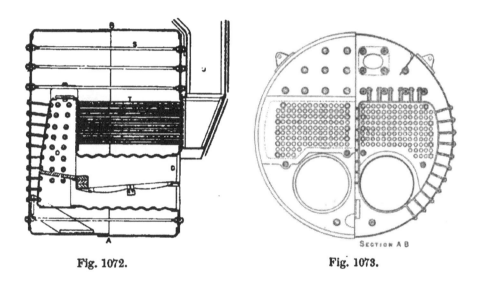

Fig. 1072. Fig. 1073.

now been successfully used on board ship for pressures up to 170 lbs. ; 160 being, however, the usual limit. Figs. 1072, 1073, show in diagram the general construction of the modern marine boiler.

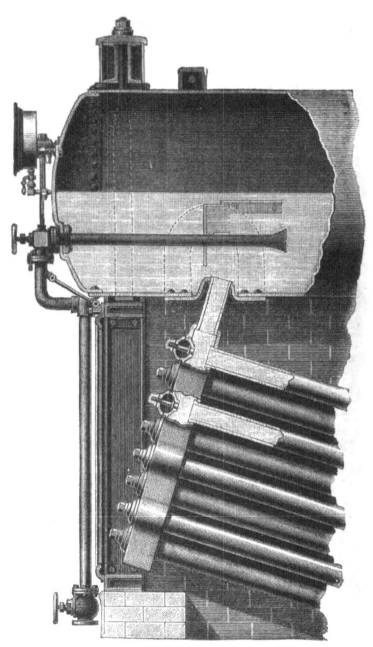

Fig. 1074.

Fig. 1075.

Water-Tube Boilers.

A number of these boilers have been designed, but only a few have been successful ; fig. 1076 shows one well-known type made by Messrs. Babcock & Wilcox. The tubes are expanded into connecting boxes in zig-zag, figs. 1074, 1075. Fig. 1076 shows the arrangement

Fig. 1076.

of flues, and fig. 1074 a partial longitudinal section taken at the front end of the boiler. A mud drum is provided, to form a receptacle for the deposit as it falls down into the more quiescent parts of the boiler. Steam can be raised very rapidly in these boilers, and they have been much used in electric lighting stations. New types of water-boilers are being now brought out for torpedo boats and small steam craft.

Lever Safety Valve.

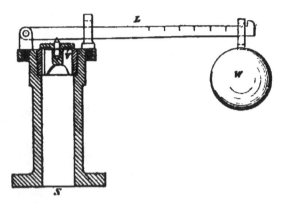

Fig. 1077.

TABLE 167.—**Dimensions of Ordinary Lever Safety Valves.**

Diameter of valve	2″	2½″	3″
Area of valve (sq. ins.) . . .	3·1416	4·9087	7·0686
Length from fulcrum to valve .	2½	2½	2½
Length of lever 60 lbs. . . .	30″	30″	30″
„ 80 lbs. . .	40″	40″	40″
Weight (in lbs.) 60 lbs. . . .	15½	24½	35¼
Diameter weight	4¾″	5⅝″	6⅜″

With the above proportions to find the length of lever for a given blow-off pressure : multiply the area of valve by the blow-off pressure, and divide by 12 ; the quotient will be the required length in inches from the fulcrum.

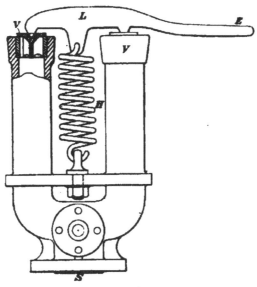

Fig. 1078.

TABLE 168.—Dimensions of Ramsbottom's Safety Valves
(Fig. 1078).

Diameter of valves . . .	$1\frac{1}{2}$	$1\frac{3}{4}$	$2\frac{1}{8}$	$2\frac{1}{2}$	3	$3\frac{1}{2}$
Diameter of flange . .	$7\frac{1}{4}$	9	9	10	$11\frac{1}{2}$	12
Between centres of valves V	$6\frac{1}{2}$	7	$7\frac{1}{2}$	$8\frac{1}{2}$	$9\frac{1}{2}$	$9\frac{3}{4}$
Height from flange to top of casting . . .	16	$17\frac{1}{2}$	$18\frac{3}{4}$	$21\frac{1}{2}$	$23\frac{1}{4}$	$25\frac{1}{2}$
Thickness of lever . .	$\frac{9}{16}-\frac{5}{16}$	$\frac{5}{8}-\frac{3}{8}$	$\frac{3}{4}-\frac{7}{16}$	$\frac{7}{8}-\frac{1}{2}$	$\frac{7}{8}-\frac{1}{2}$	$\frac{7}{8}-\frac{1}{2}$
Total length of lever . .	$16\frac{1}{4}$	$17\frac{3}{4}$	$18\frac{1}{2}$	26	$26\frac{3}{8}$	$26\frac{3}{4}$
Length of spring . . .	$6\frac{1}{8}$	$6\frac{7}{8}$	$6\frac{11}{16}$	$8\frac{3}{8}$	$9\frac{5}{16}$	$10\frac{7}{16}$
Diameter of spring . . .	$2\frac{1}{2}$	$2\frac{3}{4}$	3	$3\frac{1}{2}$	$3\frac{1}{2}$	$3\frac{3}{4}$
Pull on spring for 140 lbs. pres.	494·7	473·4	992·8	1374·2	1979·0	2693·8
Pull on spring for 90 lbs. pres.	318·0	432·9	638·2	883·4	1272·2	1731·7

Dimensions are given in Inches.

A loose link (not shown in the figure) is provided, to connect the lever L with the eye to which the spring is attached, so that, if the spring should break, the lever would be held by the link, and thus the valve would only blow off, but not leave the seat.

Dead-Weight Safety Valve.

Fig. 1079 represents a group of 3 dead-weight safety valves, one of the group being shown in section. This class of valve is made single, or with several valves in a group attached to the same base. The valve V is fixed in the interior of the circular casting C, on

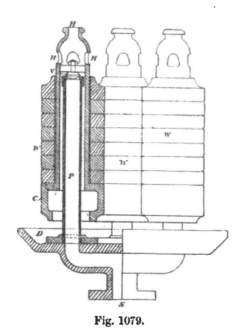

Fig. 1079.

which are placed the weights *w, w*. The seating for the valve is fixed on the top of the pipe P. The pipe in fig. 1079 is shown of wrought iron, although often made of cast iron. This type of safety valve requires no guides, as all the weights are below the valve, and therefore it returns by its own gravity to its proper place.

It is also very difficult to tamper with, owing to the large increase of weight required to make any appreciable difference to the blowing-off pressure.

TABLE 169.—Hyperbolic Logarithms.

No.	Hyp. log.	No.	Hyp. log.	No.	Hyp. log.	No.	Hyp. log.
1	0·00000	26	3·25810	51	3·93183	76	4·33073
2	0·69315	27	3·29584	52	3·95124	77	4·34381
3	1·09861	28	3·33220	53	3·97029	78	4·35671
4	1·38629	29	3·36730	54	3·98898	79·	4·36945
5	1·60944	30	3·40120	55	4·00733	80	4·38203
6	1·79176	31	3·43399	56	4·02535	81	4·39445
7	1·94591	32	3·46574	57	4·04305	82	4·40672
8	2·07944	33	3·49651	58	4·06044	83	4·41884
9	2·19722	34	3·52636	59·	4·07754	84	4·43082
10	2·30259	35	3·55535	60	4·09434	85	4·44265
11	2·39790	36	3·58352	61	4·11087	86	4·45435
12	2·48491	37	3·61092	62	4·12713	87	4·46591
13	2·56495	38	3·63759	63	4·14313	88	4·47734
14	2·63906	39	3·66356	64	4·15888	89	4·48864
15	2·70805	40	3·68888	65	4·17439	90	4·49981
16	2·77259	41	3·71357	66	4·18965	91	4·51086
17	2·83321	42	3·73767	67	4·20469	92	4·52179
18	2·89037	43	3·76120	68	4·21951	93	4·53260
19	2·94444	44	3·78419	69	4·23411	94	4·54329
20	2·99573	45	3·80666	70	4·24850	95	4·55388
21	3·04452	46	3·82864	71	4·26268	96	4·56435
22	3·09104	47	3·85015	72	4·27667	97	4·57471
23	3·13549	48	3·87120	73	4·29046	98	4·58497
24	3·17805	49	3·89182	74	4·30407	99	4·59512
25	3·21888	50	3·91202	75	4·31749	100	4·60517

Hyp. log. 10, correct to eight places of decimals, = 2·30258509.

Common logs. multiplied by 2·30258 give hyperbolic logs.

Hyp. log. 75 = 4·31749.

Hyp. log. 7·5 = 4·31749 – hyp. log. 10.

·31749 – 2·30258 = 2·01491 the hyp. log. of 7·5.

TABLE 170.—**Volumes and Pressures of a Pound of Steam.**

Temp. Fahr.	Absolute pressures in lbs. per square inch.	Volume occupied by 1 lb. of steam in cubic feet.
95	·806	404·8
104	1·06	312·8
122	1·78	192·0
140	2·88	122·0
158	4·51	80·02
176	6·86	53·92
203	12·26	31·26
230	20·80	19·03
248	28·83	14·00
266	39·25	10·48
275	45·49	9·124
293	60·40	6·992
320	89·86	4·816
329	101·9	4·280
347	129·8	3·410
356	145·8	3·057
365	163·3	2·748
374	182·4	2·476
383	203·3	2·236

INDEX.

———————

THE END.

BRADBURY, AGNEW, & CO. LD., PRINTERS, WHITEFRIARS.

7, STATIONERS' HALL COURT,
LONDON.

A SELECTION

FROM THE

CATALOGUE OF BOOKS

IN

ENGINEERING, MECHANICS, MINING, SCIENCE,

THE INDUSTRIAL ARTS, &c., &c.

PUBLISHED BY

CROSBY LOCKWOOD & SON.

MECHANICAL ENGINEERING, etc.

D. K. Clark's Pocket-Book for Mechanical Engineers.

THE MECHANICAL ENGINEER'S POCKET-BOOK OF TABLES, FORMULÆ, RULES AND DATA. A Handy Book of Reference for Daily Use in Engineering Practice. By D. KINNEAR CLARK, M.Inst.C.E., Author of "Railway Machinery," "Tramways," &c. Second Edition, Revised and Enlarged. Small 8vo, 700 pages, 9s. bound in flexible leather covers, with rounded corners and gilt edges. [*Just published.*

SUMMARY OF CONTENTS.

MATHEMATICAL TABLES.—MEASUREMENT OF SURFACES AND SOLIDS.—ENGLISH WEIGHTS AND MEASURES.—FRENCH METRIC WEIGHTS AND MEASURES.—FOREIGN WEIGHTS AND MEASURES.—MONEYS.—SPECIFIC GRAVITY. WEIGHT AND VOLUME.—MANUFACTURED METALS.—STEEL PIPES.—BOLTS AND NUTS.—SUNDRY ARTICLES IN WROUGHT AND CAST IRON, COPPER, BRASS, LEAD, TIN, ZINC.—STRENGTH OF MATERIALS.—STRENGTH OF TIMBER.—STRENGTH OF CAST IRON.—STRENGTH OF WROUGHT IRON.—STRENGTH OF STEEL.—TENSILE STRENGTH OF COPPER, LEAD, ETC.—RESISTANCE OF STONES AND OTHER BUILDING MATERIALS.—RIVETED JOINTS IN BOILER PLATES.—BOILER SHELLS.—WIRE ROPES AND HEMP ROPES.—CHAINS AND CHAIN CABLES.—FRAMING.—HARDNESS OF METALS, ALLOYS AND STONES.—LABOUR OF ANIMALS.—MECHANICAL PRINCIPLES.—GRAVITY AND FALL OF BODIES.—ACCELERATING AND RETARDING FORCES.—MILL GEARING, SHAFTING, ETC.—TRANSMISSION OF MOTIVE POWER.—HEAT.—COMBUSTION: FUELS.—WARMING, VENTILATION, COOKING STOVES.—STEAM.—STEAM ENGINES AND BOILERS.—RAILWAYS.—TRAMWAYS.—STEAM SHIPS.—PUMPING STEAM ENGINES AND PUMPS.—COAL GAS, GAS ENGINES, ETC.—AIR IN MOTION.—COMPRESSED AIR.—HOT AIR ENGINES.—WATER POWER.—SPEED OF CUTTING TOOLS.—COLOURS.—ELECTRICAL ENGINEERING.

*** OPINIONS OF THE PRESS.

"Mr. Clark manifests what is an innate perception of what is likely to be useful in a pocket-book, and he is really unrivalled in the art of condensation. . . . It is very difficult to hit upon any mechanical engineering subject concerning which this work supplies no information, and the excellent index at the end adds to its utility. In one word, it is an exceedingly handy and efficient tool, possessed of which the engineer will be saved many a wearisome calculation, or yet more wearisome hunt through various text-books and treatises, and, as such, we can heartily recommend it to our readers, who must not run away with the idea that Mr. Clark's Pocket-book is only Molesworth in another form. On the contrary, each contains what is not to be found in the other; and Mr. Clark takes more room and deals at more length with many subjects than Molesworth possibly could."—*The Engineer*, Sept 16th, 1892.

"Just the kind of work that practical men require to have near to them."—*English Mechanic.*

B

MR. HUTTON'S PRACTICAL HANDBOOKS.

Handbook for Works' Managers.

THE WORKS' MANAGER'S HANDBOOK OF MODERN RULES, TABLES, AND DATA. For Engineers, Millwrights, and Boiler Makers; Tool Makers, Machinists, and Metal Workers; Iron and Brass Founders, &c. By W. S. HUTTON, Civil and Mechanical Engineer, Author of "The Practical Engineer's Handbook." Fourth Edition, carefully Revised and partly Re-written. In One handsome Volume, medium 8vo, price 15s. strongly bound.

☞ *The Author having compiled Rules and Data for his own use in a great variety of modern engineering work, and having found his notes extremely useful, decided to publish them—revised to date—believing that a practical work, suited to the* DAILY REQUIREMENTS OF MODERN ENGINEERS, *would be favourably received.*

In the Fourth Edition the First Section has been re-written and improved by the addition of numerous Illustrations and new matter relating to STEAM ENGINES *and* GAS ENGINES. *The Second Section has been enlarged and Illustrated, and throughout the book a great number of emendations and alterations have been made, with the object of rendering the book more generally useful.*

⁎⁎ OPINIONS OF THE PRESS.

"The author treats every subject from the point of view of one who has collected workshop notes for application in workshop practice, rather than from the theoretical or literary aspect. The volume contains a great deal of that kind of information which is gained only by practical experience, and is seldom written in books."—*Engineer.*

"The volume is an exceedingly useful one, brimful with engineers' notes, memoranda, and rules, and well worthy of being on every mechanical engineer's bookshelf."—*Mechanical World.*

"A formidable mass of facts and figures, readily accessible through an elaborate index . . . . Such a volume will be found absolutely necessary as a book of reference in all sorts of 'works' connected with the metal trades."—*Ryland's Iron Trades Circular.*

"Brimful of useful information, stated in a concise form, Mr. Hutton's books have met a pressing want among engineers. The book must prove extremely useful to every practical man possessing a copy."—*Practical Engineer.*

New Manual for Practical Engineers

THE PRACTICAL ENGINEER'S HAND-BOOK. Comprising a Treatise on Modern Engines and Boilers: Marine, Locomotive and Stationary. And containing a large collection of Rules and Practical Data relating to recent Practice in Designing and Constructing all kinds of Engines, Boilers, and other Engineering work. The whole constituting a comprehensive Key to the Board of Trade and other Examinations for Certificates of Competency in Modern Mechanical Engineering. By WALTER S. HUTTON, Civil and Mechanical Engineer, Author of "The Works' Manager's Handbook for Engineers," &c. With upwards of 370 Illustrations. Fourth Edition, Revised, with Additions. Medium 8vo, nearly 500 pp., price 18s. Strongly bound.

☞ *This work is designed as a companion to the Author's "*WORKS' MANAGER'S HAND-BOOK.*" It possesses many new and original features, and contains, like its predecessor, a quantity of matter not originally intended for publication, but collected by the author for his own use in the construction of a great variety of* MODERN ENGINEERING WORK.

The information is given in a condensed and concise form, and is illustrated by upwards of 370 Woodcuts; and comprises a quantity of tabulated matter of great value to all engaged in designing, constructing, or estimating for ENGINES, BOILERS, *and* OTHER ENGINEERING WORK.

⁎⁎ OPINIONS OF THE PRESS.

"We have kept it at hand for several weeks, referring to it as occasion arose, and we have not on a single occasion consulted its pages without finding the information of which we were in quest." *Athenæum.*

"A thoroughly good practical handbook, which no engineer can go through without learning something that will be of service to him."—*Marine Engineer.*

"The author has collected together a surprising quantity of rules and practical data, and has shown much judgment in the selections he has made. . . . There is no doubt that this book is one of the most useful of its kind published, and will be a very popular compendium."—*Engineer.*

"A mass of information, set down in simple language, and in such a form that it can be easily referred to at any time. The matter is uniformly good and well chosen and is greatly elucidated by the illustrations. The book will find its way on to most engineers' shelves, where it will rank as one of the most useful books of reference."—*Practical Engineer.*

"Full of useful information and should be found on the office shelf of all practical engineers. —*English Mechanic.*

Practical Treatise on Modern Steam-Boilers.

STEAM-BOILER CONSTRUCTION. A Practical Handbook for Engineers, Boiler-Makers, and Steam Users. Containing a large Collection of Rules and Data relating to Recent Practice in the Design, Construction, and Working of all Kinds of Stationary, Locomotive, and Marine Steam-Boilers. By WALTER S. HUTTON, Civil and Mechanical Engineer, Author of "The Works' Manager's Handbook," "The Practical Engineer's Handbook," &c. With upwards of 300 Illustrations. Second Edition. Medium 8vo, 18s. cloth.   [*Just published.*

☞ THIS WORK *is issued in continuation of the Series of Handbooks written by the Author, viz :—*"THE WORKS' MANAGERS' HANDBOOK" *and* "THE PRACTICAL ENGINEER'S HANDBOOK," *which are so highly appreciated by Engineers for the practical nature of their information ; and is consequently written in the same style as those works.*

The Author believes that the concentration, in a convenient form for easy reference, of such a large amount of thoroughly practical information on Steam-Boilers, will be of considerable service to those for whom it is intended, and he trusts the book may be deemed worthy of as favourable a reception as has been accorded to its predecessors.

*** OPINIONS OF THE PRESS.

"Every detail, both in boiler design and management, is clearly laid before the reader. The volume shows that boiler construction has been reduced to the condition of one of the most exact sciences ; and such a book is of the utmost value to the *fin de siècle* Engineer and Works' Managers."—*Marine Engineer.*

"There has long been room for a modern handbook on steam boilers ; there is not that room now, because Mr. Hutton has filled it. It is a thoroughly practical book for those who are occupied in the construction, design, selection, or use of boilers."—*Engineer.*

"The book is of so important and comprehensive a character that it must find its way into the libraries of everyone interested in boiler using or boiler manufacture if they wish to be thoroughly informed. We strongly recommend the book for the intrinsic value of its contents."—*Machinery Market.*

"The value of this book can hardly be over-estimated. The author's rules, formulæ, &c., are all very fresh, and it is impossible to turn to the work and not find what you want. No practical engineer should be without it."—*Colliery Guardian.*

Hutton's "Modernised Templeton."

THE PRACTICAL MECHANICS' WORKSHOP COMPANION. Comprising a great variety of the most useful Rules and Formulæ in Mechanical Science, with numerous Tables of Practical Data and Calculated Results for Facilitating Mechanical Operations. By WILLIAM TEMPLETON, Author of "The Engineer's Practical Assistant," &c. &c. Sixteenth Edition, Revised, Modernised, and considerably Enlarged by WALTER S. HUTTON, C.E., Author of "The Works' Manager's Handbook," &c. Fcap. 8vo, nearly 500 pp., with 8 Plates and upwards of 250 Illustrative Diagrams, 6s., strongly bound for workshop or pocket wear and tear.

*** OPINIONS OF THE PRESS.

"In its modernised form Hutton's 'Templeton' should have a wide sale, for it contains much valuable information which the mechanic will often find of use, and not a few tables and notes which he might look for in vain in other works. This modernised edition will be appreciated by all who have learned to value the original editions of 'Templeton.'"—*English Mechanic.*

"It has met with great success in the engineering workshop, as we can testify ; and there are a great many men who, in a great measure, owe their rise in life to this little book."—*Building News.*

"This familiar text-book—well known to all mechanics and engineers—is of essential service to the every-day requirements of engineers, millwrights, and the various trades connected with engineering and building. The new modernised edition is worth its weight in gold."—*Building News.* (Second Notice.)

"This well-known and largely-used book contains information, brought up to date, of the sort so useful to the foreman and draughtsman. So much fresh information has been introduced as to constitute it practically a new book. It will be largely used in the office and workshop."—*Mechanical World.*

Templeton's Engineer's and Machinist's Assistant.

THE ENGINEER'S, MILLWRIGHT'S, and MACHINIST'S PRACTICAL ASSISTANT. A collection of Useful Tables, Rules and Data. By WILLIAM TEMPLETON. 7th Edition, with Additions. 18mo, 2s. 6d. cloth.

"Occupies a foremost place among books of this kind. A more suitable present to an apprentice to any of the mechanical trades could not possibly be made."—*Building News.*

"A deservedly popular work. It should be in the 'drawer' of every mechanic."—*English Mechanic.*

Steam Engine.

TEXT-BOOK ON THE STEAM ENGINE. With a Supplement on Gas Engines, and PART II. ON HEAT ENGINES. By T. M. GOODEVE, M.A., Barrister-at-Law, Professor of Mechanics at the Normal School of Science and the Royal School of Mines; Author of "The Principles of Mechanics," "The Elements of Mechanism," &c. Eleventh Edition, Enlarged. With numerous Illustrations. Crown 8vo, 6s. cloth.

"Professor Goodeve has given us a treatise on the steam engine which will bear comparison with anything written by Huxley or Maxwell, and we can award it no higher praise."—*Engineer.*
"Mr. Goodeve's text-book is a work of which every young engineer should possess himself."
—*Mining Journal.*
"Essentially practical in its aim. The manner of exposition leaves nothing to be desired."—*Scotsman.*

Gas Engines.

ON GAS-ENGINES. Being a Reprint, with some Additions, of the Supplement to the *Text-book on the Steam Engine,* by T. M. GOODEVE, M.A. Crown 8vo, 2s. 6d. cloth.

"Like all Mr. Goodeve's writings, the present is no exception in point of general excellence. It is a valuable little volume."—*Mechanical World.*

Steam Engine Design.

THE STEAM ENGINE : A Practical Manual for Draughtsmen, Designers, and Constructors. Translated from the German of HERMANN HAEDER; Revised and Adapted to English Practice by H. H. P POWLES, A.M.I.C.E., Translator of Kick's Treatise on "Flour Manufacture." Upwards of 1,000 Diagrams. Crown 8vo, cloth.   [*In the press*

Steam Boilers.

A TREATISE ON STEAM BOILERS: Their Strength, Construction, and Economical Working. By ROBERT WILSON, C.E. Fifth Edition. 12mo, 6s. cloth.

"The best treatise that has ever been published on steam boilers."—*Engineer.*
"The author shows himself perfect master of his subject, and we heartily recommend all employing steam power to possess themselves of the work."—*Ryland's Iron Trade Circular.*

Boiler Chimneys.

BOILER AND FACTORY CHIMNEYS; Their Draught-Power and Stability. With a Chapter on *Lightning Conductors.* By ROBERT WILSON, A.I.C.E., Author of "A Treatise on Steam Boilers," &c. Second Edition. Crown 8vo, 3s. 6d. cloth.

"Full of useful information, definite in statement, and thoroughly practical in treatment."—*The Local Government Chronicle.*
"A valuable contribution to the literature of scientific building."—*The Builder.*

Boiler Making.

THE BOILER-MAKER'S READY RECKONER & ASSISTANT. With Examples of Practical Geometry and Templating, for the Use of Platers, Smiths and Riveters. By JOHN COURTNEY, Edited by D. K. CLARK, M.I.C.E. Third Edition, 480 pp., with 140 Illusts. Fcap. 8vo, 7s. half-bound.

"A most useful work. . . . No workman or apprentice should be without this book."—*Iron Trade Circular.*
"Boiler-makers will readily recognise the value of this volume. . . . The tables are clearly printed, and so arranged that they can be referred to with the greatest facility, so that it cannot be doubted that they will be generally appreciated and much used."—*Mining Journal.*

Locomotive Engine Development.

THE LOCOMOTIVE ENGINE AND ITS DEVELOPMENT. A Popular Treatise on the Gradual Improvements made in Railway Engines between the Years 1803 and 1892. By CLEMENT E. STRETTON, C.E., Author of "Safe Railway Working," &c. Second Edition, Revised and much Enlarged. With 94 Illustrations. Crown 8vo, 3s. 6d. cloth. [*Just published.*

"Students of railway history and all who are interested in the evolution of the modern locomotive will find much to attract and entertain in this volume."—*The Times.*
"The volume cannot fail to be popular, because it contains, in a condensed and readable form, a great deal of just the kind of information that multitudes of people want."—*Engineer.*
"The author of this work is well known to the railway world as one who has long taken a great interest in everything pertaining thereto. No one probably has a better knowledge of the history and development of the locomotive. It is with much pleasure we welcome the volume before us . . . which, taken as a whole, is most interesting, and should be of value to all connected th the railway system of this country as a book of reference."—*Nature.*

CIVIL ENGINEERING, SURVEYING, etc.

MR. HUMBER'S VALUABLE ENGINEERING BOOKS.

The Water Supply of Cities and Towns.

A COMPREHENSIVE TREATISE on the WATER-SUPPLY OF CITIES AND TOWNS. By WILLIAM HUMBER, A-M.Inst.C.E., and M. Inst. M.E., Author of "Cast and Wrought Iron Bridge Construction," &c. &c. Illustrated with 50 Double Plates, 1 Single Plate, Coloured Frontispiece, and upwards of 250 Woodcuts, and containing 400 pages of Text. Imp. 4to, £6 6s. elegantly and substantially half-bound in morocco.

List of Contents.

I. Historical Sketch of some of the means that have been adopted for the Supply of Water to Cities and Towns.—II. Water and the Foreign Matter usually associated with it.—III. Rainfall and Evaporation.—IV. Springs and the water-bearing formations of various districts.—V. Measurement and Estimation of the flow of Water —VI. On the Selection of the Source of Supply.—VII. Wells —VIII. Reservoirs.—IX. The Purification of Water.—X. Pumps. — XI. Pumping Machinery. — XII. Conduits.—XIII. Distribution of Water.—XIV. Meters, Service Pipes, and House Fittings.—XV. The Law and Economy of Water Works. XVI. Constant and Intermittent Supply.—XVII. Description of Plates. — Appendices, giving Tables of Rates of Supply, Velocities, &c. &c., together with Specifications of several Works illustrated, among which will be found: Aberdeen, Bideford, Canterbury, Dundee, Halifax, Lambeth, Rotherham, Dublin, and others.

"The most systematic and valuable work upon water supply hitherto produced in English, or in any other language. . . . Mr. Humber's work is characterised almost throughout by an exhaustiveness much more distinctive of French and German than of English technical treatises."—*Engineer.*

"We can congratulate Mr. Humber on having been able to give so large an amount of information on a subject so important as the water supply of cities and towns. The plates, fifty in number, are mostly drawings of executed works, and alone would have commanded the attention of every engineer whose practice may lie in this branch of the profession."—*Builder.*

Cast and Wrought Iron Bridge Construction.

A COMPLETE AND PRACTICAL TREATISE ON CAST AND WROUGHT IRON BRIDGE CONSTRUCTION, including Iron Foundations. In Three Parts—Theoretical, Practical, and Descriptive. By WILLIAM HUMBER, A.M.Inst.C.E., and M.Inst.M.E. Third Edition, Revised and much improved, with 115 Double Plates (20 of which now first appear in this edition), and numerous Additions to the Text. In Two Vols., imp. 4to, £6 16s. 6d. half-bound in morocco.

"A very valuable contribution to the standard literature of civil engineering. In addition to elevations, plans and sections, large scale details are given which very much enhance the instructive worth of those illustrations."—*Civil Engineer and Architect's Journal.*

"Mr. Humber's stately volumes, lately issued—in which the most important bridges erected during the last five years, under the direction of the late Mr. Brunel, Sir W. Cubitt, Mr. Hawkshaw, Mr. Page, Mr. Fowler, Mr. Hemans, and others among our most eminent engineers, are drawn and specified in great detail."—*Engineer.*

Strains, Calculation of.

A HANDY BOOK FOR THE CALCULATION OF STRAINS IN GIRDERS AND SIMILAR STRUCTURES, AND THEIR STRENGTH. Consisting of Formulæ and Corresponding Diagrams, with numerous details for Practical Application, &c. By WILLIAM HUMBER, A-M.Inst.C.E., &c. Fifth Edition. Crown 8vo, nearly 100 Woodcuts and 3 Plates, 7s. 6d. cloth.

"The formulæ are neatly expressed, and the diagrams good."—*Athenæum.*

"We heartily commend this really *handy* book to our engineer and architect readers."—*English Mechanic.*

Barlow's Strength of Materials, enlarged by Humber.

A TREATISE ON THE STRENGTH OF MATERIALS; with Rules for Application in Architecture, the Construction of Suspension Bridges, Railways, &c. By PETER BARLOW, F.R.S. A New Edition, revised by his Sons, P. W. BARLOW, F.R.S., and W. H. BARLOW, F.R.S.; to which are added, Experiments by HODGKINSON, FAIRBAIRN, and KIRKALDY; and Formulæ for Calculating Girders, &c. Arranged and Edited by WM. HUMBER, A-M.Inst.C.E. Demy 8vo, 400 pp., with 19 large Plates and numerous Woodcuts, 18s. cloth.

"Valuable alike to the student, tyro, and the experienced practitioner, it will always rank in future, as it has hitherto done, as the standard treatise on that particular subject."—*Engineer.*

"There is no greater authority than Barlow."—*Building News.*

"As a scientific work of the first class, it deserves a foremost place on the bookshelves of every civil engineer and practical mechanic."—*English Mechanic.*

Statics, Graphic and Analytic.

GRAPHIC AND ANALYTIC STATICS, *in their Practical Appli-cation to the Treatment of Stresses in Roofs, Solid Girders, Lattice, Bowstring and Suspension Bridges, Braced Iron Arches and Piers, and other Frameworks.* By R. HUDSON GRAHAM, C.E. Containing Diagrams and Plates to Scale. With numerous Examples, many taken from existing Structures. Specially arranged for Class-work in Colleges and Universities. Second Edition, Revised and Enlarged. 8vo, 16s. cloth.

"Mr. Graham's book will find a place wherever graphic and analytic statics are used or studied." —*Engineer.*

"The work is excellent from a practical point of view, and has evidently been prepared with much care. The directions for working are ample, and are illustrated by an abundance of well-selected examples. It is an excellent text-book for the practical draughtsman."—*Athenæum.*

Practical Mathematics.

MATHEMATICS FOR PRACTICAL MEN: Being a Common-place Book of Pure and Mixed Mathematics. Designed chiefly for the use of Civil Engineers, Architects and Surveyors. By OLINTHUS GREGORY, LL.D., F.R.A.S., Enlarged by HENRY LAW, C.E. 4th Edition, carefully Revised by J. R. YOUNG, formerly Professor of Mathematics, Belfast College. With 13 Plates. 8vo, £1 1s. cloth.

"The engineer or architect will here find ready to his hand rules for solving nearly every mathematical difficulty that may arise in his practice. The rules are in all cases explained by means of examples, in which every step of the process is clearly worked out."—*Builder.*

"One of the most serviceable books for practical mechanics. . . It is an instructive book for the student, and a text-book for him who, having once mastered the subjects it treats of, needs occasionally to refresh his memory upon them."—*Building News.*

Hydraulic Tables.

HYDRAULIC TABLES, CO-EFFICIENTS, and FORMULÆ *for finding the Discharge of Water from Orifices, Notches, Weirs, Pipes, and Rivers.* With New Formulæ, Tables, and General Information on Rainfall, Catchment-Basins, Drainage, Sewerage, Water Supply for Towns and Mill Power. By JOHN NEVILLE, Civil Engineer, M.R.I.A. Third Ed., carefully Revised, with considerable Additions. Numerous Illusts. Cr. 8vo, 14s. cloth.

"Alike valuable to students and engineers in practice; its study will prevent the annoyance of avoidable failures, and assist them to select the readiest means of successfully carrying out any given work connected with hydraulic engineering."—*Mining Journal.*

"It is, of all English books on the subject, the one nearest to completeness. . . . From the good arrangement of the matter, the clear explanations, and abundance of formulæ, the carefully calculated tables, and, above all, the thorough acquaintance with both theory and construction, which is displayed from first to last, the book will be found to be an acquisition."—*Architect.*

Hydraulics.

HYDRAULIC MANUAL. Consisting of Working Tables and Explanatory Text. Intended as a Guide in Hydraulic Calculations and Field Operations. By LOWIS D'A. JACKSON, Author of "Aid to Survey Practice," "Modern Metrology," &c. Fourth Edition, Enlarged. Large cr. 8vo, 16s. cl.

"The author has had a wide experience in hydraulic engineering and has been a careful observer of the facts which have come under his notice, and from the great mass of material at his command he has constructed a manual which may be accepted as a. trustworthy guide to this branch of the engineer's profession. We can heartily recommend this volume to all who desire to be acquainted with the latest development of this important subject."—*Engineering.*

"The standard-work in this department of mechanics."—*Scotsman.*

"The most useful feature of this work is its freedom from what is superannuated, and its thorough adoption of recent experiments; the text is, in fact, in great part a short account of the great modern experiments."—*Nature.*

Drainage.

ON THE DRAINAGE OF LANDS, TOWNS, AND BUILD-INGS. By G. D. DEMPSEY, C.E., Author of "The Practical Railway Engineer," &c. Revised, with large Additions on RECENT PRACTICE IN DRAINAGE ENGINEERING, by D. KINNEAR CLARK, M.Inst.C.E. Author of "Tramways: Their Construction and Working," "A Manual of Rules, Tables, and Data for Mechanical Engineers," &c. Second Edition, Corrected. Fcap. 8vo, 5s. cloth.

"The new matter added to Mr. Dempsey's excellent work is characterised by the comprehensive grasp and accuracy of detail for which the name of Mr. D. K. Clark is a sufficient voucher."—*Athenæum.*

"As a work on recent practice in drainage engineering, the book is to be commended to all who are making that branch of engineering science their special study."—*Iron.*

"A comprehensive manual on drainage engineering, and a useful introduction to the student." —*Building News.*

Water Storage, Conveyance, and Utilisation.

WATER ENGINEERING : A Practical Treatise on the Measurement, Storage, Conveyance, and Utilisation of Water for the Supply of Towns, for Mill Power, and for other Purposes. By CHARLES SLAGG, Water and Drainage Engineer, A.M.Inst.C.E., Author of " Sanitary Work in the Smaller Towns, and in Villages," &c. With numerous Illusts. Cr. 8vo, 7s. 6d. cloth.

"As a small practical treatise on the water supply of towns, and on some applications of water-power, the work is in many respects excellent."—*Engineering*.

"The author has collated the results deduced from the experiments of the most eminent authorities, and has presented them in a compact and practical form, accompanied by very clear and detailed explanations. . . . The application of water as a motive power is treated very carefully and exhaustively."—*Builder*.

"For anyone who desires to begin the study of hydraulics with a consideration of the practical applications of the science there is no better guide."—*Architect*.

River Engineering.

RIVER BARS: The Causes of their Formation, and their Treatment by " Induced Tidal Scour;" with a Description of the Successful Reduction by this Method of the Bar at Dublin By I. J. MANN, Assist. Eng. to the Dublin Port and Docks Board. Royal 8vo, 7s. 6d. cloth.

"We recommend all interested in harbour works—and, indeed, those concerned in the improvements of rivers generally—to read Mr. Mann's interesting work on the treatment of river bars."—*Engineer*.

Trusses.

TRUSSES OF WOOD AND IRON. Practical Applications of *Science in Determining the Stresses, Breaking Weights, Safe Loads, Scantlings, and Details of Construction,* with Complete Working Drawings. By WILLIAM GRIFFITHS, Surveyor, Assistant Master, Tranmere School of Science and Art. Oblong 8vo, 4s. 6d. cloth.

"This handy little book enters so minutely into every detail connected with the construction of roof trusses, that no student need be ignorant of these matters."—*Practical Engineer*.

Railway Working.

SAFE RAILWAY WORKING. A Treatise on Railway Accidents: Their Cause and Prevention; with a Description of Modern Appliances and Systems. By CLEMENT E. STRETTON, C.E., Vice-President and Consulting Engineer, Amalgamated Society of Railway Servants. With Illustrations and Coloured Plates. Third Edition, Enlarged. Crown 8vo, 3s. 6d. cloth.

"A book for the engineer, the directors, the managers; and, in short, all who wish for information on railway matters will find a perfect encyclopædia in 'Safe Railway Working.'"—*Railway Review*.

"We commend the remarks on railway signalling to all railway managers, especially where a uniform code and practice is advocated."—*Herepath's Railway Journal*.

"The author may be congratulated on having collected, in a very convenient form, much valuable information on the principal questions affecting the safe working of railways."—*Railway Engineer*.

Oblique Bridges.

A PRACTICAL AND THEORETICAL ESSAY ON OBLIQUE BRIDGES. With 13 large Plates. By the late GEORGE WATSON BUCK, M.I.C.E. Third Edition, revised by his Son, J. H. WATSON BUCK, M.I.C.E.; and with the addition of Description to Diagrams for Facilitating the Construction of Oblique Bridges, by W. H. BARLOW, M.I.C.E. Royal 8vo, 12s. cloth.

"The standard text-book for all engineers regarding skew arches is Mr. Buck's treatise, and it would be impossible to consult a better."—*Engineer*.

"Mr. Buck's treatise is recognised as a standard text-book, and his treatment has divested the subject of many of the intricacies supposed to belong to it. As a guide to the engineer and architect, on a confessedly difficult subject, Mr. Buck's work is unsurpassed."—*Building News*.

Tunnel Shafts.

THE CONSTRUCTION OF LARGE TUNNEL SHAFTS: A *Practical and Theoretical Essay.* By J. H. WATSON BUCK, M.Inst.C.E., Resident Engineer, London and North-Western Railway. Illustrated with Folding Plates. Royal 8vo, 12s. cloth.

"Many of the methods given are of extreme practical value to the mason; and the observations on the form of arch, the rules for ordering the stone, and the construction of the templates will be found of considerable use. We commend the book to the engineering profession."—*Building News*.

"Will be regarded by civil engineers as of the utmost value, and calculated to save much time and obviate many mistakes."—*Colliery Guardian*.

Student's Text-Book on Surveying.

PRACTICAL SURVEYING: A Text-Book for Students preparing for Examination or for Survey-work in the Colonies. By GEORGE W. USILL, A.M.I.C.E., Author of "The Statistics of the Water Supply of Great Britain." With Four Lithographic Plates and upwards of 330 Illustrations. Second Edition, Revised. Crown 8vo, 7s. 6d. cloth.

"The best forms of instruments are described as to their construction, uses and modes of employment, and there are innumerable hints on work and equipment such as the author, in his experience as surveyor, draughtsman, and teacher, has found necessary, and which the student in his inexperience will find most serviceable."—*Engineer.*

"The latest treatise in the English language on surveying, and we have no hesitation in saying that the student will find it a better guide than any of its predecessors . . . . Deserves to be recognised as the first book which should be put in the hands of a pupil of Civil Engineering, and every gentleman of education who sets out for the Colonies would find it well to have a copy."—*Architect.*

Survey Practice.

AID TO SURVEY PRACTICE, for Reference in Surveying, Levelling, and Setting-out; and in Route Surveys of Travellers by Land and Sea. With Tables, Illustrations, and Records. By LOWIS D'A. JACKSON, A.M.I.C.E., Author of "Hydraulic Manual," "Modern Metrology," &c. Second Edition, Enlarged. Large crown 8vo, 12s. 6d. cloth.

"Mr. Jackson has produced a valuable *vade-mecum* for the surveyor. We can recommend this book as containing an admirable supplement to the teaching of the accomplished surveyor."—*Athenæum.*

"As a text-book we should advise all surveyors to place it in their libraries, and study well the matured instructions afforded in its pages."—*Colliery Guardian.*

"The author brings to his work a fortunate union of theory and practical experience which, aided by a clear and lucid style of writing, renders the book a very useful one."—*Builder.*

Surveying, Land and Marine.

LAND AND MARINE SURVEYING, in Reference to the Preparation of Plans for Roads and Railways; Canals, Rivers, Towns' Water Supplies; Docks and Harbours. With Description and Use of Surveying Instruments. By W. D. HASKOLL, C.E., Author of "Bridge and Viaduct Construction," &c. Second Edition, Revised, with Additions. Large cr. 8vo, 9s. cl.

"This book must prove of great value to the student. We have no hesitation in recommending it, feeling assured that it will more than repay a careful study."—*Mechanical World.*

"A most useful and well arranged book for the aid of a student. We can strongly recommend it as a carefully-written and valuable text-book. It enjoys a well-deserved repute among surveyors."—*Builder.*

"This volume cannot fail to prove of the utmost practical utility. It may be safely recommended to all students who aspire to become clean and expert surveyors."—*Mining Journal.*

Field-Book for Engineers.

THE ENGINEER'S, MINING SURVEYOR'S, AND CONTRACTOR'S FIELD-BOOK. Consisting of a Series of Tables, with Rules, Explanations of Systems, and use of Theodolite for Traverse Surveying and Plotting the Work with minute accuracy by means of Straight Edge and Set Square only; Levelling with the Theodolite, Casting-out and Reducing Levels to Datum, and Plotting Sections in the ordinary manner; setting-out Curves with the Theodolite by Tangential Angles and Multiples, with Right and Left-hand Readings of the Instrument: Setting-out Curves without Theodolite, on the System of Tangential Angles by sets of Tangents and Offsets; and Earthwork Tables to 80 feet deep, calculated for every 6 inches in depth. By W. DAVIS HASKOLL, C.E. With numerous Woodcuts. Fourth Edition, Enlarged. Crown 8vo, 12s. cloth.

"The book is very handy; the separate tables of sines and tangents to every minute will make it useful for many other purposes, the genuine traverse tables existing all the same."—*Athenæum.*

"Every person engaged in engineering field operations will estimate the importance of such a work and the amount of valuable time which will be saved by reference to a set of reliable tables prepared with the accuracy and fulness of those given in this volume."—*Railway News.*

Levelling.

A TREATISE ON THE PRINCIPLES AND PRACTICE OF LEVELLING. Showing its Application to purposes of Railway and Civil Engineering, in the Construction of Roads; with Mr. TELFORD's Rules for the same. By FREDERICK W. SIMMS, F.G.S., M.Inst.C.E. Seventh Edition, with the addition of LAW's Practical Examples for Setting-out Railway Curves, and TRAUTWINE's Field Practice of Laying-out Circular Curves. With 7 Plates and numerous Woodcuts. 8vo, 8s. 6d. cloth. *⁎* TRAUTWINE on Curves may be had separate, 5s.

"The text-book on levelling in most of our engineering schools and colleges."—*Engineer.*

"The publishers have rendered a substantial service to the profession, especially to the younger members, by bringing out the present edition of Mr. Simms's useful work."—*Engineering.*

Trigonometrical Surveying.

AN OUTLINE OF THE METHOD OF CONDUCTING A TRIGONOMETRICAL SURVEY, for the Formation of Geographical and Topographical Maps and Plans, Military Reconnaissance, Levelling, &c., with Useful Problems, Formulæ, and Tables. By Lieut.-General FROME, R.E. Fourth Edition, Revised and partly Re-written by Major General Sir CHARLES WARREN, G.C.M.G., R.E. With 19 Plates and 115 Woodcuts. Royal 8vo, 16s. cloth.

"The simple fact that a fourth edition has been called for is the best testimony to its merits. No words of praise from us can strengthen the position so well and so steadily maintained by this work. Sir Charles Warren has revised the entire work, and made such additions as were necessary to bring every portion of the contents up to the present date."—*Broad Arrow.*

Field Fortification.

A TREATISE ON FIELD FORTIFICATION, THE ATTACK OF FORTRESSES, MILITARY MINING, AND RECONNOITRING. By Colonel I. S. MACAULAY, late Professor of Fortification in the R.M.A., Woolwich. Sixth Edition. Crown 8vo, with separate Atlas of 12 Plates, 12s. cloth.

Tunnelling.

PRACTICAL TUNNELLING. Explaining in detail the Setting-out of the works, Shaft-sinking and Heading-driving, Ranging the Lines and Levelling underground, Sub-Excavating, Timbering, and the Construction of the Brickwork of Tunnels, with the amount of Labour required for, and the Cost of, the various portions of the work. By FREDERICK W. SIMMS, F.G.S., M.Inst.C.E. Third Edition, Revised and Extended by D. KINNEAR CLARK, M.Inst.C.E. Imperial 8vo, with 21 Folding Plates and numerous Wood Engravings, 30s. cloth.

"The estimation in which Mr. Simms's book on tunnelling has been held for over thirty years cannot be more truly expressed than in the words of the late Prof. Rankine :—' The best source of information on the subject of tunnels is Mr. F. W. Simms's work on Practical Tunnelling.'"—*Architect.*

"It has been regarded from the first as a text-book of the subject. . . . Mr. Clark has added immensely to the value of the book."—*Engineer.*

Tramways and their Working.

TRAMWAYS : THEIR CONSTRUCTION AND WORKING. Embracing a Comprehensive History of the System ; with an exhaustive Analysis of the various Modes of Traction, including Horse-Power, Steam, Compressed Air, Electric Traction, &c.; a Description of the Varieties of Rolling Stock; and ample Details of Cost and Working Expenses. New Edition, Thoroughly Revised, and Including the Progress recently made in Tramway Construction, &c. &c. By D. KINNEAR CLARK, M.Inst.C.E. With numerous Illustrations. In One Volume, 8vo. [*In preparation.*

"All interested in tramways must refer to it, as all railway engineers have turned to the author's work 'Railway Machinery.'"—*Engineer.*

"An exhaustive and practical work on tramways, in which the history of this kind of locomotion, and a description and cost of the various modes of laying tramways, are to be found."—*Building News.*

"The best form of rails, the best mode of construction, and the best mechanical appliances are so fairly indicated in the work under review, that any engineer about to construct a tramway will be enabled at once to obtain the practical information which will be of most service to him."—*Athenæum.*

Curves, Tables for Setting-out.

TABLES OF TANGENTIAL ANGLES AND MULTIPLES for Setting-out Curves from 5 to 200 Radius. By ALEXANDER BEAZELEY, M.Inst.C.E. Fourth Edition. Printed on 48 Cards, and sold in a cloth box, waistcoat-pocket size, 3s. 6d.

"Each table is printed on a small card, which, being placed on the theodolite, leaves the hands free to manipulate the instrument—no small advantage as regards the rapidity of work."—*Engineer.*

"Very handy ; a man may know that all his day's work must fall on two of these cards, which he puts into his own card-case, and leaves the rest behind."—*Athenæum.*

Earthwork.

EARTHWORK TABLES. Showing the Contents in Cubic Yards of Embankments, Cuttings, &c., of Heights or Depths up to an average of 80 feet. By JOSEPH BROADBENT, C.E., and FRANCIS CAMPIN, C.E. Crown 8vo, 5s. cloth.

"The way in which accuracy is attained, by a simple division of each cross section into three elements, two in which are constant and one variable, is ingenious."—*Athenæum.*

MARINE ENGINEERING, etc.

Pocket-Book for Marine Engineers.

A POCKET-BOOK OF USEFUL TABLES AND FOR-MULÆ FOR MARINE ENGINEERS. By Frank Proctor, A.I.N.A. Third Edition. Royal 32mo, leather, gilt edges, with strap, 4s.

"We recommend it to our readers as going far to supply a long-felt want."—*Naval Science.*
"A most useful companion to all marine engineers."—*United Service Gazette.*

Introduction to Marine Engineering.

ELEMENTARY ENGINEERING: A Manual for Young Marine Engineers and Apprentices. In the Form of Questions and Answers on Metals, Alloys, Strength of Materials, Construction and Management of Marine Engines and Boilers, Geometry, &c. &c. With an Appendix of Useful Tables. By John Sherren Brewer, Government Marine Surveyor, Hong-kong. Second Edition, Revised. Small crown 8vo, 2s. cloth.

"Contains much valuable information for the class for whom it is intended, especially in the chapters on the management of boilers and engines."—*Nautical Magazine.*
"A useful introduction to the more elaborate text-books."—*Scotsman.*
"To a student who has the requisite desire and resolve to attain a thorough knowledge, Mr. Brewer offers decidedly useful help."—*Athenæum.*

Navigation.

PRACTICAL NAVIGATION. Consisting of The Sailor's Sea-Book, by James Greenwood and W. H. Rosser; together with the requisite Mathematical and Nautical Tables for the Working of the Problems, by Henry Law, C.E., and Professor J. R. Young. Illustrated. 12mo, 7s. strongly half-bound.

Drawing for Marine Engineers.

LOCKIE'S MARINE ENGINEER'S DRAWING-BOOK. Adapted to the Requirements of the Board of Trade Examinations. By John Lockie, C.E. With 22 Plates, Drawn to Scale. Royal 8vo, 3s. 6d. cloth. *[Just published.*

"The student who learns from these drawings will have nothing to unlearn."—*Engineer.*
"The examples chosen are essentially practical, and are such as should prove of service to engineers generally, while admirably fulfilling their specific purpose."—*Mechanical World.*

Sailmaking.

THE ART AND SCIENCE OF SAILMAKING. By Samuel B. Sadler, Practical Sailmaker, late in the employment of Messrs. Ratsey and Lapthorne, of Cowes and Gosport. With Plates and other Illustrations. Small 4to, 12s. 6d. cloth. *[Just published.*

SUMMARY OF CONTENTS.

Chap. I. The Materials used and their Relation to Sails.—II. On the Centre of Effort.—III. On Measuring.—IV. On Drawing.—V. On the Number of Cloths required. | —VI. On Allowances.—VII. Calculation of Gores.—VIII. On Cutting Out.—IX. On Roping.—X. On Diagonal-Cut Sails.—XI. Concluding Remarks.

"This work is very ably written, and is illustrated by diagrams and carefully-worked calculations. The work should be in the hands of every sailmaker, whether employer or employed, as it cannot fail to assist them in the pursuit of their important avocations."—*Isle of Wight Herald.*
"This extremely practical work gives a complete education in all the branches of the manufacture, cutting out, roping, seaming, and goring. It is copiously illustrated, and will form a first-rate text-book and guide."—*Portsmouth Times.*

Chain Cables.

CHAIN CABLES AND CHAINS. Comprising Sizes and Curves of Links, Studs, &c., Iron for Cables and Chains, Chain Cable and Chain Making, Forming and Welding Links, Strength of Cables and Chains, Certificates for Cables, Marking Cables, Prices of Chain Cables and Chains, Historical Notes, Acts of Parliament, Statutory Tests, Charges for Testing, List of Manufacturers of Cables, &c. &c. By Thomas W. Traill, F.E.R.N., M. Inst. C.E., Engineer Surveyor in Chief, Board of Trade, Inspector of Chain Cable and Anchor Proving Establishments, and General Superintendent, Lloyd's Committee on Proving Establishments. With numerous Tables, Illustrations and Lithographic Drawings. Folio, £2 2s. cloth, bevelled boards.

"It contains a vast amount of valuable information. Nothing seems to be wanting to make it a complete and standard work of reference on the subject."—*Nautical Magazine.*

MINING AND METALLURGY.

Metalliferous Mining in the United Kingdom.

BRITISH MINING: A Treatise on the History, Discovery, Practical Development, and Future Prospects of Metalliferous Mines in the United Kingdom. By ROBERT HUNT, F.R.S., Keeper of Mining Records; Editor of " Ure's Dictionary of Arts, Manufactures, and Mines," &c. Upwards of 950 pp., with 230 Illustrations. Second Edition, Revised. Super-royal 8vo, £2 2s. cloth.

"One of the most valuable works of reference of modern times. Mr. Hunt, as keeper of mining records of the United Kingdom, has had opportunities for such a task not enjoyed by anyone else, and has evidently made the most of them. . . . The language and style adopted are good, and the treatment of the various subjects laborious, conscientious, and scientific."—*Engineering.*

"The book is, in fact, a treasure-house of statistical information on mining subjects, and we know of no other work embodying so great a mass of matter of this kind. Were this the only merit of Mr. Hunt's volume, it would be sufficient to render it indispensable in the library of everyone interested in the development of the mining and metallurgical industries of this country."—*Athenæum.*

"A mass of information not elsewhere available, and of the greatest value to those who may be interested in our great mineral industries."—*Engineer.*

Metalliferous Minerals and Mining.

A TREATISE ON METALLIFEROUS MINERALS AND MINING. By D. C. DAVIES, F.G.S., Mining Engineer, &c., Author of "A Treatise on Slate and Slate Quarrying." Fifth Edition, thoroughly Revised and much Enlarged, by his Son, E. HENRY DAVIES, M.E., F.G.S. With about 150 Illustrations. Crown 8vo, 12s. 6d. cloth. [*Just published.*

"Neither the practical miner nor the general reader interested in mines can have a better book for his companion and his guide."—*Mining Journal.* [*Mining World.*

"We are doing our readers a service in calling their attention to this valuable work."—

"A book that will not only be useful to the geologist, the practical miner, and the metallurgist but also very interesting to the general public."—*Iron.*

"As a history of the present state of mining throughout the world this book has a real value, and it supplies an actual want."—*Athenæum.*

Earthy Minerals and Mining.

A TREATISE ON EARTHY & OTHER MINERALS AND MINING. By D. C. DAVIES, F.G.S., Author of "Metalliferous Minerals," &c. Third Edition. Revised and Enlarged, by his Son, E. HENRY DAVIES, M.E., F.G.S. With about 100 Illusts. Cr. 8vo, 12s. 6d. cl. [*Just published.*

"We do not remember to have met with any English work on mining matters that contains the same amount of information packed in equally convenient form."—*Academy.*

"We should be inclined to rank it as among the very best of the handy technical and trades manuals which have recently appeared."—*British Quarterly Review.*

Mining Machinery.

MACHINERY FOR METALLIFEROUS MINES, including Motive Power, Haulage, Transport, and Electricity as applied to Mining. By E. HENRY DAVIES, M.E., F.G.S., &c. &c. [*In preparation.*

Underground Pumping Machinery.

MINE DRAINAGE. Being a Complete and Practical Treatise on Direct-Acting Underground Steam Pumping Machinery, with a Description of a large number of the best known Engines, their General Utility and the Special Sphere of their Action; the Mode of their Application, and their merits compared with other forms of Pumping Machinery. By STEPHEN MICHELL. 8vo, 15s. cloth.

"Will be highly esteemed by colliery owners and lessees, mining engineers, and students generally who require to be acquainted with the best means of securing the drainage of mines. It is a most valuable work, and stands almost alone in the literature of steam pumping machinery."—*Colliery Guardian.*

"Much valuable information is given, so that the book is thoroughly worthy of an extensive circulation amongst practical men and purchasers of machinery."—*Mining Journal.*

Mining Tools.

A MANUAL OF MINING TOOLS. For the Use of Mine Managers, Agents, Students, &c. By WILLIAM MORGANS, Lecturer on Practical Mining at the Bristol School of Mines. 12mo, 2s. 6d. cloth limp.

ATLAS OF ENGRAVINGS to Illustrate the above, containing 235 Illustrations of Mining Tools, drawn to scale. 4to, 4s. 6d. cloth.

"Students in the science of mining, and overmen, captains, managers, and viewers may gain practical knowledge and useful hints by the study of Mr. Morgans' manual."— *Colliery Guardian.*

"A valuable work, which will tend materially to improve our mining literature."—*Mining Journal.*

Prospecting for Gold and other Metals.

THE PROSPECTOR'S HANDBOOK: A Guide for the Prospector and Traveller in Search of Metal-Bearing or other Valuable Minerals. By J. W. ANDERSON, M.A. (Camb.), F.R.G.S., Author of "Fiji and New Caledonia." Fifth Edition, thoroughly Revised and Enlarged. Small crown 8vo, 3s. 6d. cloth.

"Will supply a much felt want, especially among Colonists, in whose way are so often thrown many mineralogical specimens the value of which it is difficult to determine."—*Engineer.*

"How to find commercial minerals, and how to identify them when they are found, are the leading points to which attention is directed. The author has managed to pack as much practical detail into his pages as would supply material for a book three times its size."—*Mining Journal.*

Mining Notes and Formulæ.

NOTES AND FORMULÆ FOR MINING STUDENTS. By JOHN HERMAN MERIVALE, M.A., Certificated Colliery Manager, Professor of Mining in the Durham College of Science, Newcastle-upon-Tyne. Third Edition, Revised and Enlarged. Small crown 8vo, 2s. 6d. cloth.

"Invaluable to anyone who is working up for an examination on mining subjects."—*Iron and Coal Trades Review.*

"The author has done his work in an exceedingly creditable manner, and has produced a book that will be of service to students, and those who are practically engaged in mining operations."—*Engineer.*

"A vast amount of technical matter of the utmost value to mining engineers, and of considerable interest to students."—*Schoolmaster.*

Miners' and Metallurgists' Pocket-Book.

A POCKET-BOOK FOR MINERS AND METALLURGISTS. Comprising Rules, Formulæ, Tables, and Notes, for Use in Field and Office Work. By F. DANVERS POWER, F.G.S., M.E. Fcap. 8vo, 9s. leather, gilt edges.]*Just published.*

"The book seems to contain an immense amount of useful information in a small space, and no doubt will prove to be a valuable and handy book for mining engineers."—C. LE NEVE FOSTER, Esq.

"Miners and metallurgists will find in this work a useful *vade-mecum* containing a mass of rules, formulæ, tables, and various other information, the necessity for reference to which occurs in their daily duties."—*Iron.*

"A marvellous compendium which every miner who desires to do work rapidly and well should hasten to buy."—*Redruth Times.*

"Mr. Power has succeeded in producing a pocket-book which certainly deserves to become the engineer's *vade-mecum.*"—*Mechanical World.*

Mineral Surveying and Valuing.

THE MINERAL SURVEYOR AND VALUER'S COMPLETE GUIDE, comprising a Treatise on Improved Mining Surveying and the Valuation of Mining Properties, with New Traverse Tables. By WM. LINTERN, Mining and Civil Engineer. Third Edition, with an Appendix on "Magnetic and Angular Surveying," with Records of the Peculiarities of Needle Disturbances. With Four Plates of Diagrams, Plans, &c. 12mo, 4s. cloth.

"Mr. Lintern's book forms a valuable and thoroughly trustworthy guide."—*Iron and Coal Trades Review.*

"This new edition must be of the highest value to colliery surveyors, proprietors, and managers."—*Colliery Guardian.*

Asbestos and its Uses.

ASBESTOS: Its Properties, Occurrence, and Uses. With some Account of the Mines of Italy and Canada. By ROBERT H. JONES. With Eight Collotype Plates and other Illustrations. Crown 8vo, 12s. 6d. cloth.

"An interesting and invaluable work."—*Colliery Guardian.*

"A valuable addition to the architect's and engineer's library."—*Building News.*

Explosives.

A HANDBOOK ON MODERN EXPLOSIVES. Being a Practical Treatise on the Manufacture and Application of Dynamite, Gun-Cotton, Nitro-Glycerine, and other Explosive Compounds. Including the Manufacture of Collodion-Cotton. By M. EISSLER, Mining Engineer and Metallurgical Chemist, Author of "The Metallurgy of Gold," "The Metallurgy of Silver," &c. With about 100 Illusts. Crown 8vo, 10s. 6d. cloth.

"Useful not only to the miner, but also to officers of both services to whom blasting and the use of explosives generally may at any time become a necessary auxiliary."—*Nature.*

"A veritable mine of information on the subject of explosives employed for military, mining, and blasting purposes."—*Army and Navy Gazette.*

"The book is clearly written. Taken as a whole, we consider it an excellent little book and one that should be found of great service to miners and others who are engaged in work requiring the use of explosives."—*Athenæum.*

ELECTRICITY, ELECTRICAL ENGINEERING, etc.

Electrical Engineering.

THE ELECTRICAL ENGINEER'S POCKET-BOOK OF MODERN RULES, FORMULÆ, TABLES, AND DATA. By H. R. KEMPE, M.Inst.E.E., A.M.Inst.C.E., Technical Officer, Postal Telegraphs, Author of "A Handbook of Electrical Testing," &c. Second Edition, thoroughly Revised, with Additions. With numerous Illustrations. Royal 32mo, oblong, 5s. leather. [*Just published.*

"There is very little in the shape of formulæ or data which the electrician is likely to want in a hurry which cannot be found in its pages."—*Practical Engineer.*

"A very useful book of reference for daily use in practical electrical engineering and its various applications to the industries of the present day."—*Iron.*

"It is the best book of its kind."—*Electrical Engineer.*

"Well arranged and compact. The 'Electrical Engineer's Pocket-Book' is a good one."—*Electrician.*

"Strongly recommended to those engaged in the various electrical industries."—*Electrical Review.*

Electric Lighting.

ELECTRIC LIGHT FITTING: A Handbook for Working Electrical Engineers, embodying Practical Notes on Installation Management. By JOHN W. URQUHART, Electrician, Author of "Electric Light," &c. With numerous Illustrations. Crown 8vo, 5s. cloth.

"This volume deals with what may be termed the mechanics of electric lighting, and is addressed to men who are already engaged in the work or are training for it. The work traverses a great deal of ground, and may be read as a sequel to the same author's useful work on 'Electric Light.'"—*Electrician.*

"This is an attempt to state in the simplest language the precautions which should be adopted in installing the electric light, and to give information, for the guidance of those who have to run the plant when installed. The book is well worth the perusal of the workmen for whom it is written."—*Electrical Review.*

"We have read this book with a good deal of pleasure. We believe that the book will be of use to practical workmen, who will not be alarmed by finding mathematical formulæ which they are unable to understand."—*Electrical Plant.*

"Eminently practical and useful. . . Ought to be in the hands of everyone in charge of an electric light plant."—*Electrical Engineer.*

"Altogether Mr. Urquhart has succeeded in producing a really capital book, which we have no hesitation in recommending to the notice of working electricians and electrical engineers.'—*Mechanical World.*

Electric Light.

ELECTRIC LIGHT: Its Production and Use. Embodying Plain Directions for the Treatment of Dynamo-Electric Machines, Batteries, Accumulators, and Electric Lamps. By J. W. URQUHART, C.E., Author of "Electric Light Fitting," "Electroplating," &c. Fifth Edition, carefully Revised, with Large Additions and 145 Illustrations. Crown 8vo, 7s. 6d. cloth. [*Just published.*

"The whole ground of electric lighting is more or less covered and explained in a very clear and concise manner."—*Electrical Review.*

"Contains a good deal of very interesting information, especially in the parts where the author gives dimensions and working costs."—*Electrical Engineer.*

"A miniature *vade-mecum* of the salient facts connected with the science of electric lighting."—*Electrician.*

"You cannot for your purpose have a better book than 'Electric Light,' by Urquhart."—*Engineer.*

"The book is by far the best that we have yet met with on the subject."—*Athenæum.*

Construction of Dynamos.

DYNAMO CONSTRUCTION: A Practical Handbook for the Use of Engineer Constructors and Electricians-in-Charge. Embracing Framework Building, Field Magnet and Armature Winding and Grouping, Compounding, &c. With Examples of leading English, American, and Continental Dynamos and Motors. By J. W. URQUHART, Author of "Electric Light," "Electric Light Fitting," &c. With upwards of 100 Illustrations. Crown 8vo, 7s. 6d. cloth. [*Just published.*

"Mr. Urquhart's book is the first one which deals with these matters in such a way that the engineering student can understand them. The book is very readable, and the author leads his readers up to difficult subjects by reasonably simple tests."—*Engineering Review.*

"The author deals with his subject in a style so popular as to make his volume a handbook of great practical value to engineer contractors and electricians in charge of lighting installations."—*Scotsman.*

"'Dynamo Construction' more than sustains the high character of the author's previous publications. It is sure to be widely read by the large and rapidly-increasing number of practical electricians."—*Glasgow Herald.*

"A book for which a demand has long existed."—*Mechanical World.*

INDUSTRIAL ARTS, TRADES AND MANUFACTURES.

Soap-making.

THE ART OF SOAP-MAKING: *A Practical Handbook of the Manufacture of Hard and Soft Soaps, Toilet Soaps, etc.* Including many New Processes, and a Chapter on the Recovery of Glycerine from Waste Leys. By ALEXANDER WATT, Author of "Electro-Metallurgy Practically Treated," &c. With numerous Illustrations. Fourth Edition, Revised and Enlarged. Crown 8vo, 7s. 6d. cloth.

"The work will prove very useful, not merely to the technological student, but to the practical soap-boiler who wishes to understand the theory of his art."—*Chemical News.*

" Really an excellent example of a technical manual, entering, as it does, thoroughly and exhaustively, both into the theory and practice of soap manufacture. The book is well and honestly done, and deserves the considerable circulation with which it will doubtless meet."—*Knowledge.*

"Mr. Watt's book is a thoroughly practical treatise on an art which has almost no literature in our language. We congratulate the author on the success of his endeavour to fill a void in English technical literature."—*Nature.*

Paper Making.

THE ART OF PAPER MAKING: *A Practical Handbook of the Manufacture of Paper from Rags, Esparto, Straw, and other Fibrous Materials.* Including the Manufacture of Pulp from Wood Fibre, with a Description of the Machinery and Appliances used. To which are added Details of Processes for Recovering Soda from Waste Liquors. By ALEXANDER WATT, Author of "The Art of Soap-Making," "The Art of Leather Manufacture," &c. With Illustrations. Crown 8vo, 7s. 6d. cloth.

" This book is succinct, lucid, thoroughly practical, and includes everything of interest to the modern paper-maker. The book, besides being all the student of paper-making will require in his apprenticeship, will be found of interest to the paper-maker himself. It is the latest, most practical, and most complete work on the paper-making art before the British public."—*Paper Record.*

" It may be regarded as the standard work on the subject. The book is full of valuable information. The 'Art of Paper-making,' is in every respect a model of a text-book, either for a technical class or for the private student."—*Paper and Printing Trades Journal.*

Leather Manufacture.

THE ART OF LEATHER MANUFACTURE. Being a Practical Handbook, in which the Operations of Tanning, Currying, and Leather Dressing are fully Described, and the Principles of Tanning Explained, and many Recent Processes Introduced ; as also the Methods for the Estimation of Tannin, and a Description of the Arts of Glue Boiling, Gut Dressing, &c. By ALEXANDER WATT, Author of " Soap-Making," "Electro-Metallurgy," &c. With numerous Illustrations. Second Edition. Crown 8vo, 9s. cloth.

"This volume is technical without being tedious, comprehensive and complete without being prosy, and it bears on every page the impress of a master hand. We have never come across a better trade treatise, nor one that so thoroughly supplied an absolute want."—*Shoe and Leather Trades' Chronicle.*

Boot and Shoe Making.

THE ART OF BOOT AND SHOE-MAKING. A Practical Handbook, including Measurement, Last-Fitting, Cutting-Out, Closing, and Making, with a Description of the most approved Machinery employed. By JOHN B. LENO, late Editor of *St. Crispin,* and *The Boot and Shoe-Maker.* With numerous Illustrations. Third Edition. 12mo, 2s. cloth limp.

" This excellent treatise is by far the best work ever written on the subject. The chapter on clicking, which shows how waste may be prevented, will save fifty times the price of the book."—*Scottish Leather Trader.*

Dentistry Construction.

MECHANICAL DENTISTRY: *A Practical Treatise on the Construction of the various kinds of Artificial Dentures.* Comprising also Useful Formulæ, Tables, and Receipts for Gold Plate, Clasps, Solders, &c. &c. By CHARLES HUNTER. Third Edition, Revised. With upwards of 100 Wood Engravings. Crown 8vo, 3s. 6d. cloth.

" The work is very practical."—*Monthly Review of Dental Surgery.*

" We can strongly recommend Mr. Hunter's treatise to all students preparing for the profession of dentistry, as well as to every mechanical dentist."—*Dublin Journal of Medical Science.*

Wood Engraving.

WOOD ENGRAVING: *A Practical and Easy Introduction to the Study of the Art.* By WILLIAM NORMAN BROWN. Second Edition. With numerous Illustrations. 12mo, 1s. 6d. cloth limp.

" The book is clear and complete, and will be useful to anyone wanting to understand the first elements of the beautiful art of wood engraving."—*Graphic.*

Horology.

A TREATISE ON MODERN HOROLOGY, in Theory and Practice. Translated from the French of CLAUDIUS SAUNIER, ex-Director of the School of Horology at Mâcon, by JULIEN TRIPPLIN, F.R.A.S., Besançon Watch Manufacturer, and EDWARD RIGG, M.A., Assayer in the Royal Mint. With 78 Woodcuts and 22 Coloured Copper Plates. Second Edition. Super-royal 8vo, £2 2s. cloth; £2 10s. half-calf.

"There is no horological work in the English language at all to be compared to this production of M. Saunier's for clearness and completeness. It is alike good as a guide for the student and as a reference for the experienced horologist and skilled workman."—*Horological Journal.*

"The latest, the most complete, and the most reliable of those literary productions to which continental watchmakers are indebted for the mechanical superiority over their English brethren —in fact, the Book of Books, is M. Saunier's 'Treatise.'"—*Watchmaker, Jeweller and Silversmith.*

Watchmaking.

THE WATCHMAKER'S HANDBOOK. Intended as a Workshop Companion for those engaged in Watchmaking and the Allied Mechanical Arts. Translated from the French of CLAUDIUS SAUNIER, and considerably enlarged by JULIEN TRIPPLIN, F.R.A.S., Vice-President of the Horological Institute, and EDWARD RIGG, M.A., Assayer in the Royal Mint. With numerous Woodcuts and 14 Copper Plates. Third Edition. Crown 8vo, 9s. cloth.

"Each part is truly a treatise in itself. The arrangement is good and the language is clear and concise. It is an admirable guide for the young watchmaker."—*Engineering.*

"It is impossible to speak too highly of its excellence. It fulfils every requirement in a handbook intended for the use of a workman. Should be found in every workshop."—*Watch and Clockmaker.*

"This book contains an immense number of practical details bearing on the daily occupation of a watchmaker."—*Watchmaker and Metalworker* (Chicago).

Watches and Timekeepers.

A HISTORY OF WATCHES AND OTHER TIMEKEEPERS. By JAMES F. KENDAL, M.B.H.Inst. 250 pp., with 88 Illustrations, 1s. 6d. boards; or 2s. 6d. cloth gilt.   [*Just published.*

"Mr. Kendal's book, for its size, is the best which has yet appeared on this subject in the English language."—*Industries.*

"Open the book where you may, there is interesting matter in it concerning the ingenious devices of the ancient or modern horologer. The subject is treated in a liberal and entertaining spirit, as might be expected of a historian who is a master of the craft."—*Saturday Review.*

Electrolysis of Gold, Silver, Copper, etc.

ELECTRO-DEPOSITION : A Practical Treatise on the Electrolysis of Gold, Silver, Copper, Nickel, and other Metals and Alloys. With descriptions of Voltaic Batteries, Magneto and Dynamo-Electric Machines, Thermopiles, and of the Materials and Processes used in every Department of the Art, and several Chapters on Electro-Metallurgy. By ALEXANDER WATT, Author of "Electro-Metallurgy," &c. With numerous Illustrations. Third Edition, Revised and Corrected. Crown 8vo, 9s. cloth.

"Eminently a book for the practical worker in electro-deposition. It contains practical descriptions of methods, processes and materials as actually pursued and used in the workshop."—*Engineer.*

Electro-Metallurgy.

ELECTRO-METALLURGY; Practically Treated. By ALEXANDER WATT, Author of "Electro-Deposition," &c. Ninth Edition, Enlarged and Revised, with Additional Illustrations, and including the most recent Processes. 12mo, 4s. cloth boards.

"From this book both amateur and artisan may learn everything necessary for the successful prosecution of electroplating."—*Iron.*

Working in Gold.

THE JEWELLER'S ASSISTANT IN THE ART OF WORKING IN GOLD: A Practical Treatise for Masters and Workmen, Compiled from the Experience of Thirty Years' Workshop Practice. By GEORGE E. GEE, Goldsmith and Silversmith, Author of "The Goldsmith's Handbook," &c. Crown 8vo, 7s. 6d. cloth.   [*Just published.*

"This manual of technical education is apparently destined to be a valuable auxiliary to a handicraft which is certainly capable of great improvement."—*The Times.*

"This volume will be very useful in the workshop, as the knowledge is practical, having been acquired by long experience, and all the recipes and directions are guaranteed to be successful if properly worked out."—*Jeweller and Metalworker.*

𝔚eale's 𝔕udimentary 𝔖eries.

LONDON, 1862.

THE PRIZE MEDAL

Was awarded to the Publishers of

WEALE'S SERIES

RUDIMENTARY SCIENTIFIC, EDUCATIONAL, AND CLASSICAL.

Comprising nearly Three Hundred and Fifty distinct works in almost every department of Science, Art, and Education, recommended to the notice of Engineers, Architects, Builders, Artisans, and Students generally, as well as to those interested in Workmen's Libraries, Literary and Scientific Institutions, Colleges, Schools, Science Classes, &c., &c.

☞ "WEALE'S SERIES includes Text-Books on almost every branch of Science and Industry, comprising such subjects as Agriculture, Architecture and Building, Civil Engineering, Fine Arts, Mechanics and Mechanical Engineering, Physical and Chemical Science, and many miscellaneous Treatises. The whole are constantly undergoing revision, and new editions, brought up to the latest discoveries in scientific research, are constantly issued. The prices at which they are sold are as low as their excellence is assured."—*American Literary Gazette.*

"Amongst the literature of technical education, WEALE'S SERIES has ever enjoyed a high reputation, and the additions being made by Messrs. CROSBY LOCKWOOD & SON render the series more complete, and bring the information upon the several subjects down to the present time."—*Mining Journal.*

"It is not too much to say that no books have ever proved more popular with, or more useful to, young engineers and others than the excellent treatises comprised in WEALE'S SERIES."—*Engineer.*

"The excellence of WEALE'S SERIES is now so well appreciated, that it would be wasting our space to enlarge upon their general usefulness and value."—*Builder.*

"The volumes of WEALE'S SERIES form one of the best collections of elementary technical books in any language."—*Architect.*

"WEALE'S SERIES has become a standard as well as an unrivalled collection of treatises in all branches of art and science."—*Public Opinion.*

PHILADELPHIA, 1876.
THE PRIZE MEDAL

Was awarded to the Publishers for

Books: Rudimentary, Scientific,

"WEALE'S SERIES," ETC.

CROSBY LOCKWOOD & SON,

7, STATIONERS' HALL COURT, LUDGATE HILL, LONDON, E.C.

*** Catalogues post free on application.

CABOT SCIENCE LIBRARY

DEC 1 2 1995

Lightning Source UK Ltd.
Milton Keynes UK
UKOW06f1009261114

242203UK00007B/191/P

9 781295 838677